# Translating
# and
# Interpreting Conflict

APPROACHES TO TRANSLATION STUDIES
Founded by James S. Holmes

Edited by    Henri Bloemen
             Dirk Delabastita
             Ton Naaijkens

Volume 28

# Translating and Interpreting Conflict

Edited by
Myriam Salama-Carr

Amsterdam - New York, NY 2007

Cover image: tile from Palácio Nacional da Pena, Sintra.

Cover design: Studio Pollmann

The paper on which this book is printed meets the requirements of "ISO 9706:1994, Information and documentation - Paper for documents - Requirements for permanence".

ISBN-13: 978-90-420-2200-3
©Editions Rodopi B.V., Amsterdam – New York, NY 2007
Printed in The Netherlands

# CONTENTS

Introduction     1
    *Myriam Salama-Carr*

**Part I**
**Interpreters and Translators on the Front Line**
    Interpreting and Translation for Western Media
    in Iraq     13
       *Jerry Palmer*

    The Practice of Translation and Interpreting During
    the Conflicts in the Former Yugoslavia (1991-1999)     29
       *Mila Dragovic-Drouet*

    Translators and Interpreters During the Opium
    War between Britain and China (1839-1842)     41
       *Lawrence Wang-chi Wong*

**Part II**
**Intertwining Memory and Translation**
    The Grammar of Survival. How Do We Read
    Holocaust Testimonies?     61
       *Piotr Kuhiwczak*

    The Troy of Always: Translations of Conflict in
    Christopher Logue's *War Music*     75
       *Paschalis Nikolaou*

**Part III**
**Language and Ideology**

   Ideological Independence or Negative Mediation: BBC Mundo and CNN en Español's (translated) Reporting of Madrid's Terrorist Attacks     99
     *Roberto A. Valdeón*

   One Nation, Two Translations: China's Censorship of Hillary Clinton's Memoir     119
     *Red Chan*

**Part IV**
**Translation and Conflict Awareness**

   Encounters with Cross-Cultural Conflicts in Translation     135
     *Jun Tang*

   Translating Conflict. Advertising in a Globalised Era     149
     *Maria Calzada Pérez*

**Part V**
**Manipulating and Rewriting Texts**

   The Translation of William Le Queux's *The Invasion of 1910:* What Germany Made of Scaremongering in *The Daily Mail*     169
     *Ian Foster*

   Ferdinand Freiligrath, William Wordsworth, and the Translation of English Poetry into the Conflicts of Nineteenth Century German Nationalism     183
     *John Williams*

Translating the Enemy: A 'hip-hop' Translation of
a Poem by the Russian Futurist Poet Velimir
Khlebnikov (1885-1922)     199
*Brian Chadwick*

## Part VI
## Conflict and the Translator in Fiction
*L'étrange destin de Wangrin* or the Political
Accommodation of Interpretation     223
*Sathya Rao*

The Embedded Translator: a Coming Out Story     233
*Beverley Curran*

## Part VII
## The Translator's Visibility
The Translator's Visibility: the Rights and
Responsibilities Thereof     253
*Carol Maier*

**Notes on contributors**     267
**Index of names**     273

# Introduction

*Myriam Salama-Carr*

The notion of 'conflict' is part and parcel of contemporary discourse on translation and interpreting, wherein debates are frequently couched in terms of dichotomies, tensions and cultural differences, or conflicting allegiances. Perhaps the most persistent form of tension is that illustrated by the "general conflict between source-focused and target-focused approaches" (Pym 1995: 594), but the representation of translation itself as an aggressive act (Steiner 1975), or even as a violent one (Venuti 1995) is also a familiar theme. Descriptive and systemic approaches to translation (Even-Zohar 1990; Hermans 1985, 1994; Toury 1995) highlighted and contextualised the role played by translation in cultural dynamics, and emphasis on institutional and ideological factors was further pursued by the so-called 'cultural turn' of translation studies (Lefevere 1992; Bassnett and Lefevere 1998). More recently postcolonial approaches to translation (see Robinson 1997) have interrogated the role of translation in the construction and dislocation of empires. The institutional role that interlingual mediation plays in relations of power and in the construction of identities, potentially "figure[s] in ethnic discrimination, geopolitical confrontations, colonialism, terrorism, war…" (Venuti 1995: 18-19).

Paradoxically, whilst it is widely recognised that translation and interpreting are sites of conflict, the prevailing view of the roles of the translator and the interpreter seems to remain ones of negotiation and 'neutral' mediation, which entail a number of manageable risks, but are performed from a position of 'in-between'.[1]

This volume brings together selected papers from the first international conference on *Translation and Conflict,* hosted by the University of Salford in November 2004, and a number of invited essays on the same theme. Throughout these essays 'conflict' refers to those situations of political, cultural and ideological confrontation in which the translator and the interpreter can be involved, rather than serving as a metaphor for the tension and resistance which are inevitably present in intercultural communication.

In an increasingly polarised world conflict is a powerful and pervasive narrative, whether one subscribes to the conflict-oriented world view that is illustrated in Samuel P. Huntingdon's thesis on the clashes of civilisations

(Huntingdon 2002), or one dismisses this as a myth of confrontation which is fuelled by the reality and intensity of localised conflicts. Recent events have brought to the fore the challenges that are faced by the language mediator in situations of conflict, and the essays which make up this volume explore the agency of the translator/interpreter in these contexts, and also when s/he deals with texts and discourses which narrate, report on or otherwise engage with conflict. The essays thus contribute to a critical debate of the way ideological constraints, 'embeddedness', and the prevalence of certain discourses and narratives (for instance that of globalization) are brought to bear on the work of translators and interpreters, and on their fictional portrayal 'in conflict', when control over language becomes a key priority.

The interdisciplinary nature of Translation Studies is reflected in the diversity of approaches (historical, sociological and communication-oriented, literary, or based on self-reflexive practice) which underlie the essays. The translator and the interpreter's agency and subjectivity as individuals positioned within networks of power relationships are discussed through the prisms of globalisation, political unrest, censorship, and the fictional representation of conflict. Although a wide variety of genres are examined by the contributors to the present volume, ranging from news reporting and advertising to poetry, the essays share a number of themes such as the inevitability of a degree of 'embeddedness' for the translator and interpreter of conflict and the ensuing ethical engagement.

**Translators and interpreters on the frontline** is the focus of investigation of Jerry Palmer's essay, "Interpreting and Translation for Western Media in Iraq", and of Mila Dragovic-Drouet's "The practice of translation during the conflicts in former Yugoslavia (1991-1999)". Drawing on interviews carried out with a number of journalists who have worked in Iraq since 2003, Palmer discusses the interaction that takes place between news providers and translators. He examines the conditions of work of translators and interpreters as 'fixers' caught up in the realities of a military conflict at the time of the US-led invasion and occupation of Iraq in 2003. The fact that they were expected to undertake a multiplicity of roles in order to ensure the flow of information contributes further to the invisibility of the translation 'event'. For her part, Dragovic-Drouet explores how the bitter conflict that led to, and followed the dismantling of the former Yugoslavia in the 1990s, created a need and a demand for interpreting and translating services between hitherto mutually intelligible language varieties. The frontline translators and interpreters embedded in the Iraqi situation are a case in point to illustrate the problematics of neutrality that is expected of the "honest spokesperson" (Harris 1990: 118). Palmer's analysis shows how media theory views the role of translators and interpreters as that of intermediaries, but one of the many elements which are instrumental in the flow of information. The 'local' embeddedness of the translators ensures a valuable network of contacts for the journalist but, by the same token, it reinforces the risk of allegiance of the translators to their own community and can 'form' the journalist's interpretation of events. In the same vein, Dragovic-Drouet argues that theoretical and professional requirements which underpin translation and interpreting training (for instance, those taught in the prestigious *École Supérieure d'Interprètes et de Traducteurs* in Paris) can fall foul of the contingencies of war and of entrenched ethnic and religious loyalties and allegiances. Translators and interpreters appear to be rooted in one culture, inevitably enmeshed in what they describe, and both essays put paid to the assumption that they are positioned comfortably in the middle. They sometimes have to witness abuses of human rights, which can shatter the capacity to act in a detached manner, and undermine the observance of strict impartiality and expected unobtrusiveness. They are also often caught in the impossible role of the "double agent" (Tymoczko and Gentzler 2002: xix).

The translators and interpreters whose work is chronicled in Lawrence Wong's essay "The Translators/Interpreters During the Opium War between Britain and China, 1839-1842" were operating as much on the frontline as they were intervening within the corridors of power for both parties to the conflict. Using a historical-descriptive approach, Wong foregrounds their agency and multiple roles, arguing that the fact that they played a crucial role, which went beyond 'impartial' mediation and affected the outcome of the Opium War, has been overlooked in the historical record of that conflict.

The conflicts which underpin Piotr Kuhiwczak's, and Paschalis Nicholaou's essays are located at the junction of direct experience and memory, and their accounts provide telling examples of the **intertwining of memory and translation**. It has been argued that it is impossible to write about the Holocaust without referring to translation (Hirsch 1997), and Piotr Kuhiwczak's essay "The Grammar of survival. How do we read Holocaust testimonies?" shows how the study of the Holocaust and the interpretation of testimonies, from both victims and perpetrators, have largely taken place in English. The essay discusses the role of translation in shaping representations and discussions of the Holocaust, and on a more general level, in drawing the boundaries of our knowledge of the past. The potential of translation to remember and rewrite conflict, is shown in "The Troy of always: translations of conflict in Christopher Logue's *War* Music", Nikolaou's study of Logue's poetry which translates past conflicts into the present. The translator's memory of the conflicts he has experienced, and of the brutal lessons of history, is brought to bear on his work, which can be seen as a commentary on war and its rhetoric, and constitutes an intense interrogation on the role(s) of translation as it engages with the constancy of conflict.

Roberto Valdeón's essay highlights the **ideological use** that can be made of language in reporting on conflict, emphasising the deceptive neutrality of words. The language of the news directs the readers' perception of the events which are related, and can be "impregnated with ideology" (Fowler 1991: 24). The essay draws on Fairclough's Critical Discourse Analysis model to examine the ideological implications of the lexical choices made for English-speaking TV news channels (BBC Worldwide and CNN), and for the Spanish versions of these, with specific reference to the aftermath of the Madrid terrorist attacks in March 2004. Valdeón's essay illustrates the limits of impartiality, and suggests that a number of the lexical choices found in these news reports are instances of 'negative mediation'. This echoes Roland Barthes' commentary on the language which was used by the French (right-wing) media to describe and analyse France's major imperial conflict in Algeria (Barthes 1957).

Red Chan's essay, "One Nation, Two Translations: China's Censorship of Hillary's Memoir" focuses on two translations into Chinese of Hillary Clinton's Memoir, *Living History*. Compared with the Taiwanese version, the shorter and simpler version produced for Mainland China presents a number of omissions and shifts of tones which can point to ideological conflict and pressures exerted by censorship. But Chan warns against a monolithic view of censorship as state-centred, and argues that, in the instances when the translators were faced with translating conflict (for example, as embodied in the US Senator's criticism of Mainland China's treatment of its political dissidents), a complex set of constraints were at play. These included self-censorship, in great part, and also market-driven publishing constraints. Self-censorship is an indication that the translators have identified sites of potential ideological confrontation, which is the theme developed in the following two essays by María Calzada Pérez and Tang Jun.

By focusing on **conflict-awareness** in the choice of translation strategies, Tang Jun and María Calzada Pérez' contributions go someway towards outlining the interface between conceptualisation and practice. Looking at translation itself as a potential site of conflict, Tang Jun's essay "Conflicts in Cross-Cultural Communication: Challenges for a Translator" draws on Le Baron's distinction between 'soft' and 'hard' conflicts in order to discuss the strategies which are used by translators to address and negotiate conflict situations. Tang Jun stresses the need for conflict-awareness in her essay, which takes globalisation as the context for translation practice. This is done with reference to contemporary translation from and into Chinese, and to what is seen as an asymmetrical relationship between China and the West in terms of cultural distribution and exchange.

Calzada Pérez moves the discussion one step forward, starting from the assumption that translators can contribute to the debate on advertising and conflict. In her essay "Translating Conflict. Advertising in a Globalised Era" she examines the contents of a Webpage entitled "The McDonald's Theory of Conflict Resolution", and unpacks the confusion of genres which converge to create a message that is ultimately ideological and globalising. The discussion is illustrated by a number of case studies of advertisements, including McDonald's web pages, which cater for a number of countries and adopt different localisation strategies. She concludes her essay by calling on the translator to engage in 'conflict transformation' and to feel empowered to fight for a citizen's world.

The translator's agency in the **manipulation and rewriting of conflict** is demonstrated in Ian Foster's discussion of the German translation of an English work of popular fiction. In his essay "What Germany made of scaremongering in *the Daily Mail*: the translation of William Le Queux's *The Invasion of 1910*", Foster examines the imperial and nationalist agenda which underpinned the writing of an invasion story, belonging to the genre of popular fiction. Foster shows how the German translator's editing and abstracting strategies transformed what was, in essence, an argument in favour of greater preparation for war by the British, and reconstructed it, in his translation, as a prophecy of impending German victory.

It can be argued that John R. William's essay "Ferdinand Freiligrath: translating English conflicts into 19th Century German Nationalism" provides yet another example of translation which can re-invent conflict, in order to give voice to new political preoccupations and concerns and to confront issues of nationalism and patriotism. Williams examines the dissemination of Wordsworth's poetry in nineteenth-century Germany, and discusses Freiligrath's selection and translation of Wordsworth's poetry, with reference to the translation constructs of Schleiermacher and Steiner, and also to the wider context of the translator's political engagement.

Conflict (in its social, military and aesthetic forms) underpins and generates the material discussed in Brian Chadwick's "Translating the Enemy: A 'hip-hop' translation of a poem by the Russian Futurist poet Velimir Khlebnikov (1885-1922)". In order to foreground the conflictual relationship that Russian Futurism had with its contemporary literary norms and aesthetics, and its representation of social transgression against the backdrop of the Bolchevik revolution and the civil war, Chadwick, as an English translator of Khlebnikov's poetry, explores the unchartered territory of rap poetry. The essay suggests that the potential of rap poetry to disrupt literary canons is a possible mapping for the tensions of the Russian poems. This self-reflexive account is framed in terms of Venuti's construct of foreignising and domesticating translation.

Thus far the essays have addressed the translator and interpreter's intervention in varying degrees of immediacy. The next two essays, by Sathya Rao and Beverley Curran, focus on the **fictional translator** who is embroiled in narratives of conflict. The hero of Amadou Hampâté Bâ's novel, which is the object of study of Rao's essay "Wangrin or the political accommodation of translation", operates in the context of French colonial authority over Africa, and of the ensuing conflict between coloniser and colonised, which preceded decolonisation and its choice of orientations. Rao argues that Wangrin's approach is one of 'accommodation', which transcends geopolitical and geolinguistic boundaries, and goes beyond mere opposition, constituting a truly complex and dynamic illustration of conflict. As in Rao's essay, the notion of 'fidelity' or 'loyalty' as a cornerstone of traditional writing on translation is unpacked and dislodged in Curran's "The Embedded Translator: A Coming Out Story". This essay examines the figure of the translator as portrayed in recent Canadian novels that explore World War II and its aftermath. The figure that emerges from Michael Ondaatje's *The English Patient*, and Kerri Sakamoto's *The Electrical Field* is that of an enigmatic, complex and manipulative agent whose conflicting loyalties and allegiances counter the unproblematic representation which is often made of the translator.

The ethical implications of much of the above cannot be overestimated. To claim that the translator and the interpreter are constantly confronted with decisions that are essentially ethical in nature is not new. The works of Henri Meschonnic (1970, 1973) and Antoine Berman (1984, 1985), which hinge on the question of fidelity, are a case in point. In the same vein, the translation project of feminist translators has articulated the ethical take. So has Lawrence Venuti's forceful plea for a visible translation and for more social and ideological commitment. A "return to ethics" was argued in Pym 2001. The 'ethical responsibility' of the translator and the interpreter can take different forms with regard to conflicts, be they real or fictional. As the essays included in this volume demonstrate, this responsibility goes beyond, and indeed sometimes against, the more narrowly defined realm of 'professional ethics' and 'good practice'. It may reside in awareness, in testimony, or in open ideological commitment and involvement.

It is to the increased **visibility and accountability** of translators and interpreters, and to the very real risks that this entails[2], that Carol Maier turns, drawing on her own practice of translation, on actual stances taken by translators and interpreters, and on figures of fictional translators in narratives of conflict. Maier frames and problematises the issue of responsibility in "The Translator's Visibility and the Rights and Responsibilities thereof", arguing that the increased visibility of the translator has not led to a stronger awareness of his/her responsibilities. Questioning the universal applicability of the metaphor of translation as 'in-betweeness' and 'bridge-building', her essay is an overarching plea for translators and trainers to be prepared to "address[ing] the presence of conflict as an integral part of much translation practice".

As this volume illustrates, translators and interpreters can be confronted with many different forms and varying degrees of immediacy of conflict. They may be operating as agents placed on the frontline of war zones, with all the occupational hazards which the posting entails. They could also be dealing with highly-charged texts which narrate and comment on current and past conflicts, albeit from a 'safer' distance', but where neutrality is not necessarily an option, and they may feel compelled to 'overstep' their brief. Any of these situations will call for a degree of intervention, which is inevitably linked with ethical issues.

The essays in this volume span a variety of historical, linguistic and literary contexts, raising issues which are as relevant to high profile cases, such as those of the GCHQ translator Katherine Gunn, and the FBI translator Sibel Edmonds, as they are to the work of the less visible translator or interpreter.

Pierre Bourdieu has called on intellectuals to recognise that they are social actors as well as observers. And the time may have come to accept that the mediation of translators and interpreters, who themselves are social actors, is not always that of detached observers. The relatively new phenomenon of activist networks amongst translators and interpreters, together with an increased awareness of the use of translation and interpreting to serve institutional and political agendas have begun to be addressed in translation and interpreting studies. This does not mean that the professional requirement for neutrality should be challenged, or that advocacy should become the norm, but these issues should nevertheless be problematised. Evidence suggests that neutrality can easily mask complicity and unilaterality. When, in the wake of the 11th September 2001 attacks on New York, the editor of an online translation journal call for translators to "keep in mind the moral distinction between unintended 'collateral damage' in the course of military operations and the deliberate slaughter of civilians"[3], it can be argued that the juxtaposition of 'neutral' euphemistic language and emotionally-charged terms contradicts the plea for neutrality, itself defined in the statement as 'not taking sides in political disputes'. Further, when the need for such 'neutrality' is underpinned by the argument put forward in the statement that "we, ordinary citizens (sic) do not have all the information available to our readers", it does not seem to be dictated by an ethical stand, and the *need to know* becomes even more pressing for the language mediator.

Nudler 1990, proposes a pattern of conflict resolution stages to address the clash of 'worlds' and 'frames' as sets of assumptions and principles, identifying 'primitive Conflict', 'coexistence', 'dialogue' and 'restructuring', where this last stage means that '[n]ew forms of conflict may emerge and new cycles of conflict resolution may then occur' (*ibid*: 178). Drawing on this proposed pattern I would like to suggest that the translator and the interpreter's intervention occurs precisely at this stage of restructuring, whereby their mediation can lead to conflictive representations as much as it can ensure dialogue and conform with the much used metaphor of translation as 'bridge-building'.

The realities of social and political allegiance and commitment, and the ethical stakes of language mediation when personal and collective discourses can sometimes clash, which are increasingly foregrounded within and without translation studies, as evidenced by the growing number of conferences on the subject[4], and the search for new research paradigms, sought mostly from within social sciences[5], must be addressed more explicitly both in the practice of, and in the teaching of translation and interpreting.

---

1 See for instance the following definition of 'neutrality' encountered on a professional translation website: "The concept that establishes that the translator's job is to convey the meaning of the source text and under no circumstance may he or she allow personal opinion to tinge the translation". On line at: http: barinas.com (consulted June 2005).
2 The recent Sydney Pollack's film thriller *The Interpreter* provides a snapshot of this increased visibility (with a dose of glamour to boot!) and illustrates how both vulnerable ("you're only the interpreter") and powerful ("words are slower than guns. But they are better") the position of the linguistic mediator can be.
3 On line at: www.accurapid.com/journal/18editor.htm (consulted 3.8.2006).
4 As evidenced, for instance, by the recent Salford, Manchester and Kent State *Translation and Conflict II* conference (November 2006) and the forthcoming Granada *Translation and Activism* conference (April 2007).
5 The most recent example being Mona Baker's convincing use of the concept of narrative as expounded in social theory (Baker 2006).

## References
Baker, Mona. 2006. *Translation and Conflict. A Narrative Account.* London and New York:Routledge
Barthes, Roland. 1957. 'Grammaire africaine' in Barthes, Roland (1957) *Mythologies*. Paris: Éditions du Seuil.
Bassnett, Susan and André Lefevere (eds). 1998. *Constructing Cultures. Essays on Literary Translation.* Clevedon etc.: Multilingual Matters.
Berman, Antoine. 1984. *L'épreuve de l'étranger – Culture et traduction dans l'Allemagne Romantique*. Paris: Gallimard.
——1985. 'La traduction et la lettre – ou l'auberge du lointain' in Berman *et al* (eds) *Les tours de Babel – Essais sur la traduction*. Mauvezin: Trans-Europ-Repress. 35-91.
Even-Zohar, Itamar. 1990. *Poetics Today* 11(1).
Fowler, Roger. 1991. *Language in the News: Discourse and Ideology in the Press*. London and New York: Routledge
Harris, Brian. 1990. 'Norms in Interpretation' in *Target* 2: 115-119.
Hermans, Theo (ed.). 1985. *The Manipulation of Literature. Studies in Literary Translation*. London and Sidney: Croom Helm.
——1994. 'Translation between Poetics and Ideology' in *Translation and Literature* 3. 138-145.
Hirsch, Marianne. 1997. 'Kraut und Ruben, Choux et navets, kaposta ès répak' in Grenoble, Lenore A. and John M. Kopper (eds) *Essays in the Art and Theory of Translation*. Queenston, Lampeter: The Edwin Mellen Press. 25-33.
Huntingdon, Samuel. 2002. *The Clash of Civilizations and the Remaking of the World Order.* Free Press.

Levefere, André. 1992. *Translation, Rewriting and the Manipulation of Literary Fame*. London and New York: Routledge.
Meschonnic, Henri. 1970. *Pour la poétique*. Paris: Gallimard.
——. 1973. *Pour la poétique II.*. Paris: Gallimard
Nudler, Oscar. 1990. 'On Conflicts and Metaphors: Toward an Extended Rationality' in Burton, John (ed.) *Conflict: Human Needs Theory*. New York: St Martin's Press. 177-201.
Pym, Anthony. 1995. 'Translation as a Transaction Cost' in *Meta* 40(4): 564-605.
——(ed.). 2001. *The Return to Ethics*. Manchester: St Jerome Publishing. Special issue of *The Translator* 7(2).
Robinson, Douglas. 1997. *Translation and Empire. Postcolonial Theories Explained* Manchester: St Jerome Publishing.
Salama-Carr, Myriam (ed.). 2007. *Translation and Conflict*. Special issue of *Social Semiotics* 17(1).
Steiner, George. 1975. *After Babel*. London: Oxford University Press.
Toury, Gideon. 1995. *Descriptive Translation Studies and Beyond*. Amsterdam & Philadelphia: John Benjamins.
Tymoczko, Maria and Edwin Gentzler. 2002. 'Introduction' in Tymoczko, Maria and Edwin Gentzler (eds) *Translation and Power*. Amherst and Boston: University of Massachusetts Press. xi-xxviii.
Venuti, Lawrence. 1995. *The Translator's invisibility. A History of Translation*. London & NewYork: Routledge.

# Part I

# Interpreters and Translators on the Front Line

# Interpreting and Translation for Western Media in Iraq

*Jerry Palmer*

This essay deals with the role of interpreters/translators working for Western media organisations in Iraq since the Anglo-American invasion of 2003. The fault-lines in the political situation in Iraq post-2003 mean that any Iraqi working for Western media – or indeed, any Western organisation – is placed in a situation characterised by potentially conflicting loyalties; and create a situation in which other Iraqis are apt to make different evaluations of their role. The paper deals with the uses to which translation and translators are put rather than the question of the translator's choices concerning their role. For resource reasons it is based on interviews with a number of Western journalists – mostly UK and French – who have worked in Iraq since 2003. It is thus concerned with the uses to which translation is put in particular circumstances: newsgathering in a conflict situation, and therefore in a particular 'target culture', the professional sub-culture of journalism.

Key words: news, fixers, embedding.

The role of the interpreter or translator can be regarded in many ways. At one end on a continuum of possibilities, the interpreter can be seen as little more than a technical relay, that which is necessary in order to ensure the transparent transition of information from one language to another, where translation would be "a uniform and generalized means of exchange, a transparent medium of fluid exchange" (Cronin 1998: 152). In this "conduit theory" of translation (Wadensjö 1998: 7-8), the translator would be replaceable by a machine, should a sufficiently sophisticated one be developed. At the other end of the continuum of possibilities lies the translator who operates in a situation where his or her own cultural belonging is a problematic element in the act of translation. In a recent paper, Cronin gave the example of Henry O'Kane, the Irishman who in 1798 acted as an interpreter for the French Republican Army that invaded what is now the Republic of Ireland to help the United Irishmen in their uprising against British rule: his role - as is clear from contemporary accounts – was both that of a military/political figure in the uprising/invasion and as a translator, interpreting between French and Gaelic. Under these circumstances, the relationship between political commitment and interpreting is clearly a key element in the translator's role. Cronin quotes Charles Taylor, to the effect that such a position clearly means that we must "… recover an understanding of the agent as engaged, as embedded in a culture", in other words as an "embodied agent" (Cronin 2004). Alternatively, we could say that in such situations, the translator is suspended between cultures, since neutrality is close to impossible. Of the two commitments, (s)he may contingently make a commitment to either (or all) of the sides to the conflict.

By the same token, others engaged in the same situation may ask him/her to undertake a variety of different roles, from translator in the limited technical sense, through informant to committed activist: in other words, they may find a variety of uses for this person's translation skills. The commitment that is made is largely responsible for the use to which the act of translation is put. In terms of translation theory, one could say that this involves attention to the "expectations and needs of a target culture" rather than to translation as a technical process (Wadensjö 1998: 5). Additionally, the target culture(s) may well make varied evaluations of the role of the 'interpreter': O'Kane was both admired and feared by different groups in the Irish population - admired as a committed orator, feared as a recruitment agent who placed people in positions of difficult choice about allegiance. The British could potentially have considered him as rebel/traitor; however, as he wore French military uniform, he was treated as a soldier after the suppression of the uprising and was sent to France (Cronin 2004).

There are many combinations and intermediary positions along this continuum of possibilities for interpretation/translation and the uses to which the translator is put. This paper deals with one such: the role of interpreters/translators working for Western media organisations in Iraq since the Anglo-American invasion of 2003.[1]

The fault-lines in the political situation in Iraq post-2003 mean that any Iraqi working for Western media – or indeed, any Western organisation – is placed in a situation characterised by potentially conflicting loyalties; and create a situation in which other Iraqis are apt to make different evaluations of their role. The paper deals with the uses to which translation and translators are put rather than the question of the translator's choices concerning their role. For resource reasons it is based on interviews with a number of Western journalists – mostly UK and French – who have worked in Iraq since 2003. It is thus concerned with the uses to which translation is put in particular circumstances: newsgathering in a conflict situation, and therefore in a particular *target culture*, the professional sub-culture of journalism.

In media theory, the role of the translator or interpreter is that of an intermediary in the flow of information between events and the publication of news (and ultimately therefore the public). Journalists are rarely eye-witnesses of events unless they know in advance that they are occurring, or unless the event is of sufficient duration for them to arrive while it is ongoing.[2] Commonly, either they are informed that an event will occur – e.g. a press conference, a demonstration – or they must seek out direct witnesses who can inform them – e.g. survivors and the emergency services after an accident; the generic name for such intermediaries is *sources*.[3] In either case, the nature of the intermediary is problematic, as their structural position in society, their motives and their interests may influence the account they give. This is especially true of those who are professionally engaged in producing the profiles of events for public consumption, such as communications officers and public relations practitioners, who have extensively developed strategies for dealing with information flows into the public realm (see e.g. Palmer 2000; Davis 2002). The analysis of the relationships between journalists and their sources – or, sources and their journalists – is an integral element of the theory of journalism, as well as a matter of intense practical concern for journalists engaged in attempts to provide reliable accounts of events; there is an extensive literature on the subject. From this point of view translators are a further element or stage in the information flow. The context in which they work, their motives and interests in the process, constitute an element in the flow in the same way as sources' context, motives and interests. Their role can be seen in the following diagram of information flow:

[→ indicates the flow of information]

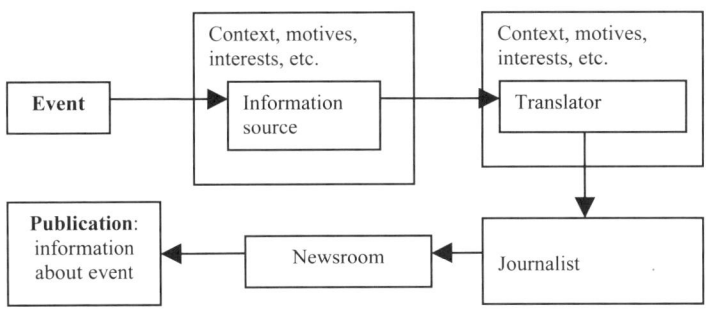

This diagram omits the possibility that the translator might in fact intervene in the process at more than one point, something to which we shall return. It also omits the question of journalists' motives, etc: for the purposes of this argument, the latter are considered simply as a function of news-gathering.

Currently (autumn, 2004), the question of the context and the motives of translators has arisen in the form of a set of concerns that have been raised with regard to their role. They are:

1. The safety of media personnel, including interpreters
2. The trustworthiness of the interpreters (and other Iraqi personnel)
3. The extent to which using them produces biased journalism

In the period March, 2003 to late October 2004, 36 journalists and 13 co-workers such as interpreters, drivers and fixers were killed in Iraq; some 20 have been kidnapped (CPJ 2004).[4] The deterioration of the security situation in Iraq since (roughly) November 2003 has put extra pressures on Iraqi journalists and media workers. Many places in Iraq are now too dangerous for European and US journalists, and substantial amounts of reporting are done by Iraqis employed by Western media in a variety of ways, usually as stringers or as fixers, some of whom have become proxy journalists (Campagna and Sabra 2004; Boldrick 2004).[5] In addition to the murders of Western and Iraqi journalists, Iraqi translators and fixers have been the victims of murders and death threats (Prothero 2004; Boldrick 2004). Roughly half the media personnel killed in Iraq have been Iraqi nationals (Feuilherade 2004). While the major cause of the murder of Iraqi personnel is no doubt to make life more difficult for the occupation forces, in at least one case the American journalist in question found that other Iraqis approved of the murder because the translator – an Iraqi woman – appeared excessively western to them, as she did not wear a veil in public and drove a car (Borkgren 2004).

The second concern is the reliability of translators and interpreters. The attacks of 9/11 and the Iraq war led the US army and intelligence services to rapidly increase the number of Arabic speaking personnel available to them, with ambiguous results: some Arabic interpreters at Guantanamo Bay have been accused of sabotaging interviews with prisoners through mistranslation (Boulet 2003). The US military had considerable difficulty in recruiting translators and interpreters with sufficient speed to cope with the new circumstances (Dinan and Taylor 2003), and one of the tactics used was to outsource these facilities, notably to the Titan Corporation. Titan's performance led to complaints about the competence of the personnel they hired (Washburn 2004), and it was subsequently announced that the Titan contract was being reviewed (Bigelow 2004). Although there is a substantial Arabic-speaking population in the USA, it has been suggested that many of them are unwilling to be involved with US organisations in Iraq, or more largely in the 'war on terror', although there is evidence of Arab-speaking US citizens working in Iraq (Soza 2003; Garwood 2004). In parallel, US military personnel have voiced doubts about the trustworthiness of Arabic-speaking personnel hired locally in Iraq, in relation to security issues: it has been alleged that - whether deliberately or by mistake - interpreters have given US soldiers false information (Marting 2004; Sperry 2004).

Thirdly, the increasing use of Iraqi stringers and fixers as correspondents for Western media has led some editors to express doubts about the viability of the journalism that is the result (Boldrick 2004). Some neo-conservative American commentators have suggested that post-invasion reliance on Iraqis with links to the previous regime has led to biased reporting of the situation (Rubin 2004; Foreman 2003).

In Iraq, the dependence on translators should be seen in the context of a further form of dependence: 'embedding' with military units, the process by which a journalist is attached to a particular unit who are responsible for his (and occasionally her) safety, and whose activities the journalist records, subject to military restrictions on the publication of information.[6] The embedded journalist does not normally require an interpreter, and where the need arises the military supply one.[7] The policy purpose of embedding is a greater degree of transparency in the dealings between military and media, with the longer term aim of securing public consent to the military activity in question (Tumber and Palmer 2004: Part 1). The 'dependence' in question, and the concerns about information flows to which it gives rise, are essentially these:

- The journalist may become emotionally attached to the unit to which (s)he is attached, and thus lose the necessary professional critical distance.
- The journalist will inevitably see things from the unit's side of the lines, which may affect their perspective in the broader sense of the word.

However, it is clear from an incident in the fighting in Falluja in November 2004, that embedding does not inevitably produce reporting that is *on message* from the military point of view: an NBC cameraman/reporter embedded with a US Marine unit filmed a Marine shooting an apparently unarmed and clearly badly wounded Iraqi; at the time of writing this incident is subject to US military investigation. In any event, an analysis of the coverage of the invasion of Iraq in 2003 indicates that neither embedding nor other forms of dependence upon official sources necessarily produces coverage in line with policy intentions (Tumber and Palmer 2004: 103-6). However, the Pentagon expressed its satisfaction at the results of the embedding arrangements in the period after the invasion (*ibid.*: 58-61).

Seen from the point of view of media theory, embedding is part of the context in which journalists are able to witness events and gain access to sources. Any element of dependence involved is potentially a form of *noise* in the information channel. In a context such as the current circumstances in Iraq, journalists are often placed in a position in which they must choose between high levels of personal danger, dependence upon the military in the form of embedding or dependence upon an interpreter/translator. For instance, in the US attack upon Falluja (early November, 2004) the overwhelming majority of journalists covering events were embedded with US forces: very few journalists published by English language media covered them from the other side of the front line (Feuilherade 2004). Therefore, in considering the uses to which translation is put under these circumstances, we will pay close attention to the extent to which dependence upon translation affects information flows.

For this paper, 17 journalists were interviewed, roughly evenly divided between French and British, and between audio-visual and print media. The interviews were semi-structured, with a check-list of questions that were sent in advance. Of these journalists, the overwhelming majority spoke no or very little Arabic and all asserted that few Western journalists had an adequate level of language competence for journalism.[8] Most knew the names of the few Arabic-speaking journalists in their organisations (where there were any), which suggests the rarity of the skill. Only one journalist I interviewed was fluent in Arabic (from birth). All of the non-Arabic-speaking journalists had used interpreters, and even the native Arabic speaker needed one on occasions, as the Iraqi version of Arabic is sufficiently different from his for him to need help in complex interviews about political topics. In most cases, the interpreter was also a *fixer*, i.e. performing a range of duties beyond interpretation/translation; this is an important element in the situation, and one which will be considered at length. In practice, it was clear from the interviews that it was the interpreters' capacity as fixers that determined their employment.

In the pattern of fixer recruitment, there was one systematic difference between French and UK journalists. The majority of the French-employed fixers had been relatively closely associated with the Saddam regime, in the sense of having had an official post of some description. The French fixers were ex-military in many cases, some of them quite highly placed (a general, a colonel), or former employees of the Ministry of Information. However, my informants stressed that this did not mean that they had been implicated in human rights abuses or other negative aspects of the previous regime; indeed, one of their criteria for employing them was that they had an honourable record under the Saddam regime. Nor did it necessarily mean that their fixers were pro-Saddam; some were, and openly discussed their sympathies with their new employers; others were anti-Saddam (or now claimed to have been). French journalists did not regard their pasts as a problem, rather as a useful way of opening doors in Iraqi society, while taking note of the extent to which their pasts might inflect the way in which they carried out their work. The UK-employed fixers were in the majority either not linked to the Saddam regime, or only peripherally so: typically, they were ex-students or professionals (a teacher, a doctor, a non-official tour guide, for example).

The purposes for which interpreters and fixers are used are detailed below:
- interpreting in interviews and translating local media;
- arrangimg interviews, including - within limits - selecting the interviewee;
- background briefings about the identities of potential interviewees, situations, social groups, etc.;
- some reporting, especially summaries of events to which the European journalist cannot have access; also some interviews, especially 'vox pops';
- security assessments, due to the level of danger caused by the degradation of the security situation;
- access to networks of local contacts;
- protection for journalists via the fixers' links with local networks of influence, and - if necessary - negotiation with kidnappers;
- spying on other journalists (one case only).

Local media are used - in conjunction with the Western news agencies - as background for journalistic initiatives and as part of the search for newsworthy events. Fixers' local knowledge is a precious resource in terms of background information about personalities, situations, and organisations or social groups: in an interview, knowledge of the identity of the speaker is an integral part of understanding the meaning of their words. Interpretation in interviews frequently takes the form of a mixture of summary and translation, rather than word-for-word interpretation. The same consideration applies in the arranging of interviews: the fixer has the language skills and the contacts necessary to arrange an interview, and this may extend to being better able than the western journalist to select the exact individual who best corresponds to the journalistic demands of the situation.

The deterioration in the security situation (which my informants dated from autumn 2003) has led to security assessments being an integral part of the fixer's role: he is better able than a westerner to assess whether going to a particular place in order to get material is likely to be possible, or excessively dangerous.

Access to networks of local contacts is regarded as one of the most important attributes of a fixer. In part this is due to the security situation, where intimate, highly localised knowledge is crucial. However, it is also due to the nature of Iraqi society, where religious, tribal, political and personal affiliations are crucial in the creation of trust. The interaction of this traditional structure with the security situation makes detailed local knowledge most important. This judgement was common among my informants, however we shall see that the conclusions that they drew from it were somewhat varied.

The point about protection, and - if necessary - negotiation - was made only by French journalists. This may be because historically they have been more vulnerable than UK ones, or it may be that they are more likely to have fixers who are useful in this respect than their UK equivalents. One French journalist told me that the French Embassy in Baghdad had contacted his fixer and asked him to act as an intermediary in negotiations with the kidnappers of two French journalists working in Iraq.[9]

Under these circumstances, trust is clearly a paramount issue. There have been complaints that fixers, interpreters and other personnel employed by the coalition forces or by the Iraqi Government may have betrayed personnel movements to the insurgents (for example, after the murder of 50 newly trained Iraqi soldiers on October 24, 2004 [Howard 2004]; see also Hilsum 2004). All my informants stated that they trusted their fixers, and several made the point that they regularly trusted him/her with their lives.

We have seen what the roles of interpreters and fixers are. Next we consider the risks that journalists think arise from dependence upon them. Briefly stated, they are these:

- Mistranslation and/or omission of significant material
- Inability to *blend in* with the local population and to understand the local culture
- Excessive dependence on the fixer
- The fixer *forming* the journalist's view of the situation

Firstly, trust also extends to trust in professional competence as translators and interpreters. Most of the people used as interpreters in Iraq do not meet the normal standards of professional competence of trained interpreters. Indeed, Kevin Hendzel, of the American Translators Association complained that even bilingual command of the relevant languages is not enough to bring professional competence in this respect (Washburn 2004). Under these circumstances, the risks of mistranslation are apparent. My informants said that in general they did not expect word-for-word translation, and that summaries were generally enough. The reasons given were various, but the chief considerations appear to be: (a) much of the information sought from ordinary Iraqis is simple, of the order: where were you? What did you see? Several journalists contrasted this kind of information with an interview with a leading politician, where the exact nuances of his/her words would be of central importance; (b) full length translation would cause delays, which would be unproductive and possibly dangerous, especially in a tense situation; (c) (but this came from one journalist only, albeit one who is learning Arabic) Arabic conversation is so full of linguistic "detours" that summary is preferable.

Clearly, opting for something between summary and translation creates the possibility of misinformation entering the communication chain; interviewees were well aware of this possibility, and they had various techniques for dealing with it. Firstly, they checked the translation/summary by asking the same question several times in different ways, until they were sure that the information they were getting was consistent. Secondly, they would check with other journalists whether their fixer had a good reputation - this last was used by the French journalists, who pointed out that the francophone group was small and everybody knew each other well. Thirdly, they checked the information they were getting against another source. Logically, this does not confirm the accuracy of the translation, only of the information; clearly the informants were not interested in the niceties of interpretation, only in the usefulness of the information they were given. In general, the journalists were happy that risks of mistranslation were small enough not to be significant. Commonly, they trusted the translations because of the fixer's track record with them and their colleagues.

However, mistranslation is not the only risk: clearly omission of significant material is also relevant, and several journalists pointed to the risk of losing useful information from things like the little conversational asides between translator and interviewee which would get left out of the summary as not being part of the question-and-answer. A good example was given by an English journalist who speaks a little Arabic: in a conversation about the ongoing violence with a group of people in the street, he heard one of them use the Arabic word for 'resistance', and several others chide the speaker for his choice of word. This was omitted from the summary by the interpreter, but the journalist was able to ask for clarification. Also mentioned as a problem was that lack of Arabic meant that the journalist could not blend in through the use of common forms of politeness and other elementary elements of manners: such techniques can be used to reduce the distance between journalist and informant, and the impossibility of using them means that the journalist is unable to try to gain the informant's confidence in one of the usual ways.

If this point is taken in combination with the earlier point about checking information against other sources, it is easy to see how a purely functional attitude towards translation can lead to omission of potentially relevant material. The 'functional' attitude towards translation leads to a focus on verifiable facts; the attitude manifest in the English journalist's search for clarification shows a concern for background material that may help to illuminate facts through reference to elements of local culture. In general, many of the journalists noted that lack of linguistic competence led to lack of understanding of the local culture, with all its associated risks of not understanding what is said when it is translated, and even not understanding events and situations.

Journalists were aware that fixers might bring their own agendas to bear on the interactions that they made possible for the journalist, thus effectively transforming the journalist into a propagandist on their behalf; however, those who mentioned it did so primarily as a theoretical possibility rather than a real threat. Another possibility noted was that constant use of a single fixer would lead to the fixer either intentionally or otherwise "forming the horizon" of the journalist through a consistent pattern of interpretation of events and of contacts with the local population. One UK journalist said he preferred not to use them for this reason, but nevertheless acknowledged the importance of the fixer's contacts. It is a particular risk in a context where the security situation is so dangerous that the journalist depends upon the fixer for an assessment of the possibility of actually being in a particular place. Several journalists reported having to lean on their fixers not to be excessively timid in their security assessments - in one case, this amounted to refusing to accept the assessment and spending four days trying to find a gap in the US military encirclement of Najaf at the height of the confrontations with the "Mahdi Army" of Moqtada Al Sadr in the summer of 2004 (with eventual success).

Clearly the risk of the fixer *forming* the journalist is the obverse of the advantage of the fixer having a network of local contacts: this access is structured by the fixer's own identity. At one level, this may take the form of the relatively inaccessible nature of particular parts of Iraq for individual fixers due to their religious identity, in particular Sunni versus Shia. Several journalists said that a Sunni fixer could not get into Shia areas (and vice-versa), but others asserted that this was far from the norm. One French journalist argued that the legacy of the *Ba'ath* party included a section of Iraqi society which was broadly secular and nationalist in outlook, and therefore relatively immune to religious intolerance; however, it should be remembered that the French journalists in my sample had fixers with relatively formalised and extensive contacts with the previous regime, and who would therefore have had access to precisely the section of Iraqi society in question; whether the same would be true under other circumstances is open to question. Several journalists queried the centrality of the religious divide, arguing that tribal affiliation and local contacts were much more important; these journalists had examples of fixers being able to cross the religious divides without difficulty. The ability or willingness of fixers to cross such boundaries would influence the range of contacts available to the journalist; however, journalists working for major broadcasting organisations had several fixers.

At another level, it is less a question of the direct effect of contacts, accessibility, etc., and more a question of outlook: the place the fixer occupies in social networks is clearly influential in forming their own view of the world, and this may be presumed to play into the way in which they interpret the world around them when offering background information to the journalist about the identity or significance of such-and-such an individual or group.

In analysing the risks involved in dependence upon fixers, I have also analysed the techniques used to avoid adverse effects deriving from this dependence. I have spoken of these techniques as if they were evenly distributed among my informants, but in fact this was not so; individual differences between journalists could be observed at these points. There were no systematic differences (except for the one analysed above, re recruitment). The individual differences I take to indicate that at the points where they occur there are particularly acute pressures on the journalistic process, sufficiently acute to produce different analyses of the situation from journalists.

The main points at which differences occurred were linked to two questions:
- Reliability of information as it passed down the chain of source – translator - journalist;
- The influence of the fixers' network of local contacts on the journalistic process.
- Lack of understanding of local culture stemming from lack of linguistic competence.

In other words, the forms of dependence and the techniques for dealing with them were more or less universal; differences arose at the point where journalists evaluated the significance of these elements of the process.

Where reliability of information was concerned, the difference between journalists lay in their evaluation of how much impact dependence on translation would have. All agreed about how to minimise it, but differed in the degree of their optimism about how much difference these techniques made. One group was robust in their assertion that ultimately journalistic skills were of so much greater importance than linguistic skills that dependence upon translation was of minimal importance. Others felt that having to depend upon translation was a real disadvantage, not in the sense of competitive disadvantage, since so few Western journalists speak Arabic, but in the sense of closing off avenues of approach to journalistic work that would be open to them if they did. This included analysis of the desirability of having an intuitive understanding of the culture of the country: some felt that speaking Arabic would give them an insight into the culture that would not be available without the language skills; others felt either that this was not that important, or even that it might be a positive disadvantage, because excessive familiarity with the local culture might lead to the journalist becoming excessively assimilated into it, and losing the critical distance necessary to preserve journalistic professionalism: assimilation readily leads to judgments about the relative interest of events and people dictated by local concerns rather than Western ones. One journalist even made both sets of assertions at different times. It is worth noting that these journalists were predominantly reporters who were sent to Iraq (and other places) for relatively brief tours of duty, rather than people permanently based there, or even in the Middle East.

Similarly opposed views of the fixers' network of contacts emerged, as we have seen. On the one hand, virtually all the journalists stressed the productivity of working with a fixer with a good range of contacts, as well as its role in creating security. On the other, some saw no disadvantages in this, while others could see that there was a downside as well as an upside: the downside is the extent to which the structured nature of the fixers' range of contacts might skew the journalists' vision of events.

**Conclusion.**

In the circumstances with which this essay is concerned, the translator, interpreter or fixer is an intermediary in a process whose efficacy depends largely upon a certain porosity: as information passes down the chain linking (and separating) event from publication, the less it is changed, the better it is. This corresponds to the conduit model of translation, with the proviso that it is not the adequacy of the translation that is really at issue so much as the adequacy of the information referred to by the translation. If each link in the chain is completely porous, so that information passes through it unchanged, the chain will not functionally damage the information; if at each stage changes are introduced, the opposite is true. Each stage is in fact a person or an institution, socially constituted and laden with all the baggage that implies: each person is embedded in a culture (or suspended between different commitments), each piece of knowledge – including the technical competence to translate – is embodied in an individual or a group of individuals or an institution, which may well have made decisions about the purposes for which the information should be used, and developed corresponding exclusions of purposes. In the case of Iraq, the culture within which Iraqi nationals working as fixers are embedded - their original, parent culture - is fraught with conflicts which directly affect their capacity to do their job, notably through the level of danger that they face.

The only systematic element in the relationship between translators' context, motives and interests derives from the difference in patterns of recruitment between French and UK-employed fixers. According to French journalists, their fixers' backgrounds did not have any negative effect upon their usefulness. The only way to check whether the difference in fixers' backgrounds had any impact upon reporting would be a systematic comparison between French and UK media coverage of post-invasion Iraq to ascertain whether there were differences that could be imputed to the nature of the fixers. However, even this would not be proof of their role because of the other variables in the information flows between events and journalists.

By the same token, those who employ translators and interpreters do so for reasons that are similarly embedded. In this instance, the embedding is in a professional culture[10,] which acts as the target culture for the translator. What features of this professional culture are implicated in the way in which the act of translation is used by journalists in Iraq?

Firstly, the act of translation is not highly valued: very few of the people employed by journalists are exclusively translators/interpreters; the overwhelming majority are employed as fixers, whose tasks include translation. Indeed, translation does not figure as the major competence sought; the main competences are a good network of contacts and the capacity to see things through the prism of journalism. Although journalists have some concerns about the competence of translators, these did not figure very prominently in discussions with them, and did not worry them very much. Qualifications as translators were not even mentioned in these discussions – the only thing that counted in this respect was track record. In other words, the act of translation is aimed at a target culture rather than a target language. However, it may be that the nature of the target languages in this sample was an important element of the calculation: both English and French are widely spoken by educated Iraqis, and therefore there is no shortage of potential interpreters; had the target language been a less frequently spoken language, the situation might have been different.[11]

Secondly, the capacity to provide contacts and to interpret situations was highly valued: a good general knowledge of Iraqi society combined with a bulging address book was the key element. In other words, it is the very embeddedness of the translator that is his/her most valuable attribute. Yet at the same time, this is also the source of what journalists see as one of the major risks involved in dependence on the fixer: the fixer may determine, to some extent, what the journalist sees. It is at this point that differences between journalists become apparent in the interviews – they give different evaluations of the risks. Clearly, this is a point of tension in their understanding of the situation: the prime positive qualities of the fixer are also the potentially negative ones.

Thirdly, some journalists at least were well aware of the disadvantage of cultural distance from the host country, and the attendant risk of partial or mis-understanding. At one level, this is an unavoidable given, since their linguistic competence is what it is; on the other hand, it can be evaluated in different ways, as we have seen, and the evaluations are clearly a product of the professional sub-culture of journalism. The different orientations towards cultural (mis)understanding no doubt play into other aspects of the fixer-journalist relationship and in particular the extent to which the journalist seeks interpretive information about events from the translator.

1 The invasion period is not analysed, as interview and media output evidence suggests that the Western journalists working on the Anglo-US side of the lines did not need or use translators during this phase of the Iraq crisis. Journalists working on the Iraqi side did so, if only because a condition of working in Saddam's Iraq was working with a 'translator' cum minder supplied or approved by the Ministry of Information. Western journalists considered these people as a kind of police of their activities. Non-Western journalists accompanying the Anglo-US forces may well have had translation difficulties: a journalist I interviewed in the course of preparing this paper said that a Japanese TV journalist he knew visibly understood little of what American soldiers were saying.
2 Any greater degree of precision would involve careful definition of what constitutes an 'event', which is sociologically complex. In particular, the 'news cycle' of 24 hours leads to a distinction of events based on this periodicity. Journalists make informed guesses about the prolongation of event sequences over a period of time which leads them to actively seek information about potential events in the future (Palmer 2000: 125-33).
3 Journalists sometimes reserve the term 'sources' for the specially cultivated relationships they have with a limited number of informants whom they trust; media sociologists use the term generically.
4 The International News Safety Institute and the International Federation of Journalists give slightly different figures. Variations are probably due to different definitions of what constitutes a journalist or media worker, as well as different dates of compilation.
5 'Stringer' means a local journalist who is employed on a part-time or piece-work basis by some other non-local news channel; 'fixer' means someone who does a variety of jobs for a journalist – see below.
6 See Tumber and Palmer, 2004, Part 1, for an extended discussion of the embedding process and the rules attached to it. In general, journalists who have been embedded regard the restrictions as a minimal inconvenience when balanced against the improved access given by this arrangement.
7 Several journalists I spoke to had had interpreters supplied by the Anglo-US military in Iraq.
8 Several interviewees said they were learning Arabic, as they felt it was likely to be a useful journalistic skill in the future and one of the organisations employing two of the journalists I spoke to had recently set up a training course in Arabic.
9 The journalists have subsequently been released by their kidnappers.
10 Which in its turn is embedded in the wider culture commonly called 'modern industrial Western' culture. The latter is of course widely shared – at least in its general orientation – across a wide spectrum of nations, ethnic groups, etc., outside of its origins, although far from universally so. However, at the moment of its importation into any new context, it may well meet with at least partial resistance; this is likely to be especially fraught at points where its introduction is accompanied by force. The extent to which these general considerations apply in Iraq, or more generally in the Middle East, is beyond the scope of this paper.
11 Some of the journalists interviewed had also worked in the Darfur region of Sudan during the recent (2004) humanitarian crisis; they spoke of multi-stage translation, involving two translators: English/French – Arabic – local language.

# References

Beaumont, Peter. 2004. 'The Final Battle?' in *The Observer* (14 November 2004).
Bigelow, Bruce. 2004. 'Iraq: Titan's Army contract under review', in *The San Diego Union Tribune* (27 May 2004). On line at: http://www.corpwatch.org/article.php?id=11339 (consulted 01.11.2006).
Boldrick, John. 2004. 'Editing conflicts in the post-9/11 world', Overseas Press Club of America panel report. On line at: http://www.opcofamerica.org/events/articles/9-1_091504.php (consulted 01.08.2004).
Borkgrel, Sherrlyn. 2004. 'In the Shadows: Ashcraf's Bullet', *Digital Journalist*, July. On line at: http://www.digitaljournalist.org/issue0407/dis_borkgren.html (consulted 01.08.2004).
Boulet, Jim. 2003. 'The Peril of Perfidious Translators. A Clintonian problem' in *The National Review* (8 October 2003). On line at: http://www.nationalreview.com/comment/boulet2003-10080856.asp (consulted 01.08.2004).
Campagna, Jod and Sabra, Hani. 2004. 'Under Threat: Iraqi Journalists Face Hazards', on line at: http://www.cpj.org/Briefings/Iraq/iraq_reports.html (consulted 01.08.2004).
CPJ (Committee for the Protection of Journalists). 2004. 'Briefing'. On line at: www.cpj.org/briefings/2003/gulf03/iraq_stats.html. (consulted 01.08.2004).
Cronin, Michael. 1998. 'The cracked looking glass of servants', *The Translator* 4 (2): 145-62.
-----2004. 'Global agency and local resistance: a microcosmopolitan perspective'. Paper presented at Conference on 'Translation and Conflict', (University of Salford, 26-28 November 2004).
Davis, Aeron. 2002. *Public Relations Democracy. Public Relations, Politics and the Mass Media in Britain.* Manchester: Manchester University Press.
Dinan, Stephen and Taylor, Gary. 2003. 'Pentagon rushed Arabic translators' in *The Washington Post* (14 October 1992). On line at: http://washingtontimes.com/national/20031014-114241-5856r.htm (consulted 01.08.2004).
Feuilherade, Peter. 2004. 'Reporting Falluja - "America's second war" in Iraq', BBC Monitoring Services report. On line at: www.nnthaewssafety.com/stories/bbc/iraq9.htm (consulted 01.08.2004).
Foreman, Jona. 2003. 'Bad reporting in Baghdad', *Weekly Standard.* Quoted Project for a new American century. On line at: www.newamericancentury.org/iraq-20030505.htm (consulted 01.08.2004).
Garwood, Paul. 2004. 'U.S. Troops Face Language Barrier in Iraq' in *Associated Press/LATimes* (26 January 2004). On line at: www.occupationwatch.org/article.php?id=2807 (consulted 01.08.2004).
Hilsum, Lindsay. 2004. 'Falluja can only be won when the battle ends and people have water' in *The Observer* (7 November 2004).
Howard, Michael. 2004. 'Massacre of 50 Iraqi soldiers. National guards shot in back of head' in *The Guardian* (25 October 2004).
IFJ (International Federation of Journalists). 2003. 'Justice Denied On the Road To Baghdad'. On line at http://www.ifj.org (consulted 01.08.2004).
IFJ 2004. Press release 02.11.2004. On line at: www.ifj.org/default.asp?index=2769&Language=EN (consulted 01.08.2004).
Marting, Susan. 2004. 'Shortage of interpreters foreshadowed prison excesses' in *The St Petersburg Times* (20 May 2004). On line at: www.globalsecurity.org/org/news/2004/040520-interpreters-shortage.htm (consulted 01.08.2004).
OPC (Overseas Press Club of America). 2004. On line at: www.opcofamerica.org/events/articles/9-11_091504.php (consulted 01.08.2004).
Palmer, Jerry. 2000. *Spinning into Control. News Values and Source Strategies*. London: Continuum.
Plunkett, John. 2003. 'CNN star reporter attacks war coverage' in *The Guardian* (16 September 2003).
-----2004. 'Western journalists quit Falluja' in *The Guardian G2* (9 November 2004).

Prothero, P.Mitchell. 2004. 'Letter from Iraq', *Dangerous Assignments*, Winter/Fall. On line at: http://www.cpj.org/Briefings/2004/DA_fall04/Iraq_Prothero_DA_fall04.html (consulted 01.11.2006).
Rubin, Michael. 2004. www.nationalreview.com/rubin/rubin200406210825.asp (consulted 1.11.2006).
Soza, Samuel A. 2003 'Interpreters role in Iraq more important than ever', submitted by Marine expeditionary force, Pfc. Soza, story identification: 2003851 5541.
Sperry, Paul. 2004. 'Army interpreters betraying soldiers. U.S. resorts to hiring ex-Saddam loyalists to gather intelligence' in *WorldNetDaily.com*, (10 February 2004). On line at: www.worldnetdaily.com/news/article.asp?ARTICLE_ID=37039 (consulted 01.08.2004).
Tumber, Howard and Palmer, Jerry. 2004. *Media at War: the Iraq Crisis*. London: Sage.
Wadensjö, Cecilia. 1998. *Interpreting as Interaction*. Harlow, Essex: Addison Wesley Longman.
Washburn, David. 2004. 'Contractor Titan's hiring faulted' in *The San Diego Union Tribune* (May 21 2004). On line at: http://www.signonsandiego.com/news/metro/20040521-9999-1n21titan.html (consulted 01.08.2004).

# The Practice of Translation and Interpreting During the Conflicts in the Former Yugoslavia (1991-1999)

*Mila Dragovic-Drouet*

This essay investigates translation and interpreting in a conflict situation, with specific reference to practice in the former Yugoslavia after the dislocation of the federal state in 1991. I examine the tasks that translators and interpreters were required to perform, and discuss the practical limitations on their role as mediators. Some of the recommendations and norms which are set out when translation and interpreting is taught will be confronted with examples drawn from the author's own practice and experience, that of other professionals, and from media coverage.

Key words: mediation, misinformation, professional norms

When the late Danica Seleskovitch lectured to postgraduate students at the École Supérieure d'Interprètes et de Traducteurs in Paris, she stressed the three prerequisites of professional translation: knowledge of the source and the target languages, knowledge of the topic, and above all *professional methodology*. The latter, acquired through training, consisted, amongst other things, in making a future translator fully aware that (s)he is a neutral mediator in someone else's communication, that mutual understanding should be prioritised and that the professional mediator's own opinion and stance should never be either evident or communicated.

The practice of translation in the Yugoslavian conflicts during the 1990s offers, unfortunately, more than one example of how these theoretical prerequisites can be contravened in a conflict situation, where inadequate linguistic knowledge and skill in both translators and interpreters was frequently a problem, as was their subjectivity when they were personally related to the parties in conflict.

Peter Newmark writes that translators "must be seen as key figures in promoting better understanding among peoples and nations. [...] They have the authority to mediate between parties, and they have their own responsibility to moral as well as factual truth" (Newmark 1989: 24-25). The illustrations below indicate that to put these recommendations into practice is far from being easy, when understanding amongst peoples and nations gives way to a conflict situation in which moral and factual truth often falls foul to an agenda of war propaganda.

Discussion of translation and interpreting in the Yugoslavian conflicts has to be situated within the overall linguistic context: excepting that between Serbs and Albanians in 1998-99 (which will be taken into consideration later), the conflicts took place between speakers of the same mother tongue, i.e. Serbo-Croatian. As language is a major element of community identity, it is often an important factor in the political aims of independence movements, which may wish to create and emphasise differences between idioms that originally were considered as being no more than regional dialects of the same language. This is why the fragmentation of the federal state of Yugoslavia led to the splitting of the common language into "Bosnian", "Croatian", "Serbian", and even "Montenegrian". But languages, unlike countries, cannot be created by decree.

The case of a Serbian film entitled *Rane* ('The Wounds'), which was shown with "Croatian" subtitles to a Zagreb cinema audience, provides an interesting example of the gap that can exist between official language policy and its (ironic) acceptance by ordinary speakers. At the beginning of the film the Serbian to Croatian "translator", who remains anonymous, used considerable inventive powers to coin new words that sounded "Croatian", but, as the script progressed he gave up the effort, and contented himself with transliterating words from "Serbian" into "Croatian" solely on the basis of differences in pronunciation. This obvious attempt at constructing artificial linguistic differentiation provoked gales of laughter from the audience.[1]

With reference to the fact that neither translation nor interpreting was necessary between the parties in conflict, and that on the international level (i.e. for negotiations, peace conferences, trials etc…) all translation and interpreting was carried out in accordance with international professional norms, further considerations will be confined to: (1) The translation of information about the conflict, performed for foreign consumption; (2) Liaison interpreting, for foreign media reporters, for non-governmental organisations, and for the peace-keeping forces.

**1. Translating information about the conflict**
Information on a conflict includes both relating immediate events and analysing their causes. In both cases, amongst the public interested in receiving information on the Yugoslavian conflicts, very few could access first hand sources in the original language. Thus, the foreign media and the publishing houses were expected to act as mediators, together with the translators who worked for them. However, the translators' mediation was only indirect, as they had no control over the selection of information to be communicated.

It is interesting to mention that the published writings: the "Islamic Declaration" by Alija Izetbegovic, president of Bosnia-Herzegovina between 1990 and 2000, and the "Wastelands – Historical Truth" by Franjo Tudjman, president of Croatia in the same period, were mistranslated in their English and French versions.[2] Consequently the fundamentalist contents of the former and the anti-Semitic substance of the latter were minimized in the Western media. Furthermore the translated versions of the well-known *Memorandum* - the Serbian text which allegedly advocated "ethnic cleansing" in order to establish a "Greater Serbia", not only misquoted it, but also wrongly attributed it to Slobodan Milosevic. This text was in fact a working document, produced by a group of members of the Serbian Academy of Science and Arts in September 1986 (i.e. before Milosevic's election as leader of the Serbian communist party), about the necessity of reforming federal institutions in the prevailing economic and political situation. It only uses the phrase "*etnički čisto Kosovo*" ('ethnically clean Kosovo') twice, and then it is to denounce the claims of Albanian independence movements in the province. Furthermore the phrase "Greater Serbia" does not occur at all.

Translators could hardly be held responsible for conveying misinformation, as they operated before the information was disseminated, in a process dictated by the *modus operandi* of the Western media. Statements and speeches made in a given language are frequently reported or paraphrased by journalists, to give the impression that their original utterance had been in the language of the reporter (see Biardzka 2004). However this is not to say that journalists were necessarily the ones at fault in all cases. Another example of the truth becoming subordinate to political involvement is quoted by Lord David Owen, the special representative of the European Union in Bosnia-Herzegovina. In his book *Balkan Odyssey* Owen mentions the massacre which took place in the Sarajevo market place in February 1994, and which was widely attributed to the Serbian forces. According to Lord Owen UN ballistic experts tended to believe that:

> [...] the mortar had been fired from a Bosnian army position. When this highly charged information reached the UN in New York on Tuesday everything was done to clamp down on the number of people who saw it as to reduce the chance of press leak. (Owen 1996: 260-61, also quoted in Collon 1998: 47)

The above examples call into question Newmark's statement that translators should be seen as key figures who convey moral as well as factual truth. In fact, in most cases, they are not given the chance to influence public opinion: it is their employers and commissioners who do this. In the journalist Jacques Merlino's 1994 book, *Les vérités yougoslaves ne sont pas toutes bonnes à dire* ('Truths about Yugoslavia are not always good to tell'), one of these "truths" concerns the important role played by public relation agencies in shaping public opinion. "Ruder Finn Global Public Affairs" was one such agency, which worked on behalf of both the governments of Croatia and Bosnia-Herzegovina, and additionally for the parliamentary opposition in Kosovo. Merlino quotes an interview he had with the director of Ruder Finn, who claimed not to be over-concerned with the accuracy of information, but rather proudly stressed the achievement of his agency in having successfully targeted Jewish world opinion (Merlino 1994: 128-9). Merlino's text indicates the many ways in which information can be used as a weapon.

Although translation for news media represents a particular site of conflict in a geopolitical context, the world of literary publishing was also affected. Translations of literary works that were related geographically to the conflict area were re-issued whilst the conflicts were in progress. In France works about Bosnia by the Yugoslav novelist Ivo Andric (a Nobel prize winner in 1961) were republished (see Andric 1963; Caillé 1963). Two of his most famous novels (*Na Drini ćuprija* and *Travnička hronika*), were written during World War II and first published in 1945. These were subsequently translated into French initially in 1956 and published as respectively *Le Pont sur la Drina* ('*The Bridge on the Drina*') and *La Chronique de Travnik* ('*Bosnian Story*'). The former was re-published in a re-translated French edition in 1994, whilst the latter was initially re-published in 1994, and then a re-translated edition was issued in 1997. One could infer from the forewords and postscripts to the re-translations which were issued in the 1990s, that the French publishers' sudden revival of interest in Andric's works may have been motivated more by recent political events than by the wish to promote an understanding of the literary value of the works themselves (Dragovic-Drouet 2003: Appendix 3).

Naturally many of the books on the conflict, which included ones by key figures who were involved in it, for instance that by Lord Owen, were only written and translated after the events they described had occurred. However whilst the conflict was ongoing publishers were particularly keen on testimonies which were written by civilians or soldiers who were either participants in or witnesses to the conflict. *Le Journal de Zlata*, the translated version of a diary by a girl named Zlata Filipovic (Filipovic 1993), an account of a young girl's life in embattled Sarajevo, was popular in France, and it undoubtedly had a considerable impact on public opinion there. The book is not dissimilar to the classic *Le Journal d'Anne Frank* (*The Diary of Anne Frank*), and it was published in paperback in March 1999, just before the NATO aerial bombing campaign was unleashed on Serbia.

The book was widely studied by French schoolchildren, and even in November 2004 several hundred web sites which were dedicated to the Filipovic text could still be found. Publications such as this diary, rather than being literary works, are not too dissimilar from target-oriented pragmatic texts, which are defined by Jean Delisle as "[...] texts whose fundamental purpose is to convey information and in which aesthetics are of secondary importance" (Delisle 1988: 8), and which:

> [...] generally do have a practical and immediate application. As instruments of communication, they are more or less ephemeral, at least as far as the useful life-span of their content is concerned. (*ibid.* : 9).

Yet in publications such as Zlata's *Journal,* unlike other pragmatic texts, the name of their author, and in this case that of the translator, are highlighted by the publisher in an attempt to authenticate the content. However the translator is not necessarily aware of amendments that may have been introduced prior to, or after, his/her own intervention, and so cannot be held responsible for the text once it has been published. For instance, one web site (http://www.ac-rouen.fr/pedagogie/equipes), does state that the book "donne parfois l'impression d'avoir été réécrit par quelqu'un de plus âgé que Zlata" ['sometimes gives the impression that it has been rewritten by someone older than Zlata'].

## 2. Liaison interpreting during the conflict

The massive influx of the media, international organisations, NGOs and peace-keeping forces into former Yugoslavia after 1991 led to an acute shortage of interpreters, and consequently non-professionals were recruited in droves. It is unsurprising that issues such as professional methodology and ethics, and even language competence were not foremost in the demands of commissioners. Michael Cronin speaks of autonomous and heteronomous systems of interpreter recruitment :

> An autonomous system is one where colonizers train their own subjects in the language or languages of the colonized. A heteronomous system involves the recruitment of local interpreters and teaching them the imperial language. (Cronin 2002: 393)

Notwithstanding the colonial context of Cronin's discussion, his distinction between two different methods of interpreter recruitment can be mapped onto the situation in former Yugoslavia. An autonomous system of recruitment was not an option for most of the organisations clamouring for staff, as very few translators who had been trained in western countries could work with Serbo-Croatian as the target language. Any conference interpreters who had received specific training were usually already employed by international organisations. In theory, untrained emigrants of Yugoslav origin could be employed in the capacity of interpreters, but the situation was complicated by issues such as lack of training and divided loyalties. Moreover, 'regime-change' may well have occurred in their region of origin after they had emigrated. This would correspond to the situation described by Cronin, whereby the interpreter is returned to his language and culture of origin, having retraced the path from his B language (possibly English) to his

A language, finds that his origins have become uncertain and "the potential duplicity of interpreters" (*ibid.* .: 392) is signalled.

There were not any translation agencies in the former Yugoslavia, nor any training schools that provided training for interpretation into any foreign language, so the heteronomous recruitment was also problematic. The best port of call for a prospective employer who wished to find a translator or interpreter were the translators' associations, whose members were normally qualified with a Masters degree in a foreign language. However these people had varying degrees of experience in only either technical or in literary translation, but their competence as interpreters was an unknown quantity, as some of them were merely familiar with the foreign language. Once all the translators with experience had all been recruited, the employers' search had to be broadened to include language teachers who, at least theoretically, were proficient in the foreign language, but whose translating or interpreting competence could be limited, or even non-existent. Even after inclusion of the latter the demand for liaison interpreters was still not satisfied. An illustration of this was provided by one trained professional interpreter, who was requested by her employers to recruit scores of "assistant-interpreters" for the approximately 60,000 members of the UN peace-keeping forces (SFOR) who arrived in Bosnia-Herzegovina after the Dayton agreement in 1995. High unemployment brought about by the civil war, and the proffered high pay rates attracted numerous candidates. But their linguistic ability was often inadequate, and their translating competence, following hasty improvised and insufficient training, was mostly acquired only after they had begun practising. As the majority of western media organisations did not have foreign correspondents in place, only those who did, i.e. the main press agencies (*AFP*, *Associated Press*, and *Reuters*), could rely on access to established translators. These translators, long associated with the profession, were usually bilingual, *au fait* with journalistic constraints, and could boast good local grounding.

Visiting journalists faced a number of problems beyond that of the recruitment of linguists, including those of mobility, personal security, and their lack of familiarity with the local situation. Once they had found someone to act as their assistant-interpreter, or 'fixer', they were heavily reliant on their resourcefulness and goodwill to deal with the above. Although foreign journalists were generally well accepted in Croatia and Bosnia-Herzegovina physical danger was never far, nor was it the only problem that they could face. Usually journalists were assigned 'official' translators, who had been chosen by the local authorities precisely because of their allegiance. In an interview for the Swiss newspaper *Le Matin*, the

American journalist Peter Brock described this taking place in Croatia in 1991-92:

> La plupart des correspondants qui arrivaient ne parlaient pas serbo-croate, (ils) ont eu tendance à compter sur les porte-parole dynamiques des gouvernements. Le ministère de l'Information de Zagreb a rapidement retenu les services de douzaines de publicistes anglophones et le gouvernement bosniaque a également loué les services de dizaines de 'manipulateurs' pour médias occidentaux. (Collon 1994: 43, quoting *Le Matin* - 17 January 1993)
>
> [The majority of newly arrived correspondents couldn't speak Serbo-Croatian, so tended to count on the government 'pro-active' spokespersons. The Ministry of Information in Zagreb recruited dozens of English-speaking publicists, and the Bosnian government also hired dozens of 'fixers' for western media.]. (My translation)

This example implies that the reporter was firmly 'embedded', all his/her reports being censored, or even modified by the 'translator'. On occasions mistranslation which had obviously occurred through the interpreter's allegiance to one party could be identified by television viewers, who were able to understand Serbo-Croat themselves whilst hearing the soundtrack and reading the subtitled 'translation' on the television screen. Michel Collon quotes an example of this, taken from an RTL-TV1 TV-news broadcast in the autumn of 1993. On a road crowded with thousands of refugees who were leaving Bosnia, Charles Neuforge, a journalist from Luxembourg, interviewed an elderly woman through his 'fixer':

> *The elderly woman (in a sad tone):* "We've had a hard time finding food, and the water has been cut off. In this icy winter, things are getting worse by the day."
> *The translator (venomenously):* "The Serbs left us to die like dogs."
> *The elderly woman:* "We couldn't do anything else, we didn't have any choice."
> The translator: "The Serbs chased us out, destroying everything."
> (Collon 1994:44) (My translation)

Misinterpretation could affect the journalist's trust in the interpreter, but if the former suspected lack of professionalism or incompetence, and bypassed his interpreter by only conducting interviews with people who could speak the journalists own language, however badly, this could impair the confidence of the interviewee who was obliged to express him/herself in a foreign language, and be thus placed at a disadvantage. Danica Seleskovitch refers to this type of situation when she claims that

> Dans sa propre langue, on plie sa langue à sa pensée, dans une langue étrangère on plie sa pensée à sa langue. Être forcé de parler la langue de l'autre c'est à tous égards et en toutes circonstances être mis en situation d'infériorité. (Seleskovitch 1983: 5)
>
> [When you are expressing yourself in your own tongue you adapt the language to express your thoughts, but in a foreign tongue you adapt your thoughts to the

language. If you are obliged to express yourself in a foreign tongue then you are always in a weaker situation. (My translation)

Thus the quality of the inter-personal relationship between the reporter and interpreter was crucial. There were also instances of them being obliged to face together the problems of the acceptability of the topic by the media headquarters abroad. Foreign news desks sometimes 'ordered' unrealistic journalistic stories. For example, in 1991, a French television crew asked if the interpreter-fixer could find an excavation of a mass grave, such an item being deemed by the Paris news desk as an appropriate item for the evening news of the day!

Whether working for the media, or for NGOs, translators and interpreters were often faced with situations which made it difficult for them to maintain impartiality. On one hand, they were operating in tandem with professional logisticians whose brief was to accomplish humanitarian missions away from their own homelands, whilst the translators and interpreters were faced with the misery of their own community in need, and required to maintain cold professionalism and refrain from showing too much empathy for the sake of the mission. On the other hand, translators could hardly avoid establishing close personal relationships with their employers, when on the road together.

The peace-keeping forces constantly required large numbers of interpreters for their contacts with the local population. The translation situation was at its most intricate in Kosovo, where the two communities in conflict had different mother tongues, Serbo-Croatian and Albanian. The following was reported to the author by a fellow Serbian professional translator who had left Kosovo in December 1999. This was six months after the arrival in the region of NATO military forces, and when the UN civilian mission (UNMIK) had been installed there for five months.

Members of the two international missions, who numbered roughly twenty thousand, sought a large number of interpreters. As each unit required interpretation and translation to take place in two language directions, they sought a large number of linguists. The UN missions had brought in their translators from Croatia and Macedonia, but needed to recruit other staff from the local Serbian and Albanian communities. With time, the peace-keeping forces introduced cost-cutting measures, and the only interpreters to be retained were Albanians. The Serbian population could not speak Albanian, whereas the Albanians could speak Serbian, or at least claimed to be able to do so. However the reasons why many Serbian interpreters stopped working were not confined to linguistics or to economics. Some female interpreters resigned due to the psychological strain of having to deal with harrowing situations and the grisly minutiae of criminal investigations. Some Serbian interpreters, and we have mentioned that many of these interpreters language teachers who spoke fluent English, were forced to abandon their posts because they had been physically threatened and consequently they were obliged to flee their native region, the peace-keeping forces being unable to guarantee their protection.

Some of the *ad hoc* interpreters who had been hastily recruited from the local Albanian population were dismissed because of their poor linguistic ability. In the context of a criminal investigation to misinterpret and say "he used his fist" instead of "he used his palm" could be a vital error. However the sacked interpreters were usually replaced quickly, as candidates were frequently provided by established networks of intermediaries associated with the Kosovar Liberation Army (KLA). Unsurprisingly though, this did not necessarily lead to an improvement in the standard of interpretation, which also included some instances of apparently deliberate misinterpretation. Usually this was carried out through either exaggerating or attenuating the source discourse. Furthermore it was argued that the loyalty of Albanian interpreters towards their local authorities may have led a number of them to use knowledge which they had gained whilst working to expose interviewees to subsequent intimidatory visits from units of the KLA. All the above illustrate how the three pre-requisites of professional translation and interpreting which were discussed by the conference interpreting trainer Danica Seleskovitch, that is to say linguistic knowledge, subject knowledge and methodology, are far from being mapped onto the reality of practice in conflict situations.

**Linguistic knowledge**:
In theory, translation into the mother tongue, i.e. from the B (or source) language into the mother tongue, or A language, is considered to be the best professional option, as it minimises the risk of language errors. Marianne Lederer argues that "translation into the B [language] should never be an option when there are translators available who can produce translations into their A language." (Lederer 2003: 178). However, she also notes that, with the increased importance of the English language as a world *lingua franca*, "It is not realistic to assume that native speakers of English will learn a sufficient number of languages to eliminate the necessity to translate into B" (*ibid.* : 158). In other words, even with widespread learning of a *lingua franca*, a requirement for translation activities to be developed will still remain.

Given that demand, as illustrated by the case of the former Yugoslavia, cannot be met through the autonomous recruitment of imported translators, the drawbacks of the necessity of heteronomous recruitment can only be overcome by specific training for translation into non-mother tongues. Far beyond relevance merely to conflict situations, this issue has become all the more important since new countries with languages of limited diffusion have joined the European Union.

**Subject knowledge**:
It can certainly be argued that a particular conflict, in itself, cannot be an area in which it is possible for translators or interpreters to specialise in. However this is not to say that the conflict that erupted in the former Yugoslavia did not provide lessons, which may be applicable by specialists who have to work in regional conflict zones in the future. Politically-based language manipulation can create a minefield for interpreters and translators, particularly so when meanings are still in a state of flux, which they are by definition when language is used as a weapon. Care should especially be taken when using terms (such as proper nouns), which over time change their meaning, so that they come to signify different things to specific groups.

One example is that of the term 'Bosnian', which was used in the whole of former Yugoslavia to denote the territorial origin of all of the three groups of citizens living in the region of that name: Croats, Serbs and 'Muslims'. Since the independence of Bosnia-Herzegovina in 1992 the term, 'Bosnian' in English, or '*bosniaque*' in French, has gained a second, supplementary meaning, one which refers specifically to the Muslim ethnic community. In foreign languages this ambiguity offers the possibility of political manipulation, whilst in Serbo-Croatian two distinct terms can be used: '*Bosanac*' in the first case, and '*Bošnjak*' for a Muslim who inhabits Bosnia.

Another example is provided by the shortening of the full name of the state of 'Bosnia-Herzegovina'. The second part of the name is a territorial reference, in the same way as the original meaning of 'Bosnian'. Thus Herzegovinians can be Croats, Serbs or Muslims from the region of Herzegovina. However, as the Muslims are under-represented in Herzegovina, it furthers the national interests of this group to use the term 'Bosnian' as per its second meaning. In other words, when the western media refer to 'Bosnia', merely in order to shorten a long name, this is not a neutral use of the term, as it can suggest implicit alignment with the Muslim community's perspective.

Finally, the adjective '*Kosovar*' does not pre-date the Albanian community's claims for the independence of Kosovo. In the former Yugoslavia, official texts referred to the 'Albanian minority from Kosovo' ('*albanska manjina na Kosovu*'), in order to denote that the Albanian community had a mother state outside Yugoslavian territory, and Serbs from Kosovo do not describe themselves as '*Kosovars*'. When the latter is used rather than the phrase 'from Kosovo' the choice of term attributes specific political identity, anticipating an independent Kosovo in accordance with the claims of the Albanian community.

These examples indicate how ideological positions can be articulated through language, and bring to mind the words of Albert Camus which were used as an epigraph in Merlino's book: "Mal nommer les choses c'est contribuer au malheur du monde" [*To misname things contributes to the world's woes*].

**Professional methodology**
The issue of responsibility must be viewed within the context of allegiance, in any discussion of the mediating role of translators and interpreters. This has been acknowledged in Translation Studies, as the role which is frequently assumed by interpreters when diplomatic exchanges take place. Here, loyalty becomes paramount and can be regarded as more crucial than optimal language competence, which means that translation can take place into the B language. Christopher Thiéry, chief interpreter in the French ministry of Foreign Affairs writes:

> La règle diplomatique veut que chaque interprète soit le porte-parole de son Chef d'Etat; cela aboutit souvent à une situation peu satisfaisante où l'interprète est amené à s'exprimer dans une langue autre que sa langue maternelle, les bilingues vrais étant assez rares. C'est pourquoi, lorsque les interprètes se connaissent bien, ils échangent parfois leurs roles, chacun interprétant vers la langue de son propre Chef d'Etat (Thiéry 1990: 48).
>
> [Diplomatic protocol requires that each interpreter be the spokesperson of his or her Head of State; this often leads to a rather unsatisfactory situation where the interpreter has to speak in a language other than his or her mother tongue. This explains why interpreters, when they know each other well, swap roles, each interpreting into the language of their own Head of State.]   (My translation)

The principle that an autonomous interpreter may on occasions be replaced by a heteronomous one does indeed exist, but in practice it is limited only to situations wherein there is mutual trust between professionals. Trust is particularly difficult to maintain and safeguard when exacerbated tensions exist, and there is a considerable gap between the theoretical and methodological expectations of the trainers of translators and interpreters, and the reality of practice in conflict situations.

---

1 See 'Balkans-Forum'. On line at: http://www.politikforum.de/forum/archive/ 22/2002/08 /4/20020 (consulted May 2006).
2 The original text of the "Islamic declaration" was published in Sarajevo in 1970, and republished in 1990. As for "Wastelands", the second edition of the original title '*Bespuca – povijesne zbiljnosti*' was issued in Zagreb in 1989. Later issues were expurgated of the offending excerpts. See Dérens and Samary (2000). See also Collon (1998) for excerpts of both Tudjman's and Izetbegovic's writings.

## References

Andric, Ivo. 1963. 'L'auteur et la traduction de son oeuvre' in *Babel* 9 (4): 174-176.
Biardzka, Elzbieta. 2004. 'Les échos du Monde: polyphonie en traduction' in Gouadec, Daniel (ed.) *Mondialisation, localisation, francophonie(s)* Paris: La Maison du dictionnaire. 41-48.
Bugarski, Ranko. 1997a. 'A problem of language identity: The comparative linguistics of Serbo-Croatian' in Ahlqvist, Anders Al and Vera Capkova (eds) *Dan do Oide: Essays in Memory of Conn R.O Cléirigh.* Dublin: The Linguistics Institute of Ireland. 67-73.
------1997b. 'Language-internal conflict and language dissolution' in Wölck, Wolfgang (ed.) *Recent Studies in Contact Linguistics.* Bonn: Dümmler (Plurilingua, XVIII). 29-35.
Caillé, Pierre-François. 1963. 'Propos sur la traduction: Entretien avec Ivo Andric.' in *Babel* 9 (1-2): 140-142.
Collon, Michel. 1998. *Poker menteur. Les grandes puissances, la Yougoslavie et les prochaines guerres.* Brussels : EPO.
Cronin, Michael. 2002. 'The Empire Talks Back: Orality, Heteronomy and the Cultural Turn in Interpreting Studies' in Pöchacker, Franz, and Miriam Shlesinger (eds) *The Interpreting Studies Reader.* London : Routledge. 386-397.
Delisle, Jean. 1988. *Translation: an interpretive approach* (tr. Patricia Logan and Monica Creery). Ottawa: University of Ottawa Press.
Dérens, Jean-Arnault and Catherine Samary. 2000. *Les Conflits yougoslaves de A à Z.* Paris : Editions de l'Atelier.
Dragovi-Drouet, Mila .2003. *Évaluation de la qualité des traductions éditoriales.* UnpublishedDoctoral Thesis, ESIT, Paris III.
Filipovic, Zlata. 1993. *Le Journal de Zlata* (tr. Alain Cappon). Paris: Robert Laffont; 1999. Paris: Pocket Junior; 2004. Paris: Pocket Jeunesse.
Kuhiwczak, Piotr. 1999. 'Translation and language games in the Balkans' in Anderman, Gunilla and Margaret Rogers (eds) *Liber Amicorum for Peter Newmark: Word, Text, Translation.* Clevedon: Multilingual Matters. 217-224.
Lederer, Marianne. 2003. *The Interpretive Model* (tr. Ninon Larché). Manchester: St Jerome Publishing.
Merlino, Jacques.1994. *Les vérités yougoslaves ne sont pas toutes bonnes à dire.* Paris : Albin Michel.
Newmark, Peter. 1989. 'Introductory Survey' in Picken, Catriona (ed.) *The Translator's Handbook.* 2nd edition. London: ASLIB. 1-26.
Owen, David. 1996. *The Balkan Odyssey.* New York: Harcourt.
Seleskovitch, Danica. 1983. 'Introduction' in *Traduire 116 (Faut-il sauver les langues nationales? Rôle de la traduction et de l'interprétation).* 5-6.
Thiéry, Christopher. 1990. 'Interprétation diplomatique' in Lederer, Marianne (ed.) *Études traductologiques en hommage à Danica Seleskovitch.* Paris: Minard, Lettres modernes. 45-59.

# Translators and Interpreters During the Opium War between Britain and China (1839-1842)

*Lawrence Wang-chi Wong*

In the First Opium War, 1839-1942, the Chinese and British, with such huge cultural and language differences, had to rely heavily on a few exceptional individuals for translation and interpretation. The Chinese employed the *tonshi,* compradors (trade intermediaries) and merchants, some of whom were barely competent in the two languages, whilst the British recruited colonial administrators and missionaries. Some in the British camp not only collected and analyzed piecemeal materials, but also assumed active parts in shaping the course of events. The paper attempts to portray the roles played by the translators and interpreters of both parties, and the backgrounds of individuals and the position they enjoyed in their respective camp will be analyzed to determine the different attitudes that the two camps held towards translators and interpreters.

Key words: Translation studies, Opium War, Robert Morrison, Gutzlaff, Bao Peng,

> As for his ability to speak the Chinese language
> both in its standard form and its various dialects,
> that was but a minor accomplishment.
> Moreover, what should not be forgotten are his efforts
> in promoting communications between China and Britain.
> (Ride 1996: 136-137)

## Introduction

The First Opium War in 1839-42 was such an important event in Chinese history that it has been taken to mark the beginning of a new era, the *Jindai,* or the 'Early modern period', roughly from 1842 to 1911. The war represented the first successful attempt of the Western powers to force open Imperial China, the egocentric Celestial Empire that had long eluded outside contact. Badly defeated, China was forced into accepting humiliating peace terms - the Treaty of Nanking (1842) required that she pay a huge indemnity, cede Hong Kong for 150 years, and open five other ports to external trade and residence (Mayers 1877: 1-4).

Obviously, in diplomatic and military intercourse such as that which occurred during the Opium War, the services of translators and interpreters were indispensable. But no attempt has been made to identify the roles and contributions made by them in this first major hostility between the two greatest powers in the East and the West. The role assumed by the translators/interpreters who worked for the British went far beyond that of impartial middlemen who merely provided communication services. Rather, they greatly affected the course of the war, responsible for the collection, collation and interpretation of a great deal of military intelligence. The present paper examines the foremost translators and interpreters of the time, their political and military roles, and examines the vast difference in their treatment by the conflicting parties.

**1. The Chinese in Preparation for War**
The first translation patron of Western works in early modern China was Lin Zexu, who was appointed by the Emperor as Commissioner to Guangzhou (Canton), in order to wipe out opium smuggling before the war.[1] Educated in the traditional Confucian tradition, Lin, like most of his countrymen, had little or no knowledge of Westerners. In a memorandum to the throne, written after his arrival at Guangzhou, that is after he had actually met a number of foreigners, Lin still reported that tea was an essential food for the British, and that Westerners, having spent so much time at sea, were unable to walk well on land (Lin 1965 II: 676, 861). However, he was quick to realize his limitations and was eager to improve.

He displayed particular insight when he adopted translation as a means to "know the strengths of the barbarians to control the barbarians". During the brief period of his commissionership, he sponsored the translation of excerpts from English newspapers and magazines published in Guangzhou, Macao and even Singapore. He also commissioned the translation of Hugh Murray's *The Cyclopaedia of Geography* (1834), in order to learn more about the outside world. Lin commissioned work on Emerich de Vatell's (1714-1767) *Le droit des gens* (*Laws of Nations*). This was of some significance, notwithstanding the fact that only three paragraphs of the work were actually translated, as this was the first time the concept of international law has been introduced into China, and there is evidence that Lin made use of these works when he came to deal with the westerners.

At that time very few Chinese wanted to learn a foreign language. They, with a strong cultural and literary heritage of their own, looked down upon foreigners as barbarians. Translation and interpretation work was left in the hands of *tongshi*, the 'linguists'. Unfortunately most, if not all of them were actually linguistically incompetent, as well as being thoroughly unprofessional. William Hunter, who was in Guangzhou and had firsthand experience of dealing with them mentions that they "knew nothing of any language but their own" (Hunter 1882: 50). He also reported a trial, in which a Lascar seaman was accused of entering Chinese territory unlawfully after a shipwreck. The Chief Linguist, Old Tom, who virtually knew not the slightest of the language, made up the questions and answers for interrogation with the assistance of a trunk and box-maker who had managed to pick up some Hindustani. The whole situation was described as pathetically farcical (Hunter 1855: 21-30). As the linguists could neither read nor write in English or Chinese, they were quite unsuitable to be members of Lin Zexu's translation team, which he formed after making strenuous efforts.

The membership of Lin's team was first reported in a postscript to an article called 'Crisis in the Opium Traffic', published in the June 1839 issue of the *Chinese Repository*, an English publication in Macao:

> The commissioner has in his service four natives, all of whom have made some progress in the English tongue. The first is a young man, educated at Penang and Malacca, and for several years employed by the Chinese government at Peking. The second is an old man, educated at Serampore. The third is a young man who was once at the school at Cornwall, Conn., U.S.A. The fourth is a young lad, educated in China, who is able to read and translate papers on common subjects, with much ease, correctness, and facility. (Chinese Repository 1839a: 77)

In fact, with the exception of the last one, there is no information or mention of the translators in primary Chinese sources, which reflects the low status in which were held.[2] Lin's team was reputably not a weak one, none of them having been recruited from the local linguists, and the members had all lived abroad for relatively lengthy periods. The quotation given above is actually incorrect as regards the fourth member of the team. He, Liang Jinde, was really the son of the first Chinese Protestant apologist Liang Fa, and had spent three years in Singapore after learning English with Bridgman in Guangzhou. As for the others, the first was Yuan Dehui, a schoolmate of William Hunter at Malacca's Anglo-Chinese College. He had worked at the Lifanyuan, the Office of Foreign Affairs, and then he had accompanied Lin Zexu to Guangzhou. The second interpreter, whose mother was an Indian, had studied in India for over ten years. The third, Liaou Ahsee, with the English alias of William Botelho, was probably the first Chinese who studied in the United States (Britton 1933: 31). Hence, unlike the linguists they had all received a formal education in English. According to Hunter, Yuan Dehui, apart from having a high command of English, was even well versed in Latin (Hunter 1855: 260-261).[3]

However, it is still doubtful whether Lin Zexu's translators and interpreters really possessed a strong command of English. The July 1839 issue of the *Chinese Repository* contained a proclamation to foreigners which Lin had given to the editor of the journal. According to the latter it was "the first document which ever came from the Chinese in the English language" (*Chinese Repository* 1839b: 168). But the "English" was opaque, to say the least. The first "sentence" – or rather the first "paragraph" – reads as follows:

> For the managing opium on the last spring being stopped trade for present time till the opium surrendered to the government than ordered be opened the trade the same as before. (167)

Then the proclamation continued with two long paragraphs, of sixteen and eleven lines respectively, without one single punctuation mark. The editor of the *Chinese Repository* commented:

> Its idioms are perfectly Chinese; and, like all the documents in their own language, it is without punctuation. If our readers should be able to understand what it means, they will here see the [...]. (168)

According to the editor, this piece of writing had been translated into English by "the commissioner's senior interpreter, who has for many years been in the employment of the government, at Peking" (168). The senior interpreter was Yuan Dehui, who was supposed to have a good command of English. Interestingly, it seemed that Lin Zexu did not have great confidence in him though, as in at least two cases, he had tried various means of checking the reliability of Dehui's translations. After a translation of the *Laws of Nations* had been produced by him, Lin invited Dr. Peter Parker (1840-1888), an American medical missionary in Guangzhou, to translate the same paragraphs again. Both versions, though are regarded as unsatisfactory (Chang 1950: 13; Hsü 1960: 123-124). Another case is that of the famous letter from Lin Zexu to Queen Victoria of England. Lin asked his translator for an English version, and he had the English back translated into Chinese by William Hunter (Hunter 1855: 262-263). Lin also asked Peter Parker to translate the original into English (Gulick 1973: 90). However, even this version was not flawless. Doctor. Hill, s surgeon on the British ship *Sunda*, complained that it was "written in their usual high flowing strain" and "some parts of it we could make neither head nor tail of" (*Chinese Repository* 1840: 485).

Lin Zexu's translators produced a rather impressive quantity of work, but unfortunately their activities were brought to an abrupt end when war broke out. The Emperor blamed Lin for mishandling the foreigners and exiled him. Lin's patronage of translation had lasted for about twenty months, from March 1839 to November 1840 (Lin 1985: 130). Worse still, he was criticised by his successor, Qi Shan, for "spying for the barbarians", which harmed the dignity of an Imperial Commissioner and brought disgrace to the Empire. Though we do not know what happened to Lin's translators and interpreters, it was reported that the disgraced Lin once recommended Liang Jinde to Qi Shan. However it appears that the latter, tin charge of foreign affairs attempted to perform his job without any translating or interpreting staff.

## 2. Field interpreters, military advisors and local magistrates: The multiple roles of translators and interpreters on the British side

Before the outbreak of the Opium War, the British were fortunate to have more than one outstanding translator/interpreters, the most prominent of these being Robert Morrison (1782-1834). Remembered in history as the first Protestant missionary in China, hence "father of the Chinese mission" (Paquette 1987: 101), Morrison produced the first Chinese version of the Bible (1819), compiled the first Chinese-English dictionary, *A Dictionary of the Chinese Language* (*Huaying zidian*, 1815), and set up the Anglo-Chinese College, the first of its kind in the world (1820). He had started to learn Chinese before his arrival in China in 1807, and his first appointment was in 1809, as Chinese Secretary and Interpreter for the East Indian Company. By 1816 he had worked for the British government at diplomatic level in the Lord Amherst Mission. He must have played an active part because he was mistaken by the Chinese as the deputy Ambassador (Xiao 1988: 7-9). Unfortunately, the mission was a complete failure because the two sides had difficulties even agreeing on the formalities with which the ambassadors were to greet the Chinese emperor. The British had regarded the mission as a normal diplomatic exchange between sovereign states of equal status, whilst the Chinese saw the visitors as no more than tributary envoys. When the mission ended Morrison continued to act as an interpreter for the East Indian Company until December 1833, when the trading monopoly of the Company was abolished. Shortly after, in 1834 on the appointment of a new Chief Superintendent of British Trade in China, Lord William John Napier, Morrison was appointed the Chinese Secretary and Interpreter. Whilst he took great pride in the appointment (Morrison 1839), his work during the nerve-racking decades had been demanding and stressful. He died at the age of fifty-one, after less than two weeks in the new post.

Charles Gutzlaff (1803-1851), was a Protestant missionary who spoke competent Chinese. Having arrived in China in 1831, he was seen as "a rare bird" (Beeching 1975: 61) in Guangzhou because he spoke not only Mandarin, the official Chinese language, but also several dialects. The fact he was could use the Fujianese dialect put him in a favourable position when the westerners wanted to open up the coast for their trading activities. According to many descriptions, Gutzlaff even looked Chinese. William Hunter, who claimed a kind of "fellow-feeling" with Gutzlaff, both having studied at Malacca, stated that he "resembled a Chinese very much, while they themselves declared him to be a "son of Han in disguise!" (Hunter 1882: 70), and reports from Chinese sources confirm this. Furthermore a chinese poet claimed that Gutzlaff was "of Chinese origin, born at the illicit intercourse between a Chinese in Guangdong and a foreign woman" (Xu 1957: 24). Other sources regard this as a misconception in both senses, but it is undeniable that Gutzlaff was eager to identify himself with the Chinese. He adopted the name of Ai Han Zhe, which literally means 'China Lover', and once claimed that even before his arrival in China, when he was in Siam, he:

> became a naturalized subject of the Celestial Empire, by adoption into the clan or family of Kwo [Guo], from the Tung-an district in Fuhkeen [Fujian]. I took, also, the name Shih-lee [Shili], - wore, occasionally, the Chinese dress, - and was recognized (by those among whom I lived) as a member of the great nation. (Gutzlaff 1834: 71)

However, Gutzlaff's proclaimed love for China is qualified by his chequered record. He probably genuinely believed that in converting China to Christianity he was doing the greatest good for the Chinese. He should also be credited for his attempts to import modern western knowledge, for such ventures as editing the first Chinese periodical on Chinese soil (1833), taking an active part in "The Society for the Diffusion of Useful Knowledge in China" (Guangzhou, 1834), and publishing on the west extensively in Chinese. But Gutzlaff's famous "three voyages along the coast of China", not to mention his participation in the Opium War on the British side, make him the target of severe censure in mainland Chinese historical discourse. He had arrived in June 1831 in a junk from Bangkok, which had sailed all the way along the Chinese coast to Tianjin. This was not only adventurous and bold, but also perilous as it was against Chinese law, and it brought him fame among westerners. Within three months, he found himself making a second journey along the Chinese coast aboard the *Lord Amherst* of the East Indian Company. Later he was to make a third voyage, this time for the Matheson Jardine Company, in an opium smuggling ship called the *Slynph*. He has been accused by Chinese historians of being an opium smuggler himself, and a spy who charted the Chinese coast and gathered information for future aggressive actions – charges that he was a conspirator who aided the British in their invasion of China which are reported by Gu (1985: 59).

On his first voyage Gutzlaff's sole purpose was to preach - as a newcomer he was unconnected to any body or organization in China. The conditions he experienced on the voyage were harsh in the extreme, and he described the "cabin" assigned to him as "a hole, only large enough for a person to lie down in" (Gutzlaff 1834: 68). He said almost every one on board was "long habituated to opium-smoking" (68-69), and that some of the sailors wanted to kill him to seize his property (95).

Nor can we be sure that the second and third of his voyages were directly related to subsequent British military actions in China. Gutzlaff was paid extremely handsomely for his service as interpreter and guide on these journeys. It was reported that he received £1,000 for the second voyage (Paquette 1987: 100). It would appear that this was initiated for purely commercial purposes, and as Gutzlaff was rewarded generously by the company, this suggests that there were no ulterior motives. This second voyage was made at the behest of Charles Marjoribanks, President of the Select Committee of the East Indian Company's branch at Canton, who instructed Hugh Lindsay, whom he appointed leader of the venture:

> to ascertain how far the northern ports of this Empire may gradually be opened to British Commerce, which would be most eligible, and to what extent the disposition of the Natives and local government would be favourable to it. (Marjoribanks 1833, quoted in Paquette 1987: 90)

At the beginning of his journal Gutzlaff also mentioned that the expedition was "to facilitate mercantile enterprise, and "to acquire information respecting those ports where commerce might be established" (Gutzlaff 1834: 153). However, the voyage was disapproved of in London by the directors of the company, who castigated Marjoribanks for incurring a financial loss of £5,647 (Waley 1958: 224). This was obviously not a military enterprise, but having said that, it must be admitted that the *Lord Amherst* was armed, and that Gutzlaff's journal did mention the inspection of some military establishments (Gutzlaff 1834: 293-296).

The third voyage, on board the *Sylph*, also resulted in Gutzlaff being paid a substantial fee, as well as him subsequently receiving "large present[s]", which ensured his loyalty to the Jardine and Matheson company after he became an official government interpreter (*ibid.* :93-96). Gutzlaff only wrote briefly about the activities of the people on board during the voyage, which is understandable as the journey does appear to have been closely related to opium trafficking. He said that he was reluctant to undertake it, and embarked on the vessel "after much consultation with others, and a conflict in my own mind" (Gutzlaff 1834: 413), but given the circumstances it would have been surprising if his journal had mentioned him doing anything other than distributing books and pamphlets.

Gutzlaff was to make several more voyages along the Chinese coast, all of which involved opium trafficking, and was to interpret numerous illicit opium deals, and hence he is remembered "as the person in whom the contradictions of humanitarianism and the opium traffic reached their most astonishing embroilment" (Coates 1966: 150). But Gutzlaff was not spying for the British government. If he was a spy, then he was serving Jardine, Matheson and Company, not the British government, and if he was spying for the Jardine Company, then he spied not on China but on the British. As one study says, Gutzlaff aided them "by keeping the Company informed of any intelligence he gleaned from his various governmental activities" (Paquette 1987: 98). He was not directly involved in the political developments of the Sino-British relationship until his appointment as the official government interpreter in 1835. Then later, during the Opium War, he made great contributions to the British government in his capacity as a translator/interpreter.

Gutzlaff was not the only translator/interpreter who worked for the British in the war. John Morrison (1814-1843) was the son of Robert Morrison.[4] Described by Ride as "the outstanding offspring" (Ride 1996: 236), initially John R. Morrison aided Gutzlaff as a deputy interpreter, but gradually he assumed a much wider role. He had been born in Macao, and spent most of his formative years in China, and almost from the start had been trained as "a Chinese scholar" (Morrison 1839 II: 104). He began learning Chinese at the age of ten (Leung 2001: 22), first with his own father in London for two years (1824-1826), then in Guangzhou (1826), and subsequently at the Anglo-Chinese College in Malacca (1827). At the college, he learned not only Mandarin, the official Chinese language, but also a number of dialects. After spending about three years in Malacca, he returned to Guangzhou at the instruction of his father.

In October 1830, at the mere age of sixteen John Morrison became "Chinese Interpreter to the British Merchants", and little more than two years later he worked as a private secretary for the American delegation to Cochin-China (Vietnam) and Siam (Thailand), which operated from December 1832 to May 1833. Apart from taking part in negotiations between the American delegates and local officials, he translated such important documents as a letter from the American President, Andrew Jackson, to the King of Siam, and on occasions worked as the chief representative of the envoy. The Naval Surgeon Benajah Ticknor, reported that John Morrison had played an important role and performed very well:

> In transacting the business of the two interviews of which I have given an account, Mr. Morrison was the medium of communication between the two parties; and the conference was carried on wholly in writing; and the use of the Chinese characters. This young gentleman appeared as familiar with the Chinese written language, as the Mandarins themselves, and translated with such facility, that the parties experienced but little delay in communicating with each other. The interpreter who accompanies the Mandarins had consequently very little to do. (Hodges 1994: 209-210)

On the death of his father in 1834, John Morrison was invited by Napier, the Chief Superintendent, to become the Chinese Secretary and Interpreter, and he continued to work as such under the following three Chief Superintendents. One, Captain Charles Elliot, who took up the post in June 1836, fulsomely expressed his thanks to John Morrison for "rendering his knowledge of the Chinese language as useful to his neighbours as possible" (87).

Although Morrison was the interpreter/translator of the British, he was responsible for translating all the correspondence between the two sides. As mentioned earlier, the first document which came from the Chinese written in English was the one published in 1839. It was barely intelligible. Hence, in the early phases of Anglo-Chinese diplomacy the original Chinese documents were merely passed to the British (Liu 1999: 131), while "the Chinese government knew only the Chinese originals of their own dispatches, and recognized only the Chinese translations of those prepared and presented to them by the British" (Wong 1984: 8). The translators and interpreters from the British, thus Morrison at the time, provided these documents.

Among the documents translated by John Morrison is one of great historical importance: the bond Lin Zexu demanded from all western traders in Guangzhou, requiring that they would never again import opium, and that any breach of this should be punishable by confiscation of the cargo and the execution of the persons involved. Chang Hsinpao, in his book on Lin Zexu and the Opium War, argues that John Morrison, in his translation misled the westerners, with the vague expression "the parties shall be left to suffer death at the hands of the Celestial Court", into believing that "the capital punishment prescribed in the draft of the bond would involve innocent men". Allegedly the vague translation gave the impression that all westerners would be executed, and consequently Morrison was responsible for the war (Chang 1964: 180).[5] This charge is seen as unjustifiable by Leung in a recent study, who pointed out that John Morrison soon re-translated the bond and made it clear that only "the offender who had brought it [opium] would be put forward for capital punishment". Further there was yet another version of the bond published in *The Chinese Repository* which stated clearly that only the transgressor should be delivered to the Chinese authorities and punished by death. The western traders would not have been misled or misinformed (Leung 2001: 120-122).

In addition to documents that were officially dispatched to the British government, throughout the war John Morrison also translated large volumes of Chinese material, including imperial edicts, decrees, and memoranda, as well as other information on Sino-western dealings. Though he never mentioned the source, it is believed that he relied mainly on *Jingbao* [*the Peking Gazette*], a newspaper published with the permission of the Beijing provincial government to disseminate information about daily events in the capital (Leung 2001: 107).

In reality John Morrison was collecting and providing confidential information for the British camp. By analyzing the exchanges between the emperor and the senior officials, he obtained a great deal of military intelligence regarding military actions and troop deployment, which was of much use to the British. A senior Chinese negotiator, She Ying (Ch'i-ying), complained to the Emperor that the British:

> every day read the *Peking Gazette* (*Ching-pao*). Since the officials of Kiangnan [Jiangnan] and Chekiang [Jiejiang] all have its news, it is more difficult to estimate from what ultimate source it is circuitously transmitted to the [British] rebels. (Quoted in Fairbank 1969: 89)

However, if John Morrison gathered intelligence mainly through the *Peking Gazette*, Charles Gutzlaff was even more daring in securing information: he simply went out bribing informants quite openly.[6] In official Chinese records, there were statements made by a considerable number of informants who were in Gutzlaff's service (Waley 1958: 222-224). With widely differing backgrounds, most of them were in financial difficulties, and Gutzlaff would pay a dollar or two for each piece of information. These included details on troop deployment, plans of military movements, and the names of rich people out of whom money could be squeezed (237). He also provided information on pawnshops which would provide rich pickings for raids, and on which influential people were against the British (236-238).

The British interpreters/translators had access to the Chinese language, and thus they could obtain local information. Consequently they asserted great influence in the course of the war, though they did not take part directly in the fighting. It is reported that John Morrison advised Pottinger to attack Hangzhou after capturing Ningbo (Leung 2001: 170-171). Morrison even drew up a plan, and a sketch of the city, helping the British army to capture Nanjing (187-190). Likewise, Gutzlaff played a central role in the expedition that took Zhoushan in July 1840 (Endacott 1964: 107).

It is, of course, rather logical that British interpreters/translators would act as military advisers. But it is harder to understand why they became local magistrates in occupied areas. This happened more than once with Gutzlaff, who after the capture of Zhoushan became the civil magistrate there for about six months (this has been described by one historian as "a perfect farce" [Welsh 1997: 102]). When in October 1841 the British captured Ningbo, he was made magistrate of the city until May 1842. Then in July of that year he became the magistrate at Qianjiang, and later, between November 1842 and the autumn of 1843, the Superintendent of Trade at Dinghai, Zhoushan (Waley 1958: 229-232). However, strange though these numerous postings may appear, Gutzlaff seems to have performed well in them. In a highly approving tone, a local poet in Ningbo eulogised on how well Gutzlaff handled legal cases (Xu 1957: 24). He was, as suggested by one historian, the "undisputed king of the place", and the only westerner there who knew Chinese (Fay 1975: 319).

In addition to the various roles which Morrison and Gutzlaff played during the War, they managed the negotiations for a peace settlement consummately. As mentioned above, the translators and interpreters on the Chinese side were the 'linguists', whose performance was far from satisfactory. So often the Chinese sometimes simply did not send an interpreter, but relied on the British. For instance, as late as August 1842, the Chinese sent Zhang Xi (Chang Hsi), a '*jiaren*' (experienced retainer) of the Imperial Commissioner Yilibu (I-li-pu, 1772-1843) on board Pottinger's ship at Nanjing to negotiate a peace settlement. Zhang, though considered to be "the pre-eminent barbarian expert" (Fairbank 1969: 99), did not speak English. Hence, in the end, he for the most of the time spoke with John Morrison – this he recorded in detail both in his *Diary of Pacifying the Barbarians* (*Fuyi riji*) and his "Petitions on Handling the Barbarians" (*Tanyi shuiti*).[7]

Therefore it is no exaggeration to say that, in most cases, the interpreters who worked for the British, and especially John Morrison, actually played the role of negotiators, especially in the eyes of the Chinese. Memoranda from the High Imperial Commissioner Yilibu to the Emperor speak of Morrison being highly manipulative as a negotiator (Yilibu 1857: 379-380), and it is not wholly unsurprising that the Chinese took him to be the prime enemy (Qi 1957: 475-476). A handsome sum – some sources said fifty thousand teals of silver, others twenty thousand teals – was put on his head by the Chinese emperor (*The Chinese Repository* 1841: 111-115), and upon news of his death, the Chinese rejoiced at it as a punishment from heaven for the crimes he committed against China (Qi 1957: 476).

Conversely the British regarded Morrison's services as invaluable. William Dallas Bernard, who was on board of *The Nemesis* with him, remarked that the value of his services throughout the war "is impossible too highly to appreciate" (Bernard 1847: 139). To this, a Captain Hall added a remark:

> Not only on this, but on many other occasions, these gentlemen were personally exposed to the fire of the enemy, little less than either soldiers or sailors. They showed the utmost coolness and personal courage: and it is but justice to them to remark that their presence was always the greatest value in every operation, even though unarmed, and, as non-belligerents, unnoticed. Their knowledge of the language and their good judgment frequently enlisted in our favour the people of the country, who might have offered great annoyance, and they were often able to mitigate the hardships even of war itself (*ibid.*)

John Morrison's premature death at the age of twenty-eight, on the 29th of August 1843, caused great sorrow to the British community in the Far East. Pottinger called it "an irreparable national calamity". All the ships in the harbour at Hong Kong dropped their colours, and the steamer *The Proserpine*, ferried people from Hong Kong to Macao for his funeral, which was attended by almost the entire foreign community there (Leung 2001: 248). In the funeral, "every heart melted - and after the service was read, no man thought of moving" (*ibid.* :270).

## 3. Bao Peng: Traitor or Translator?

The Chinese could not handle foreign affairs without the assistance of translators and interpreters. Whilst Lin Zexu had recruited his translators mainly from people who had studied abroad, his successor, Qi Shan, chose a linguist, Bao Peng to assist him in negotiating a peace settlement. Neither Qi nor Bao could cope, and accepted the humiliating Treaty of Nanjing. One can understand why Qi Shan was penalised for agreeing to cede Chinese territory without the permission of the Emperor, but it appears less than just that his assistant should also be penalised.

However Bao Peng does seem to have been a thoroughly disreputable character. He was born at Xiangshan near Macao, and began learning foreign languages at an early age. He became a comprador in 1829, working for an American merchant, and by 1836 he had taken over his cousin's work as comprador to the opium dealer Lancelot Dent. His regular salary was about sixty dollars, but Bao usually made an extra two to three hundred dollars a month on the side. From 1837 on he expanded his activities, to take commissions for supplying opium. In 1839 he came into conflict with another linguist who, demanding money, threatened to denounce him as an opium supplier. Bao fled and sought refuge in Shandong province, with his friend Zhao Ziyong, who was a magistrate there. After a while Zhao recommended Bao to the governor, Tuo Hunbu, and when a foreign ship appeared off the coast Bao was instructed to board it and send it away. Qi Shan heard about this and requested that Bao should come to Guangzhou to work as an interpreter.

John Elliot Bingham, who had taken part in the War and published a "narrative of the expedition to China", wrote:

> On one of his [Bao Peng's] trips to Macao, he had visited his old master, Mr. Dent, and then went to see his late fellow-servants, who very soon began to jeer him on his increased consequence, when jumping up with his right arm extended, and hand clenched, he thus broke forth: - "You thinkee my one smallo man? you thinkee my go buy one catty rice, one catty fowl? No! my largo man, my have catchee peace, my have catchee war my hand, suppose I opee he, makee peace, suppose I shutee he, must makee fight." It loses much in relating: the fellow's manner must be seen to be understood. (Bingham 1843: II: 40-41)

Bingham called Bao "a most intolerable liar" (I: 249), who was always making up stories and excuses to extract money (256-257). However unpleasant he might have been, his behaviour was not untypical of most 'linguists' at that time. Some sources have also argued that Bao was an agent working for the British. A Taiwanese historian, Lin Chongyong, himself a descendent of Lin Zexu, suggests that Bao had been sent by George Elliot to serve Qi Shan, in order to secure information for them (1967: 467-474). Chongyong cites a letter from Lin Zexu calling him a "*hanjian*" (traitor), Bingham mentions that he knew Bao Peng when he was a comprador, and there were a number of private meetings between Bao and Elliot. But though he is openly negative about Bao, Bingham never hinted that he was a British spy. Lin Chongyong's speculation is not entirely convincing (Hao 1970: 290).

The term '*hanjian*' bears further examination, it being widely used in the nineteenth century. In more recent times, for instance, during the Second World War when the Chinese fought against the Japanese, people in general interpreted the term as "traitors to the Chinese", implying that it was a reference to someone who indulges in spying and treachery, but there appears to be historical confusion about its meaning. Gutzlaff's many informants were certainly traitors, but the figures about the numbers of people who were described as *hanjian* at that time are astonishing. For instance, it was said that in one exercise Chinese officials successfully tracked down over three thousand *hanjian* in Hong Kong, which then had a population of about five thousand (Eitel 1895: 171). There were also reports that in the entire province of Jiejiang, "half of the population were *hanjian*" and that "in the Guangdong province, *hanjian* were everywhere". In the city of Ningbo there were only about a thousand foreign troops, whilst there were over three thousand *hanjian* (Zheng 2004: 92-104). Could there be that many spies or secret agents around, or was it merely a term of disparagement? Arthur Waley, in *The Opium War Through Chinese Eyes*, discusses the meaning of the term:

> Over and over again in the documents of this period there occurs the term *Han-chien* [*hanjian*], meaning literally "Chinese evil-doers", as opposed to *I-chien* [*yijian*], "foreign evil-doers". It was applied, long before the War, to Chinese who entered the service of foreigners, learnt foreign languages, corresponded with foreigners or made friends with them in any way. There were, of course, licensed compradors and interpreters who theoretically were not *Han-chien*; but they were under constant suspicion, as were also the licensed guild-merchants, through whom the foreigners conducted their trade. After the war started, whole new classes of *Han-chien* arose: those who obtained maps and sea-charts for the enemy, who passed on political and military information to them, acted as pilots, worked as craftsmen on board foreign warships and so on. Later the expression became a term of abuse for anyone who favoured appeasement rather than war to the death, it often being assumed that, if he did so, it must be because he was in the foreigners' pay. (Waley 1958: 222)

One should distinguish between the various types of *hanjian* - some labelled thus were perhaps spies or secret agents, others had just come into the slightest connection with foreigners, and the term could perhaps also be translated as 'evil-doer'. People were, as Waley suggests, "under constant suspicion", which explains why the figures of *hanjian* reported by the officials were so incredibly high, and it is hardly surprising that Bao did not escape being so labelled. The fact, that Bao was accused of being a "boyfriend" of Dent [Liang 1959: 50]) complicated matters further. Lin Zexu saw "*hanjian*" thus:

> Foreign traders from various countries come to China to do business, the cargo ships enter the harbour, and those foreign traders staying in Guangzhou and Macao are all allowed to hire compradors and servants for

> assistance. This is permitted in our laws. But there is a kind of evil-doers who are not employed on a business basis. They secretly had contacts and intercourse with the foreigners, colluding with them for illicit businesses by ways and means. They are come to be known as hanjian in the inner areas (Lin 1963: 41)

However, Bao Peng, though despicable, was regarded, even by Bingham as "a shrewd clever fellow". His Pidgin English was also acknowledged as rather fluent (Bingham 1843: II: 40), and he was well connected to the foreign community. When he first came to Guangzhou Qi Shan had been warned by Tuo Hunbu, the governor of Shandong, that Bao was not trustworthy (Tuo 1954: 380).

## Conclusion

Translators and interpreters in the opposing camps were given very different roles and status. As the British were well aware that their translators provided indispensable military intelligence and advice, they were regarded highly, were rewarded well and were given administrative posts. When, after the war, the British established rule in Hong Kong, their translators and interpreters were given important positions in government. John Morrison was initially made the Chinese Secretary and acting Colonial Secretary by Pottinger, then a Justice of the Peace and a member of the first Legislative and Executive Councils. Gutzlaff was given similar positions, and in 1844 he succeeded John Morrison as the Chinese Secretary and Interpreter in the Hong Kong government. At the same time he was the Officiating Chinese Secretary and Interpreter (*Chinese Repository* 1844: 8-10), and he was the Chief Secretary in the Chinese Department at the foreign office from 1845 to 1851 (*Chinese Repository* 1845: 13; 1849: 10; 1850: 11; 1851: 11). In appreciation of his services, a street in the Central District was named after him during his lifetime.

In sharp contrast, in the early to mid Nineteenth century translators and interpreters on the Chinese side was precarious, to say the least. Their tragedy lay not in their incompetence, but in the low status that the profession occupied in Chinese society and culture. Almost by definition they were taken to be traitors or evil-doers, anyone having any connection with foreigners being condemned as *hanjian*. Had the Chinese been aware of the importance of training qualified interpreters/translators, the outcome of the Opium War may well have been quite different.

---

1 For a detailed discussion of Lin Zexu as the first translation patron of Western works, see Lin 1985: 118-137; or Wong 2001: 94-127.

2 Nevertheless Dr. Hill, a Surgeon on the British bark *Sunda*, reported that amongst the linguists there was one young Chinese who had spent eight years in London. "He speaks English remarkably well, much better, indeed, than any Chinese whom I have ever met with".
3 According to Hunter, Yuan Dehui (Hunter called him Shaow-Tih [Xiaode]) "spoke a robust Mandarin dialect", "applied himself to the study of the English language, not lightly but profoundly, and when I left for Canton he had made wonderful progress. Everyone in the College referred to him as 'the reader', from the attention he gave to his studies" (Hunter 1855: 261).
4 I am indebted to Ms Leung Chung-yan for materials on John Robert Morrison. See Leung 2001, which is a very well-written M.Phil. thesis.
5 Chang also argues that John Robert Morrison mistranslated Lin's Zexu's second edict to the foreigners in Guangzhou (Chang 1964: 143, 261 n.79).
6 John Morrison allegedly had also secured information from the local people. See Ouchterlony: 428-428; Leung 2001: 187-188.
7 Zhang 1869; Zhang 1957: 335-352. For a translation of the *Diary of Pacifying the Barbarians*.

## References

Beeching, Jack. 1975. *The Chinese Opium Wars*. London: Hutchinson & Co.
Bernard, William Dallas. 1847. *The Nemesis in China: Comprising a History of the late War in That Country: With an Account of the Colony of Hong Kong: From Notes of Captain W.H. Hall and Personal Observations*. London: Henry Colburn.
Bingham, J. Elliot. 1843. *Narrative of the Expedition to China, From the Commencement of the War to Its Termination in 1842*. London: Henry Colburn, Second Edition, 2 Vols.
Board of Punishments. 1957. "Memorial from the Board of Punishments" (Xingbu zouzhe) in Qi Xihe (et al.) (eds) *Corpus of Material about the Opium War* (*Yapian zhanzheng ziliao congkan*). Shanghai: Shanghai renmin chubanshe, III, 380-382.
Britton, Roswell S. 1933. *The Chinese Periodical Press, 1800-1912*. Shanghai, Hong Kong and Singapore: Kelly & Walsh Ltd.
Broomhall, Marshall. 1924. *Robert Morrison: A Master-Builder*. London: Church Missionary Society.
Chang Hsin-pao. 1964. *Commissioner Lin and the Opium War*. Cambridge, Mass.: Harvard University Press.
*Chinese Repository*. 1834. "Society for the Diffusion of Useful Knowledge" in *Chinese Repository*, III. 378-384.
——1839a. "Crisis in the Opium Traffic" in *Chinese Repository*, VIII. 1-8, 12-37, 57-83.
——1839b. "Great Imperial Commissionary's Governor's of Two Kwang Province Lieutenant-governor's of Canton Earnest Proclamation to Foreigners Against Issued" in *Chinese Repository*, VIII, 167-168.
——1840. "Loss of the British Bark *Sunda*" in *Chinese Repository*, VIII, 478-486.
Coates, Austin. 1966. *Prelude to Hongkong*. London: Routledge & Kegan Paul.
Eitel, E.J. 1895. *Europe in China: The History of Hong Kong from the Beginning to the Year 1882*. London: Luzac & Co.
Endacott, George B. 1964. 2nd ed. *A History of Hong Kong*. Hong Kong: Oxford University Press.
Fairbank, John K. 1969. *Trade and Diplomacy on the China Coast: The Opening of the Treaty Ports, 1842-1854*. Stanford: Stanford University Press.
Fay, Peter Ward. 1975. *The Opium War, 1840-1842*. Chapel Hill: The University of North Carolina Press.
Gu, Zhangsheng. 1985. *From Robert Morrison to John Leighton Stuart: Critical Biographies of Protestant Missionaries in China* (*Cong Malixun dao Situ Leideng: Laihua xinjiao chuanjiaoshi pingzhuan*). Shanghai: Shanghai renmin chubanshe.

Gulick, V. Edward. 1973. *Peter Parker and the Opening of China*. Cambridge, Mass.: Harvard University Press.
Gutzlaff, Charles. 1834. *Journal of Three Voyages Along the Coast of China in 1831, 1832 & 1833*. London: Frederick Westley & A.H. Davis.
Hao, Yen-P'ing. 1970. *The Comprador in Nineteenth Century China: Bridge Between East and West*. Cambridge, Mass.: Harvard University Press.
Hodges, Nan Powell (ed.) 1994. *The Voyage of the Peacock: A Journal by Nenajah Ticknor, Naval Surgeon*. Ann Arbor: University of Michigan Press.
Hunter, C. William. 1855. *Bits of Old China*. London: Kegan Paul, Trench, & Co.
——. 1882. *The "Fan Kwae" at Canton Before the Treaty Days, 1825-1844*. London: Kegan Paul, Trench, & Co.
Hsu, Immanuel, C. Y. 1960. *China's Entrance into the Family of Nations: The Diplomatic Phase, 1858-1880*. Harvard: Harvard University Press.
Leung, Chung-yan. 2001. "A Bilingual British 'Barbarian' – A Study of John Robert Morrison (1814-1843) as the Translator and Interpreter for the British Plenipotentiaries in China Between 1939 and 1943". Unpublished M.Phil. thesis, Hong Kong Baptist University.
Liang Tingnan. 1959. *Notes on the Barbarians (Yifen wenji)*. Beijing: Zhonghua shuju.
Lin Chongyong. 1967. *A Biography of Lin Zexu (Lin Zexu chuan)*. Taibei: Commercial Press.
Lin Yongyu. 1985. "On the Translation Activities Organized by Lin Zexu" (*Lun Lin Zexu zuzhide yiyi gongzuo*) in History Research Institute, Social Sciences Academy of Fujian (ed.), *Lin Zexu yu Studies on Lin Zexu and the Opium War (Yapian zhanzheng yanjiu lunwenji)*, Fuzhou: Fujian renmin chubanshe. 118-137.
Lin Zexu. 1963. *Writings of Lin Zexu: Official Letters [Lin Zexuji: Gongdu]*. Beijing: Zhonghua shuju.
——1965. *Writings of Lin Zexu: Memorials [Lin Zexuji: Zougao]*. Beijing: Zhonghua shuju, 3 Vols.
Liu, Lydia H. 1999. "Legislating the Universal: The Circulation of International Law in the Nineteenth Century" in Liu, Lydia H (ed.). *Tokens of Exchange: The Problem of Translation in Global Circulations*. Durham: Duke University Press. 127-164.
Lutz, Jessie G. 1985. "Karl F.A. Gutzlaff: Missionary Entrepreneur" in Barnett, Suzanne Wilson & Fairbank, John King (eds). *Christianity in China: Early Protestant Missionary Writings*. Cambridge, Mass. and London: Harvard College. 61-87.
Mayers, William Frederick. 1877. *Treaties Between The Empire of China and Foreign Powers*. Shanghai and London: J. Broadhurst Tootal & Trubner & Co.
Morrison, Elizabeth Armstrong. 1839. *Memoirs of the Life and Labours of Robert Morrison, DD*. London: Longman, Orme, Brown, Green and Longmans, 2 Vols.
Ouchterlony, John. 1844. *The Chinese War: An Account of All the Operations of the British Forces from the Commencement to the Treaty of Nanking*. London: Saunder & Otley.
Paquette, Jean. 1987. "An Uncompromising Land: The London Missionary Society in China, 1807-1860". Unpublished PhD dissertation, University of California, Los Angeles.
Qi Ying. 1957. "Memorial to the Emperor" in Qi Xihe (et al.) (eds). *Corpus of Material about the Opium War (Yapian zhanzheng ziliao congkan)*. Shanghai: Shanghai renmin chubanshe, III. 475-476.
Ride, Lindsay & Ride, May. 1996. *An East Indian Company Cemetery: Protestant Burials in Macao*. Hong Kong: Hong Kong University Press.
Teng, Ssuyu. 1944. *Chang Hsi and the Treaty of Nanking, 1842*. Chicago: Chicago University Press.
Tuo, Hunbu. 1957. "Memorial from Tuo Hunbu" (Tuo Hunbo zouzhe) in Qi Xihe (et al.) (eds). *Corpus of Material about the Opium War (Yapian zhanzheng ziliao congkan)*. Shanghai: Shanghai renmin chubanshe, III. 379-380.
Waley, Arthur. 1958. *The Opium War Through Chinese Eyes*. London: George Allen & Unwin.
Welsh, Frank. 1997. *A History of Hong Kong*, London: HarperCollins Publishers.
Wong, Lawrence Wang-chi. 2001. "Power and Translation: A Study of Translation Patronage in

the Late Qing" (*Quanli yu fanyi: wanqing fanyi huodong zhanzhuren de kaocha*) in *Chung Wai Literary Monthly* (*Zhongwai wenxue*), 30 (7): 94-127.

Xiao, Xie. 1988. *The Record of Sino-western Relations* (*Zhongxi jishi*). Changsha: Yuelu shuwu..

Xu Shidong. 1957. 'At the Terrace' (*Lin Gaotai*) in Ah Ying (ed.). *Opium War Literature* (*Yapian zhangzhen wenxueji*). Beijing: Guji chubanshe, 24.

Zhang Xi. 1869. *Diary of Pacifying the Barbarians* (*Furi yiji*). Taibei: Wenhai chubanshe.

——1957. "Petitions on Handling the Barbarians" (Tanyi shuiti) in Qi Xihe (et al.) (eds). *Corpus of Material about the Opium War* (*Yapian zhanzheng ziliao congkan*). Shanghai: Shanghai renmin chubanshe, V. 335-352.

Zheng Jianshun. 2004. *The Study of the Late Qing Period* (*Wanqing shi yanjiu*). Changsha: Yuelu shushe.

# Part II

# Intertwining Memory and Translation

# The Grammar of Survival. How Do We Read Holocaust Testimonies?

*Piotr Kuhiwczak*

The Holocaust was a European phenomenon. English was not the first language of either the victims or the perpetrators, but the study of the Holocaust and the debates about its implications have taken place mainly in English-speaking countries. English is therefore the main medium through which the phenomenon has been represented to the world. As a result, large quantities of primary source material have been translated into English, and many conclusions have been drawn from texts read only in translation. My aim is to discuss how far translation has altered the nature of these primary sources, and how linguistic-and hence cultural-mediation has influenced interpretations of the Holocaust. The paper concentrates primarily on the evidence of eyewitnesses, because these eyewitness accounts have been often used by researchers to support or discredit a variety of contradictory interpretations of events.
Apart from its immediate historical context, the paper will question the role of translation in shaping our knowledge about the past.

Key words: Holocaust, memory, testimony.

A reputable Holocaust historian has recently made a claim that every day a new publication is added to an already vast collection of books and articles devoted to the Holocaust. His claim was based on a search in the Library of Congress, and probably does not include publications in many lesser known languages.[1] But even if the figures are not entirely accurate, we must agree that the Holocaust receives a lot of scholarly attention. Indeed, there are voices implying that the Holocaust receives too much attention considering that the event took place sixty years ago. For instance, in his controversial, but well publicized book, *The Holocaust Industry*, Norman G. Finkelstein suggests that the memory of the terrible events is treated in an instrumental way with no consideration for genuine survivors, like the authors' parents , former inmates of Auschwitz. Finkelstein's line (2000: 41), "I sometimes think that American Jewry "discovering" the Nazi Holocaust was worse than its having been forgotten", has been quoted repeatedly by the media and adopted by many anti-Semites as a useful motto.

What is striking about the above statements as well as other similarly controversial debates about the Holocaust is not so much their merit, but the very fact that they are expressed in English - one of the European languages that was of marginal importance either to the victims or to the perpetrators. Britain was not an occupied country and there were few English-speaking prisoners kept in the Nazi concentration camps, the exception being a little known episode when in 1944 a group of around four hundred British POWs held near Auschwitz worked for six months alongside Jews in the same factory (Heller 1992: 2-4). So the reasons why English became so important in Holocaust studies had nothing to do with the war itself, but rather what happened when the war came to an end.

First of all, many of the remaining European Jews found asylum in the United States, Australia and the United Kingdom. Over the years this immigration initially stimulated general public interest in the survivors' predicament, and then genuine scholarship devoted to the Holocaust. The other reason is not connected with the Holocaust itself, but with the English language, which grew in importance after 1945 and in equal measure has dominated the discourse of the most trivial mass media and the most respectable academic institutions.[2] This combination of geographical, political and linguistic circumstances has led to the colonization of Holocaust debates by the English language to such a degree that that the knowledge, views and arguments must be disseminated in English if they are going to attract public attention and stimulate further discussion. I do not want to suggest that this colonization should be viewed only negatively, because it cannot be denied that without the disseminating power of some *lingua franca* many local issues of global importance would never have been properly aired.

For instance, a wide-ranging international debate about the murder of several hundred Jews in a Polish village of Jedwabne in 1941 became possible only after a book on the subject written in Polish by an American professor of Jewish history, Jan Gross ( 2001), was translated into English. Equally important was the role of American or British historians, to name only Christopher Browning (1992) and Daniel Goldhagen (1996) in stimulating German debates about the responsibility for the Holocaust. Even the Holocaust denying, if undertaken in English, seems to have more weight than denying the Holocaust in smaller languages. David Irving's denial of the Holocaust for instance, has overshadowed many other attempts at revising the history and re-igniting pre-Second World War anti-Semitic ideas.[3]

If this is the case, then perhaps we should accept this linguistic colonization and go along with it like everybody else does – physicists, mathematicians, medics, social scientists and more and more often, literary critics. And yet the Holocaust is problematic precisely because the issues of language and communication are some of its most distinctive and important features. In a way this should be obvious. Ghettos and concentration camps themselves constituted frighteningly mixed communities. People of countless nationalities and social backgrounds were packed together into improbably small spaces. Although a vast majority were classified as Jews, for many, until the moment of deportation, Jewishness was not a concept which either defined or dominated their identity. Indeed for many urban and assimilated Jews the very thought of falling back on the idea of some essential Jewishness was not a viable option. The 2002 Nobel Prize winner, Imre Kertesz (2004: 4-9), talks explicitly about his immense reluctance with which he, a teenage Hungarian, had to confront the fact that he was Jewish when the situation of the Hungarian Jews became precarious towards the end of the Second World War. Equally ambiguous were the feelings of a Polish teenager, Janina Bauman when she realized that she belonged to the same ethnic group as the orthodox and Yiddish-speaking patients of her father. In her memoir *Winter in the Morning* Bauman reflects on a trip to a *shtetl* she made one summer in 1930s:

> I can still remember little children sitting in the dusty road in front of their shabby cottages, playing with used flypapers black with dead flies. Live flies buzzed in their curly black hair, crawled on their filthy arms and legs. The children did not seem to mind. Their fathers were pedlars or poor craftsmen. They had long beards and wore black gabardines. Their mothers wore untidy wigs. They all spoke a foreign language I could not understand. Their Polish was funny. (Bauman 1991: 3)

If the gap was so vast between the people who grew up in one country, and often in the same city, then what was it like when Jews from other countries found themselves forcibly deported to Poland? We get some sense of this difference even long before the outbreak of the war. For an emancipated Jew from Western Europe a contact with *Ostjuden* was a totally unfamiliar experience. In his travel journal *A Journey to Poland* written in 1924 a German-Jewish writer Alfred Döblin gives vent to his complex feeling when he meets the people who are Jewish like him and yet speak a foreign language and live as if little had changed since the Middle Ages. At one point he compares this new cultural experience with what was familiar to him in Germany:

> I can't help thinking as I go out: What an impressive nations Jews are. I didn't know this nation; I believed what I saw in Germany, I believed that the Jews are the industrious people, the shopkeepers who stew in their sense of family and slowly go to fat, the agile intellectuals, the countless insecure unhappy refined people. Now I see that those are isolated examples, degenerating remote from the core of the nation that lives here and maintains itself. (Döblin 1991: 102)

But what had a certain romantic appeal in the 1920s, became an insurmountable barrier with the outbreak of the war. Many accounts of the relations between the deported German Jews to the Polish ghettos and concentration camps testify to the impossibility of communication between the Jews who considered themselves German and the Orthodox Jews who by that time held in contempt not only the assimilationist attitudes but also the German culture. The deportees from the German cities were not considered as "real Jews" but "half-Jews" who lost their identity in the process of assimilation (Engelking and Leociak 2001: 309-310) These differences were not lost on the Nazis, who exploited them to their own ends, since any strategy that helped to keep the ghetto population under control until the final deportations was useful. In his memoir a Warsaw resident, Stefan Ernest quotes a German soldier expressing a condescending surprise that not as many Polish Jews as their counterparts in Vienna and Prague committed honourable suicides on the day of the Nazi invasions: "Ostjuda [Der Ostjude] ist ein besonderer Unmensch mit grösster Würdelosigkeit". (Ernest 2003: 198) Many witnesses and historians emphasize how carefully orchestrated were all restrictive measures that the Nazis mounted against the Jews in occupied Europe (Ernest 2003: 25-45), and in Holocaust museums we can see copies of public notices by means of which the Nazis were announcing their exterminatory policies. Little is known however, apart from the accounts of the work of Jewish Councils in larger cities, how the restrictive measures were actually communicated to the non-German speaking ghetto population. A rare example of this can be found in Marcel Reich-Ranicki's memoir *Mein Leben* (*The Author of Himself*), who was recruited by the Jewish Council in Warsaw to translate documents between German and Polish in order to keep the flow of Nazi decrees into the Ghetto and Jewish reports to the headquarters of SS and Police in return. Eventually, as the author explains, the vast bulk of correspondence compelled the Warsaw Jewish Council to establish a fully fledged department of translation. Reich-Ranicki does not supply many details concerning his department's daily tasks, but there is one moment in his narrative, that reflects the dilemma of somebody in a position of a language expert and mediator under such dramatic circumstances. The episode took place on July $22^{nd}$ 1942, when an SS Sturmbannfürher Hermann Höfle came to the Jewish Council to announce the first major wave of deportations of the ghetto inhabitants to Treblinka. Höfle, who read out the deportation decree to the leaders of the Jewish Council in German, ordered Reich-Ranicki to take down the text simultaneously then translate it quickly into Polish so that the decree about, what was called "resettlement" could be posted up in the streets as soon as possible. The episode gives some insight into the intricate cultural complexities of the power relations under the Nazis as well as into the linguistic obfuscation the Nazis deliberately mounted to disguise their real intentions. While characterizing Höfle Reich-Ranicki (2001: 65) remarks: "Even the man's language, with his unmistakable Austrian accent, testifies to the ruthlessness and vulgarity. He came, as I learned much later, from

Salzburg where he had allegedly been employed as a motor mechanic". Then Reich-Ranicki continues:

> From time to time Höfle looked at me to make sure I was keeping up. Yes, I was keeping up all right. I wrote down that 'all Jewish persons' resident in Warsaw, 'regardless of age or sex' were to be resettled in the east. What did the word 'resettled' mean? And what was meant by 'east'? For what purpose were the Warsaw Jews to be taken there? Nothing was said about this in Höfle's 'Information and Tasks for the Jews' Council. (Reich- Ranicki 2001: 65)

This is the author's confrontation with the new languages, which despite his bi-lingualism he finds utterly incomprehensible and untranslatable. Victor Klemperer (1999), the author of *The Language of the Third Reich* would probably classify the words "resettle" and "the east" as cover-up words - that is terms that were used to obscure the policies and actions that the Nazis were implementing. In Warsaw, in the same way as years earlier in Klemperer's Dresden the strategy of covering up continued unabated even when the truth behind the opaque terms became obvious. As the news of the war horrors was gradually unveiling the cover up words were getting even a tighter grip not only on the official but also on the colloquial German. In his diary *I Will Bear Witness*, Klemperer (1999: 203) gives a vivid examples of these daily accommodations between reality and bureaucratic language: letters delivered to the Jews who had been already deported from Dresden to the concentration camps in Poland were returned to senders with either the innocuous remark '*emigrated*', or more often '*left*' ('*abgewandert*'), which means 'gone away'- and gone away out of their own will without any external encouragement.

If such was the linguistic complexity of the ghetto communities, then what was it like in the concentration camps, particularly the largest ones like Auschwitz-Birkenau, Mauthausen or Bergen-Belsen. Primo Levi's (1988: 68-83) essay 'Communicating' gives a good insight into the intricacies and pitfalls of communicating in Auschwitz, where German was not only the official language but the only code that the Nazis recognized as language. Levi makes it clear that without having very basic German he acquired while studying chemistry, his fate would have been quite different. Italian turned out to be of little use, as did French in a place dominated by Yiddish, Polish, Russian and Hungarian – the main 'non-languages' (as Levi puts it) spoken at Auschwitz. He concludes that

> whoever did not understand or speak German was barbarian by definition; if he insisted on expressing himself in his own language, indeed, his non-language, he must be beaten into silence and put back in his place, pulling, carrying and pushing, because he was not a *Mensch*, not a human being. (Levi 1988: 71)

Levi's observations have been confirmed by little-known research on what Polish and German linguists call *Lagerszpracha* - a restricted communicative code based on German vocabulary adapted to the rules of Polish grammar. Danuta Wesołowska (1996) and Walter Oschlies (1985) carried out detailed linguistic analysis of the memoirs, interviews and other documents that are lodged in Auschwitz museum. Their findings, I think, are of fundamental importance for our understanding of communication not only in the Nazi and by analogy, Stalinist camps, but in all situations where large numbers of people are exposed to prolonged, extreme violence. Wesołowska compiled a substantial corpus of texts with a considerable number of expressions characteristic of the Lagerszpracha. The corpus and its analysis give us a good general insight into what happens to language under extreme social circumstances. Apart from trying to define and classify this type of restricted code, Wesołowska takes the issue further and asks questions which go far beyond the specific historical context of the Nazi concentration camps. In particular, she is concerned with the very function of language in the camps, and then with a possibility of communicating the knowledge about the conditions under which this type of language emerged.

I think it is the second question that is of particular concern to us, because it touches on the issue of the transfer of knowledge, feelings and experience about the situations to which most of us have been fortunate not to have had direct access.

Wesołowska's argument includes the striking case of a small child who protested when somebody called one of the Polish doctors in Auschwitz 'die Artzt' – that is, doctor in German. "This woman is not Artzt, she is a doctor insisted the child [using the Polish word]. Mengele is Artzt". What we have here is not a difference between Polish and German, says Wesołowska (1996: 155), but a classification of reality based on the speakers' prolonged experience. The young child spent a very long period in Auschwitz and the concentration camp was for him the only reality he could remember. The author's conclusion, derived from examples like this one, is that the concentration camps constituted an environment where the language users, apart from the guards and their superiors, did not have human status. This may mean that despite well intentioned attempts, the concentration camp reality cannot be successfully expressed in what she calls 'human language', that is, the langue we normally use. Whether we accept or not the foundations of this argument, the fact is that the inability to communicate the extreme experience is at core of writing on the Holocaust, and Adorno (1967) and Steiner's (1967) views on this subject have been very influential. The inability to communicate the experience is also recognized as a part, of what just after the war the Polish psychiatrists termed 'the concentration camp syndrome'.[4] This is well illustrated by a British prisoner of war, who was held for a while in a camp near Auschwitz and witnessed some horrific events taking place on the other side of the barbed wire. He said the following:

> When I came back to England it was very strange, like coming back
> to a foreign country. I did tell people – but I found that the average
> person you speak to about these things, they can't really understand it
> or they are not particularly interested. It's finding people to who want
> to hear that's been a problem'. I 've never wanted to get it out of my
> system – it's still part of my system now. (Heller 1992: 3)

Survivors' testimonies abound in statements like this one. Over the years, the inability to communicate the traumatic experience was viewed mainly as a psychological phenomenon. The therapeutic work with the survivors has allowed the researchers to identify oral and written forms of witnessing as a therapeutic process that allows the survivors to partially overcome the trauma. Since then, for better or worse, the findings have been used extensively by historians and literary critics, particularly of the Lacanian brand.

Considering the fact that a majority of the victims came from Europe and that English was not for them their first language, it is surprising to see that in a huge body of writing devoted to trauma and witnessing, there is little attention paid to the question whether bilingualism, or often multilingualism plays any role in accounts given of the past. So far the closest anyone gets to the problem is through indirect allusion, or general statement about the relation of trauma to language. For instance, in his book *On Listening to Holocaust Survivors* Henry Greenspan writes:

> For survivors whom we shall hear, memory and selfhood *are* rooted
> in the Holocaust. But they are also rooted elsewhere: in the past as
> personal as any of our own. As we listen to their words, therefore,
> we hear more than voices from Auschwitz or Treblinka, let alone
> confront "embodiments" of such places. Rather, along with the echoes
> of screams and silences, we also hear the distinctive accents of Bialystock,
> Budapest and Lvov. Within and around memories of collective destruction
> are fully personal memories of one who had been a schoolgirl in the
> Carpathians and of another who was once a factory worker in
> Galicia, who dreamed, and still dreams, of planting trees in Palestine.
> (Greenspan 1998: 5)

Here is acknowledgement that the survivors are rooted both in the traumatic reality of the Holocaust but also in the life preceding this period, but this pre-traumatic life fact is acknowledged only as a backdrop, an unusual accent superimposed on the English phonetic pattern – not the linguistic key which could perhaps unlock the door to fruitful exploration of the traumatic past.

A similar example comes from Dominick La Capra's book *Writing History, Writing Trauma*. In the chapter entitled 'Holocaust Testimonies: Attending to the Victims' Voice', the author investigates the validity of the testimony as a source for the historian and as a personal and therapeutic narrative. Language is the central issue in La Capra's argument, but again, language is viewed here as an abstract code, unrelated to any particular linguistic reality. At one point La Capra states:

> In testimonies the survivor as witness often relieves traumatic events and is possessed by the past. These are the most difficult parts of testimony for the survivor, the interviewer, and the viewer of testimonies. Response is a pressing issue, and one may feel inadequate or be confused about how to respond and how to put that response into words.
> (La Capra 2002: 97)

La Capra talks here about the moments when all parties involved in the act of witnessing have no adequate words to express the past and respond to it, and the survivors' testimonies abound in such moments of communicative disruption. However, when the disruption happens in a second language, we are left wondering whether the issue is only emotional, or perhaps what cannot be expressed in a second language could have been expressed in the native one?

In her book *Dinner with Persephone* Patricia Storace (1997: 163) remarked "Nothing destroys fluency faster than the presence of anger – only the truly native speaker or linguist of long standing can manage both anger and grammar". If this is the case under the relatively normal circumstances Storace describes, than what happens to the grammar of somebody 'possessed by the past' when the possession is being expressed in the second language? And taking this questioning further we might ask would the survivor, interviewer and the viewer of the testimony respond differently if the session were carried out in the survivor's first language?

Claude Lanzmann's (1988) monumental documentary *Shoa* provides a partial answer to this question. Multilingualism and interpretation are key issues in his work. On the screen all the linguistics and visual forces are at play. The intentionally visible work of the interpreters on the screen, and the emotions with which language is charged, provide an alternative approach to the project of witnessing the Holocaust. In the words of Shoshana Felman (1992: 212)

> The film places us in the position of the witness who *sees* and *hears*, but *cannot understand* the significance of what is going on until the later intervention, the delayed processing and rendering of the significance of the visual/acoustic information by the translator, who also in some ways distorts and screens it, because (as is attested by those viewers who are native speakers of the foreign tongues which the translator is translating, and as the film itself points out by some of Lanzmann's interventions and corrections), the translation is not always absolutely accurate. (Felman 1992: 212)

If to acknowledge the linguistic reality of the Holocaust opens up such an empathic way of receiving the past, then why hasn't this reality been exploited earlier? To answer this question, we probably need to turn to the medical profession, because for some time after the end of the war, interviews with the Holocaust were carried out first as a form of therapy. Only much later the interviews were videoed and treated as historical material. A family therapist, Charlotte Burck (1997: 64-85) stresses the fact that in systematic therapy the experience of bilinguals has not been given much attention despite the fact that research has shown that bilinguals' narratives vary depending on which language they use. In her article Burck quotes cases of traumatised bilingual patients who in the course of a single therapeutic session switched between languages, either to distance themselves from the events, or to challenge the past by re-claiming the language in which the trauma took place. Burck (1997: 84-85) concludes that the lack of language awareness in the therapeutic environment is closely linked to what she calls a "deficit model of bilingualism" that has prevailed in Britain for a long time. Until relatively recently similarly negative perceptions of bilinguals have been common in the United States. It might pertinently be asked how far these attitudes may have contributed to the fact that the bilingualism of the survivors has never been explored.

But to research this question today would only be of historical value. The memory of the Holocaust is now at a turning point. We are losing touch with the lived experience narrated by the witnesses and begin to rely on records, which inevitably turn it into the event deeply buried in a distant past.
This transition from the oral to the written may perhaps explain why interest in the Holocaust memoirs is currently so strong. How else should we account for the ever increasing number of new memoirs coming out particularly in the United States? Norman Finkelstein (2000: 81), whom I mentioned at the beginning of this article, attributes this increase to conscious manipulation and forgery. He makes this claim on the authority of his mother who used to say "If everyone who claims to be a survivor actually is one, who did Hitler kill"? Finkelstein's (2000: 55-63) attention is drawn to Jerzy Kosinski and Binjamin Wilkomirski, two writers who do seem to have used the Holocaust as the means to attract public attention. But this is a tendentious argument, which does not take into account a number of factors that have impacted on the publication of the memoirs. In the first case, many books appearing in English are just delayed translations from other languages. The best example is *The Pianist* by Władysław Szpilman (1999) - originally published in Warsaw in 1946 under the title *Śmierć Miasta* and translated into English from a German version. There is no doubt that the film adaptation of the book will lead to the translation of other memoirs, as did Steven Spielberg's film *Schindler's List*.

Then there is an issue of the memoirs that were lodged for decades in east European archives. Many manuscripts were not published there for political reasons, and now, although local resources are limited, institutions like the Jewish Historical Institute in Warsaw and the State Museum in Auschwitz are collaborating with publishers to bring out manuscripts of often outstanding historical and literary value. Undoubtedly the most important titles will eventually be published in English, thus adding to the odd impression that the number of publications is in reverse proportion to the number of survivors.

But not all memoirs are translations - or perhaps, taking into consideration the complex ontology of these texts, it would be safer to say that often we are not sure whether we are dealing with a translations or not. *The Pianist* by Szpilman is a good example. The original manuscript has a dual authorship, and from the preface to the book we know that Szpilman's co-author, Jerzy Waldorff, put down on paper the story Szpilman (1946: 5-8) told him. Forty years later the book suddenly appeared in German with Waldorff's name removed, some alterations in the order of events, and with a new preface by Szpilman's son, Andrzej. The son emphasized the fact that this was now a new and authoritative version of his father's memoir, substantially changed from the censored version published in Warsaw.[5] The remark about the communist censorship made by Andrzej Szpilman (2000: 7) remains a mystery, because there is nothing in the new versions of the book that one can find in the Polish original.

The *Pianist* is a conspicuous but by no means the most complex case of a Holocaust memoir in transfer. Janina Bauman's (1986) outstanding book *Winter in the Morning* was written forty years after the end of the Second World War and in English, the language she was learning painstakingly just after her expulsion from Poland and arrival in England in 1968. As Bauman confessed in a private conversation,[6] it was a tortuous enterprise to write such a personal book in a foreign language. By comparison, translating the book some years later into Polish was sheer pleasure. Then with her second book *The Dream of Belonging* (1988) the process was reversed. Bauman recalls that writing the second volume of her memoir in English was a pleasurable task but translation into Polish turned out to be hard not so much because of linguistic but because of the cultural difficulties. While writing about the post-war communist Poland for the English readers Bauman was subconsciously expanding on the things that otherwise would have been incomprehensible. In Polish all the elaborate explanations became obsolete down to simple items like the names of institutions which in Polish could be labelled with generally recognizable acronyms. So instead of translating, says Bauman, "I really had to write the book again".

There is no doubt that translingualism, as Steven Kellman (2000) calls the phenomenon of writing in one's second or often third language, is an important feature of Holocaust memoirs. But there are also other forms of text production like transcription of oral accounts, co-authorship, or editing which often disguises a radical re-writing and translation. Then there are multiple translation procedures, for instance, from Yiddish into a modern European language and then into English, but this complicated transformation is not always obvious and we can only find it out by tracing the Yiddish original in the archives. Imre Kertesz (2004), who writes in German and Hungarian, casts a further doubt on the survivors' memoirs when he claims that their stories are written in "borrowed languages" - languages that do not belong to the Jews but to other European nations. This statement which expresses deep pain of incomplete assimilation and then subsequent rejection of the Jews by European nation states, adds another dimension to the complexity of the Holocaust writing.

One may ask then what is the impact of these complex operations both on the text and on the reader, and what exactly do we lose and gain on the way. If the Holocaust cannot be either described or expressed in a human language, as some survivors claim, then what do we, the readers, get from these books? Sanitized versions of something so horrific that it cannot be expressed in words, or what modern literary criticism calls *representation* or a *construction* of reality that cannot be directly accessible, and which in fact was obliterated in the 1940s?

For an average reader who is not a historian verifying the facts, the Holocaust memoir is not necessarily a source of information. What makes the reading of these text compelling is an urge to understand the world in which the horrific events took place, and perhaps eventually to find an answer to the question how was it possible?

Only some authors, co-authors and translators have managed to satisfy this need by conveying at least some of the specificity of the places and the people involved in the tragedy of extermination. This has been done by different means, for instance, by retaining often crucial Polish, Yiddish or German words to show the communication gaps and the function of language as an instrument of coercion, or by careful characterization in order to make sure that the victims belong to a *shtetl* and not to a small market town in southern England. In a word, what we need is the preservation of what Antoine Berman (1999:287) aptly calls a "Babelian proliferation of languages" which is such a strong feature of the memoirs. It is very likely that within few decades the Holocaust memoirs will be read differently. Their historical specificity will give way to a more universal response to the issue of what psychological price we pay for surviving under extreme circumstances. And yet one feels that without understanding this complex 'Babelian' feature of the Holocaust it will be difficult to understand its universal significance. There is a danger that some general empathy will replace the present restless search for explanation.

In his 1984 Aquinas Lecture entitled *The Reality of the Historical Past*, Paul Ricoeur talked about our relation to the past. He contrasted sympathy with curiosity as mental attitudes that determine how we conceive of the past and relate it to the present.

> We return in this way to the enigma of *temporal distance*, an enigma overdetermined by the axiological distancing that has made us strangers to the attitudes of past ages, to the point that the otherness of the past in relation to the present overrides the survival of the past in the present. When curiosity takes over from sympathy, the foreigner becomes foreign. The distance that separates is substituted for the difference that joins together.
> (Ricoeur 1984: 21)

It is just this - interplay of the sympathy and curiosity that perhaps may bring us a little bit closer to the understanding of the past which is deemed incommunicable.

The recognition of the multilayered texture of the Holocaust memoirs may perhaps help us to convert the alienating otherness into the difference, that in Ricoeur's words 'joins together'.

---

1 Conversation held in November 2005 with Gunnar S. Paulson, author of *Secret City*, Yale University Press, New Haven, 2000.
2 The seriousness of the problem is well illustrated by the debate about the use of English in Scandinavian universities. For instance, Oslo University has formed an academic committee to develop a language policy to cope with the use of English in teaching and research. See Buscal, John. 'Fears for Norwegians as English papers rewarded' in *The Times Higher Education Supplement* (10 February 2006).
3 A good account of Irving's case can be found in Lipstadt, Deborah. 2005 *History on Trial; My day in Court with David Irving*. London: Harper Collins World.
4 Early research on the KZ-syndrome was published in a journal *Zeszyty Oswiecimskie* (Auschwitz Journal). More on the subject is available in Kepinski, Antoni. 1978. *Rytm Zycia*. Krakow: Wydawnictwo Literackie
5 The English translation that claims to be translated from the 1946 Polish edition, is actually a translation from the German.
6 Unrecorded personal conversations with Janina Bauman in 2001.

## References

Adorno, W. Theodor. 1967. *Prisms* (tr. S. and S. Weber). Camb. Mass.: MIT Press.
Bauman, Janina. 1988. *A Dream of Belonging*. London: Virago Press.
——1986. *Winter in the Morning*. London: Virago.
——1989. *Zima o Poranku*. Kraków: Znak.
Browning, Christopher. 1992. *Ordinary Men: Reserve Batallion 101 and the Final Solution in Poland*. London: Penguin Books.
Burck, Charlotte. 1997. 'Language and narrative' in Papadopolous, Renos K. and John Byng-Hall (eds) *Multiple Voices*. London: Duckworth. 16-41.

Berman, Antoine. 2000. 'Translation and the trials of the foreign' in Venuti, Lawrence (ed.) *The Translation Studies Reader*. London: Routledge. 284-297.
Döblin, Alfred. 1991.*Journey to Poland* (tr. J. Neugrischel). New York: Paragon House.
Engelking, Barbara and J. Leociak. 2001. *Ghetto Warszawskie. Przewodnik po nieistniejącym mieście*. Warszawa: IFiS PAN.
Ernest, Stefan. 2003. *O Wojnie Wielkich Niemiec z Zydami Warszawy*. Warszawa: Czytelnik.
Felman, Shoshana and Dori Laub. 1992. *Testimony*. London: Routledge.
Finkelstein, G. Norman. 2000. *The Holocaust Industry*. London: Verso.
Goldhagen, Daniel. 1996. *Hitler's Willing Executioners: Ordinary Germans and the Holocaust*. London: Abacus.
Greenspan, Henry. 1998. *On Listening to Holocaust Survivors*. London: Praeger.
Gross, Jan. 2001. *The destruction of the Jewish Community in Jedwabne, Poland*. Princeton University Press.
Heller, Zoë. 1992. 'Out of Silence' in *The Sunday Times* (15 March 1992)
Kellman, Steven G. 2000. *The Translingual Imagination*. Lincoln: University of Nebraska Press.
Klemperer, Victor. 1999. *I Will Bear Witness* (tr. M. Chalmers). New York: Random House.
——1999. *The Language of the Third Reich: "LTI (Lingua Tertii Imperii)" – A Philologist's Notebook* (tr. M. Brady). London: Continuum.
Kertesz, Imre. 2004. 'Słowami łatwo się bawić...' in *Nowe Książki* 11: 4-9.
——2004. *Die exilierte Sprache*. Frankfurt am Mein.
La Capra, Dominic. 2002. *Writing History, Writing Trauma*. Baltimore: The John Hopkins University Press.
Lanzmann, Claude. 1988. *Shoah: An Oral History of the Holocaust : the Complete Text of the Film*. New York: Random House.
Levi, Primo. 1988. *The Drowned and the Saved*. London: Michael Joseph.
Oschlies, Walter. 1985. 'Lagerszpracha' – Zur Theorie einer KZ-specifischen Soziolinguistik' in *Zeitgeschichte*, heft 1, Okt : 1-27.
Reich-Ranicki, Marcel. 2001. *The Author of Himself* (tr.E.Osers). London: Weidenfeld & Nicholson.
Ricoeur, Paul. 1984. *The Reality of the Historical Past*. Milwaukee: Marquette University Press.
Steiner, George. 1967. *Language and Silence*. London: Faber and Faber.
Storace, Patricia. 1997. *Dinner with Persephone*. London: Granta Books.
Szpilman, Władysław. 1946. *Śmierć miasta*. Warszawa: Czytelnik.
——2002. *The Pianist* (tr. A. Bell). London: Weidenfeld & Nicolson.
——1998. *Das wunderbare Überleben*. Berlin: Econ Verlag.
Wesolowska, Danuta. 1996. *Slowa z Piekl Rodem*. Kraków: Impuls.

# The Troy of Always: Translations of Conflict in Christopher Logue's *War Music*

*Paschalis Nikolaou*

This essay looks at Christopher Logue's dialogue with Homer's epic of war, his work-in-progress 'account' of the *Iliad* as *War Music*. I examine connections between Logue's aesthetic positions, personal circumstances –especially his post-war military experience in the Black Watch, and anti-war activity as he becomes involved in the anti-nuclear Committee of 100 and the CND Aldermaston March– and his 're-statement' of the ancient epic. Logue's is a modernist, ongoing literary project that seems ultimately driven to comment on the universality of conflict and violent constants in human nature; numerous allusions and anachronisms help create an intertextual merger of voices from many battlefields during the centuries, while a subversive sensibility translates the epic past into what is shown to still be a 'Trojan' present. *War Music* exemplifies creative translation partaking of political/social comment; it is to translation we often turn in considering our relationship with conflict, conflict that still defines modern societies and the human psyche.[1]

Key words: Christopher Logue, Homer, the Iliad, creativity and translation/re-writing, political contexts, psychologies of conflict, (auto) biographical elements.

## 1. Making Homer new

> The cold from this very large space flooded into the auditorium.
> We sat in darkness for several seconds. Then, faintly at first, rising through a full minute to a high-pitched painful shrieking, came the noise of diesel engines mixed with the grinding clatter of heavy metal tracks. As this frightening, unstoppable roar gained its maximum, the stage lights came up on an actual Tiger (PzKw 6) tank, a gigantic thing of terrible beauty, its 18 foot 6 inch gun barrel pointing at us, the audience, as it swung around on the theatre's revolving stage.
> Then the noise stopped. The turret's hutch opened. A head looked out. The play began. (Christopher Logue, 'Visiting Brecht')

In 1959, the poet Christopher Logue arrived in London following a five-year artistic exile in Paris, with three collections of poems under his belt. He soon joined London's burgeoning anti-war movement as, by then, the victors of the Second World War were mass-producing and testing nuclear bombs around the globe. 1959 was also the year that he was approached by two classicists working for the BBC, Donald Carne-Ross and Xanthe Wakefield, to work on a radio version of an extract from the *Iliad*. What appears to have been an accident of birth started taking shape in his mind as 'my Homer poem'; more than four decades later, he is still at work on what is possibly the greatest poetic rendering of Homer since George Chapman and Alexander Pope. Logue has been wise to focus all his literary powers on this project, and has not produced any new poetry 'of his own' for many years: thus, if one thinks of the poet Christopher Logue, one tends to think of the translator of the *Iliad*, the composer of *War Music*. In place of collections of poems, we are offered the *Iliad* in instalments. Recent books are: *All Day Permanent Red* (2003a; henceforward referred to as *ADPR*), roughly corresponding to books 5 and 6 of the *Iliad*, and *Cold Calls* (2005) which saw the poet –at the age of 80– receive the Whitbread Prize for Poetry.[2]

I want to explore, here, how we have come to 'Logue's Homer'; how the translating of the prototypical epic of ancient conflict itself becomes and embodies Logue's own poetics. Mainly drawing upon his memoir, *Prince Charming* (1999), I shall trace several connections between the poet's literary output and a diversity of conflicts in his own life, as they have influenced views that subtly resonate in his re-creation. Questions on the nature and workings of translation and literary creativity inevitably rise to the surface when we consider dynamics that develop between version and original, especially if the translator approaches an original with the mind-frame, priorities and objectives of a poet. At the same time, the relationship between life lived and the originals/translations that follow its expression, the extent to which verbal artefacts coincide with personal narratives, our creative autobiographies, are of interest; particularly since, in this case, we deal with a work that can offer comment on the problematic synapses between the realities of war and its aesthetic representations, its *music*.

Translation has provided us with a steady flow of Homers, especially in the Anglo-American context. Indeed, in the words of George Steiner (1996: 91), it is

> to Achilles and Odysseus, to the 'topless towers of Ilium' and the shores of Ithaka, it is to 'deep-browed Homer' that English-language sensibility turns and returns, incessantly, as if striving to appropriate to itself, to the native genius, material already, by some destined or elective affinity, its own.

Chapman's 'fourteener' *Iliad*, in its excited licentiousness and proud neologisms, facilitates an English heroic couplet. Pope explores previous translations as he works on his own *Iliad*, taking liberties in capturing 'that Rapture and Fire' of the original, to arrive at a poetic text that stands on its own as a masterpiece in English. Both renderings trace a maturation of translation as both literary enterprise as well as enabler of critical acuity. From then on, the history of English –and of translation practices– overlaps extensively with a long history of Homer re-translated (for an overview see Rosslyn 2001: 350-355). To return to Steiner,

[...] the sequence of translations from Homer provides a unique radioactive tracer. By its luminescent progress, we can follow the development of the language, of its vocabularies, syntax and semantic resources, from root to stem, from its stem to its multiple branches and leaves. Every model of English lexical and grammatical observance is visible in this chain: all the way from the most ornate and experimental, as in Chapman or Joyce, to the 'basic English' purpose in I. A. Richards's narration of the fury of Achilles. The Homeric sequence is an inventory of metrical means: we find in it alliterative verse, rhyme royal, Spenserian stanzas, heroic couplets, iambic pentameter, blank and free verse. (1996: 93-94)

In this context, creative and critical starting points often depend on the assertion of the translator's subjectivity. When the identity of the poet shapes the identity of the translation, as with Pope, Chapman or Logue, we observe the 'political incorrectness' of a mode of translating that is distinctly 'literary' in conception and execution, as opposed to more classically *responsible* approaches of, for instance, Lattimore (1951) or, more recently, Fagles (1991). While this is not to imply that the latter should be devoid of brilliance and, indeed, inventiveness in transferring the perceived 'whole' of Homer, it can be argued that the former more clearly offer us also a sense of time and place, images of an 'aesthetic personality' reading the ancient epic while the poet's known voice is re-articulated and extended through translation. As the poet-translator is visibly doing things to both translation and original, we draw a little closer to the paradox of 'creative translation'. Logue, in particular, joins a pantheon of poets who have 'co-authored' with Homer, by focusing on broadcasting impacts rather than re-articulating a sanctified shibboleth. He begins by boldly disposing of the epithets and the repetitions abundant in the *Iliad*, a consequence of the oral formulae of its conception. He then proceeds by way of compression and amplification, eliminating or re-imagining scenes: what reaches us is a 'dreamworking' of Homer, an evocative *processing* of an original that presents us with the translator-as-editor, abstracting from his primary text and distilling its essences, intensifying his understanding (and ours) through visual collages and cinematic language. In the end, a transparency between original, translation and inspiration allows his work to be simultaneously construed as a new poem in its own right, as well as 'Logue's Homer'. The added possessive, like with Chapman and Pope before him, makes and unmakes both Homer and Logue.

At the same time, no translator is an island, and no translation, however personalised, avoids participating into more communal internalisations or even, shared causes. And this is perhaps especially evident in poetic translation, where perspectivism and linguistic idiosyncracies may more readily mingle with creative and critical movements, and socio-political and aesthetic ideologies as these reach for possible platforms. Peter Fawcett's overview of thought on 'ideology and translation' (2001: 106-111) reminds us how manipulative translating tends to rise to a performance that echoes agendas often hidden behind the (ab)use of source texts. In Logue's case, his method as translator-poet owes much to the precedent of Ezra Pound –as the previous paragraph already shows–, who navigates the advances of literary modernism through works like *Cathay* or *Homage to Sextus Propertius* (as a matter of interest, J.P. Sullivan [1965] practically invents the term 'creative translation' both to describe what Pound does and in order to reclaim it as translation). Logue shares Pound's principles on translation, particularly in that *War Music* appears conceived "as a series of 'brilliant moments', both at the level of the individual phrase and in its overall architecture" (Underwood 1998: 61).

Overall, Pound expects that the poet as reader and critic will react to what has been before, that this underpins the way in which he or she conveys the present and 'makes it new'. But now more than ever this expectation applies to what is able to be imported through translation as much to originals; this shift in turn impinges on what literary translation can be *made to be*. Steven G. Yao, in his compelling study of *Translation and the Languages of Modernism* (2003) not only confirms that modernism legitimises translation as a literary mode that serves to extend central preoccupations with gender, politics and language; he also argues that translation has been midwife to –if not often coincident with– literary innovations that paved the way for the trans-lingual poetics of *The Cantos* or *Finnegans Wake*, as modernist authors proceeded to redefine and augment the operative parameters of translation. In newly discovered borderlands, both creativity and subjectivity are re-presented in visible conflicts of interest between original author and translator, with the translator emerging as power-player in terms of what is said *through* a transformed original (see Venuti 1995 also). To suggest that literary modernism 'discovers' a sense of selfhood in translation might be overstating the case; yet, with modernism, we do witness an increased awareness of what was always there. As a result, the creative potentialities of translating, usually anaesthetised in the past, are now celebrated.

It is hardly an accident that this new-found self-consciousness, which goes with a rethinking of translation as poetry gained rather than literature lost, also concurs with a recharging of the terms that portray alchemy or synergy between sensibilities: among others, a 'version', a 'homage' and, to return to Logue, an 'account'. *War Music* describes itself thus in relation to the *Iliad*, yet its poet has always been a willing participant in the definitional confusion –imitation or paraphrase, adaptation or new poem?– surrounding what he does as he inserts parts into the whole: *Patrocleia* (1962) is 'freely adapted into English'; and *ADPR* announces itself on its title page as 'the first battle scenes of Homer's *Iliad* rewritten'. While suggesting awareness of literary shapes, such tensions of naming also reflect an essential symptom of poetic translating: with respect to the ensuing formations or hybrids, it is mostly fluid descriptions of a distinctive approach that prove feasible, rather than exact designations.³ Thus *War Music* continues to present us with an instance of poetry redefining itself by way of translation exploring its creative possibilities.

Given Logue's early alignment with Pound and Eliot, and the reverberations of modernism in his original poetry –which become more obvious when he explores the variants of poster poetry and performance poetry during the 1960s– it is hardly surprising that he awakens to *War Music* as a neo-modernist work-in-progress, and comes up with something distinctly Poundian for a text for which until then only exhaustive reverence would do.⁴ What is difficult to bypass, however, is a notorious 'war record' associated with modernist values. As modernism gained momentum in its brutal confrontation with past and present, it compelled Wyndham Lewis to state that it was astonishing to find "how like art is to war, I mean 'modernist' art" (1937: 4). A host of precarious ideas were accommodated as aesthetics and politics mingled in the course of this 'first literary war'. In *Writing War in the Twentieth Century* (2000), Margot Norris suggests that as modernism proceeded to replace representation with performance, its

> self-reflexive pre-scription of the war as (energetic) formalism may thus have colluded in the phenomenology of the Great War by placing the mass dead's irrational and illogical production under an erasure that itself pre-scripted and, in a sense, pre-dicted World War II (*ibid.*: 35).⁵

In the wake of Pound and Lewis, Logue's subscription to modernist aesthetics on the one hand, and his stated endeavor of conveying Iliadic morality in *War Music* on the other, could invite criticisms of glorifying war, or of sensationalising violence. Nevertheless, Logue famously holds Eliot accountable for anti-Semitic nuances in a much-publicised correspondence in the *TLS* (his reflections on this can be found in 1999: 214-215), and he is indeed all too aware of the pitfalls that led to Pound's fascist salutes and post-war adventures:

> [...] the texts of the radio broadcasts Pound made to the American soldiers who were fighting in Italy in 1943 and 1944 [...] were worse than I had guessed. Full of anti-Semitic ravings [...] Pound was a fighter for the kind of literary art I admired, an experimental idea of beauty. And at the same time, he was advocating a perverse delusion realized through a criminal ideology. Literary commentators who try to justify, or apologize for, racist –in Pound's case– views by appealing to the poet's undoubted gifts soil themselves. In verse (as elsewhere) beauty will serve any view and give it a glamour. We should not be afraid to call it whorish. (*ibid.*: 152)

Logue's project should also be seen alongside his political outlook and overall views on art. Most of his work, not least his overtly anti-war protest poetry of the 1960s, confirms a firm belief in poetry as a force for change; the poet has always been "strongly committed to an idea that poetry should play an active part in society" (2003b: 125). Moreover, Logue's life-writing suggests that, if not an ideological charge, there *is* a certain accountability at the back of his mind while translating Homer. Arguably, his modernist 'contaminations' of *Iliad*, which I will examine in more detail shortly, manage to reset some of the encodings of modernism to another, more responsible socio-ideological agenda. At the same time, the poem/translation that calls itself *War Music* reminds us of millennia-old traffic between war and art, as it confronts us with our enduring violent tendencies, tendencies resistant to illusions of innocence.

## 2. '...The *Iliad* suits you'

> It is odd that Homer, in the thirteenth century, should have copied down the adventures of Sinbad –another Ulysses– and again after many hundreds of years have discovered forms like those of his own *Iliad* in a northern kingdom and a barbaric tongue. (Jorge Luis Borges, 'The Immortal,' tr. Andrew Hurley)

Logue's memoir shows how his formative years were marked and indeed, shaped, by military, political and ideological conflicts. The book starts with recollections of the Blitz and moves towards his prison spell in 1961 for 'civil disobedience', together with other members of the Committee of 100 against atomic weapons, led by Bertrand Russell.

Between these two demarcating experiences, we find, by Logue's account, a restless and confused young man keen to escape and perhaps join "the army commandos from where it was a short step to strange units such as Popski's Private Army, among whose heroes I imagined myself" (1999: 46). In 1944, he volunteered for the Black Watch, and began a notorious stint with the regiment as part of the British presence in what would soon become Israel. There he witnessed the onset of a conflict that was to have a strong and lasting effect on him; and, in an effort to dispose of some ill-advisedly taken army paybooks, he landed himself in a Palestine military prison for theft (*ibid.*: see esp. 58-74). During this whole period, Logue not only acquired a soldier's practical understanding of the realities of the military way of life, but also, despite never finding himself beyond battle exercises or directly engaged in actual confrontations, was able to reflect on the deeper causes and consequences, firstly of the Middle Eastern conflict in particular and, gradually, of wars in general. During the sixteenth months he spent in prison, he continued to write poetry, an activity that had first started in earnest in camp libraries. The image of the young poet writing in the library of an army unit or prison is bizarre enough; one might perhaps be forgiven for thinking of alchemies between war and the literary art already occurring in Logue's mind.

Logue's poetry, always direct, declamatory and combative, fittingly begins by drawing on his early experiences as a serviceman, and soon becomes preoccupied with the inherent absurdities of human nature and the irrationality of war. This is more evident in poems such as 'Loyal to the king', 'The Song of the Imperial Carrion' and 'The Song of the Dead Soldier' (see *Selected Poems* 1996: 14-15, 16-17 and 26-27 respectively) which recount first exposures to military exploits –the latter begins with "For seven years at school I named / our kings, their wars (if these were won)"– and take note of political betrayals of patriotic loyalty. Throughout his writings, the poet often resorts to military lexis in articulating political protest and societal discord. Also, even before work began on his 'Homer poem', characters and analogies from the *Iliad* are considered, and with hindsight, a reader is able to recognise that Logue's poetry is being gradually driven towards a perceived 'shared concern' between himself and Homer. Moreover, when *War Music* starts happening, the poet-translator becomes both 'host' and 'guest': the *Iliad*, comes to *affect* Logue's poetic stance as his voice tries to find sources for itself; at the same time, the poet, welcoming the prospects of concentration and annexation, starts to *infect* the *Iliad* with his own staccato syntax, laconic rhythms and eye for irony.

In his Paris years (1951-1956), Logue's views on a fairer, classless society became stronger and more articulated. His concerns at this time extend to the moral power and social responsibility of art and of poetry, which, however avant-garde, cannot be above politics (see 1999: 160-161 and 190-197). Then, Logue's youthful, anarchic, indeed anarchistic, left-wing enthusiasm was exposed to the anti-nuclear movement in London. At this time of Cold War, he was wary of what he and others perceived as a misguided Western defence policy and becomes convinced that a significant intellectual minority, or 'intelligentsia', that is "blessed with the power of detached, informed, analysis fails in its duty if it fails, when necessary, to criticize, as well as to support, the institutions that sustain it" (*ibid.*: 229). Thus he was quick to join the Campaign for Nuclear Disarmament (CND), which culminated in the Aldermaston March of 1958. He was part of what Alan Sinfield (see 1997: 232-277) calls the 'rise of left-culturism' in post-war Britain, rooted in liberal humanism and disaffected with the policies of the prevailing system. At one of the regular meetings held before the march itself in the house of critic Kenneth Tynan, Doris Lessing, who had recently been reading the *Iliad*, suggested to Logue that it 'suited' him (Logue recalls her saying "[s]omething to do with heroism, tragedy, that sort of thing" –1999: 221). This suggestion was made only days before Carne-Ross proposed the BBC version to Logue.

It is not hard to see why others recognised early Homer in Logue in this period of his development, when his committed, outspoken poetry of protest called for social justice and change. If the artists and writers involved in the anti-war group required a 'model' for the brutal lessons of history, a sounding board for their own stance towards it, the *Iliad* was perhaps best suited for this purpose; and Homer's poem seemed entirely to 'belong' to

Logue, whose inclination to versioning already enables the political charge of his poetry, be it a Brechtian-style pastiche of the anti-nuclear lobby ('To My Fellow Artists'; 1996: 28-32), or a chorus from *Antigone* on man's propensity for confrontation: "We long to destroy the things we have made / Finding no enemy, we become our own enemy. / As we trap the beasts, so we trap other men. / But the others strike back, trap closing on trap" (*ibid*: 6-7).

Moreover, this is a poet who was not only steeped in confrontation and activism, but was also keen on public poetry readings that, conceivably, were reminiscent of those of ancient bards. Indeed, the public orality of Logue's readings, and the speech-act immediacy of his poetry, comes to haunt his Homer. For all its stimulating visual configurations, *War Music*'s greatest asset, arguably, has to do with going back to the beginning, to a long-lost oral tradition, gathering us around what is spoken; Logue's incremental re-writing is, at the same time, a re-oralising. In this sense it is not surprising that the poet feels that work on the poem "does not end with the manuscript. For me, until I have heard it read aloud, the published text is incomplete. I made a lot of changes to the text of *Kings* after hearing the BBC Radio performance" (1993: 256). In the event, and considering its origins in radio dramatisation, its performance history and Logue's willingness to create a text that can be shared by many, his Homer may be said to redress the elitism inherent in modernism, aiming to return its poetic languages to the masses whom the avant-garde often frowned upon, and even dangerously erased.

Still, the poet begins to doubt the sincerity of his political commitment when he finds himself in prison once more with others of the Committee of 100. He reflects on what he understands as naiveté in some of his views. This is perhaps matched by his innocence when first confronted with the Iliadic world: initial impressions, such as that of Achilles as 'some kind of a Nazi', are patiently countered by Carne-Ross and Wakefield's explanations that there are no 'good' or 'bad' characters for Homer (1999: 223); and that "[t]he Greeks are not humanistic, not Christian, not sentimental [...] They are musical" (*ibid*.: 209-210). These insights echo Bespaloff's, in her classic commentary on Homer's epic:

> Who is good in the *Iliad*? Who is bad? Such distinctions do not exist; there are only men suffering, some winning, some losing. The passion for justice emerges only in mourning for justice, in the dumb avowal of silence. To condemn force, or absolve it, would be to condemn, or absolve, life itself. (2005: 50)

A kind of reassessment accelerates as the poet is immersed in Homer's world. Logue's memoir notes, for instance, a powerful sentence he comes across in W. E. Gladstone's *Studies On Homer and the Homeric Age* (1858; quoted in 1999: 274):

> [i]f we cannot conceive of freedom without perpetual discord, the faithful performance of the duty of information and advice without coercion and oppression, it is either a sign of our narrow-mindedness, or of our political degeneracy.

So while core anti-war views and political left-wing stances cannot change much, a wider complexity of the civic realities and facts that now disallow the quick changes the young activist was once so fond of are gradually accepted. Poetry should remain involved within society, yet the active political purpose of Logue's poetry cools as the poet realises "how difficult it is to bring about a set of changes that won't make matters worse" (2003b: 126).

Through this summary of relevant biographical details, I am suggesting that rather than simply 'using' the ancient text as a vessel through which to channel fully developed anti-war positions, Logue becomes enveloped in a reciprocal process. In the dialogue between original and translator, Logue's own views can mature, evolve, refine. At the same time, the unmistakably original voice and recognisable energy of the Logue of his earlier poems emerges more strongly than ever. Thus, by translating, Logue not only encounters Homer but also himself and, in that double encounter, realises that he is more creatively at home in recomposing, that is, in abstracting from what was before, than in starting from scratch (see 1999: 223-224; other reflections on poetic translation in 248-249). The case of Logue offers images of translation as creative confrontation, a clash and merging of sensibilities. As worldviews collide and inhabit each other, the poet-translator behind *War Music* engages in a process of understanding, which demands that he embrace the warrior ethic of a remote and ancient world; it is a process that also allows him, perhaps, to glimpse sources of contradiction in his own views.

In this embrace, what is essentially Homeric, the violent pre-humanistic 'music' of the *Iliad*, might only be truly retained by imaginative updating, by modern equivalences of 'that Rapture and Fire'. However, Logue's Iliadic 'installations' in our present consciousness cannot but have different effects, from plain guilt at enjoying this verse to empowering recognitions of the absurd reality of what is still happening around us. Because through the use of anachronisms or the highlighting of occasional comment, his treatment shares understandings of where we still are, politically and psychologically:

> Now I shall ask you to imagine how
> Men under discipline of death prepare for war.
> There is much more to it than armament,
> And kicks from those who could not catch an hour's sleep
> Waking the ones who dozed like rows of spoons;
> Or those with everything to lose, the kings,
> Asleep like pistols in red velvet.
>     Moments like these absolve the needs dividing men.
> Whatever caught and brought and kept them here

> Is lost: and for a while they join a terrible equality,
> Are virtuous, self-sacrificing, free:
> And so insidious is this liberty
> That those surviving it will bear
> An even greater servitude to its root:
> Believing they were whole, while they were brave;
> That they were rich, because their loot was great;
> That war was meaningful, because they lost their friends. (2001: 206)

As Logue tries to speak truth to war, the main hope he expresses for *War Music* is that it will make people "very much aware that warfare is somehow endemic to human beings. It is hopeless. We must keep trying" (2003b: 125). The political charge and core values of Logue's poetic voice, tempered now by awareness of the timelessness of conflict, and mutated through the vagaries of translational processes, are still present in his ongoing 'account'. To an extent, it is hard *not* to look for their traces when we are made aware of the context out of which *War Music* arises, and of the translator's life story.

## 3. Paint it red: life into 'account', and a timeless Troy

> Though it is noon, the helmet screams against the light;
> Scratches the eye; so violent it can be seen
> Across three thousand years. (Christopher Logue, *Pax*)

In this section I wish to consider in further detail how Logue's long-standing concerns, as outlined, continue through the detour of translation, and how they overlap with the main liberties he takes as he shapes *War Music*. These liberties, fortunately encouraged at the point of the poem's genesis by the necessity of an interlingual approach that sees the poet sifting through previous translations and word-for-word cribs rather than working from the ancient Greek original, find *War Music* often resembling a translation of translations, a literary mosaic of influences and echoes, a project that registers the textual distance travelled, the impurities and layers of reflection added in reaching, from antiquity, through (post-)modernity, towards the palimpsestic Homer of now. With Logue compensating for being able to touch everything but the ancient text itself, we become the privileged addressees of a recasting that, through the judicious use of allusions and anachronisms, rises at points to an intertextual collision of voices from many battlefields through the centuries, a perpetual mapping of relationships between literature and conflict, art and war.

Logue's Notes at the end of recent volumes (see 2001: 211-212; 2003: 39; 2005: 46) signpost many of his allusions, exposing the *bios* of a text creatively aware of itself. Among them we encounter lines and turns of phrase extracted from previous translations of the *Iliad* as well as from poems and versions of modernist forebears like Pound (from 'The Return', 'Homage to Sextus Propertius') and H.D. ('I would forego'). Insertions such as Pope's

"I am full of the god!" (in 2003a: 28) also serve to remind us of the junctures when both warring and translating collide in poetry; together with modernist fragments, they create a sense of lineage, implying a history of approaches to both classical literature and translation that pave the way to the twilight formation(s) of *War Music*.

A significant second strand of allusions may be called 'militaria': these have to do with references to historical, autobiographical and literary accounts of conflict. In the course of Logue's 'Homer poem', we have the building up of a select bibliography of war: we encounter Napoleon's cavalry commander Joachim Murat, King Ivan Kursk, phrases from (war) memoirs or Tennyson's 'The Charge of the Heavy Brigade at Balaclava'. This might be because the 'original' that Logue is trying to get his head around in his own account is *warfare itself* as much as it is the *Iliad* –warfare that, in its first literary recording, was perceived worthy of the epic form, if not actually giving rise to it, at least within the European tradition. But initially at least, a line like "Rommel after 'Alamein" following "[...] Ajax, / Grim underneath his tan as" (2001: 13) also had to do with the aesthetic needs of *War Music*, since, by Logue's admission (see 2003b: 130), he found original metaphors repetitious and unengaging.

Nevertheless, the gradual accretion of warlords, war writings and weaponry across time cannot help but reverberate the actuality of what is never too far away. Furthermore, it helps implement the relevance both of ancient epic and of subsequent war literature through an all-encompassing past present; in this past present of *War Music*, the playing out of conflict coincides with intertextual reflection on it. Together with the use of anachronisms, such elements show Logue on his way to confirming Pound's definition of the epic as 'a poem including history'. Within what is also a *translation including history*, one finds 'militaria' that come with an autobiographical weight: lines from memoirs, and reported voices that are 'there', both see and tell of a diversity of conflicts firsthand; and so Logue injects splinters of subjectivity –together, inevitably, with their respective historical moments– that have to do with a host of conflicts, from the 17th century battlefield of Edgehill and the trenches of the First World War, to the slums of Harlem. Those para-sites append themselves to the body of Logue's account, and echo a history of participating in conflict; a history of trying to understand and express what has been witnessed.

Perhaps more urgently than in 'original' writing, intertextual elements within poetic translation point to autographic imperatives of a reading consciousness. Previous literary experiences in what is an *embodied* practice of reading may claim a connection with what the poet-translator now co-authors. Furthermore, in *War Music*, we have an autobiographical fragment confidently inserted into the poetic text of *Kings* (see 1991: 54) that simply reveals Logue and his friends in the spring of 1961, observing people in the modern town of Skopje. This fragment, employed to the effect of a simile, poignantly reminds us of the subjectivity that translates original into a further poetic text, and again points towards what I believe is a latency of life-writing in many translations. (By 'life-writing' in the context of translation I do not simply have in mind only some –very rare– narrative formations, recognisable snapshots of life's 'contents', but a more general, underlying mind-set. That is, a drive to embed, in a translation, aspects of one's relationship with language, in the shape of phrasal recurrences, intertextual traces and 'favourite words' that carry a private, empirical weight and reference: the felt, idiosyncratic significances of the reading mind. Behind the words of a translation we often sense cognitions where words, languages, emotions and experiences uniquely fuse together.)

Overall, the editing of war literature fragments into Logue's version help to emphasise senses of both subjectivity and actuality: constituting an in-built reality check apparatus within his method, such fragments, reflecting the poet's readings, remind us of the reality of actual Trojan war(s) behind the *Iliad*, trace autobiographical imperatives following traumatic events and experiences of conflict, and help to convey both the horrors and history/art-making capacity of conflict across time. As the modern poet also composes through read memoirs, historical accounts of war and poetries of conflict, embedding them into *his* translation, such fragments also participate in a textual, inconspicuous autobiography, a self-translation of Logue.

The allusions and intertextual elements described above contribute to an overall strategy of immersion. Even as we are assisted in inhabiting the warrior ethic that Homer requires the modern poet to embrace, Logue perhaps hopes we also share a certain disgust of his heroes' behaviour. Moreover, for him,

> [...] even stronger than disgust, there is a kind of hopelessness. A kind of fatality. People get taken over by passions –whatever this means. I want people reading *War Music* to feel this could happen to *them*. (2003b: 123; his emphasis)

It explains perhaps why the poet of *War Music* wants us, literally, to see ourselves in the past and the past in ourselves: cinema is what, in many senses, frames his reworking throughout; this representative, universal language of modernity that could match the comparable reach of the ancient epic. The panoramas of Logue's hybrid poetry-as-cinema, its ceaseless and varied travelling and reverse shots, jump cuts and stage directing ('go there', 'follow' 'see if you can imagine how it looked'), is what ensures that we are directly, inescapably involved as the poet casts the unflinching eye of a modern medium over the ancient proceedings. Asking us to, for instance, board airplanes, or 'raise your binoculars' so we can really *see*, Logue makes of us voyeurs in the unfolding bloodshed and/or actors inhabiting his camera angles as he directs Homeric origins towards a new poetic whole. Readers of this Troy are not allowed to dissociate themselves from the inter-activity of the confrontation they find themselves in. While assisting Logue's propensity for a powerful image, *War Music*'s cinemato*graphy* helps minimise our perceived distances from causes and settings of violent confrontation. With no higher ground for both reader and translator/live action commentator to occupy, it is inevitable that 'we the army' will be often asked to join Logue and 'slip into the fighting' (2003a: 29):

> Go left along the ridge. Beneath,
> Greek chariots at speed. Their upcurled dust.
> Go low along the battle's seam.
> Its suddenly up-angled masks.
> Heading 2000 Greeks Thoal of Calydon
> A spear in one a banner in his other hand
> Has pinched Sarpédon's Lycians in a loop.
> Drop into it.
> Noise so clamorous it sucks.
> You rush your pressed-flower hackles out
> To the perimeter.
> And here it comes:
> That unpremeditated joy as you
> – The Uzi shuddering warm against your hip
> Happy in danger in a dangerous place
> Yourself another self you found at Troy –
> Squeeze nickel through that rush of Greekoid scum!

Thus we are escorted into battlegrounds of amassing armies amid the cries of their leaders, and left there to our own devices, with barely enough time to ponder the sheer inevitability of it all, to sink or swim, willed to experience the gamut of emotions we are often unaware of within our shared psychological makeup: from the paralysing fear of death to the adrenaline rush of surviving by ending the lives of others. In this inescapable *now* of an ancient epic, the question that hangs around Logue's approach, ever troubled by human conflict, is bound to be: this is what it really is about –what it feels like. Do you still want this? Which brings us to the distressing realisation that a part of us so often does.

Richard Eyre's reflections (2003) on the persistence of conflict and our ambivalent emotions towards it are of interest here. His childhood fascination with war games, his love of "the romance, the nobility, the extremity and the secrecy of war" (*ibid.*), of war as test of character and a proof of life, was gradually replaced by recognitions of its futility, the waste and irrationality of conflict, and a certainty of its eventual abolition. Later in life, this optimistic credo begins to appear, as with Logue, like a 'colossal naiveté'; nothing seems to change. Eyre's 'voilà moment' comes while watching war reportage on TV:

> After hours of homogenised 'rolling news', of reports from vicarious combatants ('embedded correspondents') talking with knowing assurance of desert strategy, rapid dominance and friendly fire, and with prurient awe of bombs, mortars, missiles and tanks, I realised that all this is happening because in some atavistic way, most of us must have a desire for the rush of adrenalin, for the smell of napalm in the morning, an appetite for war indistinguishable from the one that fuelled my childhood passion for it: the great game, tin soldiers made real. In the story of mankind, war is the one unbroken subject. (*ibid.*)

Much of Logue's project parallels such insight, his method enacting this 'unbroken subject'. From the previously encountered Rommel, or the kings asleep 'like pistols in red velvet' to the Ilian sky's gleam described "[a]s when Bikini flashlit the Pacific" (2001: 124), *War Music*'s vast armamentarium of anachronisms essentially help enunciate a sense of timelessness: they contribute to a report on human nature that remains unchanging, to an account of one ongoing conflict.

In *ADPR*, the Trojan War's 'first battle-scenes rewritten', this approach encounters, more than ever, its justification. Of course the face of battle has been phrased before, notably in *Patrocleia*'s protagonist's lethal rampage and in the battle around Patroclus's corpse in *GBH*; but *ADPR*'s sustained, autonomous onslaught, detached from any 'meaningful' narrative save the deadly advance of Hector and Diomed (Diomedes) towards each other amid inexplicable mayhem, properly identifies the *Iliad*'s actual core. In an insightful meditation on how the reality of the battlefield and mourning turns to memorial through art forms, James Tatum argues, in *The Mourner's Song* (2003), that our imagined distance from war helps us disconnect the epic's gory bulk of near-clinical descriptions of injury and killing from the few and far-between tragic moments and narrative pauses, like the parting of Hector and Andromache or the meeting of Priam and Achilles. We normally tend to focus on these, as readers and in our critical descriptions, while "blood and guts, in fact, mean everything" (*ibid.*: 116). Noting the *Iliad*'s inquisitorial descriptiveness of wounding, of how humanity and its protagonists really come to life at the point of death, and alongside wider considerations of art's willingness to reconstruct processes and points of dying (thus helping us give meaning to both life and death), Tatum relocates the poem's essence in the chaotic, gruesome presentness of fighting; it is from this that poetry, music, *has* to spring forth:

> [p]oet's song and warrior's song blend into a single melody as Patroclus turns killing itself into poetry. With apologies to Wilfred Owen, who found poetry in the pity of war, war's poetry is also to be found in the killing (*ibid.*: 119).

The expressive volatility of *ADPR* seems to share and voice such recognitions. With Espiner (2006: 25), we realise that Logue has understood "the importance of the visceral dramatic narrative complete with all its bloody, almost pornographic, detail. If the violence isn't present tense, it has the dramatic quality of an eyewitness account". Not only do wounding and dying emphatically happen in an eternal present, but Logue's experimentations with anachronism and allusions to a modern consciousness reach critical mass in *ADPR*, as we read of armies that hum "like power station outflow cables do", of Porsche-fine chariots, of Diomed's shield with "as many arrows on his posy shield / As microphones on politicians' stands", as we hear of the Greek army getting to its feet: "Then of a stadium when many boards are raised / And many faces change to one vast face. / So, where there were so many masks, / Now one Greek mask glittered from strip to ridge" (2003a: 9). These radical equivalences transport the relevance of what would be distant terrains and pre-humanistic morals into modern circumstance, enforce instant recognitions of an alien past ingenuously translated into what is still a Trojan present. Such characteristic imaginative leaps, the deployment of fragments from other war poetry, memoirs and histories, the use of anachronisms so at home in *War Music* the moment they are inserted, help to collapse our perceived distances from war, while echoing its complex, less-than-innocent interface with artistic expression.

Thus employing the *Iliad* as an essential platform, *War Music* centripetally invites the experiencing of war, its written testimonies and artistic transformations, with an ear for both its painful realities and the ways it lends itself to artistic endeavour. Logue's version of the Trojan battleground is a centre that holds; enough to involve and embed both translator and reader in the drama, as true conflict always involves all. A cursory look at the inconsistency in translating the very names of the main protagonists confirms this Troy as a timeless topos of global conflict; the original ancient Greek names are abstracted into numerous nationalities – among others, Thoal, Merionez, Gray, Boran, Chylábborak, Idomeneo. The brutal acts of this international cast acquire a universal relevance: these characters are never far away from home, never safely inhabiting Greek antiquity. Rather, they populate a place where, to borrow from Eliot, 'all time is eternally present', a porous battle plan invaded by mentions of Missouri, Iwo Jima, Castile, or Gallipoli, where snapshots of conflict across history come and go. We will at points briefly desert this theatre of war, together with our battle psychology, only to call on some of humanity's most vulgar and critical moments

> And here they come again the noble Greeks,
> Ido, a spear in one a banner on his other hand
> Your life at every instant up for-
> Gone.
> And candidly, who gives a toss?
> Your heart beats strong. Your spirit grips.
> King Richard calling for another horse (his fifth).
> King Marshal Ney shattering his sabre on a cannon ball.

> King Ivan Kursk, 22.30 hrs,
> July 4th to 14th '43, 7000 tanks engaged,
> '...he clambered up and pushed a stable-bolt
> Into that Tiger-tank's red-hot-machine-gun's mouth
> And bent the bastard up. Woweee!'
> Where would we be if he had lost?
> Achilles? Let him sulk. (2003a: 29-30)

–before we return 'back to today', this 'today' being a Troy of always. We see here why a retelling is so painfully necessary: these are choices we are still making, battles we are still fighting. Logue's work confirms, perhaps, Bespaloff's argument that it is indeed difficult to speak of a 'Homeric world' (in the same way she feels it difficult to speak of 'Balzacian', 'Tolstoyan' or 'Dantesque' ones). Simply because Homer's world "is what our own is from moment to moment. We don't step into it; we are there" (2005: 72).

In conclusion, while Logue's treatment of Homer's battle-scenes should trouble us with awareness of poetry lying in the killing, in spite of, or perhaps because of, this 'delight in violence', what ultimately underscores *War Music* as a whole is neither a glorification of war, nor overt or uncomplicated critiques of humans fighting humans. It is simply awe in the face of conflict's undeniable power to foster identity even as the individual is lost in battle formations, to create societal structures and civilisations at the same time that it drives them to obliteration. What Logue invites us to share is an understanding of the senses in which war defines our being, even while we – Logue surely, if his CV is anything to go by– want things otherwise. Through the lens of the *Iliad* and the hierophantic immediacy of its treatment in *War Music*, we are enabled to reflect on how our nations and societies are still shaped by conflict and driven towards it: Logue's 'account' demands that we recognise imagined distances from war, that we confront ourselves with difficult knowledge. We are to find ways around our very nature.

## Epilogue: translations of conflict

> When the performance unfolded under the starry sky of Epidaurus, the music took its place, the women's voices joined in an *Ode of Tears* and all became one: sounds, voices, colours, words, movement, light. In the holy area of Epidaurus, the poet's voice, the voice of transcendence, was raised once more, just as back in 451 BC, when he was striving through *Trojan Women* to turn his fellow citizens away from the insanity of war, teaching the whole world now, just like then, that there are no winners or losers in wars, only horror and madness.
>
> So then, during that evening in Epidaurus, on 31 August 2001, I saw armies of uprooted people traverse the stage of the ancient theatre slowly, silently: Armenians, Pontic people, Greeks of Smyrna, Hebrews, Kurds, Kossovars, Afghans...I saw the funeral procession of little Astyanax and wept for the genocide of the peoples...And I felt grateful that I was able to experience such a painful moment of self-knowledge...
> (Eleni Karaindrou, liner notes on *Trojan Women*, tr. Harina Deliyannis-Easty)

For nearly half a century Logue has been translating human conflict; producing, with Homer, an artistic landscape ravaged by spears, artillery shells and nuclear warheads. As I write, his series of transcendent, palimpsestic canvases of a timeless war reaches towards an end. In his *Areté* interview, Logue lets us know that *Cold Calls* will be the penultimate installment, and goes over some details of a plan to compress the considerable remainder of the *Iliad* into a further book (with the likely title *Big Men Falling A Long Way*, coming from his friend Kenneth Tynan's description of tragedy), a plan that demands at least an escalation of most strategies so far used, and probably radical changes in the mode of composition (see 2003b: 132-135). It remains to be seen whether the word 'translation' loses its application completely in terms of an evident process, but one doubts it ever will, in terms of what Logue actually achieves: Homer's life-as-war world, its heroic code and intense inhabitants are precisely understood and conveyed in ways not unrelated to the ones that spoke to an ancient audience. Arguably, the further Logue strays from the letter of the *Iliad*, the more we come to see what the ancient epic really is *about*. In the process, it is we who find ourselves on the page, we who are translated: *War Music* involves us enough for us to recognise that we still are *musical*, that conflict and violence still define us. When Logue discloses what is yet to come ("there will be a whole section on Achilles' shield, which is a big deal in the *Iliad*. It reflects Homer's world. I'm going to try and reflect our world" - *ibid*.: 134) we realise that, through allusions, borrowed fragments and anachronisms, this is already happening. Lacking in moralising or explanation, Logue's war brings home, to powerful effect, the essential implication of the Homeric epic: as he puts it, "the *Iliad* tells the truth about something very important: the propensity to violence in human males" (in Hoggard 2006: 25). The way he approaches this truth also largely confirms Steiner's insight that the "linguistic-cultural distance to the Homeric is both talismanic and liberating. We revert to Homer as, in some ways, an unattainable dawn and model. But we are sufficiently remote and free from him to answer back creatively" (1996: 105).[6]

Whether real or taking place within the artist's psyche, between aesthetic ideologies, inside art-acts as they accommodate influences or challenge the forms of the past, conflict is a condition of creativity. At the same time, violence and warfare, so defiant of reason while so ingrained in our being, lead us into art more than anything else as we attempt to come to terms with their felt absurdity and terrible persistence. Still, we should bear in mind that while art and artists provide us with the most effective condemnations of war, they have often been lured by the energies, the potential 'hygiene', the aesthetic appeal of power and confrontation, thus helping pave the way for conflicts: for every Guernica, we also have examples like Leni Riefenstahl's early career.

It is apt that *War Music* happens *in translation*, as well as incrementally: this serialised 'account' is vital in helping us not lose sight of the darkest constituencies of our nature, in gaining and retaining a necessary awareness. While there are anecdotes of mistranslation causing wars, it is perhaps because we translate that we are not fighting all the time. In contexts of conflict, from war-zone interpreters having to relate to irreconcilable convictions, to cases of prisoners of war saving their own lives by reciting the enemy's literature, translation enables us to hold contradictory viewpoints, it fosters and maintains understanding as we strive for possible reconciliation. Existing simultaneously within and beyond what is literary, translation is the mirror we hold up so that we may see ourselves across time. This is not least due to how translation relates to language:

> [...] it is in and through the process of translation that a language is made eminently self-aware. Translation constrains it to formal and diachronic introspection, to an explicit investment and enlargement of its historical, colloquial and metaphorical instruments. Simultaneously, translation puts a language under pressure of its limitation. It will solicit modes of perception and designation which that language had left underdeveloped, or had altogether discarded. (Steiner 1996: 94)

Literary translations inject us with the perception needed in dangerous periods; they quicken creative and critical capacities. It is often through (re)translations that we are enabled to sense how history and human nature repeat themselves. Seamus Heaney's recent version of Sophocles' *Antigone* (2004a) is a telling example, the poet's own comments on his translation work establishing some poignant connections: he translates in the shadow of the second Gulf War, and his source text urges him to reflect on American president George W. Bush as a modern Creon, on the ancient chorus as the American public and so on (see Heaney 2004b); such connections were of course also recognised by the critical responses to Heaney's version as its performances began in Dublin's Abbey Theatre in the spring of 2004. Further reasons why we seem to *need* translation –and its creative mutations– in contexts of conflict or when we deal with traumatic events, have to do with a ventriloquist potential inherent in its acts. Harsh realities may not be directly confronted, yet translation can coincide with self-expression as the translator therapeutically echoes shared suffering, or is able to impart criticism and much-needed reflection in times of censorship, while 'hiding' behind the literature of others.

Introducing a sourcebook on Homer (2001), Harold Bloom reflects the general impression that, post-Enlightenment, we are closer to the comic resourcefulness of the Odyssey's protagonist rather than the tragic wrath of Achilles. Admittedly, the *Odyssey*'s influence makes it "difficult to imagine an 'Achilles' by Tennyson, or a vaster *Achilles* by James Joyce" (*ibid.*: 10). Steiner is somewhat more equivocal:

> [...] the experience of the Second World War produces a counter-current. The proud cities set ablaze, the chivalric heroism of the fighter pilot or commando, restores Hector and Troy to felt immediacy. The sufferings of civilians in the bloody hands of their captors make of Hecuba and Andromache emblems all too familiar. English and American poet-dramatists turn back to 'the Trojan women', as do Hauptmann and Sartre on the Continent. Today, I would guess, the two epics are in active equilibrium of repute, though it may be that late-twentieth-century moods are more at home in the subtle variousness and questionings of the Odyssey. (1996: 100)

A decade after Steiner's reflections, a decade that saw varied conflicts following the end of the Cold War, and during the 'war on terror' which came in the wake of 9/11 –Pentagon reports recently rephrased it 'the Long War'– we register a renewed critical and creative attention to the *Iliad* (we now even have an *Achilles* –though nowhere near as vast as Joyce's *Ulysses*– from Elizabeth Cook).[7] As the current climate supports reassessments of our relationship with conflict, one's impression is that we may never be as far from Achilles' age as we would wish. In this context, and especially in reminding us of what remains unchanging and what we yet feel should be otherwise, few things can instil moments of recognition like the timely arrival of an *Antigone*, or more than four decades of *War Music*. Such classical recurrences force us to remember, as nothing else does perhaps, what Logue says in one of his poems ("O come all ye faithful" –1996: 133), repeats somewhere in his memoir (1999: 278) and subtly intimates throughout *War Music*: "all wars are civil wars".

It is something worth translating and re-translating.

---

1 Some of my views here first appeared in a review of Logue for *The London Magazine*. In their progression towards the present essay, a series of readers, gave their encouragement and critical advice: Sebastian Barker, Cecilia Rossi, Jean Boase-Beier, Clive Scott, Richard Burns and Aishwarya Subramanyam. The generous support of the Alexander S. Onassis Foundation should also be acknowledged.
2  These two volumes append themselves to the Faber & Faber edition of *War Music* (from which I quote in this essay), published in 2001. This includes the first whole of *War Music*, where *Patrocleia* (1962; Book 16), *Pax* (1967; Book 19), and *GBH* [Grievous Bodily Harm], Books 17 and 18, come together in one volume, first published by Jonathan Cape in 1981. The Faber *War Music* also includes the later additions *Kings* (1991; Books 1 and 2) and *The Husbands* (1994; Books 3 and 4). All other poetry by Logue is quoted from his *Selected Poems* (1996).
3  There are sporadic attempts: Willis Barnstone's taxonomy of literary translational approaches in *The Poetics of Translation* (see 1993: 25-30), defines Logue's project as a newly structured, 'uniquely literary', metaphrase.
4   See Yao's reflections (*ibid.*: 10-15) on how modernism's distrust of scholarship reclaims literary translation from the realm of the non-poets (scholars, critics). Pound perceives his lack

of knowing Chinese as a decided advantage rather than a hindrance; it might paradoxically enhance overall understanding. Full comprehension of the source language is not a formal requirement for an influential translation. Note how Logue can mirror Pound in those respects, in his introductory comments to *War Music* as well as in the interviews he has given. On Logue's animosity towards scholar-translators, in the name of poetry, see also Underwood (1998: 56-61)

5  The whole of Norris's first chapter is of interest, where she reflects on statements such as the 'we will glorify war – the world's only hygiene' of Marinetti's Futurist Manifesto.

6  Note that Steiner has been one of the first and staunchest defenders of Logue's approach to the *Iliad*. Fragments from the beginnings of *War Music* were included in the seminal collection of translations *Poem into Poem* (1970) that Steiner edited. See also his Introduction to the volume (21-35) for some perceptive comments on Logue.

7  It is perhaps no accident that Cook has long been interested in *War Music*, as her insightful review of Logue's project makes clear (2002).

## Primary References

Homer. 1715. *The Iliad of Homer* (tr. Alexander Pope). London: printed by W. Bowyer, for Bernard Lintott et al.

———1897. *The Iliads of Homer, Prince of poets: never before in any language truly translated, done according to the Greek* (tr. George Chapman). London: Gibbings.

———1951. *The Iliad of Homer* (tr. Richmond Lattimore). Chicago: University of Chicago Press.

———1991. *The Iliad* (tr. Robert Fagles). Harmondsworth: Penguin Books.

Logue, Christopher. 1962. *Patrocleia*. London: Scorpion.

———1967. *Pax.*. London: Rapp & Caroll.

———1981. *War Music: An Account of Books 16 to 19 of Homer's Iliad*. London: Jonathan Cape.

———1991. *Kings*. New York: Farrar, Straus & Giroux.

———1993. 'The Art of Poetry LXVI' (interview with Shusha Guppy) in *The Paris Review* 127: 238-264.

———1994. *The Husbands*. London: Faber & Faber.

———1996. *Selected Poems* (chosen and arranged by Christopher Reid). London: Faber & Faber.

———1999. *Prince Charming: A Memoir*. London: Faber & Faber.

———2000. 'Visiting Brecht' in *Areté* 2: 63-66.

———2001. *War Music: An Account of Books 1-4 and 16-19 of Homer's Iliad*. London: Faber & Faber.

———2003a. *All Day Permanent Red: War Music continued*. London: Faber & Faber.

———2003b. 'The Shortest Long Poem Ever Written: an interview with Christopher Logue' in *Areté* 13: 117-136.

———2005. *Cold Calls: War Music continued*. London: Faber & Faber.

## Secondary References

Barnstone, Willis. 1993. *The Poetics of Translation: History, Theory, Practice*. New Haven and London: Yale University Press.

Bespaloff, Rachel. 2005. 'On the *Iliad*' (tr. Mary McCarthy) in *War and the Iliad: Simone Weil-Rachel Bespaloff*. New York: New York Review Books.

Bloom, Harold (ed.). 2001. *Homer* (Bloom's Major Poets). s.l.: Chelsea House Publishers.

Borges, Jorge Luis. 1998. 'The Immortal' in *Collected Fictions* (tr. Andrew Hurley). Harmondsworth: Allen Lane/The Penguin Press. 181-195.

Cook, Elizabeth. 2001. *Achilles*. London: Methuen.

———2002. 'A Restless and Passionate Engagement'. Review of Logue (2001) in *Poetry London* 43. On line at: http://www.poetrylondon.co.uk/reviews/issue43iii.htm (consulted 22.02.2006).

Espiner, Mark. 2006. 'Troy Story' in *The Observer* (22 January 2006).

Eyre, Richard. 2003. 'My voilà moment' in *The Guardian* (12 April 2003). On line at: http://books.guardian.co.uk/review/story/0,,934764,00.html (consulted 18.02.2005).

Fawcett, Peter. 2001. 'Ideology and Translation' in Mona Baker (ed.) *The Routledge Encyclopedia of Translation Studies*. London and New York: Routledge. 106-111.

Heaney, Seamus. 2004a. *The Burial at Thebes: Sophocles' Antigone*. London: Faber & Faber.

——2004b. 'To Hellas and Back' in *The Times* (14 February 2004).

Hoggard, Liz. 2006. 'Logue in Vogue' in *The Observer* (22 January 2006).

Karaindrou, Eleni. 2002. *Euripides: Trojan Women* (Hellenic Festival, 31 August 2001). ECM Records GmbH; New Series 1810.

Lewis, Wyndham. 1937. *Blasting and Bombardiering*. London: Eyre & Spottiswoode.

Norris, Margaret. 2000. *Writing War in the Twentieth Century*. Charlottesville and London: University Press of Virginia.

Pound, Ezra. 1963. *Translations*. New York: New Directions.

Rosslyn, Felicity. 2001. 'Homer and Other Epics' in France, Peter (ed.) *The Oxford Guide to Literature in English Translation*. Oxford: Oxford University Press. 350-356.

Sinfield, Alan. 1997. *Literature, Politics and Culture in Postwar Britain*. London and Atlantic Highlands, NJ: The Athlone Press.

Steiner, George. 1970. *Poem into Poem: World Poetry in Modern Verse Translation*. Harmondsworth: Penguin Books.

——1996. 'Homer in English' in *No Passion Spent: Essays 1978-1996*. London: Faber & Faber. 88-107.

Sullivan, J.P. 1965. *Ezra Pound and Sextus Propertius: A Study in Creative Translation*. London: s.n.

Tatum, James. 2003. *The Mourner's Song: War and Remembrance from the Iliad to Vietnam*. Chicago: University of Chicago Press.

Underwood, Simeon. 1998. *English Translators of Homer: From George Chapman to Christopher Logue*. Plymouth: Northcote House in association with the British Council.

Venuti, Lawrence. 1995. *The Translator's Invisibility: A History of Translation*. London and New York: Routledge.

Yao, Steven G. 2003. *Translation and the Languages of Modernism: Gender, Politics, Language*. London and New York: Palgrave MacMillan.

# Part III

# Language and Ideology

# Ideological Independence or Negative Mediation: BBC Mundo and CNN en Español's (translated) Reporting of Madrid's Terrorist Attacks

*Roberto A. Valdeón*

In 2004 Madrid experienced the worst terrorist attack ever on mainland Europe. This event and the subsequent defeat of the conservative government featured prominently on world news websites. This paper is concerned with the coverage of the Spanish government's initial claims, and the use of terms *separatist* and *terrorist* in two English-speaking media (the BBC and the CNN) and their Spanish services. We approach English media texts drawing on Fairclough's model, borrowing also on the strategies suggested by Bell and van Dijk, to examine the ideological implications of the lexical choices made in the texts and intra-textual cohesion devices used by text producers. Spanish reports in BBC Mundo and CNN en Español are analysed. Control contexts are used to ascertain whether the patterns identified for the reports on the attacks follow standard procedures. Texts are compared in order to examine more closely the lexical choices made and the extent to which they reflect what Schelesinger and Lumley called "a journalistic ideology of independence" (1985: 325), or are, in fact, instances of "negative mediation".

Key words: Terrorist, journalist, text production, mediation, Critical discourse analysis (CDA)

## Introduction

The mediatory role which journalists can assume has been examined in recent decades by scholars within different fields of research. Media text writing involves indeed a mediation process to bring news events to the audience of the different media, radio, television, the press and, in recent years, the Internet. Very often the translation of texts produced in another language is involved. Thus, their role as mediators is twofold. The bombings that took place in Madrid on March 11 2004, three days before the Spanish general election, highlighted this double role, as the news event originated in Spain and news writers were having recourse to translation processes more often than not. This attack brought about an important number of unexpected political consequences on both a national and an international level, the first of which was the ousting of the conservative government of Jose Maria Aznar, who had supported the American-led coalition in the Iraq war. On an international level, governments, and notably European ones, seemed to have awoken to the nightmare of terror in the Old Continent with newspapers acknowledging the event as the worst terrorist attack in mainland Europe since World War II. The event fuelled the long-standing controversy regarding the ways in which Anglophone media refer to *ETA*, the Basque terrorist group that has campaigned for the independence of the Basque country from France and Spain over the last fifty years. The controversy originates from the Anglophone tendency to refer to *ETA* as a separatist organization, highlighting the political goals and toning down the violent means used by the group to achieve its objectives. Although the bombings in March 2001 were carried out by Islamist groups, *ETA* was initially blamed by the Spanish government and thus was reported internationally.

This paper studies the ambivalent role of media writers, who function both as producers of texts that provide their readers with information about a news event, and also as translators who carry out interlingual transformative acts of different kinds. An approach capable of foregrounding the connections between the linguistic, the translational and the ideological components of the texts is used. Basil Hatim and Ian Mason have covered the power implications of the lexical choices made by translators (1990: 89; 1997: 172) and have also acknowledged the importance of the study of ideology in language within TS (1997: 143). Harald Olk has underlined the fact that a critical discourse analysis applied to the field of Translation Studies (TS) can "reveal how translation is shaped by ideologies and in this way contributes to the perpetuation or subversion of particular discourse" (2002: 101). On the other hand Siobhan Brownlie believes that, contrary to what she terms as "committed approaches" (namely, postcolonial and feminist) "a critical descriptive approach" has a greater potential for questioning presuppositions than have other approaches since they tend to import their "agendas" from other disciplines (2003: 61). In this sense, Brownlie writes about the eclectic nature of this approach, although we believe it should be more aptly termed as *interdisciplinary*.

The study of the discourse of translation could certainly benefit from the insights gained by a critical analysis to primary and secondary discourses, understood here as source texts (ST)s and target texts (TT)s. For this reason, it could be a complementary tool to existing methodological approaches in order to provide us with a comprehensive reflection on language and culture. In fact, Critical Discourse Analysis (CDA) is meant to analyse discourse in its three dimensions, as text, as interaction or communication involving people, and as part of a piece of social interaction (Fairclough 1992: 10-11). These three dimensions are also present in source texts (ST)s and translated texts (TT)s, subsuming the various components of the transformative act we call translation: "language, culture, and the relationships between different peoples, different identities, and even different points in times and space" (Arrojo 1998: 44).

We shall use some of the concepts put forward by Norman Fairclough's model of CDA. In his three-dimensional approach to the analysis of communicative events, he speaks of *text, discourse practice and sociocultural practice* (1992; 1995a; 1995b; 2001). In the corpus studied the texts are written taking the form (or genre) of news reports, and the discourse practice refers to the production and subsequent consumption of the texts. This actual production process might involve correspondent reporting and/or the use of agency dispatches besides translation strategies. Finally, sociocultural practice will relate the previous two sections to the particular situation in which the texts are produced. Consequently, we shall relate the communicative events to the political and cultural situations in which they are embedded. The paper also attempts to question the policy of editorial independence used as the pretext for the lexical choices made by the news corporations, and, in particular, the assumption that these/their websites might be described as "arbiter[s] of truth" (Allan 2004: 22).

Due to the nature of this study, which concentrates on the translational aspects of news texts, we shall adapt Fairclough's model to cover the relational, expressive and experiential values of specific lexical items (2001: 94-98) in connection with the source language and culture as well as their matching versions in Spanish. In this sense, we shall focus on a smaller number of questions in Fairclough's model, namely 1, 3 and 5, since they are more closely related to experiential and expressive values of the items analysed, the existence of ideologically contested words and the presence of ideologically significant meaning relations such as hyponymy or synonymy. References to grammatical processes used in the construction of the news text will be made when appropriate, notably to provide information on the experiential and expressive values of the words (2001: 100).

The final section examines the discursive and translational findings of this paper, and the term "ideology" is used to imply a set of assumptions accepted by the participant in a given stretch of discourse (Simpson 1993: 5; Fairclough 2001: 2), (Hatim and Mason 1990: 160-161; Hatim and Mason 1997: 143-163; Puurtinen 2003: 53-54). Hatim and Mason have spoken of the "assumptions which are closely bound up with attitudes, beliefs and value systems" (1997: 144).

The terms *translation* and *mediators* have been used in the 1990s by both critical analysts and translation scholars, although not with the same implications. Fairclough often uses the term *translation* to refer to the linguistic changes operated in a given text before it is ready for consumption in the same language and for a specific readership (1995a: 61). These processes are clearly linked with production or editing techniques rather than with translational strategies as understood in TS. Allan Bell speaks of three types of media text transformations: information deletions, lexical substitutions and syntactic editing rules (1991: 70-74), whereas Teun A. van

Dijk offers a wider range of processes, including selection, reproduction (1990: 168), summarizing (169) and local transformations (170). The latter, in their turn, would be subdivided into other four types: *omissions, additions, permutations and substitutions*. Some of these strategies are common in Critical Discourse Analysis (CDA) and Translation Studies (TS), since both translators and media text producers are concerned with making changes of various types, understood as editing processes in the case of media reports, or translational processes in TS. Since some of these strategies have been used by CDA and TS researchers alike, we shall maintain those we believe to be useful for this interdisciplinary approach: adaptation, substitution, omission and addition.

As regards the term *translation*, it will be used to refer to the act of transforming the messages, views, opinions and comments expressed in a given language, taken as the source language (e.g. English), resulting in a similar text performing similar functions in the target text (e. g. Spanish). To differentiate between the two processes mentioned above, we shall be using the expression *transformative acts* when talking about both processes, whereas *transformations* will be applied to the strategies used by text-producers in their own language.

CDA and TS also share the term *mediation* in the discussion of the relationship between writer-text-reader and translator-text-reader. Fairclough argues that one important feature of the mass media is that they *mediate* between the public and the private domains (1995a: 62; 1995b: 37). The mediation process is interpreted as a chain between text producers and text consumers. The first would belong to the sphere of the public in that they use "predominantly public domain source materials" (37), whereas the latter would refer to the private domain of the home and the family. He exemplifies his discussion with an article from the *The Sun* newspaper, which presents its readership with a government document on drug-abuse. The strategies followed by the text producers aim at transforming official language into more informal varieties of English. It is precisely when discussing this particular instance of mediation that Fairclough resorts to the term *translate*: "its call is translated into colloquial discourse" (70). Drawing on Stuart Hall et al. (1978: 61), he also states that the *translation* of official viewpoints into "a public idiom" is frequent in the media (Fairclough 1995b: 71-72) and underlines that one effect of the "translation of official sources and official positions into colloquial discourse in to help legitimize these official sources and positions with the audience" (73).

Olk suggests that, within TS, the term *mediation* could be used along the same lines as in CDA. In fact, he adopts Robert de Beaugrande's definition, whereby *mediation* would refer to the ways in which a text is manipulated "according to a translator's ideology" [quoted in Olk 2002: 102]. He adds that "it seems reasonable to suggest that ideology does not necessarily have to be understood as a set of false convictions and oppressive attitudes" (2002: 102). However, it also seems reasonable to expect the translator to be capable of establishing the connection between the objectives of the source and target texts, which should not be shaped by the translator's own set of convictions. In this study, we shall use the terms *mediation* in connection with *transformative acts* involving changes into another language. Thus, we understand the role of translators to be that of "intercultural mediators" (Wolf 1995: 127; Campbell 1998: 3) who should try to optimize communication between cultures (Chesterman 1995: 149). If the translation process is to succeed, then translators must function as interlocutors between author and readership. Hatim and Mason have spoken of different types of mediation (1990: 223-238; 1997: 143-163): *minimal* (1997: 148-152), *maximal* (153-159) and *partial* (159-161), although they have also stressed the importance of translators as mediators seeking to overcome incompatibilities as regards "ideologies, moral systems and socio-political structures" (1990: 223).

For the purpose of this paper, we shall assume that media text producers also mediate between sources of information and their target readership, but the passing of information will typically involve transformative acts of various kinds with different (and not always acknowledged) goals. For this reason we could differentiate between *positive mediation* and *negative mediation*. In the former, text producers attempt some form of ideological neutrality towards the events being communicated through texts, whereas in the latter the writers would be importing external agendas that might stem from their own ideological background or, more likely, from the companies they work for.

## 1. The corpus and the procedure

The parameters used for the study were similar to those suggested by Ruth Wodak and Michael Meyer (2003: 140-141), as described below:

Firstly, we present the results of a survey on the use of the terms *terrorista* and *separatista* in the Spanish media in connection with the group called *ETA*. Anglophone news texts are examined to establish whether the terms "terrorist" or "separatist" are used.

Secondly, we investigate whether the Spanish services of the BBC and CNN, namely *BBC Mundo* and *CNN en Español* are truly Spanish services, with news texts specifically produced for a Spanish readership, or whether these services use, at least partly, translated material from the English sites. We shall refer to reports on other international news, used here as 'controls'. Control texts have been gathered during a longer period. It should be noticed that CNN cancelled its Spanish service in September 2004.

In the final section, we shall reflect upon whether the term *separatist* in English could be considered as an equivalent of the term *terrorista*, drawing on Baker's parameters for translation at word level (1992: 21-26). We shall examine the two Spanish news web sites financed by the above mentioned anglophone companies.

For our analysis we shall use the expression "text producers" (Fairclough 1992), since very often the texts are produced by agencies and later used by news websites at their own discretion, after going through various editing (and translational) processes. The corpus also includes correspondent dispatches.

To cover the three points above, we examined a total of a hundred and fifty articles, distributed as follows: seventy texts posted in nine American and British news websites, mostly published between 11 and 21 March 2004. These include *The New York Times* (nytimes.com), *The Washington Post* (washingtonpost.com), five from the CNN (edition.cnn.com), ten from *The Guardian* (guardian.co.uk), *The Observer* (observer.guardian.co.uk), *The Times* (timesonline.co.uk), *The Daily Telegraph* (telegraph.co.uk), *The Independent*, and the BBC (bbc.co.uk), covering a wide range of the political spectrum. We also examined fifty texts published in Spanish by English-speaking news sites, thirty from BBC Mundo and twenty from CNN en Español. This will help us assess the third step mentioned above.

The corpus of Spanish texts includes thirty reports: ten from conservative *Abc* (abc.es), ten from pro-Socialist Party *El País* (elpais.es) and the last ten from liberal *El Mundo* (elmundo.es).

This is part of a larger corpus of three hundred texts gathered to analyse the lexical choices and rhetorical devices used by Anglophone news media with regards to the binomial separatist-terrorist in connection with the militant group *ETA*. In that forthcoming study, we will focus on the discourse of British and American news texts whereas here we concentrate on the translational aspects of the problem. The findings of the former are summarized in the next section as a starting point for the ensuing discussion.

## 2. The 3/11 events in Spanish and English websites

Spanish news texts reporting on Madrid's terrorist attacks preferred the term *terrorista* in connection with *ETA*, that is, the standard term used by the Spanish media in all other news items about the Basque militant group. In fact, we have not encountered a single text featuring the term *separatista*. Spanish text producers might regard the political objectives of the organization as secondary and, therefore, focus on the devastating effects of their violent actions. Besides, as *ETA* is a well-known name in Spain's recent history (comparable to the IRA in Britain), it requires no identificatory pre-modifiers for a Spanish audience. For this reason, the group is always presented in a straightforward manner in most headlines, e. g. "Los ataques más sangrientos de *ETA*" (*El Mundo* 11/03/04).

The main body of the news reports might also use "la banda terrorista" as an alternative for two different reasons. In some cases, text producers resort to this expression for emphasis, as in the following extract from www.elmundo.es: "Desde 1992 un total de 143 personas habían muerto en España víctimas del terrorismo, de las cuales 138 perecieron en atentados perpetrados por la banda terrorista *ETA*".

Here the range of lexical items underlining the criminal nature of the Basque group (or "violent death vocabulary" as defined by Hartley and Montgomery 1985: 240) is very wide: "muerto", "víctimas", "terrorismo", "perecieron" and "atentados". These words seem to signal the state of mind of the writer and might also be interpreted as an attempt to impose it on the readership before spelling out the name of those being held responsible for the attacks, "la banda terrorista *ETA*". The strategy identified in all the texts examined is very similar, but what must be stressed is that writers never use superordinate items such as '*banda*' or '*organización*' ('group') as a synonym. When used, they tend to be accompanied by other sentence elements, as in "la organización terrorista *ETA*". Therefore, the experiential value of the term "terrorista" equates *ETA* to violence with no immediate reference to political goals, even if these motives are at the basis of *ETA*'s actions. That is, Spanish news companies follow similar patterns as their Anglophone counterparts when reporting on Islamic terrorism or IRA attacks.

The use of these noun phrases also serves another purpose within the text: to achieve cohesion and avoid continuous repetition. They play a grammatical function with cataphoric or anaphoric reference to *ETA*, which has been mentioned at some point in the same paragraph or text. Cohesion serves to establish links between the different parts of the text, both when considering texts in one given language (Halliday and Hasan 1976: 6ff) or in the case of the translated texts discussed in section five of this paper (Baker 1992: 180-207), so we can infer that the use of nouns phrases such as *banda terrorista* or *organización terrorista* are merely taken as synonyms for *ETA*. Thus, the substitution procedure carried out intratextually by Spanish text producers, or *reiteration* (Halliday and Hasan 1976: 283; Halliday 1994: 311), clearly points to the fact that, within the texts, those noun phrases have the same semantic value and can perform the same grammatical function(s) as *ETA*. In fact, we could also argue, following Michael Hoey (1991: 8) that the text itself creates the context for the interpretation of the lexical and grammatical relations between *ETA* and the other noun phrases, which we had initially considered as superordinates, as synonyms within the context of this news event.

As regards the English-speaking websites, we can distinguish three main strategies concerning the introduction and/or presentation of *ETA* within the main text, or story proper (Bell 1998: 67). Firstly, we have encountered sites which opt for *separatist*, although the term *terrorist* is used sparingly when presenting at least part of the news event. Secondly, we have identified a medium where text producers have opted for *terrorist* almost exclusively.

And finally, another news website prefers the term *separatist*. Let us now consider some examples for each strategy.

The majority of the media surveyed follow the first pattern, with a pervasive use of the term *separatist* performing different grammatical and semantic functions within the sentence, very often used as an explicatory pre-modifier of *ETA*. Thus, *The Guardian,* the *BBC* and *The New York Times* tend to resort to the noun phrase "the Basque separatist group *ETA*", *The Daily Telegraph* may also use "the Basque separatist movement *ETA*", and *The Washington Post* "the Basque separatist organization". These heavy noun phrases are used as a preliminary presentation of *ETA*, typically made by making reference to the geographical localization of the group, *Basque*, and to its political motivations, *separatist*. Addition is a feature of news reporting that allows the journalist or editor to provide the readership with information that might be needed for the comprehension of the text or news event. Once the *actors* of the news item (Bell 1991: 193-198) have been clearly identified, text producers will simply use either *ETA* as the subject of the sentence, as done in the Spanish reports, or might resort to other cohesion devices in order to avoid the repetition of the name. However, whereas Spanish text producers used *grupo terrorista* or *banda terrorista*, the preferred expression in the majority of the English texts is *the separatist group,* putting emphasis on the political motivations rather than on the violent actions. Following the lines of our discussion of intratextual coherence in Spanish texts, *separatist group* can, therefore, be interpreted as performing the same grammatical functions (i. e. subjects, object, complements) and as having the semantic implications as the word *ETA*. However, it is true that, occasionally, writers may use the term *terrorist*, but this is done sparingly and usually when quoting Spanish sources. Thus, Giles Tremlett in *The Guardian* uses *separatist*, although when reproducing indirectly the words of Spanish officials, he also has recourse to *terrorist*, as in the following extract: "The government was widely accused of blaming *ETA* for political reasons, because Mr Aznar's tough line on the Basque terrorist group was popular" (19/03/04).

Another recurrent feature in many of the articles from these sites is the addition of clauses to provide their readership with information about the current legal status of the group. Whereas this is never done in the Spanish articles, text producers referring to *ETA* in political terms (*separatist*), rather than as a terrorist organization, often insert phrases or clauses such as "listed by the EU and US as a terrorist group" (*The Guardian*) or "which has been designated a terrorist group by the United States and the European Union" (CNN).

As regards the second strategy identified, the preferred use of *terrorist*, this is predominantly used by *The Times*, at least during the period being examined. Although text producers also used *separatist*, this was done in combination with the terms *terror* or *terrorist*, as in "it would be the worst attack by the Basque separatist terror organisation" (11/03/04). *The Times* also boasts a wider range of alternative expressions for intratextual cohesion, including "Basque terror group *ETA*", "the Basque separatist terror organisation", "an indigenous terror group" and "the Basque terrorist group".

Finally, the third strategy is to be found exclusively in the BBC website, as in "Spain's government has blamed Basque separatist group *ETA*" (11/03/04). The range of cohesion devices here is also quite limited. For instance, text producers might use the term *separatist* with either an introductory or an identificatory function. Or else, they might favour the use of the superordinate term *group* for intratextual cohesion, as in "There has been no claim of responsibility from *ETA*, but across the political spectrum in Spain there has been widespread condemnation of the group" (11/03/04).

The BBC also differs from other news websites in that addition processes are also frequent. Whereas other texts tend to offer short identificatory elements (such premodifiers), BBC articles often provide the readership with much more ample information:

If the attack is confirmed as *ETA*'s work, it would be the deadliest one by *the group, which has killed more than 800 people in its armed struggle for independence from the Spanish state since the late 1960s.* (11/03/04) [my italics]

Here text producers have chosen to add historic information in which the scale of *ETA*'s terrorism (over 800 people killed) is minimized by expliciting the long time-span (since the 1960s) and by underlining the political agenda of the group (struggle for independence).

All in all, it could be argued that English-speaking media resort to what Philip Schelesinger and Bob Lumley called "a journalistic ideology of independence" (1985: 325).[1] However, the heterogeneity of the examples might reflect, as Fairclough points out, "the often tentative, unfinished and messy nature of change" (1995b: 60), that is, it might be revealing about the nature of change taking place within the establishment of Anglophone news corporations. Of all the news websites explored, only the BBC offers strong resistance to this "creative" nature of change (Fairclough 1995a: 78), which can also be referred to as *dynamic discursive practices*. In fact, only the BBC has a specific webpage to justify its decision not to use the term *terrorist* with regards to *ETA* (but, paradoxically, *not* for other such groups such as the IRA), implicitly acknowledging the existence of the controversy.

## 3. Spanish services or translated services?

Before we consider the actual translational aspects, let us briefly reflect upon whether the Spanish texts posted in BBC Mundo and CNN en Español can be taken as produced specifically for the Spanish services of the BBC and the CNN respectively, or are, in fact, the product of the transformative act that we have defined as *translation*.

The texts studied include most of the elements of media reporting identified by Allan Bell (1998: 64-104). Firstly, headlines are clear examples of literal translations from English. They all follow the usual pattern for English headlines (Carter and Nash 1990: 62-64; Bell 1991: 185-190; Bell 1998: 48-49), such as the omission of articles ("cinco arrestos por atentados"), of subjects ("creen haber identificado a presuntos autores...") and of other elements that would not be omitted in Spanish headlines ("cinco arrestos por los atentados [de Madrid]). The same applies to the control texts used for the study, e. g. BBCWorld's sports headline "Japan claim world classic title" was relayed as the dreadful "Japón gana clásico béisbol" in the Spanish service (21/03/06) where Spanish syntax and grammar have been turned upside down. Therefore, BBC Mundo and CNN en Español headlines do not conform to the linguistic patterns of their Spanish counterparts, which are much closer to standard sentence formation in everyday language (Hurtado 2003: 34-49).

As regards the stories proper, we have identified a number of important structural errors and mistaken lexical choices, including fragmented sentences (e. g. "...quien descartó que la vinculación de *ETA* con los atentados de este jueves", where a relative clause has not been completed), incorrect syntactic structures leading to ambiguity (as in "se encontrara una furgoneta robada con siete detonadores y una cinta con versos islámicos", which can imply that "seven detonators were found in the van" or that "the van was stolen with seven detonators"), syntacting calquing of heavy noun phrases, unnatural in Spanish (e. g. "al grupo separatista armado vasco *ETA*, responsable..."), erroneous use of prepositions, and mistaken lexical choices (such as the use of *funcionario* as a cohesion device to refer to the Spanish Interior Minister, a term that would not be used in Spanish when referring to high officials).

All these shortcomings point in the direction of text producers translating from English rather than constructing a text in Spanish (Valdeón 2005). That is, they do not seem to have the target audience in mind, but rather the source language, culture and audience. This could have a significant effect on the resulting texts and, consequently, on the perception that the target readers will have of the text producers and the two news media. We can now move on to the next stage of the paper, the study of the use of the terms *separatista* and/or *terrorista* in the Spanish websites of the BBC and the CNN.

### 4. BBC Mundo and CNN en Español texts

The importance of lexical choices in translation has been underlined by many. Basil Hatim and Ian Mason have mentioned the role of words and their power implications (1990: 89; 1997: 172). More recently, Olk has pointed out that "translators largely depend on norms to produce target texts which are likely to be accepted by the cultural communities for which they are intended" (2002: 111) and concludes that "only translators who are aware of their position and the positioning of their target text can make responsible choices" (112).

Let us begin by considering what we understand by *equivalence* in the linguistic process we call *translation*, a relevant concept for the discussion of the appropriateness of using *separatist* in English in the same contexts where Spanish has used *terrorista*, either when quoting the official line of the Spanish government or when using Spanish agency dispatches. The concept of *equivalence* itself has caused a considerable amount of controversy over the last three decades. For Gideon Toury the argument is futile because he argues that "equivalence is not a postulated requirement but an empirical fact, like TT itself: the actual relationships obtaining between TT and ST" (1981: 13). On the other hand, Christiane Nord's approach to the notion is much more critical on the grounds that it "is one of the most ambiguous concepts in translation studies" (1991: 22), and, therefore, too fuzzy to be defined precisely, a view also shared by Hans Vermeer (1996: 47-51). To avoid the controversy we shall rely on Rosa Rabadán's thorough discussion (1991: 49-99). In her attempt to define the term, she stresses that equivalence depends on two fundamental factors: the intertextual features of the texts, on the one hand, and the readers for whom the target text is intended, on the other (284). However, since we need an approach capable of working with equivalence at word level, we have turned to Baker's parameters for word, sentence and text levels. In her functionalist approach, Baker provides a categorization of some of the most common problems of non-equivalence between words (1992: 21-26). We list them below in order to apply them to the two terms under discussion:

    (a) Culture-specific concepts, that is, the concept may be unknown in the
        target culture.
    (b) The source-language concept is not lexicalized in the target language.
    (c) The source-language word is semantically complex.
    (d) The source and target languages make different distinctions in meaning.
    (e) The target language lacks a superordinate or generic term.
    (f) The target language lacks a hyponym, or specific term.
    (g) Differences in physical or interpersonal perspective.
    (h) Differences in expressive meaning.
    (i) Differences in form.
    (j) Differences in frequency and purpose of using specific forms.
    (k) The use of loan words and false friends.

As mentioned, the words being analysed emerge from the news events that took place in Spain in March 2004. Before continuing let us summarize the news event. The numerous news texts posted in the Internet reported on bloody and murderous attacks with the result of two hundred civilian casualties. The Spanish government's initial claims pointed towards a new *terrorist* attack by *ETA*, an illegal group that has been fighting for independence for the Basque country from the rest of Spain for nearly fifty years. The expression used by Spanish media was "*atentado terrorista*". The group is described by the Spanish Interior Minister in his first press conference after the blasts as "*la banda terrorista ETA*". English-speaking media had to translate from Spanish when presenting the events in English to some degree.

Consequently, the source language of the news and communicative events was Spanish. News media did report on the Spanish government's initial claims that the terrorist group *ETA* had carried out Madrid's train attacks. The term was used by non-Spanish media, which might have received the information from news agencies or might have elaborated the news texts directly. In both cases, a translation process took place. The process, therefore, might well be: Spanish>English>Spanish if the texts were produced directly from Spanish sources, from correspondents or from Spanish agencies, or English>Spanish if the texts were produced from English language sources, either agencies or correspondent dispatches. Apart from the transformations characteristic of media text production, we are faced with an additional transformative act, that of translating from a source language *and* culture into another language *and* culture.

Let us now return to Baker's parameters for word equivalence or non-equivalence, as the case may be. British and Spanish media have been familiar with violent attacks of a political nature within their national boundaries for decades and have often been forced to report on attacks carried out on their soil. Therefore, problems (a) and (b) do not apply here since terrorist attacks are neither specific to Britain or Spain, nor are the US untouched after 9/11.

Consequently, the expressions '*atentados terroristas*', ('terrorist attacks'*)* and the like are not specific to the Spanish readership or to the English-speaking audience, since both have experienced similar events in their own countries. Consequently, problem (c) does not apply either because both languages use similar terms when presenting news events that have taken place within their own boundaries: English uses *terrorist* for IRA members and Spanish for *ETA* militants.

The same is true of problems (e) and (f). Although the terms '*terrorista*' and '*terrorist*' share the same etymological origin, they could have evolved in different ways and have given way to different semantic values. However, this is not the case, as shown in dictionary entries for these terms in English and Spanish lexicons[2]. Problem (k) can also be discarded since neither of these languages is using loans or false friends, but common-core terms with similar semantic values. And, since they can both function as adjective and nouns, problem (j) is not relevant here, as neither is (i) as regards their form.

Thus, we are left with problems (d), (g) and (h). Problem (d) refers to the fact that one of the two languages might make more or fewer distinctions as regards the items. In the case of *separatist*, it might be argued that, whereas Spanish uses *separatist* only when defining the political motivations of a group or party, English might also apply it to terrorist attacks carried out by groups seeking independence from a country. However, this is merely a hypothesis. As we turn to three well-known lexicons of the English language (*Oxford*, *Cambridge* and *Collins*), the entries clearly emphasize two facts: that *separatism* is related to ideology and political beliefs, whereas *terrorism* differs in that political aims are the justification for violence. Therefore, the controversy affecting the translation of these terms does not stem from problem (d) of Baker's parameters either.

Let us now move on to category (g). Of the two differences that Baker notes, physical and interpersonal, only the latter might apply here: "Perspective may also include the relationship between participants in the discourse" (1992: 23). We might be tempted to interpret that this problem *does* arise when media text producers opt for "separatist" in the English texts, a choice influenced by their own ideological, editorial or political stand with respect to the news event. That might indeed be applicable to media texts in general. However, Baker's functional approach to translation refers here to the perspective of the participants within the discourse (or *tenors* in Halliday and Hasan's terms 1976: 22), not to the translators themselves, who must evaluate the relationship between the text (or news event in this case) and the potential readership before making the appropriate lexical choices. It might be argued that news writers are not professional translators. That is obviously true. However, let us remember that although they might not be translators, they are, in fact, acting as such when, for example, quoting their sources directly or indirectly. Therefore, the translational component is clearly present in their reporting. Following Baker's discussion, problem (g) would not apply, and, consequently, 'separatist' cannot be rendered as 'terrorist', least of all in indirect quotations of Spanish officials, unless, of course, text producers intend to infuse the articles with their own perspective, their own editorial or ideological stand.

Finally we come to problem (h), which is related to differences in expressive meaning. This is probably the most interesting point, since it refers to the connotative meaning of the two words, to the feelings, emotions or images that they may encompass, leaving aside their primary semantic value. Baker states that if a given lexical item is more neutral in the original language, translators can always add expressive meaning using a modifier or an adverb. That is, if the word does not convey the same strength as in the original, they can add it. Paradoxically enough, in the choice made by non-

Spanish text producers the word loses connotative meaning by emphasizing political aims and by toning down the violent effects of their actions. Baker stresses that, in fact, these differences "are more difficult to handle when the target-language equivalent is more emotionally loaded than the source-language item. This is often the case with items which relate to sensitive issues such as religion, politics and sex" (1992: 24). It is also paradoxical to notice that in the case of *'terrorista'* and *'separatist'*, the emotional force, because it is about human death caused by extreme violence, is present in the former, whereas the controversy arises precisely from the use of the latter. In fact, devoiding the news event of its extremely strong emotional content produces a rather anomalous situation: the lexical item, as used in the source text, carries a stronger connotative meaning, which text producers (or translators) do not even try to compensate when using 'separatist'.

In the case that we accept Spanish as the source language of the news events from which reports emanate or when dealing with indirect quotations of Spanish officials: Spanish > English > Spanish, i.e. *'terrorista'* > 'separatist' >. If English is regarded as the source language, irrespective of where the news event has taken place and without considering the translational component present in indirect quotations of the Spanish government then English > Spanish, i.e. *separatist.*

Let us now consider the choices in the Spanish services of the BBC and the CNN, beginning with the European website. Firstly, we must refer to the presentation that the British company makes of its services in Spanish. They claim that their aim is to offer impartial journalism, to provide perspective and analysis and they also underline that the service is formed by a team of experienced Spanish and Latin-American journalists. The implication is, therefore, that news reports are specifically produced for this service. If that is so, it is fairly reasonable to expect text producers of Spanish texts to take into account Baker's parameters for word equivalence, irrespective of whether they are translating already produced texts or constructing their own, since both processes will involve a translational component to some degree. It might even be reasonable to expect the use of *'terrorista'* to refer to *ETA*, not merely because their Spanish counterparts have done so in Spanish, but because the connotative, expressive and semantic values of the term can be easily equated to similar news events experienced in their own countries or in the countries where they are based, particularly in the case of the UK with respect to the IRA. We shall begin by quoting some lengthy extracts in order not only to illustrate the preferred choices but also to provide sufficient additional information about the quality of the texts for the ensuing discussion on whether they can be taken as specifically written for a Spanish-speaking readership or as translations from English source texts. The words in italics are particularly relevant for the discussion:

*Ideological Independence or Negative Mediation: BBC Mundo and CNN en Español's (translated Reporting of Madrid's Terrorist Attacks*

BBC Mundo (11/03/04)
Madrid/atentados: más de 170 muertos
Cuatro explosiones se registraron este jueves en la mañana, sin previo aviso, en el sistema ferroviario de Madrid, provocando la muerte de 173 personas y casi 600 heridos, según informó una fuente del ministerio del Interior de España.
Las autoridades españolas responsabilizaron de los atentados al grupo separatista armado vasco *ETA*, responsable de la muerte de más de 800 personas en varias décadas de violencia política. (BBC Mundo 11/03/04)

BBC Mundo (12/03/04)
Atentado: *ETA* "niega" responsabilidad
La organización separatista vasca *ETA* negó responsabilidad en los atentados del jueves en Madrid, en los cuales murieron 199 personas y más de 1.400 resultaron heridas.
Varios medios vascos, entre ellos la televisión pública y el diario Gara, recibieron llamadas de *ETA*, en las cuales niega su participación en los atentados. (…)
El gobierno inicialmente culpó a la organización separatista armada por los atentados del jueves, pero adoptó una postura más precavida luego de que en Alcalá de Henares, cerca de Madrid, se encontrara una furgoneta robada con siete detonadores y una cinta con versos islámicos. (BBC Mundo 12/03/04)

BBC Mundo (13/03/04)
España: cinco arrestos por atentados
(…) Otras hipótesis
Más temprano se había informado que fuentes del Centro Nacional de Inteligencia (CNI) español indicaron a la radio local Cadena Ser que están "99% seguros" de la validez de la hipótesis que apunta a un atentado de corte radical-islamista. (…)
Esta teoría está basada en la mochila hallada que no explotó. Fuentes de la lucha anti-terrorista citadas por el diario consideran que el material encontrado no es el utilizado por la organización separatista vasca armada *ETA* y que, hoy por hoy, no está al alcance de esa organización. (…)
El funcionario insistió en ese momento que *ETA* seguía siendo el principal sospechoso, pero agregó que la autoría de militantes islámicos que responden a la organización al-Qaeda seguía siendo considerada una posibilidad.(BBC Mundo 13/03/04)

BBC Mundo (17/03/04)
España: "identifican" autores de atentados:
(…)
En los atentados, que inicialmente habían sido atribuidos por el gobierno español a la organización separatista vasca *ETA*, murieron 200 personas y más de 1.400 resultaron heridas.
(BBC Mundo 17/03/04)

Let us now consider examples of reports published by the Spanish service of the CNN. The three texts below are quoted to have been dispatched by Reuters:

CNN en Español (12/03/04)
Millones salen a las calles de España en repulsa a los atentados de Madrid
(…)
Los españoles observaron el momento de silencio a lo largo de la península Ibérica, desde Gibraltar en el sur hasta la región vasca en el norte, a pesar de que el grupo armado vasco

113

*ETA* seguía siendo uno de los sospechosos.
*ETA*, un grupo armado vasco considerado terrorista por Estados Unidos y la Unión Europea, hamatado a más de 850 personas desde que comenzó su lucha violenta por la independencia del País Vasco en 1968. (CNN en Español: 12/03/04)

CNN en Español (13/03/04)
España entierra a víctimas de atentados; aumenta a 200 la cifra de muertos
(...)
El gobierno dijo que el grupo armado vasco *ETA* sigue siendo el principal sospechoso, pero no descartaba a grupos extremistas islámicos vinculados a la red al Qaeda. (...)
Si fuera *ETA*, significaría una escalada en las tácticas del grupo, que ha matado a más de 850 personas en su lucha violenta por la independencia del País Vasco. *ETA* es considerada un grupo terrorista por Estados Unidos y la Unión Europea. (CNN en Español: 13/03/04)

CNN en Español (14/03/04)
*ETA* niega de nuevo su participación en los atentados
MADRID (Reuters) -- El grupo armado vasco *ETA* emitió un comunicado en el que nuevamente negó cualquier implicación en los atentados que el pasado jueves dejaron en Madrid 200 muertos y más de 1.500 heridos, informó el diario vasco Gara en su página de Internet el domingo, al comienzo de la jornada electoral.
Según el diario, que publica habitualmente comunicados de la banda separatista, *ETA* dijo que el apoyo del presidente del gobierno español, José María Aznar, a la guerra liderada por Estados Unidos en Iraq, es responsable de provocar los atentados, que, agregó *ETA*, probablemente sean obra de "un grupo de origen islámico". (CNN en Español: 14/03/04)

The most important feature of the extracts is the repeated use of the term '*separatista*', with a similar introductory function as already commented upon for the English texts, although affecting the necessary changes to the syntax of the sentence. In general the structure is conspicuously similar in the majority of the cases. Text producers resort to heavy noun phrases which include geographical reference ('*vasco*') and political demands ('*separatista*'). In some extracts from BBC Mundo, text producers use the same adjectives as their counterparts in English (such as '*armado*' and '*extremista*'), whereas the CNN tends to prefer '*grupo armado vasco*', with '*banda separatista*' being used as an intratextual cohesion device. In no cases do text producers use '*terrorist'a* as part of their own reporting (or translation), and when they do it is to mention the current legal status of the group: "considerado terrorista por Estados Unidos y la Unión Europea". That is, there is a clear strategy of detachment from *ETA*'s official status *vis-à-vis* Western governments.

As we can see, both the CNN and the BBC choose to render the term *separatist* as *separatista* in Spanish. Thus, we have encountered heavy noun phrases of the type "grupo separatista armado vasco *ETA*", "organización separatista vasca armada *ETA*", "organización separatista vasca *ETA*", "grupo armado vasco" or "banda separatista". In no case is the word "terrorista" used in connection with *ETA*, although, paradoxically enough, it is used to refer to actions carried out by Al-Quaida related groups, both by the BBC and the

CNN. As we reach the final stage, we come to the following transformations and/or translations: Spanish > English > Spanish i.e. *'terrorista'* > 'separatist' > *'separatista'*, or English > Spanish, i.e. 'separatist' > *'separatista'*.

The term originated in a Spanish news item, was transformed by English-speaking media as a consequence of alleged editorial independence (or ideological preference) through substitution and adaptation processes, and finally imposed in the Spanish texts. The reluctance to use *terrorista* to refer to *ETA* becomes more obvious in the transformation process that text producers carry *out* when reporting the words of Spanish officials. In section three, we mentioned that most of the Anglophone reports on the 3/11 events followed the first strategy identified, that is, they preferred *separatist*, although they also resorted to *terrorist* when reporting official statements from the Spanish government, or when mentioning the current legal status of the group. However, it is surprising that in the Spanish services of these news websites, Spanish government officials are quoted as having used *separatista* when blaming *ETA*. Text producers are not merely following an editorial policy of independence, but are, in effect, altering a communicative and informative event to make it conform to their own political stance. We are not faced with a question of translational choices, however questionable or understandable they could be, we are faced with a clear instance of misinformation. Or, at least, it could be argued that they have filtered the words of Spanish officials, and, consequently, toned down their reference to the Basque terror group.

Consequently, text producers in the case of BBC Mundo and CNN en Español have a two-fold mediating role, as media writers, on the one hand, and as translators, on the other. As media writers, we have discussed that the quality of the mediation process can range between positive and negative. In *The Sun* article analysed by Fairclough, there was positive mediation inasmuch as text producers aimed to make officialese comprehensible to ordinary readers by incorporating an informal tone. But there was also negative mediation, as they imposed a certain ideological position in the construction of the text. The same ambivalence occurs in the extracts quoted above since, whilst the main objective is to provide information about the scale of the massacre and its effects, the substitution and addition strategies used by texts producers are instances of negative mediation. Even if they did reproduce the actual words spoken by members of the Spanish cabinet, text producers would *not* be endorsing them. However, they opted for the term *separatist*, even though it cannot be substantiated from the application of Baker's parameters for word equivalence. The use of the term *terrorist* in combination with the strategy whereby writers add information of the type "*ETA* es considerada un grupo terrorista por Estados Unidos y la Unión Europea" would have informed the potential readers of the actual words uttered by Spanish officials, and it would have also indicated the intratextual position of the writer (or the corporation) with respect to *ETA*. It is the combination of these two strategies what seems to signal ideological compromise rather than ideological independence.

Thus, considering that these texts function primarily as translations, rather than as original texts, it could also be argued that the role of the text producer as a mediator has been abused. We could define the mediation process around the following parameters:

(a) It should respect the position of the 'Other' by acknowledging the implications of lexical choices, their expressive and emotional value.

(b) It should opt for those terms which carry the same semantic value as they would apply to the same concept in their own culture.

(c) It should try to overcome incompatibilities as regards "ideologies, moral systems and socio-political structures" (Mason and Hatim 1990: 223).

(d) It should operate in the interest of the culture into which they are translating (Toury 1995: 12).

(e) It should optimize communication between cultures (Chesterman 1995: 149), between author and readership (Peeters 1999: 217-227).

The use of 'separatist' in the translated texts examined here does not reflect any of these. On one hand, text producers do not respect the position of the 'Other', understood as a democratic nation hit by terrorist attacks carried out by a group whose political aims are secondary to the use of violence and terror. They do not operate in the interest of the target culture, quite the contrary, they operate in their own interest, whether that is understood as personal, editorial or national. They certainly do not optimize communication between author and readership, as the choice is widely contested by the Spanish readership. They operate in the interest of the set of assumptions of the source culture rather than of the target culture, and, for this reason, they represent an anomaly within TS. The reason for this anomaly might well lie in the fact that, as opposed to most translated texts, the TTs analysed here are commissioned from within the source culture, source culture constraints apply to them, and the translators, even if speakers of the target language, are also embedded within the source culture. Therefore, the texts examined for this paper seem to show a tendency to work in the benefit of the source culture. Adding to this the fact that text producers are subject to editorial routines instructing them on the lexical choices they have to make in the target language, the quality of the mediation can, in our view, be said to have suffered from serious constraints imposed upon the target readership by the "source" writers. The translation process has been shaped primarily by very incoherent editorial notions of ideological independence, making the mediating role of the text writers subservient to the political position of the company, and, consequently, turning a series of texts with an informative function into controversial reports contested by the target readers.

---

1 Although media experts do not agree on what is to be understood by "independence". Lisa Taylor and Andrew Willis discuss it in connection with the changes that affected news media in the UK under Margaret Thatcher's Conservative government (1999: 132-136).
2 See, for example, the entry for *'terrorista'* in the dictionary of the *Real Academia Española* or for 'terrorist' in well-known English dictionaries such as the *Oxford Dictionary of English.*

## References

Allan, Stuart. 2004. *News Culture*. Maidenhead: Open University Press.
Arrojo, Rosemary. 1998. 'The Revision of the Traditional Gap between Theory and Practice and the Empowerment of Translation in Postmodern Times' in *The Translator* 4(1): 25-48.
Baker, Mona. 1992. *In Other Words*. London and New York: Routledge.
Beaugrande, Robert de. 2000. 'La saga del análisis del discurso' in van Dijk, Teun A. (ed.) *El discurso como escritura y proceso*. Barcelona: Gedisa. 67-106.
Bell, Allan. 1991. *The Language of News Media*. Oxford: Blackwell.
——1998. 'The Discourse Structure of News Stories' in Bell, Allan and Peter Garrett (eds) *Approaches to Media Discourse*. Oxford: Blackwell. 64-104.
Brownlie, Siobhan. 2003. 'Distinguishing Some Approaches to Translation Research' in *The Translator* 9(4): 39-64.
Campbell, Stuart. 1998. *Translation into the Second Language*. Harlow: Longman.
Carter, Ronald and Walter Nash. 1990. *Seeing Through Language*. Oxford: Blackwell.
Chesterman, Andrew. 1995. 'Ethics of translation' in Snell-Hornby, Mary, Zuzana Jettmarová, and Klaus, Kaindl (eds) *Translation as Intercultural Communication*. Amsterdam: John Benjamins. 147-157.
Fairclough, Norman. 1992. *Discourse and Social Change*. London: Polity Press.
——1995a. *Critical Discourse Analysis: the Critical Study of Language*. London and New York: Longman.
——1995b. *Media Discourse*. London: Arnold.
——2001. *Language and Power*. Harlow: Longman.
Fowler, Roger. 1996. 'On Critical Linguistics', in Caldas-Coulthard, Carmen R. and Malcolm Coulthard (eds) *Texts and Practices: Readings in Critical Discourse Analysis*. London and New York: Routledge. 3-14.
Gorman, Lyn and David McLean. 2003. *Media and Society in the Twentieth Century, A Historical Introduction*. Oxford: Blackwell.
Hall, Stuart et al. 1978. *Policing the Crisis: Mugging, the State, and Law and Order*. London: MacMillan.
Halliday, Michael A. K. 1994. *An Introduction to Functional Grammar*. London: Edward Arnold.
Halliday, Michael A. K. and Ruquaiya Hasan. 1976. *Cohesion in English*. Harlow: Longman.
Hartley, John and Martin Montgomery. 1985. 'Representations and Relations: Ideology and Power in Press and TV News' in van Dijk, Teun A. (ed.) *Discourse and Communication, New Approaches to the Analysis of Mass Media Discourse and Communication*. Berlin and New York: Walter de Gruyter. 233-271
Hatim, Basil and Ian Mason. 1990. *Discourse and the Translator*. Harlow: Longman.
——1997. *The Translator as Communicator*. London: Routledge.
Hoey, Michael. 1991. *Patterns of Lexis in Text*. Oxford: Oxford University Press.

Hurtado González, Silvia. 2003. *El uso del lenguaje en la prensa escrita*. Valladolid: Secretariado de Publicaciones de la Universidad de Valladolid.
Nord, Christiane. 1991. *Text Analysis and Translation*. Amsterdam: Rodopi.
Olk, Harald. 2002. 'Critical Discourse Awareness in Translation' in *The Translator* 8(1): 101-116.
Rabadán, Rosa. 1991. *Equivalencia y traducción. Problemática de la equivalencia traslémica inglés-español*. León: Servicio de Publicaciones de la Universidad de León.
Real Academia Española. 1992. *Diccionario de la Lengua Española*. Madrid: Unigraf.
Peeters, Jean. 1999. *La médiation de l"étranger. Une sociolinguistique de la traduction*. Paris: Artois Presses Université.
Schelesinger, Philip and Bob Lumley. 1985. 'Two Debates on Political Violence and the MassMedia: The Organisation of Intellectual Fields in Britain and Italy' in van Dijk, Teun A. (ed.) *Discourse and Communication, New Approaches to the Analysis of Mass Media Discourse and Communication*. Berlin and New York: Walter de Gruyter. 324-349.
Sheyholislami, Jaffer. 2001. *Yesterday's Separatists Are Today's Resistance Fighters: A Critical Discourse Analysis of the Representation of Iraqi Kurds in The Globe and Mail and The New York Times*. M. A. thesis. Carleton University.
Simpson, Paul. 1993. *Language, Ideology and Point of View*. London: Routledge.
Sinclair, John (ed.) 1995. *Collins Cobuild English Dictionary*. London: HarperCollins.
Soanes, Catherine and Angus Stevenson (eds). 2003. *Oxford Dictionary of English*. Oxford: Oxford University Press.
Taylor, Lisa and Andrew Willis.1999. *Media Studies: Texts, Institutions and Audiences*. Oxford: Blackwell.
Toury, Gideon. 1981. 'Translated Literature: System, Norm, Performance. Toward a TT-oriented Approach to Translation' in *Poetics Today* 2(4): 9-27.
——-1995. *Descriptive Translation Studies and Beyond*. Amsterdam: John Benjamins.
Valdeón, Roberto A. 2005. 'The Translated Spanish Service of the BBC' in *Across Languages and Cultures* 6(2): 195-220.
van Dijk, Teun A. 1990[1980]. *La noticia como discurso: comprensión, estructura y producción de la información*. Barcelona: Paidós.
——2003. *Ideología y discurso*. Barcelona: Ariel.
Vermeer, Hans J. 1996. *A Skopos Theory of Translation (Some Arguments for and against)*. Heidelberg: TextconText-Verlag.
Vidal, Bernard. 1995. 'Communication, traduction et transparence: de l'altérité du traducteur' in *Meta* XL(3): 372-378.
Wolf, Michaela. 1995. 'Translation as a Process of Power: Aspects of Cultural Anthropology in Translation' in Snell-Hornby, Mary, Zuzana Jettmarová, and Klaus Kaindl (eds) *Translation as Intercultural Communication*. Amsterdam: John Benjamins. 123-133.
Woodford, Kate and Guy Jackson (eds). 2003. *Cambridge Advanced Learner's Dictionary*. Cambridge: Cambridge University Press.
Zlateva, P. (1990). Translation: Text and Pre-Text "Adequacy" and "Acceptability" in Crosscultural Communication. In Bassnett, Susan and André Lefevere (eds) *Translation, History and Culture*. London and New York: Cassell. 29-37.

# One Nation, Two Translations: China's Censorship of Hillary Clinton's Memoir [1]

*Red Chan*

International politics is a battlefield of language, ideology, and translation. Regional as well as global peace (or conflict) is the direct result of negotiation between different national interests and cultures. In 2003 two Chinese versions of Hillary Clinton's memoir, *Living History* were published. The mainland Chinese (PRC) version is said to be a replica of the edition published in Taiwan – it claims authorship by the same group of translators. However, the two versions are different in every aspect – from book title to chapter titles to actual contents, renderings, incidents, etc. This paper discusses how translation serves to create narratives that justify or challenge particular interpretations of meanings or events in Sino-US politics. It provides an empirical study of the industry of publishing and translation in the increasingly powerful PRC today.

Key words: Sino-US relationship, translation and politics, translation of memoir, Hillary Clinton, Peoples Republic of China (PRC), Taiwan.

"I was amazed and outraged to hear about this... They censored my book, just as they tried to censor me". Thus was the protest of Hillary Clinton in September 2003, after learning that the Mainland Chinese version of her memoir, *Living History*, was not at all a faithful translation of her English original. Different interpretations arise when readers of the same text base their judgment on their own contextual, prescribed set of criteria. When different opinions are voiced about translation in a diplomatic scenario, the stakes could be high. In this paper the translation of Hillary Clinton's *Living History* (first published by Simon & Schuster in the US, 9 June 2003) is studied in light of its Mainland Chinese version in simplified Chinese. The dissatisfaction of the American Senator with her Mainland Chinese representation could be understood in terms of her perception that the Communist Regime sanctions her explicit criticism of its human rights abuses through a cleansed version of translation. The official publisher of her work, however, explained that the changes in the translation were not imposed by the government but the result of hasty production that was meant to avoid pirated versions winning the bigger share of the market.

The causes of conflict in this incident of translation are rooted not only in an ideological clash between an American, liberal, high-profile politician, and a presumably undemocratic, corrupted culture. The conflict is also the result of a cut-throat, unruly publishing market in a developing country, where only the brutal, opportunist players are rewarded – with big money. The publication of a former First Lady of America's memoir in simplified Chinese has political implications. It showcases a friendly Sino-US relationship and symbolises the Communist regime's forbearance of its international critics. The Sino-US relationship has gone through ping-pong games since the 1979 visit to Beijing by Nixon, the former US President. The visit formally started the diplomatic relationship between the PRC and the US. As far as the US is concerned, Communist China is strategically a rival and a friend. In the twentieth century, the two had fought in wars as enemies but also as allies – during World War II, they were allies; yet during the Korean and Vietnam wars, they were arch-enemies. The undeniable, unstoppable rise of Communist China following its economic reform from the late 1970s has created new tension as well as affinity between the world's two superpowers.[2] In the past twenty years or so, US presidents – from Ronald Reagan to George Bush senior, from Bill Clinton to George Bush junior – have periodically advocated either distance from, or engagement with, Communist China. Whether it was the pro-democracy movement in 1989, arms sales to Taiwan, human rights issues, nuclear power development or the PRC's membership in the World Trade Organization (WTO), they have served as platforms on which the PRC and the US negotiate and compete for economic and political power.

In 2001, Mainland China finally became a member of the WTO. This owed much to the support of former US President, Bill Clinton. Under his presidency the US and the PRC had, on the whole, become closer allies. He adopted a policy of engagement: believing the best way to make Mainland China a more open, democratic nation was to engage with its government. He paid several official and unofficial visits to the PRC during his office and his family went with him in 1998. In 1995, his wife Hillary was the Honorary Chair of the American delegation to the United Nations Fourth Conference on Women, which took place in Beijing. Those high-profile diplomatic events had turned the 'Clintons' into a household name across Mainland China. When news broke out that *Living History* would be published in the PRC, there was great interest from the public. For many, the name 'Clinton' is an object of voyeurism and fascination.

The enormous book market in Mainland China made this translation project a 'golden goose' for any publisher, legal or otherwise. It is estimated that since the 1990s about 30 percent of books published in Mainland China are translations.[3] According to a report in November 2004, Mainland China saw 10,000 translations a year for nine consecutive years. Statistics from the

China Bibliographic Library showed that over 94,400 translations were published between 1995 and 2003, a rise from the figure of 28,500 titles between the twelve-year span of 1978 and 1990.[4] The booming translation industry was a by-product of the open-door policy the reformists (under the leadership of Deng Xiaoping) adopted since the late 1970s. For several decades during the Maoist period (late 1940s through to late 1970s), Mainland Chinese readers were allowed a very small canon of propagandist books. Only revolutionary literature from Russia and former communist countries was allowed, almost all literature from Europe or Anglophone countries being banned. Dai Sijie's *Balzac and the Chinese Little Seamstress* (2002) is a powerful depiction of the deprivation which Chinese book lovers suffered during the Cultural Revolution (1967-1977).

The market-minded new regime showed little interest in a boom of foreign works in translation. In fact it only became a signatory of the international copyright treaty, the Bern Convention, as late as 1992. Following this endorsement Mainland China is required to obtain a copyright for all translations of foreign works. Many publishers (all state-controlled) would rather produce re-translations of foreign classics than seek legitimate copyright of contemporary works. In the mid 1990s, there was a frenzied wave of re-translation. One scholar reckoned that as of November 2004, there were

> at least twenty-six translated versions of Stendhal's *The Red and The Black*, and more than ten of Miguel Cervantes's *Don Quixote of La Mancha*. Some of them are of poor quality ... and some are plagiarized.[5]

It is no surprise that prior to the release of *Living History* in 2003, quite a few powerful, state-run publishers fought to earn the copyright to its translation in simplified Chinese. Yilin Press (of Nanjing, Jiangsu province) paid Simon & Schuster Inc.US$20,000 and won the exclusive right to publish the work in simplified Chinese for the Mainland market. This amount is four times the usual rate a Chinese publisher would pay for a work in English for a translation copyright. One editor of Yilin Press revealed this amount was an initial payment only, a further 10 percent copyright royalties would subsequently be paid.[6]

The Taiwan translation in traditional Chinese was published in June 2003, around the same time as the English version. The Taiwan publisher, China Times, is a leading publishing house and it assigned the project to six of its in-house, full-time translators. Yilin Press received the English version in June 2003 and its original plan was to release the translation by end of 2003. However, immediately after the traditional Chinese version came out in Taiwan, pirated copies in simplified Chinese were spreading like wildfire in Mainland China. Even national papers were serialising parts of the book without permission.[7] Yilin was in dire need to publish its official simplified

Chinese version as soon as possible. It is unclear to this writer when and how it happened – it could have been a pre-arranged plan or a last-minute change of strategy – in any case Yilin Press did not produce its own translation but bought the copyright from China Times.

On 8 August 2003, two months after the traditional Chinese version was published in Taiwan, the simplified Chinese version was officially released in the PRC. Yilin Press made an initial print run of 100,000 copies.[8] In Beijing, five hundred copies were sold in the first two hours.[9] In September 2003, a month after its official release, the book "has become the most popular foreign political memoir in Chinese history, with 200,000 copies sold in just over a month" (Kahn 2003).

## 1. Comparing the Taiwan and the Mainland Chinese versions

In its presentation the Mainland Chinese version makes it clear that it is based on the Taiwan version. But there are numerous differences between the two. The first notable difference is the book title. The Taiwan version is *Huochu Lishi*, which means 'living out history', or 'out-living history'. This title suggests a character who has outlived and perhaps outwitted the challenge of History. It is a celebration of a fighting spirit. The PRC version, *Qinli Lishi*, has a different focus. Literally it means 'first-hand experiencing of history', 'experiencing history in person', or, in translation by a *New York Times* correspondent, as '*Personal History*'. This title emphasizes more the personal aspect of experiences. It highlights the first-person perspective, hence the authenticity, of Hillary Clinton's account of her public and private lives. While the Taiwan title carries a metaphorical, symbolic register of a woman's championship against the overwhelming power of historical subjugation, the Mainland Chinese title is a straightforward, plain denotation of the book's value – that it gives the reader direct, unobstructed access to the very heart of a controversial figure.

Both books proclaim the same six translators from the International News Desk at China Times Publishing Company as authors of the translation. The Taiwan version includes a brief biography of each translator and the respective chapters translated by her/him, but the simplified Chinese version only lists their names without any biographical information. Given the differences between the two versions, it is unsettling to observe that the Taiwan translators were assigned 'translatorship' of a text over which they had virtually no control.

Another main difference in presentation is that the Taiwan version omitted Hillary Clinton's dedication on the first page. Instead there is a Foreword by the General Manager of China Times, entitled 'Remembering the Past, Imagining the Future – Decoding Hillary'. Readers of the Taiwan version are thus prescribed with a framework of interpretation. The removal of Hillary Clinton's own dedication and replacing it with a 'reader's guide' by the top man of the publisher, undermines the feminist tone embedded in the book throughout.

Overall the Taiwan version stays close to the English version. Yilin Press of the PRC version claimed that in terms of content, the translation is 99.9 percent the same as the original. But Hillary Clinton was infuriated when she learned about the changes, omissions and shifts in the simplified Chinese version. On 23 September 2003, Joseph Kahn, a *New York Times* correspondent based in Beijing, reported that upon discovery of the changes, Simon & Schuster sent a letter to Yilin Press demanding that it "recall the Chinese edition and provide a new translation that faithfully adheres to the original." Kahn highlighted several key differences between the Mainland Chinese version and the English original,

> [N]early everything Mrs. Clinton had to say about China, including descriptions of her own visits here [Beijing], former President Bill Clinton's meetings with Chinese leaders and her criticisms of Communist Party social controls and human rights policies, has been shortened or selectively excerpted to remove commentary deemed offensive by Beijing. ... Though the Chinese edition includes much of Mrs. Clinton's account of her visit to China in 1998 with President Clinton, it selectively strikes out sensitive passages, including her statement that she was 'haunted by the events at Tiananmen", the violent crackdown on a student-led pro-democracy demonstration in 1989. ...The manuscript appears to have been combed for even stray mentions of China or its leaders, though the Chinese editors did not mark or otherwise indicate where they had made changes or elisions in the 466-page text. Simon & Schuster prepared a new translation of passages dealing with China and posted them on its Web site today. (*ibid.*)

The chapter entitled 'Women's Rights are Human rights' is illustrative of the alleged censorship. In it Hillary Clinton recalls the Chinese government's sanction of political dissident Harry Wu. While the Taiwan version follows closely the English in content as well as register, the Mainland Chinese version depicts twisted facts in a manipulative tone. The chapter begins with the following paragraph:

> The arrest of a dissident is not unusual in China, and Harry Wu's imprisonment might have received scant attention in the American media. But China had been chosen to host the upcoming United Nations Fourth World Conference on Women, and I was scheduled to attend as honorary Chair of the US delegation. Wu, a human rights activist who had spent nineteen years as a political prisoner in Chinese labor camps before emigrating to the United States, was arrested by Chinese authorities on June 19, 1995, as he entered Xinjian Province from neighboring Kazakhstan. [*Living History*, 298]

In back translation[10], the Taiwan version reads:

> The arrest of dissidents is not unusual in Mainland China, and Harry Wu's imprisonment might not have received attention in the American media. But

> China had been chosen to host the United Nations Fourth World Conference on Women, and I was scheduled to attend as honorary Chair of the US delegation. Wu, a human rights activist who was condemned as a political prisoner, had spent nineteen years in Chinese labor camps before emigrating to the United States. On June 19, 1995, he was enroute to China via Kazakhstan and was arrested by the Chinese authority. [*Huochu Lishi*, 321]

In back translation, the Mainland Chinese version reads:

> Harry Wu's arrest would not have caused much media attention in the first place. But China had been chosen to host the United Nations Fourth World Conference on Women, and I was scheduled to attend as honorary Chair of the US delegation. [*Qinlin Lishi*, 263][11]

Compared with the English source text, the Mainland Chinese version is obviously much shorter and simpler. It removes all background information about Wu and his arrest. In this version Wu's arrest is perceived and presented as a marginal fact rather than being one which is central to Hillary Clinton's dilemma.

The second paragraph of the English text reads:

> Although he had a valid visa to visit China, he was charged with espionage and thrown in jail to await trial. Overnight, Harry Wu became widely known, and US participation in the women's conference was cast into doubt as human rights groups, Chinese American activists and some members of Congress urged our nation to boycott. I sympathized with their cause, but it disappointed me that, once again, the crucial concerns of women might be sacrificed. [*Living History*, 299]

In back translation, the Mainland Chinese version reads,

> Harry Wu was charged with espionage, therefore he was detained and awaiting trial. Because various groups and some members of Congress urged the US government to boycott the United Nations Fourth World Conference on Women, whether America should take part became an uncertainty. I sympathized with their cause, but it disappointed me that, once again, the crucial concerns of women might be sacrificed. [*Qinli Lishi*, 263]

The Taiwan version follows more or less the same content and narrative as they are in the English. The Mainland Chinese version, however, is rendered in a changed discourse. The affirmative tone that presumes legality of Wu's arrest leads the reader to think Wu was conducting a forbidden act, hence his arrest was legitimate. This translation achieves the opposite effect that the author means to achieve in her English version: in her account she questions the action of the Chinese government but the translation de-problematises this question altogether.

In the sixth paragraph Hillary Clinton describes how various senators were opposing her visit to China. She mentions that

> The Vatican, vociferous on the subject of abortion, joined forces with some Islamic countries concerned that the conference would become an international platform to promote the women's rights they opposed. And some on the American political left were unhappy about the prospect of US participation because the Chinese government was indicating that non-governmental organizations advocating maternal health, property rights for women, microfinance and many other issues might be excluded from the official gathering. Chinese authorities made it difficult for Tibetan activists and others to get visas to enter China. Furthermore, there was widespread discomfort, which I shared, about the host nation's dismal record on human rights and its barbaric policy of condoning forced abortions as a means of imposing its "one child policy". [*Living History*, 299]

The Taiwan version again mirrors the source text with every sentence and word translated, while the Mainland Chinese version is much reduced in length and reads, in back translation,

> Some countries were concerned that the conference would become an international platform to promote the women's rights they opposed. The Vatican, vociferous on the subject of abortion, joined forces with those countries. [*Qinli Lishi*, 264] [12]

In its abstraction the simplified Chinese version removed Hillary Clinton's critical comment of the PRC's one-child policy. The range of 'women's rights' listed in the English text is skimmed down to the subject of abortion and the Vatican is presented as the key oppositional force causing Hillary Clinton to have second thoughts about gracing the UN Conference in Beijing with her presence.

A comparison of the Taiwan and Mainland Chinese versions shows that sentences and paragraphs that are damning for the Communist regime are deleted, and changes in nuance, tone or register are plenty. Robert Barnett, Hillary Clinton's lawyer in charge of the book's domestic and international release, regarded the changes a breach of contract, as they 'had been made without consultation.' Hillary Clinton insisted she would "do everything she can to make sure that her readers in China get an accurate translation of her book." (Kahn 2003) On 23 September 2003, Simon & Schuster took measures to remedy the unauthorized changes, and placed on the web a Chinese translation of missing pages and paragraphs from the Yilin edition.[13] However, it is not clear how many Mainland Chinese readers were aware of this provision as Internet access in the PRC is under strict state control. An American writer based in Beijing wrote on 1 January 2004 that "Although the Chinese publishers did agree to produce an accurate translation of Senator Hillary Clinton's book, they did excise anything remotely critical of China.

Simon & Schuster initially put all the censored passages on their website, but China firewalled the page".[14]

In his promotion of the simplified Chinese version, Zang Zude, President of Yilin Press claimed that the purpose of

> translating the book is to give Chinese readers a chance to learn more about contemporary US society, culture and politics since, in the book, Hillary gives a quite comprehensive account of US foreign affairs, social and political events during Bill Clinton's administration.[15]

It is ironic that Hillary Clinton's demand for an accurate translation of her work was not given priority by her Mainland Chinese publisher. For Yilin Press, what mattered was the comprehensiveness of her first-hand narrative of American politics and her private life, not her opinions about Mainland China and its government. The conflict between these two parties stems from their attribution of different significance to the same text.

When Yilin Press was first confronted with allegations of having made illegitimate changes to *Living History* in the simplified Chinese version, its editorial staff denied any wrong doing. On 27 September 2003, Zang Zude made a public announcement about the dispute. He claimed that Yilin Press signed the contract with Simon & Schuster in March 2002. On 9 June 2003 the English version was released in the US. Yilin Press received the English version on 2 June 2003, which was almost two months later than their counterparts in Taiwan.[16]

> During the editorial process, Yilin Press carried out technical treatment [*jishu chuli*] in a few places for the sake of better reader reception. Meanwhile it was aware that many pirated versions – which were based on the Taiwan version – were appearing in the Mainland Chinese market. This was direct infringement of the legal rights of the author, Simon & Schuster and Yilin Press. In its urge to outrace the pirates, Yilin Press did not have time to seek consent from Simon & Schuster of the technical treatment it had made. Yilin was trying to publish the work as soon as possible because this was in the interest of all three parties.[17]

The Deputy Editor-in-Chief of Yilin Press, Liu Feng, also blamed the black market of pirated books for Yilin's failure to seek consent:

> Mrs. Clinton's book had been translated hurriedly because Yilin as the official publisher had to compete against China's vigorous black market in unauthorized versions of best-selling books. As such […] Yilin had no time to discuss changes with Simon & Schuster. (Kahn 2003)

After receiving the official complaint letter from Simon & Schuster, the Chinese publisher still maintained only a small number of technical changes were made, although it expressed sincere regrets for not having sought consent from Simon & Schuster.

## 2. Lessons learned

The worldwide success of *Living History* is testimony to the everlasting appeal of sex, money, and politics. Entitling her memoir *Living History*, Hillary Clinton seeks to engage the reader with her agenda – a commitment to women's issues, health reform, human rights and Third-World aid, in spite of insurmountable political conditions. But all this has marginal value to many of her prospective readers, whose primary aim was to get her version of her husband's sex scandals. To a certain extent the *Living History* episode represented the political entanglement between Mainland China and the US. Leaders of both countries are strong in their own beliefs, but they also recognise the necessity of their strategic partnership. The US government is as keen to enter the Mainland Chinese market as are powerful celebrities like the Clintons. For some patriotic Americans, though, reading a distorted version of their former First Lady's memoir is worse than not having read it at all.

On 13 Sept 2003, Ross Terrill published in the *New York Times* a commentary entitled 'China Censors a Senator':

> Even if they [Mainland Chinese readers] are aware the book has been edited by the thought police, they are in the position of not knowing what "anti-China" sentences have been excised, which is almost worse than having no book in their hands at all. ... The 'Living History' episode suggests backsliding. We're talking about a United States senator here, and the tampering with 'Living History' is so blatant that the Chinese must have known she would find out. Here is the nub of the issue: foreign opinion, even that of the Clintons, is less important to Beijing than keeping its grip over the minds of its citizens. China's post-Mao openness to the world, an economic strategy, remains contradicted by its fear of a free flow of non-economic information reaching the ears and eyes of the people. Citizens of the People's Republic are trusted with their money but not their minds. (Terril 2003)

In post-Mao Mainland China, state control is decentralised and one can no longer identify a direct link between censorship and the regime. Intervention in cultural production comes from various directions. Terrill himself is a victim of discriminative translation in the PRC. His biography of Jiang Qing, the 'Chinese First Lady' and wife of Chairman Mao, was published in Mainland China in the 1980s without his permission or any contract. The positive references to Jiang Qing in his book were cut out, 'In the bowdlerized version, Jiang Qing appeared responsible for all Mao's failings' (*ibid.* 2003). His discourse in the quote above is representative of some Americans who believe their government should stand firm against Communist China. His criticism of Mainland Chinese government is valid but he underestimates the power of a huge but chaotic market economy in shaping the publishing industry. In today's Mainland China, self-censorship has replaced state sanction as the form of information control. Liu Feng, Deputy Editor-in-Chief of Yilin Press, revealed that the changes in the simplified Chinese version of *Living History* were not made upon government censorship or guidance, because "Most state-owned media companies are not subject to advance censorship, though they can be held responsible if they publish something deemed offensive to the leadership" (Kahn 2003).

One lesson from *Living History*, a case of translation and conflict, is the overriding force of market over politics. In the name of readership, or business, a publisher can alter the content, value, or significance of a text in translation. Now the market can be used as an excuse, or gateway, to bypass political agendas. It has become difficult to discern whether an act of censorship is made on political grounds or mere commercial convenience. Being a powerful state-owned publisher, Yilin Press occupies an advantageous position in securing translation projects of bestsellers from the West. In theory it should be guarding state interests and act as an ideological watchdog. However its editorial policy seemed to be driven more by business than a concern for any form of correctness. When it has bought the copyright of a foreign work, it produces the translation within a short frame of time. There is evidence it has forsaken translation quality for quick release. An example is the translation of *The Lord of the Rings*, which "was severely panned by some Tolkien fans, who even called for a boycott against the Yilin edition in several Chinese fantasy websites".[18]

Despite the rows over *Living History*, Yilin Press was still granted the rights to translate Bill Clinton's memoir, *My Life* (Alfred A. Knopf, June 2004). Robert Barnett, the lawyer in charge of Clinton's work, insisted that Yilin Press sign an agreement which entitled him to examine and return any problematic Chinese translations. His position is clear and strong in this statement, "Either give a full rendering of Clinton's book, or not having a single Chinese translation of it".[19] It is beyond the scope of this paper to investigate how effective this pre-emptive measure is in terms of securing a 'faithful' translation of Bill Clinton's work. In any case a hard fact remains: whether it is the Chinese press or the American publisher, it is money, not politics that dictate the world of publishing.

Yilin Press has not done justice to the author Hillary Clinton; it has not treated the translators fairly either. In presenting the simplified Chinese version as work of six Taiwan translators without acknowledging the changes made, it has violated the intellectual property of those translators. The general lack of respect of authorship in Mainland China can be explained by its recent history. The late Chairman Mao was sceptical of intellectuals and scornful of 'intellectual property'. Destruction of the gentry class was one prime target of the Cultural Revolution (1966-1976). When the political wind changed for the reformers in the late 1970s, a tight grip remained on the publishing industry. While the regime welcomed an influx of foreign goods it remained cautious of cultural artifacts from the West. The culture of respecting authorship is slowly being built but it will take a long while to impact on the publishing industry. The current economic condition, in conjunction with a lack of legal infrastructure, puts the rights and integrity of translators in question and their works at risk of infringement. As long as there is quick money to be made and the enforcement of law is lax, the Chinese book market will continue to be plagued by careless or illegal publications.

There is no innocence in cross-cultural interaction. In the twenty-first century, when the momentum of the PRC to outperform the US gathers more force, the former will find itself gaining more negotiation power over the latter. To understand the entanglement between these two big brothers, one can begin by investigating what, how and why translations between the two disparate societies occur. Hillary Clinton, based on her set of ideological values, disapproves of her book's Mainland Chinese version. She could take a clean moral ground in writing the book because she could leave the (sometimes ugly) business of disseminating the book in translations in the hand of her lawyer and publisher. Whether she can stop it or not, the Mainland Chinese readers who have read her book would nevertheless form their own view of her life. It was not ethical for Yilin Press to censor her work but in practice the censorship has probably helped sales as the Chinese readers are not shown her more critical interpretation of the Communist regime.

But politics and money walk hand-in-hand, as was proved when, in spite of the *Living History* fiasco, Bill Clinton's publisher still sold the translation copyright of his book, *My Life,* to Yilin Press. This is an example of a commanding US politician yielding to the temptation of conquering the world's biggest consumer market – and we can be sure that it probably won't be the last.

---

1 I would like to thank especially Carolyn Ford, who informs me on the US military culture; Yuchueh Chung, for her first-hand experience in translating *Living History*; and Shukang Ku, for alerting me of the reception and debates surrounding *Living History* in Taiwan.
2 Statistics show that in the last 20 years, the economy of the PR of China has grown at an annual rate of almost 10 percent.
3 'Veterans see ethics lost in translation' in *China Daily* (12 November 2004).
4 'Translation Sector Big But Not Strong' in *China Daily* (10 November 2004).
5 Interview of Xu Jun, Dean of the Department of Western Studies in Nanjing University, PRC. See 'Translation Sector Big But Not Strong' in *China Daily* (10 November 2004).
6 Sun Limei, 'Xi Lali jihua lai hua Mmi zizhuan' ('Hillary plans to visit China to sell her memoir') in *Xinwen Wanbao* (25 August 2003).
7 On 16 August 2003, a week after the official translation was published, a report suggested there were already 4 pirated versions, one of which was asking for a higher price than the authentic version. The four pirated versions are *Huochu Lishi: Xi Lali Huiyilu* (published by

Shijie Zhishi Chubanshe); *Huo Zai Lishi: Xi Lali Huiyilu* (published by Yuanfang Chubanshe); *Huochu Lishi: Xi Lali Huiyilu* (published by Yanbian Renmin Chubanshe) This paperback carries the name of its translators (Luo Lin, Li Yimin, Liu Minshan) and it is more expensive than the hardback official version; *Qinli Lishi: Xi Lali Huiyilu* (in the name of Yilin Press, with very similar covers and format; the printer's name was changed from the legitimate one of 'Nanjing Aide Yinshua Youxian Gongsi' to 'Nanjing Maide Yinshua Youxian Gongsi') See Cao Feng's article 'Shushi Chuxian "Xin Qixiang"' ('New Phenomenon" in the Book Publishing Industry') in *Xiandai Kuabao*,16 August 2003. On 13 September 2003, another report suggested there were altogether 6 pirated versions. See '*Qinli Lishi* Daoban Zeng Zhi Liu Zhong: Zang Zude Tanyan Chachu Kunnan' ('Pirated *Living History* has increased to six versions: Zang Zude admits it's difficult to track down and punish the pirates'), in *Beijing Yule Xinxi Bao* (13 September 2003).
8 'Hillary's Autobiography Sells Like Hot Cakes' in *China Daily* (12 August 2003).
9 Li Ying 'Xi Lali Huiyilu Liang Xiaoshi Mai Chu Wubai Ben 'Hilary's memoir sells 500 copies in 2 hours') in *Beijing Yule Xinxi Bao* (8 August 2003).
10 All back translations are mine.
11 The Chinese text:
  Wu Hongda beibu de xiaoxi yuanben buhui shoudao Meiguo meiti de taiduo guanzhu. Danshi Zhongguo yijing huoxuan wei Lianheguo di si jie funv dahui de zhubanguo, wo ye zhunbei yi Meiguo daibiaotuan rongyu zhuxi de shenfen canjia jijiang zhaokai de dahui.
12 The Chinese text:
  Youxie guojia danxin zheci dahui hui biancheng guchui tamen suo fandui de funv quanli de yige guoji jiangtan, yanli fandui duotai de Fandigang ze he zhexie guojia jiecheng lianhe zhenxian.
13 See the untitled document in Simon & Schuster website:
http://www.simonsays.com/extras/html/LivingHistory/LivingHistoryPressRelease.htm
14 *Crackpot Chronicles*, http://ellensander.com/2004_01_01_cp_archive.html
15 'Hillary's Autobiography Sells Like Hot Cakes' in *China Daily* (12 August 2003).
16 'Yili Chubanshe Chengqing *Xi Lali Huiyilu* Jiufen' ('Yilin Press clarifies on the dispute over the publication of Hilary's Memoir') in *Zhongguangwang* (28 September 2003).
17 See Yuan Nan 'Yilin She Chengqing "Shangai Jiufen"' ('Yilin Press clarifies on "Disputes over omission"') in *Yangzi Wanbao* (28 September 2003).
18 'Veterans see ethics lost in translation' in *China Daily* (12 November 2004).
19 'Qinzi Shencha Huiyilu Zhongwen Ban' ('Personally checking the Chinese version of memoir'), in *Beijing Qingnian Zhoukan* (16 June 2004). On line at: http://book.sina.com.cn/news/b/2004-06-16/3/76326.shtml

## References:
*Texts in English*
Clinton, Hillary Rodham. 2003. *Living History*. New York: Simon & Schuster Inc., London: Headline Book Publishing.
  Taiwan Translation. 2003: *Huochu Lishi: Xi La Rui Huiyilu*. Taipei: China Times Publishing Company.
  PRC Translation. 2003. *Qinli lishi: Xi La Li Huiyilu*. Nanjing: Yilin Press.
*Crackpot Chronicles*, http://ellensander.com/2004_01_01_cp_archive.html (consulted 10.04.2006).
Dai, Sijie. 2002. *Balzac and the Little Chinese Seamstress*. London: Vintage.
Editorial, 'Bill Clinton Fake Chinese Life' in *The New York Times* (24 October 2004).
'Hillary's Autobiography Sells Like Hot Cakes' in *China Daily* (12 August 2003).
Kahn, Joseph. 2003. 'Clinton History Doesn't Repeat Itself in China' in *The New York Times* (24 September 2003).

Terrill, Ross. 2003. 'China Censors a Senator' in *The New York Times* (13 Sept 2003).
'Translation Sector Big But Not Strong' in *China Daily* (10 November 2004).
http://www.simonsays.com/extras/html/LivingHistory/LivingHistoryPressRelease.htm. Untitled document on Simon & Schuster website announcing the availability of Chinese translations of deleted parts in the simplified Chinese version (consulted 10.04.2006).
'Veterans See Ethics Lost in Translation' in *China Daily* (12 November 2004).

*On-line Chinese texts (all consulted 10.04.2006):*
Cao Feng 曹锋 '书市出现"新气象"'《现代快报》 (16 August 2003). On line at: http://www.yilin.com/cn/news/news.asp?id=1426
Li Ying 李瑛 '希□ 拉里自传频遭侵权，译林社向《参考消息》讨说法'《北京娱乐信报》 (22 July 2003). On line at: http://www.yilin.com/cn/news/News.asp?p=2&id=1284
Sun Limei 孙立梅, '希□ 拉里计划来华卖自传'《新闻晚报》 (25 August 2003). On line at: http://www.yilin.com/cn/news/news.asp?id=1470
'《亲历历史》盗版增至6种： 章祖德坦言查处困难'《北京娱乐信息报》 (13 September 2003). On line at: http://www.yilin.com/cn/forum/default.asp?menu=7&board=1000
'译林出版社澄清《希□ 拉里回忆录》纠纷'《中广网》 (28 September 2003). On line at: http://www.yilin.com/cn/news/news.asp?id=1659
'克林顿自传将闪亮登场 《我的生活》出炉前后'《北京青年周刊》 (16 June 2004). On line at: http://book.sina.com.cn/news/b/2004-06-16/3/76326.shtml
Yuan Nan 袁楠 '译林社为保护独家中文版权而□ 战'《中华读书报》 (23 July 2003). On line at: http://www.yilin.com/cn/news/News.asp?p=2&id=1304
'译林社澄清"删改纠纷"',《扬子晚报》 (28 September 2003). On line at: http://www.yilin.com/cn/news/news.asp?id=1658
A proviso in the contract for Clinton's autobiography. On line at: http://book.sina.com.cn/news/b/2004-06-16/3/76326.shtml
An interview with one of the translators of Bill Clinton's autobiography in China. On-line at: http://book.sina.com.cn/1094809492_mylife/2004-10-18/3/116098.shtml
News regarding *Living History* from its official publisher, Yilin: http://www.yilin.com/cn/specia

# Part IV

# Translation and Conflict Awareness

# Encounters with Cross-Cultural Conflicts in Translation

*Jun Tang*

Drawing on the distinction in translation between soft and hard conflicts, this paper contends that in dealing with soft conflicts, conflict fluency is the preferred strategy for Chinese-English translators, whilst non-interference is the favoured option for those who work into Chinese. With regard to potential hard conflicts conflict fluency is an essential. A translator requires mindful awareness of potential conflicts and cultural difference, but beyond this there are no identifiable off the peg optimal solutions, and the individual has his/her own way in tackling intercultural conflicts.

Key words: cross-cultural conflicts; translation

It is accepted in Translation Studies that translation is a trans-cultural project that travels between languages and cultures and brings about encounters between different values, viewpoints, and ideologies (Lefevere and Bassnett 2001; Snell-Hornby 2001, etc.). This implies that translation can be a site of conflicts and misunderstandings as well as one of communication and understanding.

This essay explores the influences of conflicts in a translational context on the production of translated versions as regards the direction of translation and the asymmetrical power relations between cultures. It examines the performance of conflict-conscious and conflict-unconscious translators by analyzing examples of contemporary Chinese-English and English-Chinese translations.

## 1. Culture, Translation and Conflicts

Culture, being a sense-making, viewpoint-forming and behaviour-determining system, can be defined as "a set of internalized understandings and ways of interacting with the world" (LeBaron 2003: 42). Snell-Hornby has rightfully contended that

> The concept of culture as a totality of knowledge, proficiency and perception is fundamental in our approach to translation. If language is an integral part of culture, the translator needs not only proficiency in two languages, he must also be at home in two cultures. In other words, he must be bilingual and bicultural. (Snell-Hornby 2001: 42)

In this sense, translation is regarded as a process offering "a means of studying cultural interaction" (Lefevere and Bassnett 2001: 6), and a translator is regarded as a mediator or communicator between cultures, which means that the translator must manipulate differences, whether they concern fusion, infiltration, recognition, understanding, acculturation or tension, constraints, hatred and hostility. Said (1993: xxv) has noted that in our age, "all cultures are involved in one another; none is single and pure, all are hybrid, heterogeneous, extraordinarily differentiated, and unmonolithic". This is the natural outcome of the accumulative influences of countless translated versions on their respective target cultures, the drive for which comes from no other than the conflicts in translation because paradoxically, it is conflicts that upset the conceit of a culture in most cases. Being confronted with conflicts, a closed culture may be jolted out of its former narcissistic illusion or purposeful isolation in the end. In this respect, translators and translations play an indispensable role in manipulating conflicts and bringing about deeper understanding between cultures.

The word *conflict* conjures up negative associations - displeasure, discomfort, hurt feelings, loss of face, hostility and violence, etc. In the cultural arena "Conflict need not be openly acknowledged or named to be real", "but it must be felt and experienced before it takes on form" (LeBaron 2003: 28).

Though cultural conflict derives from cultural differences, it "does not emerge from every difference "[...] Only when some aspect of our differences becomes salient and nudges the way we hold our identity or meaning does difference translate into conflict" (*ibid.*). Once a potential cultural conflict becomes apparent then it cannot be ignored.

According to LeBaron (*ibid.:* 117-134), the management of cultural conflict involves four steps: naming, framing, blaming and taming. Naming will determine whether a conflict can be labeled as such, whether or not it is acknowledged. Framing refers to delimitation of the form, site and those parties involved in a conflict. Blaming includes all the approaches and decision processes that help to resolve the problems caused by such a conflict. Taming indicates the settlement or removing of a conflict. This four-step method is helpful in the sense that it reminds us to check the source of a conflict before we decide to do something about it when cross-cultural transmission in translation is concerned.

As LeBaron has suggested, in this global age, our world needs more than goodwill and well-meaning intentions to deal with the many kinds of conflicts which can arise. These can stem from differences in cultural tradition, system of values, ideological tendencies, and the like. Because of the cultural specificity of translation as cross-cultural communication, shapes and forms taken on by conflicts in a translational context must be analysed separately.

A variety of types of cross-cultural conflicts such as cultural, social and ideological ones can be found in a translational context. These conflicts form a continuum, ranging from a minimum of inner tension of an individual involved in the process of translation to a war or an outbreak of violence. In this sense, conflicts in translation are not always explicit and conspicuous.

A conflict can be termed a *soft* conflict if resentment on the part of the receiving audience of a given translation is kept private and invisible or, even though the resentment is shown, the disagreement is not serious enough to induce formal display of displeasure by making public speeches, publicizing various forms of writing, or resorting to force. On the other hand, a conflict can be termed a *hard* conflict if it incites social reactions not only from independent individuals but also from members of one or more than one social group or power institution, or more people on a larger scale, and the negative sentiment is no longer suppressed.

If agreement on this classification of soft and hard conflicts is reached, it can be safely said that a soft conflict is more likely to be found in a translational context that involves either literary, academic, or legal texts, or in audiovisual, advertising, or other practical products such as travel brochures, documents for the local branches of multinationals, and manuals for electronic products. If the target culture is subordinate in comparison with the source, then cultural concessions are usually expected from the receiving audience, so even if a translator foresees potential soft conflicts, s/he may choose to do nothing. Explanations are provided in the endnotes or footnotes at best where the translator sees fit. If the target culture is a dominant one, the translator may attempt to minimize or eliminate possible conflicts, unless there is a good reason for him or her to leave them alone or to highlight the textual segments that might provoke conflicts. Sometimes, soft conflicts in a translational context may rouse verbal or written objection, or even invite interference of censorship, which may facilitate the transformation of soft conflicts into hard ones. But later changes in the indigenous ideological climate may tell a different story. Also, there are times when the source author is displeased with the rewriting or omitting strategies adopted by a translator to diminish, minimize or eliminate possible soft conflicts. The author may express his or her displeasure openly, and this has nothing to do with the status of a language or culture.

Hard conflicts are more likely to arise when translation concerns international affairs or diplomatic events. Hard conflicts are often easily provoked by translational misinformation or misunderstanding at press conferences, during public speeches made by national leaders, or on similar occasions. It follows that sometimes, translation plays a part in building up ill-grounded hostility towards and misconception of another country or an immigrant community as an enemy or adversary; other times, translation sends false messages of compromise or concession. Since the linguistic competence and the political awareness of translators vary, it is possible for a translator to overlook or ignore a potential hard conflict and fail to present it properly in the translated version. Also, a translator may wish to avoid a hard conflict and choose to make changes or omissions against the wish or demand of the source author, the speaker, or the target audience. Such a choice is usually greeted by protest or objection because, generally, people wish to make potential hard conflicts known as it is one of the most effective ways to raise a problem or to display their discontent.

Even if s/he has sufficient goodwill to avoid a conflict in his or her professional practice, the translator is not always required to minimize or remove the conflict.

## 2. Globalization, Soft Conflicts and Translation in China

"Globalization is generally perceived as the result of the collapse of Soviet-style socialism, as well as the unprecedented expansion of transnational capitalism" (Liu 1998: 164). Against this context, the transnational flow of products, technology, capital and information has set up the site for the confrontation of different values, fashions, life styles, and ideological tendencies of different cultures, which gives expression to new forms of conflicts and frictions between the self and the other or the local and the global. It is in this sense that Fredric Jameson has claimed that "globalization is a communicational concept, which alternatively masks and transmits cultural or economic meanings" (Jameson 1998: 55).

It is unsurprising in this global age to find that China is caught between two conflicting pressures: the cultural domination of foreign elements over the indigenous on the material level and the desire to preserve traditional Chinese culture. What a translator chooses to do, no matter how seemingly trivial, may have far-reaching consequences because the intermediary role of translation activities determines the interactions between foreign and native elements on all of the three levels of culture—material, institutional, and spiritual.

In China, as elsewhere, people's views on *globalization* are divided. Some regard it as an economic phenomenon connected with development of the local economy, progress towards global unification, and the narrowing of the economic gap between developing and developed districts. Others emphasise negative aspects, such as the big powers' economic exploitation, cultural domination and political hegemony over less developed nations. The position which a translator adopts can be crucial with regard to the selection of a text to be translated, the choice of translational strategies and devices, or the potential impact of the translation. Translators' choices may have ideological implications for the changes or fluctuations in the social life of a given culture.

Both soft and hard conflicts in translation pose challenges for translators sandwiched between Chinese and Western cultures, as ideas and values in the two cultures differ widely. But nobody can deny that numerous Chinese versions of Western texts have contributed to many social changes in contemporary China, most of which have been motivated by soft conflicts foreseen yet left alone in cases of English-Chinese translation. This widely accepted strategy of inaction on potential soft conflicts, which has been followed by most translators since the reform and opening up of China in 1979, actually expects the Chinese audience to be cooperative in the cultural process of shedding its old self.

As a result, ongoing social changes can be observed in almost every aspect of Chinese culture, including customs, life styles, values or outlooks on life, moral principles, ways of thinking, legal practices, and the norms of scholarly writing. Any Chinese citizen born before the 1980s has witnessed and experienced the foregoing changes. Activated by the desire to share the same discourse as the Western world in fields such as law, science, finance and business, many changes and reforms concerning norms, practice, terminology, and so on have been initiated by professional translations in these fields. Influenced by the large number of translations of Western audiovisual products, the Chinese no longer stick to the thrifty life style which had previously been cherished as a part of the Confucian heritage. Parents of young persons no longer overreact to premarital sex, and a divorce is no longer regarded a shameful thing or scandal that needs to be discouraged at all costs by family members, close friends, or even immediate superiors of those parties directly involved. Fascinated by adaptation of translated versions of Western commercials and audiovisual products incorporated as part of the marketing efforts of local businesses ever since the 1980s, nowadays an urban bride usually wears a Western-style white wedding dress on her wedding ceremony instead of a traditional red gown and an urban resident will celebrate his or her birthday by the side of a candled birthday cake rather than a bowl of traditional birthday noodles. Acculturated by the translations of Western literary works (canonical and popular) as well as audiovisual products, Chinese people's aesthetic taste for architecture, household decoration, and even feminine or masculine beauty have changed.

One of the distinctive features of globalization is the dawning of the era of cultural consumption on a global scale which is characterized by the centralization of popular cultural products and the decentralization of elite cultural products, which overturns and disorders traditional value systems. China is undergoing wide cultural transformation, replacing the old value system with a plurality or diversification of values, and a translator has to tackle problems sensitively.

There is a notable contrast between the large number of translations of English source texts into Chinese and the small number of translations of

Chinese source texts into English. Furthermore most of the English texts which are translated into Chinese could be categorised as either having English canonical literature as their source or else stem from popular culture. By contrast the small number of Chinese texts translated into English originate, in the main, either from Chinese canonical literature or from introductory or informative pieces about China. This can be explained as a function of differences in status between Chinese culture and the Anglo-American counterparts. Though the Chinese-speaking population is large, Chinese culture is much less influential than are the cultures of English-speaking nations.

This gulf in status between the cultures determines the wide variation in the number of translations initiated in the different language directions. It can be seen that as English culture is so dominant the underlying purpose of many Chinese-English translations is to win recognition or understanding for Chinese culture. Conversely the West provides a variety of models representing dominant ideologies of the Anglo-American countries. Many English-Chinese translations are initiated to exert influences or induce change. Thus, the large number of publications of translations of English source texts into Chinese falls into two categories. Either the source text refers to popular cultural products - and thus serves as the vanguard of cultural infiltration, or else the text appertains to Western canonical literature - so serving as the vehicle of Anglo-American ideology. On the other hand, English translations of Chinese canonical texts and introductory or informative pieces are performed in the main for the exportation of Chinese cultural elements, in order to allow Western readers to obtain a wider understanding of Chinese culture.

A more fundamental reason for the glaring discrepancy between the number of translations which take place in each language direction lies in the difference in the distribution of cultural and educational attainment between the populations of the two cultures. If the readers of a given culture are grouped by their level of education (i.e. low, medium, or high), the shape of the cultural distribution mode of China can be compared to that of a pyramid - those with low levels of education are positioned at the bottom, medium levels in the middle, and readers with high levels of education on the top[1]. China has only had a modern educational system for little more than 100 years[2]. This pyramid shape to a Chinese model of cultural distribution means that translations must be adapted to the cultural needs of the majority of readers, who have relatively low levels of education. Most of the texts themselves are connected to commercial or recreational cultural products.

The shape of the mode of cultural distribution in Anglo-American countries can be compared to that of an olive or oval. The relatively small number of readers with low levels of education are positioned at the bottom, the majority of readers with medium levels of education are in the middle, and the minority who have high levels of education are on the top. This 'olive' shaped model means that the translations of Chinese texts can be targeted at Anglo-American readers with medium levels of education. Professionally accomplished, satisfied with their social status, and well-educated, they turn to translations of foreign texts out of sheer curiosity or for professional ends.

The so-called Chinese situation of 'cultural deficit' as regards the dominance in production of English-Chinese translations over Chinese-English ones will be difficult to change because both the Chinese 'pyramid' shaped model of cultural distribution and the Western 'olive' shaped model are relatively stable and help to consolidate the cultural mentality on a national scale. Besides, the imbalance of translation production is further guaranteed in English-speaking countries because the olive-shaped model is more resistant to external pressure. China could not hope to balance the cultural deficit of its ill-educated masses in the near future. This implies that translations of canonical literary texts must cater for the prevailing tastes of Western readers, whilst the selection of Western popular cultural texts to be translated should consider the impact of possible cultural domination on ideological tendencies.

## 3. Soft Conflicts and Chinese-English Translations

In a translational context, soft conflicts often derive from cultural differences in value systems, social conventions and ways of thinking. If the target culture is dominant, then the translator will have to handle the target text carefully to minimise potential problems of miscomprehension, cultural discomfort or resistance on the part of the receiver. Notwithstanding the fact that the source text may appear to be purpose-free, the translating act and target text are purpose-bound, and any translation must fulfill specific functions. Cultural discomfort, uneasiness or misunderstandings and unnecessary hatred or enmity are to be minimized in the target version.

In most cases translators who work from Chinese to English normally attempt to bridge or eliminate soft conflicts, but in contrast their peers who perform English-Chinese translations tend to maintain soft conflicts for Chinese culture to digest. I wish to discuss the challenges, possibilities and opportunities of the removal of soft conflicts, and consequently the present section will only deal with Chinese-English translations.

In 2002 I was asked by a friend to translate her application form for immigration to Canada. She hoped to join her husband there, who had been a Canadian citizen for several years by that time. The problem was that their case bore little resemblance to the Western concept of marriage for love's sake, if the translation was 'faithful', as required. I would like to cite a 'truthful' presentation of her answers to some of the questions on the form:

Q1: Did anyone introduce you to your sponsor? Describe the circumstances of this introduction.
A1: She was an old friend of our parents, and had been their colleague for more than 30 years. She knew the two families very well so that she introduced my husband in person to me with our parents' permission.
Q2: Was there a formal engagement ceremony?
A2: China has no tradition that requires a formal engagement ceremony. When our parents learned of our marriage plan, they arranged a gathering of the two families on September $22^{nd}$ (photos are enclosed). But we did celebrate our engagement and went out with his parents on October $22^{nd}$ (photos are enclosed) when my husband flew in from Canada in October.
Q3: Was there a traditional/customary marriage ceremony?
A3: Since my husband was too busy and only had two weeks for holiday, we did not have enough time to prepare for a traditional marriage ceremony, which should be held both at my husband's hometown—Tai'an, Shandong Province, and at my hometown—Shanghai. Besides, my husband's brother, who lives in Singapore, and my sister, who lives in Australia, wish to attend our wedding ceremony. Therefore, we decided to withhold the ceremony until September, next year, since our brother and sister will be able to come back then, and my husband will get a long holiday at that time.
Q4: Did you and your sponsor live together?
A4: We took our marriage certificate on November $1^{st}$, 2002 to become a lawful married couple. But because my husband had to go back to Canada on November $3^{rd}$, we didn't have much time to live together. But we do wish to be together again as soon as possible.

The details she was asked to provide gave the impression that they had only been together for a very short period of time before they got married, and the marriage was the result of mutual approval on the part of her and her husband's parents. Though this marriage may be understood by an immigration officer as a marriage of convenience, the case is anything but a rarity for a young Chinese person.

Lin Yutang (2000: 173), a famous writer of the 1920s, wrote about the traditional Chinese view of marriage as follows:

> It [The traditional sense of family honour in China] takes the right of contracting marriage from our hands and gives it to those of our parents; it makes us marry, not wives but 'daughters-in-law,' and it makes our wives give birth, not to children but to 'grandchildren'.

A marriage in China is not a matter concerning just two people: it also involves both families. Chinese young people have had the final say about marriage since 1949, but to marry against their parents' will is still regarded by the majority of the population as unblessed and unnatural. This fact simply reflects what is considered natural and acceptable in a culture where the word *love* had been almost always replaced by *like* until a little more than two decades ago. Those born since the 1980s react differently to the word, and are no longer too shy or conservative to avoid its usage. But there are many who stick to tradition and shrink from explicit expressions of love. My friend does love her husband, despite the fact that they haven't known each other for long, nor have been together long enough in the eyes of Westerners, and she believes that the permission and support of their parents legitimises their love. Parental opinion regarding marriage is highly regarded, as both wise and reliable, taking into account character, disposition, and background.

Given the difference between the Western and Chinese views about love and marriage, I realised that there would be much less chance of her fulfilling her dream of a reunion with her husband if the translation was performed 'faithfully'. So I explained the situation to her, discussing the conflicts in values and ideas between the two cultures, and I rewrote her answers according to Western style. This was the final version:

> Q1: Did anyone introduce you to your sponsor? Describe the circumstances of this introduction.
> A1: Yes. The introducer was a family friend, and she thought we were made for each other. Then we met as arranged and I was deeply impressed by him at the first sight.
> Q2: Was there a formal engagement ceremony?
> A2: No, there wasn't. For most Chinese young people leading a city life, a formal engagement ceremony is not necessary or indispensable. But we did go on a tour of Jiuzhai Valley, a famous scenic spot of China, to celebrate our engagement.
> Q3: Was there a traditional/customary marriage ceremony?
> A3: No, there wasn't. But we've decided to make up for it in September, next year, since our friends and relatives insist that a ceremony will brighten up our married life.
> Q4: Did you and your sponsor live together?
> A4: I don't think that there's any logical connection between living together and a happy marriage. There are married bedfellows who mean nothing to each other, and there are people who cannot be separated from their beloved ones even by death. But if my application for immigration is granted as soon as possible, my husband and I will be spared the torture of a life without each other's presence.

One day in June, 2003, my friend let me know that she had been allowed to join her husband in Canada, and thanked me for my strategy. Of course, my translation is more a piece of rewriting which eliminated potential soft conflicts that could arise from different cultural values regarding love and marriage, and tilts completely in favour of the predetermined function of the translated version rather than being an accurate translation in the widely accepted sense of the word.

In real life, practical calculations demand various degrees of rewriting. Several years ago, an Osmanthus-Flower Festival was held in Shanghai, and its promotion leaflet read:

> *Manshu jinhua, fangxiangsiyi de Jingui; huabai ruxue, xiangqipubi de Yingui; honglitouhuang, huaduo weinong de Zishagui; huase siyin, jiji youhua de Sijigui; jingxiangkaifang, zhengyapimi. Jinru Guilingongyuan, zhenzhen guihuaxiang pubi erlai.*
>
> [Golden Osmanthus is covered with golden flowers that scent the air with their fragrance; Silvery Osmanthus has snow-white flowers that greet people's nostrils with sweet smell; Zisha Osmanthus has the color of red tinged with yellow, and is thick with blossoms that give out heady perfume; Siji Osmanthus has silvery flowers that bloom every season. All the osmanthus flowers are in full bloom and vie for each other for

143

supremacy in beauty. When you enter Guilin Park, you will be met with the aroma of osmanthus flowers.][3]

The exaggerated and verbose style of writing was adopted to highlight the rich colour and fragrant smell of the osmanthus flowers. The Chinese language is perceptual, relatively tolerant of original variations in style and grammar and can accept exaggeration and redundancy. English prefers logic and concision, which makes a word-for-word translation from Chinese look like a combination of broken and ill-organized sentences. Because of the differences between the English and Chinese languages, a conservative translator may do some minor rewriting in his or her translation by omitting unnecessary modifiers and intensifying the logical structure in this way:

> All kinds of osmanthus flowers vie with each other: there are the golden and fragrant Jingui, the silvery and sweet smelling Yingui, the Zishagui thick with flowers characterized by the red color tinged with yellow, and the white Sijigui blooming every season. Guilin Park is perfumed with these flowers.

But a more adventurous translator may perform a significant degree of rewriting, focusing on relevant and important elements:

> Guilin Park is perfumed with all kinds of sweet smelling osmanthus flowers: golden Jingui, silvery Yingui, white Sijigui and Zishagui whose color is red tinged with yellow.

Of course, nothing in translation is absolute, and there are times when potential soft conflicts are too trivial to be dealt with. What must be noted is that the translator often plays the role of the dog wagged by its tail and succumbs to practical calculations in order to achieve the expected function of his or her translation.

## 4. Hard Conflicts and Translation

Generally speaking in a translational context, hard conflicts usually arise from differences in political positions or ideological tendencies. In most cases concerning political or ideological elements, the author or the speaker would not thank the translator for his or her rewriting, for fear that the translator should come up with a distorted version. The situation is often complicated if the translator is insensitive to potential hard conflicts and has created a translation that misuses strategies and induces ideologically significant miscommunication. In fact, a translator or an interpreter must be politically or ideologically sensitive or s/he may fail or commit mistakes in translating written or oral texts carrying political or ideological implications.

In 2001, the former Chinese Premier Zhu Rongji presided over a press conference. During the press conference, a Taiwanese reporter suggested that

> ...*huozheshi xiang qunian xiaban'nian qianfuzongli shuode na'yang, dalu he tanwan tong shuyu yige zhongguo, jiushi yong geng you tanxing de fangshi lai jieshi*

*yigezhongguo*

> [...or to adopt a more flexible way to explain the concept of one-China just as Vice-Premier Qian said in the second half of last year that mainland and Taiwan are two parts of China]

What the Taiwanese reporter implied by "a flexible way to look at the one-China principle" is to regard mainland and Taiwan as two parts of equal importance, which may be viewed as another presentation of *two-China* proposed by the provincial government. The political division is that the Chinese government views Taiwan as a province of China, but not a geo-political counterpart, while the provincial government of Taiwan insists that Taiwan is a sovereign or an independent nation[4]. The interpreter failed to perceive the implication in the original question, and missed the target in interpretation:

> Or, could you explain and interpret the one-China principle more flexibly to bring about the breaking of the deadlock? For instance, in the latter half of last year, Vice-Premier Qian Qichen has stated that there is but one China in the world, mainland and Taiwan are parts of one China and China's sovereignty and integrity brook no division, could such moves help solve the problem?

This translation failed as it expressed goodwill that was not in the original, such as in the phrases "to bring about the breaking of the deadlock" and "could such moves help solve the problem". Furthermore the translator obscured hidden meaning in the question—would Zhu accept "a more flexible way to look at the one-China principle"? This would, if it were to be confirmed, be a considerable political concession on the part of mainland China. This kind of mistake is diplomatically disastrous and politically unforgivable[5], but Zhu denied that there was any difference between Qian's words and those of other Chinese leaders.

Another question raised at the press conference went as follows:

> I noticed in your work report that you included several elements of Jiang Zemin's theories, including the "Three Represents" and Rule by Virtue. Since you are famous for very plain and easy-understanding language, can you explain to us what the Three Represents means to the man on the street and also what Rule by Virtue means as you plan to practice it?

Political awareness can help one to detect a note of challenge hiding behind a seemingly moderate request (i.e. "can you explain to us what the 'Three Represents' means to the man on the street and also what 'Rule by Virtue' means as you plan to practice it") that has been preceded by a compliment (i.e. "you are famous for very plain and easy-understanding language"). The political implications of the question are: Since one of the Three Represents mentions the essential rights of the people, how will the government protect and ensure these rights? In addition, how will you meet the demands of Rule by Virtue in your office?

The Chinese version did not present the challenge to its full because of its simplification of the latter part of the reporter's words—

> ... qingwen duiyu putongren lai jiang, "sange daibiao" dui tamen yiwei zhe shenme, "yi de zhiguo" dui tamen you yiwei zhe shenme?
>
> [...can you explain to us what the Three Represents and Rule by Virtue means to the man in the street?)

But Zhu was sharp enough to get the challenging note in replying

> ... danshi ni rang wo zai zhege difang lai chanming zhege sixiang, woxiang bushi shihou, yexu wo'men xuyao kai yici yantaohui.
>
> But if you want me to explain it at here, I don't think the time is right. Maybe we need to organize a seminar to make things clear.

The interpreter took the edge off the answer once again, by rendering it as "But I don't think today is the fitting occasion for me to give you a thorough elaboration. Perhaps it will need an international seminar for a thorough discussion about the question you have raised". In fact Zhu's "bushi shihou" (literally: "it's not the time") is rather cutting, whilst the interpreter's "I don't think today is the fitting occasion" is too polite to serve as a close equivalent. The following translation would be more accurate: "I'm afraid that at present any attempt to explain is ill-timed and maybe we need to hold a seminar for clarification of ideas."

A more recent example is the Chinese version for Hillary Rodham Clinton's memoirs *Living History* published by Yilin Press in 2003. The changes and omissions made by that version as regards political problems or ideological disagreements displeased Mrs. Clinton considerably, who demanded that the American publisher of the original, Simon & Schuster, should protest to Yilin Press and make them buy back copies which had been sold. The protest was presented as she wished – a translator occupies a space between conflicting political or ideological positions of different cultures, can hardly please all but s/he cannot afford to be insensitive all the time.

**Conclusion**

This essay contends that in a translational context, conflicts can be categorized into soft conflicts and hard ones. Based on this, the influences which conflicts have on the production of translations are explored with reference to the direction of translation and asymmetrical power relations between cultures.

By examining examples of contemporary Chinese-English or English-Chinese translations by conflict-conscious and conflict-unconscious translators, this paper contends that in dealing with soft conflicts, conflict fluency is the favoured policy for translators who work from Chinese, whilst translators who work into Chinese prefer not to interfere.

A conflict-unconscious translator is more likely to commit mistakes or convey misunderstanding, a fact which indicates that awareness of conflicts and cultural differences is an important quality for a translator.

---

1 Statistics show that, until 1997, 2.53% of China's population had received higher education, 9.59% had gone to senior high school, 29.62% to junior high school, 37.56% to elementary school, and 12.11% were illiterate or semi-literate. Since that time Chinese Universities have increased their enrolment levels but the overall picture has not changed.
2 The modern Chinese education system began in 1895 when Tianjin Beiyang College of Western Thoughts (*Tianjin Beiyang Xixue Xuetang*) was established. This became the University of Beiyang in 1896.
3 All translations, unless otherwise attributed, are my own.
4 See "Powell: Taiwan not Sovereign", http://www.foxnews.com/story/0,2933,136711,00.html (consulted March 06).
5 "Explanations on Draft Anti-Secession Law" Online at: http://service.china.org.cn/link/wcm/Show_Text?info_id=122118&p_qry=opposing%20and%20the%20and%20division%20and%20of%20and%20country (consulted August 2006).

## References

China Daily (16 March 2001). "Premier Zhu Meets Reporters". On line at: http://www.chinadaily.net/ highlights/ 2001npc/ news/ 316text.html (consulted 31.03.2001).

Jameson, Fredric. 1998. 'Notes on Globalization as a Philosophical Issue' in Jameson, Fredric, and Masao Miyoshi (eds) *The Cultures of Globalization*. Durham and London: Duke University Press: 54-77.

Jia, Wenbo. 2000. *Chinese-English Translations of Contemporary Texts: Analyses of 300 Translated Sentences on Politics and Economy*. Beijing: China Translation and Publishing Corporation.

LeBaron, Michelle. 2003. *Bridging Cultural Conflicts: A New Approach for a Changing World*. San Francisco: Jossey-Bass.

Lefevere, André, and Susan Bassnett. 2001. 'Introduction: Where are we in Translation Studies?' in Bassnett, Susan and André Lefevere. (ed.) *Constructing Cultures: Essays on Literary Translation*. Shanghai: Shanghai Foreign Language Education Press: 1-11.

Liu, Kang. 1998. 'Is There an Alternative to (Capitalist) Globalization? The Debate about Modernity in China' in Jameson, Fredric, and Masao Miyoshi. (ed.) *The Cultures of Globalization*. Durham and London: Duke University Press: 164-190.

Lin, Yutang. 2000. *My Country and My People*. Beijing: Foreign Language Teaching and Research Press.

Said, Edward W. 1993. *Culture and Imperialism*. New York: Alfred A. Knopf, Inc.

Snell-Hornby, Mary. 2001. *Translation Studies: An Integrated Approach*. Shanghai: Shanghai Foreign Language Education Press.

# Translating Conflict. Advertising in a Globalised Era

*María Calzada Pérez*

We are exposed to an average of 4000 advertising messages a day. Advertising does not promote isolated products any longer, but rather entire ways of life. It concocts identities *à la carte* which consumers buy more or less consciously. It has become a powerful site of ideological conflict(s), and is a highly persuasive means through which world-views are advocated or challenged. This paper consists of three main explorations. In exploration 1, definitions of key terms (i.e. translation, advertising and conflict) are presented and discussed. In exploration 2, some of the links between advertising and conflict are highlighted. In exploration 3, the topic of 'conflict transformation' is dealt with. Among the various forms of conflict transformation 'third party mediation' excels. For recognition, mediators are required to be able to listen, communicate, analyse, evaluate and make decisions. I argue that, due to their cross-cultural tasks and abilities, translators may become ideal conflict mediators. Exploration 3 provides examples of how translators listen to their own mistakes, communicate anthropoemic censorship, analyse anthropophagic censorship and evaluate (and make decisions) about zero translation and monogolossia in the context of both paper and electronic adverts. The paper ends with a discussion of covert colonizing and imperialist patterns of behaviour, their transfer into "other" (non-Anglo Saxon) cultures and the ethical role of translators.

Key words: translation, advertising, conflict, globalization, colonialism, anthropoemic censorship, anthropophagic censorship, monoglossia.

I would like to begin on a cautionary note and quote José Antonio Marina, a contemporary Spanish philosopher, who says:

> Ya sé que la ciencia no debe expresar sentimientos, pero el científico sí. (Marina 2004: 10)
>
> ["I know that science should not express feelings. The scientist, on the contrary, should do."]

Not that Translation Studies (TS) is, in any form, a particular branch of science. Roberto Mayoral (2002), amongst many others, is adamant about this. According to him, Translation Studies is, at most, a kind of technology. For that matter I am not in any way, a scientist, and my paper stems from feelings. Translation, advertising and conflict —like so many other things— are about feelings, those which we experience in the troubled and troublesome globalised world that we inhabit.

Continuing on this cautionary note, I will quote Theo Hermans:

> This is purely an exploratory essay, modest in its aim and scope. It does little more than explore a practical question: whether it is worth investigating in more detail what is best described, in its present state, as a hunch, hardly a hypothesis as yet. (Hermans 1997: 14)

Hermans' work is hardly ever modest in aim and scope. But this paper is indeed exploratory and modest. And it does depart from "a hunch, hardly a hypothesis as yet". The hunch that, as translators, we may contribute to the debate on advertising and conflict. The hunch that probably we should not only attend Translation Studies conferences in order to talk amongst ourselves (interesting though this undoubtedly is), but maybe we should enter other settings, talking to other people from other disciplines, and exploring new ground from the perspective of the translator and the translation scholar.

## Exploration 1

When I started reading for this paper, I was particularly intrigued by the term 'conflict'. I had a reasonable amount of information about 'translation'. My whole training and research revolves around translation – a complex and multifaceted term that has been attributed a wide array of definitions from the 'traditional':

> the rendering of a source text (ST) into the target language (TL) so as to ensure that (1) the surface meaning of the two will be approximately similar and (2) the structures of the ST will be preserved as closely as possible but not so closely that the TL structures will be seriously distorted. (Bassnett 1988: 2)

to the more 'radical':

> ... a parricidal dis-memory [which] intends to erase the origin, to obliterate the original. (Haroldo de Campos in Vieira 1999: 109)

Definitions of 'translation' differ widely - in 1988 Susan Bassnett had written of "conflicting attitudes towards translation" (Bassnett-McGuire 1988: 4). But this conflict seemed to have been settled by the "descriptive turn" in which Translation Studies (TS) views anything regarded as a translation to be one which deserves study. The 'translational conflict' was, in theory (and in theory only), over.

The complexities and strategies of advertising have been approached from numerous fields. Well-known ad producers (Aitchison 1999; Bassat 1993; Robinson 2001; Russell and Lane 1994; Berger 2001), best-selling analysts (Beigbeder 2000; Kilbourne 1999; Klein 2001; Twitchell 2000), inquisitive literary authors (Gopegui 2001), legal experts (Zambrana 2002, Martín el al. 1996), linguists and translation scholars (Bueno 2000; Cook 2001; Pedro

1996; Seguinot 1995; Shakir 1995; Slater 1988; Tanaka 1994; Valdés 1999, 2002a, 2002b), and numerous other researchers have studied advertising from quite dissimilar viewpoints, even 'conflicting' ones, it could be argued. In 2000 Bueno proposed this basic definition:

> Publicidad es un tipo de comunicación que pretende decidir o cambiar la opinión sobre las cosas y la acción de sus receptores por medio de unas técnicas que actúan sobre el intelecto. (Bueno 2000:28)

> [Advertising is a type of communication that attempts to decide or to change receptors' opinions of things and their actions by means of techniques that act upon their intellect.]

Bueno's definition is complemented by others, such as Beasley and Danesi's, who highlight the naturalising power of the advertising genre, which upholds certain practices, whilst abandoning and obliterating other (minoritised and excluded) forms of behaviour:

> We refer to advertising as a form of discourse in the sense that it has influenced not only the structure of language and modality of lifestyle, but also the content of routine daily acts of communicative exchanges. (Beasley and Danesi 2002:16)

It is also the case that researchers focus on a wide range of aspects of advertising. Some researchers such as Rotzoll, emphasize advertising's monetary components: "advertising must first be recognised as paid non-personal communication" (Rotzoll 1985: 94), whilst Cook (2001:9), focusing on the commercial goals, defines it as "the promotion of goods for sale through impersonal media". Others, in turn, prefer to highlight the various modes in which promotional material appears. Al Shehari (2001:10) claims that advertising is "any material written or spoken or acted upon which is published or displayed in any mass media for the purpose of persuading people to buy a product or service or to support an idea or institution". Valdés, speaking in a more generalised sense, refers to the multi-functionality of the genre:

> Por tanto, podemos afirmar que la publicidad es una arte, una ciencia y una profesión. (Valdés 2002b:17)

> [We can therefore claim that advertising is a form of art, a science and a profession]

And Kellner argues that advertising:

magically offers self-transformation and a new identity, associating changes in consumer behaviour, fashion and appearance with metamorphosis into a new person. Consequently, individuals are taught to identify with values, role models, and social behaviour through advertising which is thus an important instrument of socialization as well as a manager of consumer demand. (Kellner 1992: 163)

I will now turn to the term 'conflict'. I was aware of the "conflicting attitudes towards translation", referred to earlier. I felt that there were also conflicting approaches to advertising and, of course, I see 'conflict' around me every day. But I still lacked a definition of the term. I then looked into theories on peace and conflict, including handbooks on conflict resolution (Deutsch and Coleman 2000; Bergof *Handbook for Conflict Transformation*), and associations related to peace and conflict (Association for Conflict Resolution; Conflict Research Consortium; Unesco Chair of Philosophy for Peace located in Castellón; The *Instituto de la Paz y los Conflictos* in Granada, etc.). However, none of the references I consulted (e.g. Burgess 1997; Collins 1974; Fisher 2001; Kaldor 1992; Krauss 2000; Kimmel 2000; Miall 2001; Muñoz 2001; Reinmann 2001) provided a definition, but they only discussed or exemplified the term. For instance Deutsch and Coleman explain that:

> The black arts of conflict (such as violence, coercion, intimidation, deceit, blackmail, and seduction) are not discussed [in their handbook] except [...] in the context of how to respond or prevent the use of such tactics by oneself or others. (Deutsch and Coleman 2000: xiii)

According to *The New Oxford Dictionary of English* the term 'conflict' may be defined thus:

> **Noun** A serious disagreement or argument, typically a protracted one (The eternal conflict between the sexes)/ A prolonged armed struggle // a state of mind in which a person experiences a clash of opposing wishes or needs (bewildered by her own inner conflict, she could only stand there feeling vulnerable) // a serious incompatibility between two or more opinions, principles or interests (there was a conflict between his business and domestic life).
> **Verb** to be incompatible or at variance, clash (parents' and children's interests sometimes conflict.
>
> [as adj. **Conflicted**] N. Amer. Having or showing confused and mutually inconsistent feelings/he remains a little conflicted about Marlene).

An internet search listed more than ten pages of results that contained the phrase "theory of conflict". The sixth of these results was entitled "McDonald's Theory of Conflict Resolution". (a webpage page by Tim Lynch at http://www.lynch.st/index.html). The page referred to Thomas

L. Friedman's "Golden Arches Theory of Conflict Prevention", in which he hypothesised that no two countries with a McDonald's franchise had ever gone to war with one another:

> when a country reaches the level of economic development where it has a middle class big enough to support a McDonald's network, it becomes a "McDonald's country". And people living in "McDonald's countries" do not like to fight expensive and tiresome foreign wars any more, they prefer to queue up for burgers and fries.
> The theory states that no two countries that both had McDonald's had fought a war against each other since each got its McDonald's. [The "Golden Arches' Theory of Conflict Prevention", [in News Scan Online at http://www.newsscan.com/cgi-bin/findit_view?table=newsletter&id=11250 ]

Tim Lynch's page was, I would argue, purposefully confusing as to its presentation and as to the fact that it mixed messages. It was presented as expounding on an academic theory (Friedman's McDonald's theory of conflict resolution) —classified under politics— when it was really an advert. According to Martín et al. (1996), adverts consist of a trade mark, a logo, a message and a footnote. Indeed Tim Lynch's page complied with this. Superficially, it may be taken to be an advert for McDonalds with its brand (McDonalds), its logo ("the golden arches"), its confusing message (see above), and its footnote (which reinforced the confusion by reminding the viewer again that this is page to be classified under "Politics"). It was also confusing because, if we look into it, we realize this was a multiple advert. It advertised Tim Lynch (and his friend Dave Novak), Norwalk Pictures, Little Scoop, the Gematriculator and … the Bush and Cheney campaign. This is what makes it simultaneously confusing and consistent. If we put all the (confusing) ingredients together they all blend perfectly well to advertise the neo-conservative political ideas which Bush and Cheney represent. On the basis of Bueno's definition, this was an outright ad:

> .. a type of communication that attempts to decide or to change receptors' opinion of things and their actions [e.g. "PUT THIS ON YOUR SITE", "JOIN THE PRESIDENT'S TEAM", "DONATE TO GELAC"...] by means of techniques that act upon their intellect.

**Exploration 2**

The convergence of previously separated genres to cause confusion and conflict, as we have seen exemplified by *McDonald's Theory of Conflict Resolution*, is by no means a coincidence in our globalized world. Michael Cronin writes of "fluid modernity" (Cronin, 2003: 105) characterizing modern times. He quotes Scott Lash and John Urry, who point out that "the objects created in the post-industrial world are progressively emptied of their material content. The result is the proliferation of signs rather than material objects", and Cronin goes on to explain that these signs are of two kinds:

informational and aesthetic. And he also reflects upon the convergence of both types of signs, commenting on the ensuing hybridity of genres:

> This convergence of previously distinct types of documentation and means of distribution shows that it is increasingly difficult to separate cognitive goods from purely aesthetic ones. Such difficulty is to be expected if aestheticisation increasingly takes place in the production, circulation and consumption of goods in the new economy. (Cronin 2003: 15)

Aesthetic signs converge with informational signs, and the "production, circulation and consumption of goods in the new economy" automatically lead to the subject of advertising. Because it is through advertising -its aesthetic signs, its bold, generic confusion - that consumption is nowadays promoted to the upmost.

In 1972 John Berger, in association with Sven Blomberg, Chris Fox, Michael Dibb and Richard Hollis, wrote *Ways of Seeing*. In it Berger includes an essay on advertising, which began with the following:

> In the cities in which we live, all of us see hundreds of publicity images everyday of our lives. No other kind of image confronts us so frequently. (Berger 1972: 129)

In 1999, Jean Kilbourne could say that "the average American is exposed to over 3000 advertisements a day and watches three years' worth of television adverts over the course of a lifetime." (Kilbourne 1999: dustjacket) And a year later, Frédéric Beigbeder (2000: 57) warned that we are all bombarded with an average of 4,000 advertising messages each day. In 2003, Ramonet (2003: 72) commented that:

> Antes de alcanzar la edad de doce años, un niño habrá visto, en Francia, unos 100.000 anuncios que, subrepticiamente, van a contribuir a interiorizar las normas ideológicas dominantes. Y enseñarle criterios consensuales de lo bello, el bien, lo justo y lo verdadero; es decir, los cuatro valores morales sobre los cuales para siempre se edificará su visión moral y estética del mundo.
>
> [By the age of twelve, a child in France will have seen 100,000 adverts. This is going to contribute to his/her unconscious assimilation of dominant, ideological norms. It is also going to teach him/her widely accepted criteria about beauty, the common welfare, justice and the truth; that is, the four moral values upon which he/she will build his/her moral and aesthetic view of the world.]

Given the escalation in the number of adverts which are consumed every day, it can be argued that, if advertising is indeed related to conflict, there has been a large increase in the degree of conflict that we are exposed to. Advertisements and conflict are related in more than one way. In 'radical' terms, it has been argued by Berger (1972), Chomsky (2003) [1993] and

Ramonet (2003), for instance, that conflict is advertising's *raison d'être*. Advertising, says Chomsky "es a la democracia lo que la cachiporra al estado totalitario" [is to democracy what the truncheon is to totalitarian systems] (Chomsky 2003 [1993]: 16). Referring to Lippman, he speaks of our democracies as being nothing more than "democracias del espectador" ["Democracies of the spectator"] (*ibid.*: 12-13), there being two kinds of citizens, those belonging to:

> La clase especializada, los hombres responsables, ejercen la función ejecutiva, lo que significa que piensan, entienden y planifican los intereses comunes. (*ibid.*: 16)

> [the specialised class of responsible men, who exercise an executive role, which means that they think, understand and plan the common interests]

and those who belong to what Chomsky labels as "el rebaño desconcertado" [the puzzled flock], those whose function in our society is to be "spectators of action", and not participants. The flock is ignorant and meddlesome and has to be distracted, its attention carefully deflected away from power (*ibid.*: 15).

In 1972 Berger also said

> publicity turns consumption into a substitute for democracy. The choice of what one eats (or wears or drives) takes the place of significant political choices. Publicity helps to mask and compensate for all that is undemocratic within society. And it also masks what happens in the rest of the world. (Berger 1972: 149)

And, according to Ramonet advertising does the same. It masks what happens in the rest of the world to such an extent that

> Se puede llegar casi a considerar que los 17,4 millones de parados europeos, el desastre urbano, la precarización social, los suburbios, a punto de estallar, el saqueo ecológico, el retorno de los racismos y la marea de marginados, son simples espejismos, alucinaciones culpables y altamente discordantes en este mundo feliz que está edificando para nuestras conciencias anestesiadas, el pensamiento único. (Ramonet 2003: 61)

> [One may even think that images of 17.4 million unemployed in Europe, urban disaster, social precariousness, marginalised communities on the verge of eruption, ecological looting, the return of racism, and marginalised hordes, are merely mirages or highly disturbing hallucinations in the happy world that current one-way thinking is building for our numb consciences]

Some of the statements quoted above may be regarded as being radical, but evidence indicates that a complex relationship between advertising and conflict does exist. There is a potential relationship between advertising and conflict (in the sense of the term defined above by *the New Oxford Dictionary of English* as phenomena or realia which ignite disagreement or confusion, and cause clashes within and amongst ourselves.

Advertising can **cause** conflict, as shown in the following example drawn from Berger 2001. An advertisement for clothes featured a picture of a mass-murderer. Berger commented:

> When this upstart clothier [Zipper Head] and its mischievous agency [Gyro, Philadelphia] wanted to draw attention, their put famed murderer Charles Manson in their ad. It worked but it also caused problems. (Berger 2001: 271)

But advertising can attempt to **settle** conflict, as further examples by Berger illustrate. A tanning studio used a picture of Michael Jackson, in an advertisement with the by-line "Some people are just too white", and Berger comments "Pop singer Michael Jackson was once advertising's brightest star, but eventually became an object of ridicule" (*ibid.:* 257).

Humour was used in the above advert, but a change of perspective can also attempt to settle conflict. A poster used by the Commission for Racial Equality pictured the face of a black man, and it carried the following message: "Scared? You should be. He's a doctor" (Commission for Racial Equality. Euro RSCG Wnek Gosper, London 1999). But, as Berger (2001: 240) comments: "Race is a minefield for advertisers. This well-meaning campaign came under heavy fire for offending the people it was trying to help".

Furthermore, advertising is also the **main target of 'conflicting forces'**. Activists, such as Kalle Lasn (2000) take on, or launch conflict against the mesmerising and contradictory effect of commercials. In 1990, Ron English used a fake billboard advertisement for 'MacDonald's' which carried the statement "MacDonald's – better living through chemistry". As Berger said: "Some artists have began to use billboards both to display their work and to make anti-commercial statements; [...] Ron English takes on MacDonald" (*ibid.*: 458).

**Exploration 3**
So far, we have associated conflict with disagreement, confusion and clash. But according to Muñoz (2001), conflict should not always be viewed in negative terms, and much depends on how we engage with it. Burgess (1997) explains that there are two kinds of approaches to conflict: 'problem solving' and 'conflict transformation'. The former attempts to reach an acceptable settlement by focusing on areas of consensus, whilst avoiding disagreement. The latter tackles disagreement and aims to modify it in order to achieve long-lasting benefits. Conflict transformation requires 'recognition' and 'empowerment'. With recognition, participants are able to consider "the perspective, views and experiences of the other" (*ibid.*), whilst 'Empowerment' gives "the restoration to individuals of their own value and strength and their own capacity to handle life's problems" (*ibid.*). The

literature on conflict transformation encompasses various ways of facing disagreement, one of which is third party intervention (see Fisher 2001). Many different individuals and organisations have been regarded as appropriate third party mediators. Furthermore, many others are attributed active roles in today's globalised conflicts:

> The global presence in these wars can include international reporters, mercenary troops, and military advisers, diaspora volunteers as well as a veritable army of international agencies ranging from non-governmental organisations (NGOs) ... to international institutions ... (Kaldor 1999: 4)

However, and of particular relevance to our discussion, the translator is nowhere to be seen in the literature on conflict. This is difficult to comprehend if we agree with Kimmel (2000: 456) that conflict proliferates because:

> Most of us are unaware of the important differences between our subjective culture and those of individuals from other well-known cultures because few of us are in direct contact with such individuals.

Translators are aware of difference, they are also in contact not only with the pragmatic and symbolic texts that make up "other" cultures, but with "other" individuals. Their invisibility in the literature on conflict transformation is even more difficult to understand when we read Burgess, who stresses the need for those involved to "learn how to listen, communicate, analyse issues, evaluate alternatives and make decisions more effectively than before" (Burgess 1997). As part of their daily tasks, translators listen (or read), and communicate, an intrinsic part of their job being to analyse issues and evaluate alternatives. Translation is often described as a decision-making process.

On the basis of Kimmel's and Burgess's recommendations, translators would appear to be ideal candidates to take part in the transformation of conflict. The question is, then, how do translators achieve the transformation of conflict? I believe they can do so precisely through *recognition* and *empowerment*. On the one hand, translators may reflect on their task and on how they shed light on "the perspective, views and experiences of the other" (Burgess 1997). Based on this 'recognition', they should restore (defend) their "own value and strength and [their] own capacity to handle life's problems" (*ibid.*) before other disciplinary settings, which would correspond to 'empowerment'. In what follows I will concentrate on the process of recognition, which I believe is the basis for robust empowerment.

To achieve recognition and clarify the way translators understand other cultures, we could concentrate on the effective things we, as translators, do when dealing with "the other". Along these lines, we can examine the ways in which we listen, communicate, analyse, evaluate and make decisions. We should focus attention on how we do all this, *vis-à-vis* conflicting phenomena related to translation.

Cronin (2003) highlights two common practices which can be the cause of conflict in our globalised world. These are "Censorship" and "Zero translation".

The first, "Censorship" can itself be subdivided into "anthropoemic censorship" when "texts must be expelled from the system", and are therefore banned or prohibited, (Cronin 2003: 96); and "anthropophagic censorship", which is described as "the forcible ingestion of the other, the coercive assimilation of others so that they are no longer to be distinguished from the ingesting body." Furthermore, Cronin believes that all translations are somewhat anthropophagic (*ibid.*).

The second practice "Zero translation" is part of a process of homogenisation, which Cronin (2003) calls "clonialism" (and which I will associate with hegemonic monoglossia), where I would argue that linguistic and cultural differences are being systematically suppressed and where monoglossia rules.

To the areas of "censorship" and "zero translation", which Cronin identifies as possible causes of conflict, I suggest the addition of a third category: *outright translation mistakes*. To achieve recognition for the translator, we may reflect on how we perform *vis-à-vis* these phenomena, and how translators could share with other disciplines how to i) *listen* to translational mistakes; ii) communicate anthropoemic censorship; iii) analyse anthropophagic censorship, and iv) evaluate and make decisions about zero translation and monoglossia.

Conflict, advertising and translation take part in all these practices and the following will illustrate how translation may contribute to the transformation of conflict related to advertising.

1. *Listening* to mistakes

As part of their recognition skills, translators listen to, and profit from, previous errors. The following advertisement, promoting the services of the translation agency WordBank, refers to a translation mistake which was made regarding an utterance by Churchill:

> WHEN I LOOK AT MY BACKSIDE
> I see that it's split in two parts"
> (Quand je regarde mon derrière je vois qu'il est divisé en deux parties. OH LA LA!) What he really meant was when he looked at his past he could see it was split in two parts.
> Maybe our wartime leader should have given us a call. At WordBank, translation is handled by a national from the relevant country. In fact, we have a network of over 3,000 translators living in their own country, which eliminates the risk of embarrassing mistakes.
> If you want to make your foreign marketing and advertising make sense, call us on —. You can rest assured, our translators know their arse from their elbow. (Wordbank, Leo Burnett, London, mid-1990s)

Churchill's utterance "When I look at my past" was translated as "Quand je regarde mon derrière" ['When I look at my backside']. Translation Agency Wordbank 'listened' to a previous translating mistake, learned from it and, to quote Berger (2001: 288-9) "poke[d] fun at Churchill" to get their intended message across (i.e. that the services of a good translation agency are always advisable in intercultural communication exchanges). In short the translators at Wordbank transform potential conflict by 'listening' to translational mistakes.

2. Communicating anthropoemic censorship

Anthropoemic censorship is the eradication of the "other" by boycotting its appearance. If, as Cronin (2003: 96) argues, translators are sometimes involved in anthropoemic censorship, then they are well placed to identify it and communicate it, and to warn of its consequences. Anthropoemic censorship is often only spotted with the bicultural material that translators work with. For instance, monolingual Spanish consumers would not be able to identify censorship if they only had access to the following advert for perfume in Spanish, with the English byline "The funny side of myself for the Spanish-speaking consumer". But juxtaposition of this with its English counterpart "The funny side of myself for the English-speaking consumer" shows that the female body which appears in the English version is removed in the Spanish advert, to be replaced by a lollipop, and anthropoemic censorship can be identified.

3. Analysing anthropophagic censorship

Anthropophagic processes, where some participants ingest the production of other participants and expel it in their own terms, are not exclusive to translators. Advertising is also important site for such cannibalistic practices. However, because translators 'devour' foreign texts in their professional practice, and because translation scholars are accustomed to discussing this forcible 'ingestion of the other', Translation Studies has at its disposal a wide variety of methodologies to analyse conflicting 'anthropophagic censorship' in advertising.

Drawing on Barthes, and inspired by Al Shehari (2001), I will attempt to expose the mechanics of the countermyth in order to analyse the degree of success of some 'advertising binges'.

According to Roland Barthes the myth may be the third step in the semiotic system of signification, coming after denotation and connotation:

SIGNIFYING                           SIGNIFIED
SIGN/SIGNIFYING =*DENOTATION [FORM]*    *SIGNIFIED[CONCEPT]*=**CONNOTATION**
SIGNIFICATION = **MYTH**
(Barthes 1972 [1957])

Myths, for their part, may be ingested and expelled as countermyths. The following advertisement is a clever and controversial attempt by Guiness to promote their product through the use of a countermyth. The picture of a pint of Guiness with a 'head' has a by-line "The head of the British Intelligence". The controversial mechanics of the cannibalistic countermyth which may be seen to sustain Guiness's campaign can perhaps be explained as follows:

3.1 There is a highly controversial myth in England which claims that the Irish are stupid, and as a result of this they are frequently the butt of jokes.

3.2 Guinness beer is Irish. The advertising campaign uses on play on words "The head of British intelligence" to refer to their Irish product, whilst subverting the previous underlying myth.

3.3 It may be argued that, through metonymic strategies, the Irish themselves may be taken to be "the head of British intelligence".

3.4 The initial English myth is completely subverted and turned into this controversial countermyth, whereby "the Irish are the head of British Intelligence".

3.5 This countermyth is not designed anew by Guiness. For some, James Joyce and Oscar Wilde, for instance, have always been 'the best' of 'English (- speaking)' writers.

4. Evaluating zero translation and monoglossia

Translators are accustomed to making and evaluating decisions, and are often confronted with the increasingly homogenising trend of zero translations and English monoglossia, which contributes to "clonialism", to use Cronin's term (Cronin 2003: 128). English monoglossia is especially apparent in adverts for the non-English audience(s). For instance, in a relatively recent advertisement, Bang and Olufsen advertises one of its luxurious television sets by iconically presenting it as the American statue of liberty and by verbally referring to this fact with the statement "STATUE OF LIBERTY". No other word (or prominent image is) used in the ad. The same image and the same verbal message in English ("STATUE OF LIBERTY") become an appeal for the Spanish-speaking audience(s), although the advertisement could have perfectly used a verbal 'equivalent' in Spanish ('*ESTATUA DE LA LIBERTAD*') instead of the English wording. Incidentally, a Spanish-speaking iconic comparison would have also been possible.

At any rate, in this case, as in anthropoemic censorship, the realisation of the advertisement's monoglossic strategy relies on the juxtaposition of equivalent texts in other languages. And this is why the work of translators and translator scholars, who always face cross-cultural material, is vital.

However, the most conflicting cases of monoglossia and "clonialism" are to be found in adverts for multinational companies, such as those for McDonald's. This company has its webpages localised for different markets, and its strategy is in accordance with Napthine's remark that "To take a purely commercial point, it has been said, with reason, that while you can buy in any language you can't sell in any language" (Napthine 1983: 21)

McDonald's produces web-pages for 59 countries in the world, each of them on the basis of localised strategies. All the EU countries have their own 'unique' pages which are in their own languages. Some of the pages for these countries (i.e. Spain and Britain) favour majoritarian languages (i.e. Spanish or English), other countries (for instance Belgium) have bilingual pages (i.e. French and Dutch). Far East Asian countries (Japan, China, Taiwan, South Korea etc.), together with Australia and New Zealand also get 'unique' pages in their official languages. India gets two 'personalised' pages in English, (one for the "West Region" and one for the "North Region"). Most other (non-EU) European countries also have their own pages (ranging from Switzerland –with pages in German by default and in French as an alternative, to Eastern European countries such as Bulgaria, Russia or the Czech Republic which have pages in their official languages).

Latin America is an interesting case. McDonald's designs "unique" pages in Spanish for countries such as Colombia, Chile, Argentina, Brazil or Mexico. But they provide standard pages for other Central and South American countries (such as Guatemala, Peru, Paraguay, and Uruguay). Most standard pages have English by default, but offer an alternative in Spanish. It is also interesting to see that for Latin America, pages are often used to introduce the country. The webpage for Uruguay gives the impression that the standard page is not addressed to the locals but to foreigners (Americans?) travelling to these countries.

McDonald's strategy for Arabic-speaking countries is worth mentioning. All of these countries get standard pages which are written in English only. In this case, the format is always the same: In the case of Egypt, McDonald's insists on the fact that it is Muslim-run (though its webpages say nothing about the company's being US owned). Furthermore, there is a standard comment on McDonald's involvement in the local community.

On these webpages, the Arabic language has completely disappeared, even in so-called "westernised" cases such as Egypt or Morocco. Most African countries are non-existent as far as Mc Donald's web coverage is concerned.

It appears that McDonald's classifies countries in three overall groups: richer nations, which get unique pages, less developed nations which merely get standardised pages, and the rest. Certain members of the second group (i.e. some Latin American countries) can access the pages in their own languages, but if the country is in the third group (mainly ones in Africa) the language is quite likely to be totally disregarded.

The study of McDonald's localisation strategies for their advertising pages goes beyond the scope of this paper. But I would like to argue that translators have, at their disposal, the tools to evaluate the degree of conflict that this commercial strategy may provoke.

## Conclusion

This paper has argued that advertising and conflict were closely connected and that translators had the tools to participate in conflict transformation, recognition and empowerment. The questions which arise are whether translators should do this, and whether conflict transformation is also part of the definition of translation.

I answer in the affirmative. Cronin (2003: 67) proposes that translators should claim "value-added components" in our globalised world. These may include conflict transformation of different kinds, such as conflict and advertising. I refer to 'conflict translation' rather than 'problem-solving' as I am particularly interest in the translator's ability to actually tackle conflict, rather than avoid it in a search for a consensus.

Finally, the participation of translators in conflict transformation could hopefully contribute towards establishing a more dignified world which has no place for the stratified globalised world of "McDonald's countries" where multinationals distinguish between the rich, the developing, the standardised and the non-existent. Furthermore, our participation in conflict transformation could, as Marina - the Spanish philosopher with whom I started the paper - claims:

> necesitamos vivir en un mundo digno, donde se respete nuestra dignidad personal, porque sólo así podremos abrir un espacio seguro para realizar nuestros propios proyectos de felicidad, o al menos intentarlo. (Marina, 2004: 15)
>
> [we need to live in a dignified world, where our personal dignities are respected because this is the only way we will be able to establish a safe place in order to put (or try to put) in practice our own projects of happiness.]

And personal happiness, according to Marina again, is only possible if we care for social and political happiness. Our awareness of cultural difference, our access to otherness, our tools for translating and analyzing translation all make us valuable candidates to fight for a citizen's world rather than a 'McDonald's world'. As Chomsky (2003 [1993]: 53) exclaims:

> La respuesta a estas cuestiones está en gran medida en manos de gente como usted y como yo
>
> [The answer to these questions are, to a large extent, in the hands of people like you and me]

## References

Aitchison, Jim. 1999. *Cutting Edge Advertising. How to Create the World's Best Print for Brands in the 21$^{st}$ Century*. Singapore: Prentice Hall.

Al Shehari, Khalid. 2001. *The Semiotics and Translation of Advertising Texts: Conventions,*

Constraints and Translation Strategies with Particular Reference to English and Arabic. Unpublished Thesis. Manchester: UMIST.
Apter, Emily. 2001. 'On translation in the global market', *Public Culture*, 13(1). On line at: http://www.uchicago.edu/research/jnl-pub-cult/current/apter1.html (consulted 30.10.2003).
Association for Conflict Resolution, 'Frequently Asked Questions about Conflict Resolution', http://www.acrnet.org/about/CR-FAQ.htm, 1-4. (consulted 24.07.2006).
Barthes, Roland. 1972 [1957]. *Mythologies*. New York: Hill and Wang.
Bassat, Lluis. 1993. *El libro rojo de la publicidad (Ideas que mueven montañas)*. Madrid: Espasa Calpe.
Bassnett-McGuire, Susan. 1988. *Translation Studies*. London and New York: Routledge.
Beasley, Ron and Danesi Marcel. 2002. *Persuasive Signs. The Semiotics of Advertising*. Berlin: Mouton de Gruyter.
Beigberder, Frédéric. 2000. *13'99 euros*. Barcelona: Anagrama.
Berger, John. et al. 1972. *Ways of Seeing*. London: Penguin.
Berger, Warren. 2001. *Advertising Today*. London: Phaidon.
Bueno, Antonio. 2000. *Publicidad y traducció*. Soria: Vertere. Monográficos de la Revista Hermeneus, 2, Diputación de Soria. 1-239.
Burgess, Heidi. 1997. 'Transformative Mediation'. On line at: http://www.colorado.edu/conflict/transform/tmall.htm (consulted 24.07.2006).
Burgess, Heidi et al. 1997. 'Transformative Approaches to Conflict'. On line at: http://www.colorado.edu/conflict/transform (consulted July 2006).
Chandler, Daniel. 2002. *Semiotics. The Basics*. London and New York: Routledge.
Chomsky, Noam. 2003 [1993]. 'El control de los medios de comunicación', in Chomsky, Noam and Ignacio Ramonet. *Cómo nos venden la moto*. Barcelona: Icaria. Más Madera, 7-54.
Collins, Randall. 1974. *Conflict Sociology*. New York: Academic Press. 56-61.
Cook, Guy. 2001. *The Discourse of Advertising*. 2nd ed. London and New York: Routledge.
Cronin, Michael. 2003. *Translation and Globalization*. London and New York: Routledge.
Danesi, Marcel. 2002. *Understanding Media Semiotics*. London: Arnold.
Deutsch, Morton and Peter T. Coleman. 2000. 'Preface' in Deutsch, Morton and Peter T. Coleman (eds) *The Handbook of Conflict Resolution*. San Francisco: Jossey-Bass. xi-xiii.
Fisher, Ronald. 2001. 'Method of Third-Party Intervention', Bergof Handbook for Conflict Transformation. Berlin: Bergof Research Centre for Constructive Transformation. On line at: http://www.bergof-handbook.net (consulted August 2006).
Goddard, Barbara. 1998. *The Language of Advertising*, London and New York: Routledge.
Gopegui, Belén. 2001. *Lo real*. Barcelona: Anagrama.
Hatim, Basil. 1996. 'The Method in their Adness: the Juggling of Texts, Discourse and Genres in the Language of Advertising and Implications for the Translator' in Amparo Hurtado (ed.) *La enseñanza de la traducción*. Castellón: Universidad Jaume I.
Hermans, Theo. 1997. 'The Task of the Translator in the European Renaissance: Explorations in a Discursive Field' in Bassnett, Susan (ed.) *Translating Literature*. Cambridge: D.S. Brewer. 14-40.
Kaldor, Mary. 1999. *New and Old Wars: Organised Violence in a Global Era*. Stanford, Ca.: Stanford University Press.
Kellner, Douglas. 1992. 'Popular culture and the construction of postmodern identities' in Lash, Scott and Jonathan Friedman (eds) *Modernity and Identity*. Oxford: Blackwell.
Kilbourne, Jean. 1999. *Can't buy my love. How Advertising Changes the Way We Think and Feel*. New York: Simon and Schuster.
Kimmel, Paul R. 2000. 'Culture and Conflict', in Deutsch and Coleman (2000): 453-474.
Klein, Naomi. 2001. *No logo*. Barcelona: Paidós.
Krauss, Robert M. 2000. 'Communication and Conflict' in Deutsch and Coleman (2000): 131-143.
Lasn, Kalle. 2000. *Culture Jam. How to Reverse America's Suicidal Consumer Binge – and Why We Must*. New York: Quill.
LeBaron, Michelle. 2001. 'Transforming Cultural Conflict in an Age of Complexity' in Bergof

*Handbook for Conflict Transformation*. Berlin: Bergof Research Centre for Constructive Transformation. 1-20. On line at: http://www.berghof-handbook.net (consulted 24.07.2006).
Lynch, Timothy, 'McDonald's Theory of Conflict Resolution'. On line at: http://www.lynch.st /index.html (consulted 30.10.2003). (Tymothy Lynch's blog can now be accessed at http://timothylynch.blogspot.com/index.html -consulted 24.07.2006).
Marina, José Antonio. 2004. *Aprender a vivir*. Barcelona: Ariel.
Martín, Jacinto et al. 1996. *Los lenguajes especiales*. Granada: Comares.
Mayoral, Roberto. 2002. '¿Existe la teoría de la traducción?' in *Apuntes* 10(4): 12-13.
Miall, Hugh. 2001. 'Conflict Transformation. A Multi-dimensional Task' in *Bergof Handbook for Conflict Transformation*, Berlin: Bergof Research Centre for Constructive Transformation. On line at: http://www.berghof-handbook.net (consulted 30.06.2006).
Molina, Rueda, Beatriz and Francisco A. Muñoz (2004). *Manual de Paz y Conflictos*. Granada: 1-554.
Muñoz, Francisco A. 2004. 'Qué son los conflictos' in Molina and Muñoz (2004): 143-170.
Napthine, Anne. 1983. 'Training of Translators' in Picken, Catriona (ed.) *The Translator's Handbook*. London: Aslib. 21-32.
News Scan Online at http://www.newsscan.com/cgi-bin/findit_view?table=newsletter&id=11250 (consulted 1.11.2006).
Pedro, Raquel de. 1996. 'Beyond the Words: the Translation of Television Adverts' in *Babel* 42(1): 27-45.
Ramonet, Ignacio. 2003. 'Pensamiento único y nuevos amos del mundo' in Chomsky, Noam and Ignacio Ramonet (2003) *Cómo nos venden la moto*. Barcelona: Icaria. Más Madera, 55- 98.
Reinmann, Cordula. 2001. 'Assessing the State-of-the-Art in Conflict Transformation' in *Bergof Handbook for Conflict Transformation*. Berlin: Bergof Research Centre for Constructive Transformation.
Robinson, Mark. 2001. *The Sunday Times Hundred Greatest TV ads*. London: Harper Collins.
Rotzoll, Kim. 1985. 'Advertisements' in van Dijk, Teun A. (ed.) *Discourse and Communication*. Berlin and New York: Walter de Gruyter. 94-105.
Russell, J. Thomas and W. Ronald Lane. 1994. *Kleppner Publicidad*. México: Prentice Hall Hispanoamericana.
Seguinot, Candice. 1995. 'Translation and Advertising: Going Global' in Schäffner, Christina and Helen Kelly-Holmes (eds) *Cultural Functions of Translation*. Clevedon: Multilingual Matters. 55-71.
Shakir, Abdullah. 1995. 'The Translation of Advertisements: Registeral and Schematic Constraints' in *Meta* 40(1): 62-72.
Slater, John. 1998. 'The Image as Text: Some Considerations for Translating Print Advertisements' in Nekeman, Paul (ed.) *Translation, Our Future. Proceedings of the XIth World Congress of FIT*. Maastricht: Euroterm. 389-391.
Stam, Robert et al. 1992. *New Vocabularies in Film Semiotics: Structuralism, Post-Structuralism and Beyond*. London: Routledge.
Tanaka, Keiko. 1994. *Advertising Language. A Pragmatic Approach to Advertisements in Britain and Japan*. London and New York: Routledge.
'The Golden Arches' Theory of Conflict Prevention'. On line at: http://www.newsscan.com/cgi-bin/findit_view?table=newsletter&id=11250 (consulted 30.10.2003).
Twitchell, James B. 2000. *Twenty Adverts that Shook the World*. New York: Crown Publishers.
Valdés, Cristina. 1999. *La traducción publicitaria: comunicación y cultura*. Unpublished PhD Thesis: Universidad de Oviedo.
——2002a. 'Parámetros teóricos en la traducción: un enfoque interdisciplinar' in Corpas, Gloria et al (eds) *En torno a la traducción-adaptación del mensaje publicitario mensaje publicitario*. Málaga: Universidad de Málaga. 87-102.
——2002b. 'Estrategias traductoras en publicidad' in Corpas *et al* (2002): 103-114.
Vieira, Else. 1999. 'Liberating Calibans: readings of *Antropofagia* and Haroldo de Campos'

poetics of transcreation' in Bassnett, Susan and Harish Trivedi (eds) *Post-Colonial Translation*. London and New York: Routledge. 95-113.

Zambrana, Rafael. 2002. 'Ordenamiento jurídico de la publicidad en España' in Corpas et al. (2002): 13-48.

# Part V

# Manipulating and Rewriting Texts

# The Translation of William Le Queux's *The Invasion of 1910*: What Germany Made of Scaremongering in *The Daily Mail*.

*Ian Foster*

Between 1900 and 1906 there was a shift in the 'Tale of the Next Great War', a popular fictional genre that had become established following the success of George Chesney's *The Battle of Dorking* in 1873. Chesney's narrative exploited the speed of Prussian victory in France to present the emergent German Empire as a new challenge to British Imperial interests, one that might even threaten the homeland. It was, however, France that remained the principal enemy in the tales of Chesney's imitators. In 1900, France still featured in six novels as the perceived threat, where Germany only featured in three. With the signing of the *Entente Cordiale* in 1904 and more importantly the visit of Kaiser Wilhelm II to Tangier in 1905 that sparked the so-called *Morocco Crisis*, attention shifted to the German Empire. The owner of the *Daily Mail* Lord Northcliffe had founded his newspaper in 1896 as a mouthpiece of the Imperial idea. In 1906, Northcliffe commissioned William Le Queux, a colourful figure, would-be spy and author to write an invasion story that would campaign for greater spending on the armed forces. Le Queux's story *The Invasion of 1910* ran from March to July 1906, a period in which sales of the *Daily Mail* rose by 80 000. A book edition subsequently sold over a million copies and was widely translated. Despite its widespread influence, there has been little detailed examination of the book itself. I look at the German translation of the story, *Der Einfall der Deutschen*, which offers a far from straightforward rendering of the English novel.

Key words: invasion scares, future war, genre, scaremongering.


In the last decades of the nineteenth century a distinctive genre of science fiction story emerged in Western Europe, a genre that reflected the rising national rivalries of the era. This popular form came to be known in English as the 'Tale of the Next Great War', in German more pithily as the '*Zukunftskrieg*', or 'future war'. The first and perhaps best known English example was George Chesney's *The Battle of Dorking*, published in serial form in *Blackwood's Magazine* in 1871. Chesney's dramatic narrative exploited the speed of the recent Prussian victory over France to present the unified German Empire under Bismarck as a new challenge to British Imperial interests, one that might even threaten the homeland itself. It was an instant and much imitated publishing success.

In Britain in particular the 'Tale of the Next Great War' came to be a format for advancing an argument from 'defects to disaster', in the phrase coined by I F Clarke in his classic pioneering study of the genre, *Voices Prophesying War*. Writers of this type of novel would imagine what a military conflict between their own country and a foreign power might look like, given the existing or likely technologies of war. The narrative would then describe the imagined future war in terms that reflected a partisan view of the shortcomings of one's own side. Tales of impending military defeat served as arguments in favour of greater spending on whatever the author felt to be the likely weakness. In England such stories, following Chesney's model, tended to take the form of invasion scares. Ten years before the Schlieffen plan and the reality of the '*blitzkrieg*', major wars were being fought out in a fertile strand of popular novels and on the pages of mass market newspapers. These paper wars were not purely internal affairs of nations addressing their own fears and pro-military campaigners. A key and under-examined aspect of the genre is that the novels were frequently translated.

The raw statistics tell of the growing fears and expectations of those years. From 1888 to 1914 Britain, France and Germany alone saw the publication of over 200 novels of this type. In 1906, twelve novels of this kind were published in Britain, France and Germany; this figure rose to nineteen in 1907, fell back to sixteen in 1908 and reached a peak of twenty in 1909 (Clarke 2001: 2).

Significantly, between 1900 and 1906 there was a shift in the content of the novels published. In British novels of the early 1900s, France outweighed Germany as the enemy of choice for warfare fantasies. In 1900 the ratio was 6:3. The signing of the *Entente Cordiale* in 1904 inaugurated a public change of attitude between France and once perfidious Albion, the oldest and best-established enemies. Interestingly enough, the most prolific French author of future wars, Edouard Driant, continued to envisage the British Empire as the principal foe right up to the outbreak of the First World War itself. More future-minded authors, like the Frenchman Albert Robida, would introduce novelties like the air transport of troops, mechanized war vehicles and the like. Such flights of fantasy were less common than the more prosaic-minded works of many of the authors concerned who saw the essence of the Future War novel as lying in the playing out of a war game scenario between existing armies and navies.

In the most successful examples of the genre there is often an element of opportunism, of identifying and latching on to contemporary fears and concerns. This combines with a growing awareness of the potential of a mass market publication to affect political discourse, particularly in view of the rise of mass literacy after the Education Act of 1872 (Lopes 2004: 3). If there was one thing that transformed the future war story and made it a powerful political instrument then it was the birth of the popular mass newspaper. Chesney's invasion scare story, for all its success, was written for a middle-class readership. After 1890, future war stories would seek to appeal to a much broader readership. Given this context, it is important to consider the contribution of Lord Northcliffe's *Daily Mail*.

It would be no exaggeration to say that *The Daily Mail* was the first modern British mass newspaper. The newspaper was launched in 1896 with a cover price half of that of its rivals (a halfpenny rather than one penny), promising "All the news in the smallest space" and styling itself "The Busy Man's Paper" (Mackenzie 1921: 20). *The Daily Mail* was unashamedly pro-Empire in its editorials, explicitly describing itself as the 'mouthpiece of the Imperial idea'. It was from the first extremely successful, with circulation figures rising from 170 000 steadily to 700 000 before the First World War (peaking at over one million briefly during the Boer War) and reaching 1.3 million in 1921. The success of *The Mail* made its founder an extremely wealthy man, secured him and his brother seats in the House of Lords and was the cornerstone of a media conglomerate that later included even the venerable *Times* itself.

Lord Northcliffe's early career before the founding of *The Mail* is the stuff of legends. His first successful publication was the magazine *Answers* (originally *Answers to Correspondents on Every Subject under the Sun*), which began in June 1888. It had used innovative prize competitions and gifts to build up its circulation. *Answers* reflected its owner's association with the many Imperial organisations of the period, like the conservative Primrose League and the Navy League. Such organisations flourished in the 1890s and campaigned for greater military expenditure to prepare Britain for possible war.

In 1894, to boost the circulation of *Answers* and further views sympathetic to his own, Northcliffe commissioned the writer William Le Queux to write a series of stories imagining the invasion of England by Russia and France three years hence. The original title was 'The Poisoned Bullet' and featured instalments with titles like 'The Massacre of Eastbourne' and the 'Battle of Beachy Head'. These tales were collected as *The Great War in England in 1897* and formed the first of a series of works financed by Northcliffe with the intention of advancing the cause of military reform. *The Great War in England in 1897* found a sequel in March 1895 when Northcliffe, who was at the time of course still humble Alfred Harmsworth and thus eligible to enter the House of Commons, announced that he would stand as Conservative candidate for Portsmouth (Lee Thompson 2000: 27). The Harmsworth Press acquired the local Portsmouth paper, the *Evening Mail* and began to publish 'The Siege of Portsmouth', a serial that reran the alliance between France and Russia as an imminent threat to British security in 1897. Episodes included the 'Startling Appearance of a French Man o'War at Spithead', 'The Battle of Eddystone' and 'The Battle of Spithead' (Lee Thompson 2000: 28). In every case the navy and army failed as a result of the floundering of a Liberal government under its Prime Minister Henry Campbell-Bannerman. Northcliffe failed to win over the voters even of conservative-minded Portsmouth with its substantial naval vote, but the relationship with Le Queux persisted and was to be reawakened in the remarkable campaign surrounding the future war story *The Invasion of 1910*.

The visit of the German Emperor Wilhelm II to Tangier in April 1905 resulted in a diplomatic crisis when the Kaiser criticised French ambitions in North Africa and demanded equal treatment for German business in what he somewhat disingenuously argued was an independent country. The ensuing 'Morocco Crisis', as it came to be known, led ultimately to the resignation of the French Foreign Minister Delcassé. This was perhaps the decisive event that shifted the attention of the British press and with it the writers of future war stories to the German Empire. Although evidence of growing investment in the German navy had been noted in the British press from the appointment of von Tirpitz in 1897, and the German naval spending plans announced in 1900 triggered a wave of alarm, it was not until the repercussions of the Morocco Crisis that Germany began to be presented publicly as a serious threat. It is interesting to observe that one of the most famous future war novels of all, perhaps the only major text of the genre from this period that is still widely read today, prefigured these developments: Erskine Childers's *The Riddle of the Sands*, first published in 1903.

With a conference scheduled to be convened in January 1906 in Algeciras in Spain to settle the issues arising from the Morocco Crisis, Northcliffe again turned to William Le Queux in the autumn of 1905 and commissioned him to write a new invasion story that would reflect the changed international situation and campaign for greater spending on the navy and reorganisation of the defensive forces to guard England in case of attack. The enemy was now to be Germany.

According to Le Queux's biographer, the author recruited a number of military men to help him in developing the ideas for the story, a Colonel Cyril Field and a Major Matson (St Barbe Sladen 1938:192). For four months, beginning in winter 1905, Le Queux reconnoitred the East coast of England, looking for the most vulnerable points for a likely invasion. In total, he claimed to have travelled some 10,000 miles by car and was appalled to find he had spent over £3000, which Northcliffe paid in full, apparently without comment. Le Queux worked on the text of his novel until the spring of the following year. The resulting story *The Invasion of 1910* ran in *The Daily Mail* from March to July 1906, during which time sales of the newspaper rose by 80 000. A book edition subsequently sold over a million copies. There was even an abridged pocket edition in the Everett's Library Series. Significantly, the book was translated into 27 languages.

There are conflicting views of this book and its subsequent reception. The most noted collector and critic of future war stories I F Clarke, for example, goes out of his way to dismiss the novel. He writes: "...there was alarm and anger when the ridiculous story began to appear in the *Daily Mail*" (Clarke 1966: 22). While Clarke does mention that questions were asked in parliament regarding the novel, his version of the political response to the publication of the novel differs somewhat from the official record. Clarke refers to the idea that that the story was "calculated to inflame public opinion abroad and alarm the more ignorant public at home" (*ibid.*: 22). Le Queux's biographer also makes rather more of the political repercussions than the facts would seem to warrant (see St Barbe Sladen 1938:193). Le Queux is reported as having immediately written to the Prime Minister to ask if Campbell-Bannerman had meant that the British public was less-informed than the public abroad? There is reference to a reply stating the Prime Minister of course had meant no such thing and that Le Queux was invited to visit Downing Street.

The official version can be found in a *Hansard* entry for 13 March 1906 under the title 'Fiction and Foreign Relations'.[1] A Mr Lehman, MP for Market Harborough, asks whether the Prime Minister's attention has been drawn to an advertisement in the morning papers announcing *The Invasion of 1910*, and whether "the Government can take any steps or express any opinion which will discourage the publication of matter of this sort, calculated to prejudice our relations with other Powers". Campbell-Bannerman's reply is a classic piece of British political rhetoric:

> I was greatly surprised to see the publication to which my hon. Friend has referred appearing in some newspapers, even in newspapers of which but a few years ago we were all proud. I do not know what step the Government can take in the matter; I am afraid they can do nothing. We can safely leave it, I think, to be judged by the good sense and good taste of the British people.

Clarke does not include an excerpt from the novel in his representative anthology *The Tale of the Next Great War 1871-1914* (Clarke 1995).

*The Invasion of 1910* was launched with a bold advertising strategy: veterans dressed in Prussian uniform, including the distinctive '*Pickelhaube*', or spiked helmet, appeared on the streets of London carrying sandwich boards with the news that Le Queux's story was about to appear. Regional newspapers owned by Harmsworth printed invasion maps showing likely routes to be taken. The wider public reaction is frequently dismissed as no more than a 'scare'. Also, the idea has somehow been passed on that the route of Le Queux's invading Germans was altered to boost sales in particular parts of the country. This appears to be untrue. The substantial political campaigns inspired in part by Le Queux and *The Daily Mail* in favour of a nationally organised defence force and the support he actively sought from Field Marshall Lord Roberts and the National Defence League and the Navy League require more serious comment.

By any standards we might care to apply, this novel was one of the most popular tales of the Future War genre. But it has received a decidedly uneven critical treatment. *The Invasion of 1910* was not only more widely read than most similar stories of the genre, both in the original and in its many translations, it also inspired more parodies and variants. For example, P G Wodehouse's humorous play *The Swoop, or how Clarence saved England* and Heath-Robinson's numerous satirical drawings of German spies clearly play upon the enormous popularity of Le Queux and his obsession with a spy threat. To simply dismiss the content of Le Queux's novel out of hand is in effect to follow those "Liberals and Labourists" who, in the words of Robert Blatchford, a contemporary Socialist thinker, believed Germany to be "pacific and dove-like", despite all the evidence to the contrary (Blatchford 1910: 7). Many in the British establishment were essentially pro-German and found the idea of hostile intentions on the part of Kaiser Wilhelm II and his advisers inconceivable.

Those who drew negative inferences from German attitudes to the British during the Boer War or towards France during the Morocco Crisis were openly mocked as chauvinists and jingoists. Drawing the obvious conclusions from the scale of the German naval build-up, the existence of the million-member strong lobby group in support of its navy, the '*Flottenverein*', which had influential Imperial and aristocratic patrons, was not a particularly popular viewpoint. Major engineering projects like the fortification of Heligoland and the widening of the Kiel canal that would permit the swift passage of dreadnought class ships from the Baltic to the North Sea had clear implications for British naval power. To dismiss populist attempts to raise these matters by attempting to reconstruct them retrospectively as 'anti-German propaganda' is both misguided and historically inaccurate. Indeed, in the rhetoric of the time one may also discern a degree of snobbery towards the *Daily Mail* and its readership that we would do well to avoid. To ask the question whether the issues that Northcliffe, Field Marshall Roberts and their supporters raised were indeed matters that should have concerned the government of the day is not the same as to approve their methods.

The question therefore remains then as to whether the idea of an invasion of England and Le Queux's imagined version was in any sense 'ridiculous'? Clearly, there were many senior naval officers who did not find the idea so far-fetched. Admiral Sir John Fisher, for example, First Sea Lord from 1904, perceived the rise of German sea power to be a major threat. Fisher, who had been present at the Hague Peace Conference of 1899 and met his German counterparts at that time, was by common consent 'in a position exceeding by far in personal power the influence of even the most highly placed civilian ministers' (Gollin 1960: 32) Fisher's recorded view was that an initial defeat at sea would mean certain invasion and the destruction of the Empire. Now there were others who took a different view, but when it came to the question of the plausibility or otherwise of Le Queux's scenario in *The Invasion of 1910* it is evident that the author drew on well-established ideas and backed them up with strategic military advice.

The credibility or otherwise of Le Queux's outline in hindsight is not the point. It was taken seriously at the time and that is what matters. Not that it was ridiculed. What is perhaps surprising is that, despite its widespread influence, there has been relatively little examination of the original text or its translations. I propose therefore, in the rest of this essay to look more closely at Le Queux's invasion-scare novel and its German translation.

When it comes to the translation of the text into German we know, as is so often the case, relatively little. Le Queux's biographer reports that negotiations for the German rights were conducted while the author was absent in Naples (see St Barbe Sladen 1938: 196-197). Le Queux's literary agent A P Watt dealt exclusively with a representative of the German Concordia Verlags-Gesellschaft. The translator who carried out the work, Traugott Tamm (1860-1938) was a novelist and historian.

It is remarkable how often the translation of a title can reveal a good deal about the expectations of an intended audience.

Fig.1 English Frontispiece of *The Invasion of 1910*

# THE INVASION OF 1910

### WITH A FULL ACCOUNT OF THE SIEGE OF LONDON

BY

WILLIAM LE QUEUX

NAVAL CHAPTERS BY H. W. WILSON

INTRODUCTORY LETTER BY
FIELD-MARSHAL EARL ROBERTS, K.G., K.P., ETC.

LONDON
EVELEIGH NASH
1906

Ian Foster

The full English title of Le Queux's original when published as a novel was: *The Invasion of 1910. With a Full Account of the Siege of London.* A line below the author's name noted "Naval Chapters by H. W. Wilson" (see Fig. 1). This point is elaborated in the author's preface, where Le Queux refers to the "invaluable assistance of my friend Mr H. W. Wilson" in deciding upon the naval portion of the campaign. The German translation of the title reads as follows: '*Die Invasion von 1910. Einfall der Deutschen in England*' (see Fig. 2). Now one might argue that the difference in the subtitle can be accounted for in the change of target audience – the Germans perhaps being less concerned with the fate of London and more interested in the general pattern. One might also argue that the word *Invasion* was perceived

Fig. 2  Frontispiece to German Edition of *The Invasion of 1910*

as a *'Fremdwort'* and therefore required reinforcement from the Germanic equivalent *'Einfall'*, but the German subtitle explicitly mentions the combatant nations – something which imparts a distinct overtone to the title[2]. Also, the word *'Einfall'* has a more common primary meaning. In colloquial German it means a 'bright idea'. So a back translation of the German title might impart an altogether different flavour! There is still more to be said about the wording of this frontispiece. Where the English acknowledges the contribution of Mr H. W. Wilson, the German text has "Die Seeschlachtkapitel von Admiral H. W. Wilson", chapters on naval battles by *Admiral* Wilson. Le Queux's friend Wilson was a humble civilian, long-time editor at *The Daily Mail*, a journalist and naval historian. This may be a case of genuine confusion but there can be little doubt that a future war written by an enemy admiral would have greater pulling power for a mass audience. The source of the confusion may have been Sir Arthur Knyvet Wilson (1842-1921), one of the greatest naval commanders of the nineteenth century, who was Commander of the Home and Channel Fleets from 1901 to 1907, then First Sea Lord from 1910. Knyvet Wilson developed the British tactic of deploying from columns into a single line for attack later used to great effect by Jellicoe in 1916 and his name would have been known to the German naval campaigners (see Davis and Weaver 1927: 579-581).

It is perhaps worth commenting on titles and subjects in future war stories at this point. Where the broad sweep of the British "tale of the next Great War" typically focussed on invasion scares, as mentioned at the start of this essay, and this is plainly evident in many of the titles, German fantasies of the same era directly projected the force of German arms. Briefly, if one contrasts some of the titles, the point is obvious. British examples range from *The History of the Sudden and Terrible Invasion of England by the French*, a short story of 1851, through *The Battle of Dorking* (1871), various channel tunnel fantasies inspired by the proposal to build a tunnel in 1882, for example, *How John Bull Lost London* or *The Taking of Dover* to Le Queux's own contributions in the 1900s. Typical German titles of the same era include: Die Abrechnung mit England (1901), 'The Reckoning with England', August Niemann's *Der Weltkrieg. Deutsche Träume* (1904), literally 'The World War. German Dreams' but translated into English as *The Coming Conquest of England*, or Carl Bleibtreu's *Die 'Offensiv-Invasion gegen England* (1907), literally 'The Offensive Invasion of England'. While it is possible to explain these differences by virtue of Britain being the pre-eminent power and an island to boot, the same differences remain highly suggestive of a different function for the future war in the two countries. Even if one accepts a degree of paranoia in the English response and the obsession with invasion threats, the old saw remains – just because you're paranoid, it doesn't mean they're not out to get you.

On closer comparison, the German text of Le Queux's novel is far from being a 'faithful translation'. The German text is considerably shorter, at 273 pages than the original English book version of *The Invasion of 1910*, which ran to 550 pages. The 26 chapters of Le Queux's English text are divided into three 'books': 'The Attack', 'The Siege of London' and 'The Revenge'. Tamm's version has 37 shorter chapters, no subdivisions and lacks a preface of any kind. In addition, the English novel featured 22 maps and 16 mock-ups of proclamations and pages of newspapers which are absent from the translation. While this may have been a matter of simple economic expediency, it does mean that the German reader's experience is considerably less vivid as a result.

Fig. 3 Example of graphical material incorporated into the text of the English original

THE FIRST NEWS IN BERLIN OF THE
GERMAN VICTORY.

In the remaining part of this essay I would like to focus on two telling sections in particular in the English text and examine how they are dealt with in the German translation. But before I do so, I need to set the scene briefly. The story of the invasion runs as follows. A surprise landing by German troops in East Anglia, Lincolnshire and Yorkshire is aided by German spies, one of Le Queux's pet themes (most mocked in Heath-Robinson's caricatures). The spies cut communications with London. The narrative is mediated through journalists working for national newspapers, who are the first to realise that there is something untoward afoot. As the tale proceeds a number of other narrative models are employed – the accounts of eyewitnesses, the letters of a dead German soldier and reports of war correspondents to name but a few. The effect of a collage of voices is enhanced through the invented documents, proclamations, newspaper headlines, tactical maps and so on inserted into the text. The land invasion is coordinated with a surprise attack at sea, commencing with the sinking of a disguised freighter in the Medway that bottles up a significant portion of the British fleet in Chatham. The remainder of the Home Fleet is outclassed by superior German gunnery at sea.

One of the early land engagements is symbolically a modern Battle of Maldon. In the historical Battle of Maldon in 991AD the Earl of Northumbria Brithnoth was defeated by the invading Danes. Over eleven chapters, some 200 pages and there is little in the way of good news for the defenders of the British Empire until chapter XII, which bears the title 'Defence at Last'. However, the defence is short-lived and by chapter XVII Britain is "In the Enemy's Hands" and London encircled.

It is at this point that the English and German texts decisively diverge. Where the original is rich in place names throughout, growing ever more complex in its use of local colour and detail, the German text grows sketchier and more abstract. The German text closes with the "Fall of London", in which a heavy artillery bombardment is depicted in a bloody and realistic fashion, with large numbers of civilian dead. The remaining 180 pages of the English original describe the birth of a "League of Defenders", a militia that wages a guerrilla campaign against the invaders. The remains of the British Navy also rally to launch a counter-attack at sea. Needless to say, the British Empire emerges at the end weakened but intact.

The German translation closes the tale at the high point of the German forces' victory. In order to do this it effectively edits sections of the original together, removing key emphases and comments in order to reverse the original message – that lack of preparedness could lead to defeat and this will not be because the British lack the will to fight. One may find a good example of this editing technique in the first passage I would like to consider which describes the Fall of London. The original is as follows:

> All the barricades had been broken.
> London lay burning – at the mercy of the German eagle.
> And as the darkness fell the German Commander-in-Chief looked again through his glasses, and saw red flames leaping up in dozens of places, where whole blocks of shops and buildings, public institutions, whole streets in some cases, were being consumed.

> London – the proud capital of the world, the "home" of the Englishman – was at last ground beneath the iron heel of Germany!
> And all, alas! due to one cause alone – the careless insular apathy of the Englishman himself! (356)

The German version offers a good translation but removes the key sentence at the end:

> Alle Barrikaden waren in der Hand des Feindes.
> Brennend lag London da – in den Klauen des deutschen Adlers...
> Und als die Dunkelheit sich über die unglückliche Stadt legte, blickte der deutsche Höchstkommandierende wiederum durch sein Fernrohr und sah an unzähligen Stellen rote Flammen aufzüngeln, denen ganze Häuserblocks und Straßenzüge zum Opfer fielen.
> Endlich lag London, die stolze Hauptstadt der Welt, an der das Herz jedes Engländers hängt, unter der Eisenferse Deutschlands... (259)

The omission of the final sentence changes the message from the warning "argument from defects to disaster" – that the English have been too apathetic in their insularity to notice and counter the coming threat – to a triumphalist prophecy of Germany victory. The three dots replacing the exclamation mark become a suggestion of the future hegemony of Germany rather than the patriot's despairing cry.

A second passage that illustrates the character of the changes made is the section depicting the encounter between the German general von Kleppen. Like the majority of the enemy officers in *The Invasion of 1910* von Kleppen speaks excellent English and is scrupulously polite and fair:

> Von Kleppen gave the Lord Mayor a message from Von Kronhelm, and urged him to issue a proclamation forbidding any further opposition on the part of the populace of London. With the three officers Sir Claude talked for a quarter of an hour, while into the Mansion House there entered a strong guard of men of the 2nd Magdeburg, who quickly established themselves in the most comfortable quarters. German double sentries stood at every exit and in every corridor, and when a few minutes later the flag was hauled down and the German Imperial Standard run up, wild shouts of triumph rang from every throat of the densely packed body of troops assembled outside.
> The joyous "hurrahs!" reached the Lord Mayor still in conversation with Von Kleppen, Von Mirbach and Frölich, and in an instant he knew the truth. The Teutons were saluting their own standard. The civic flag had, either accidentally or purposely, been flung down into the roadway below, and was trampled in the dust. A hundred enthusiastic Germans, disregarding the shouts of their officers, fought for the flag and it was instantly torn to shreds, and little pieces preserved as souvenirs.
> Shout after shout in German went up from the wildly excited troops of the Kaiser when the light wind caused their own flag to flutter out, and then as with one voice the whole body of troops united in singing the German National Hymn.
> The scene was weird and most impressive. London had fallen. (367)

The same scene in German is conveyed in a very different way:

Der Lord Mayor legte seine Amtskette ab und übergab sie seinem Diener zur Verwahrung. Nachdem er auch seine Robe abgelegt hatte, trat er wieder vor den deutschen General, der ihn aufforderte, eine Proklamation anschlagen zu lassen, die der Bevölkerung von London jeden weiteren Widerstand untersagte.

Gleich darauf rückte auch eine starke Wache in das Mansion House ein; deutsche Doppelposten standen an jedem Ausgang und auf jedem Korridor, und als einige Minuten später die englische Fahne niedergeholt und die deutsche gehißt wurde, ertönten wilde Hurrarufe aus den Kehlen der draußen aufgestellten Truppen.

In den schweigenden engen Straßen der City war kein einziger Engländer mehr zu sehen. Außer dem Lord Mayor und seinen Beamten war alles geflohen.

Ohne Verzug wurde noch in dieser Nacht eine deutsche Verwaltung in London eingesetzt, an deren Spitze ein deutscher Gouverneur trat. ( 265)

The German text emphasises the acquiescence of the Lord Mayor with a description of the removal of the symbols of office. The English "urged" becomes "*uffordern*" in German, which is a little milder: He is "asked' to issue a proclamation. Instead of the quarter-hour discussion between the Mayor and the German officers, things happen immediately (*"Gleich darauf"*). The conversation in the German version is already over when the German Imperial standard is raised. The entire incident concerning the tearing up of the civic flag is excised altogether. And, needless to say, "*Deutschland, Deutschland über alles…*" is not mentioned at all. In English, the reader is left with the impression of the scene as "weird and most impressive". In German we are assured that a German military governor will be in place that very night to guarantee order.

My title promises what Germany made of this mass-market invasion story. To some extent this question can be answered by looking at the changes made to reconstruct a populist argument in favour of greater British preparedness for war as a triumph for German arms. However, further areas remain for research: contemporary reactions in the German press, the original version in the *Daily Mail*, and translations into other languages.

1 *The Parliamentary Debates*, Series 4, 1892-1909, entry for 13 March 1906 under 1120.
2 William Jervis Jones does not list *Invasion* in his *Lexicon of French Borrowings in the German Vocabulary 1575-1648*. Nor does the word appear in volume 10 of Jacob and Wilhelm Grimm's famous *Deutsches Wörterbuch* of 1877. However, the *Deutsches Fremdwörterbuch* by Hans Schulz of 1913 cites the word *Invasion* as having been in use in the seventeenth century. From this we might infer that it was clearly perceived as a *Fremdwort* at the time.

**Primary References**
Blatchford, Robert. 1910. *Germany and England*. London: The Daily Mail.
Capitaine Danrit (Edouard Driant). 1902-1903. *La guerre fatale. France-Angleterre.* Paris: Flammarion. 3 vols.
Erskine Childers, Robert. 1903. *The Riddle of the Sands. A Record of Secret Service Recently Achieved.* London: Smith, Elder & Co.
Le Queux, William. 1894. *The great war in England in 1897*. London: Tower Publishing Company.
——1906a. *The Invasion of 1910. With a Full Account of the Siege of London*. London: Eveleigh Nash.
——1906b. *Die Invasion von 1910. Einfall der Deutschen in England*. Berlin: Concordia Deutsche Verlags-Anstalt.
——1906c. *The Invasion*. London: Everett & Co. Ltd.
——1909. *Spies of the Kaiser Plotting the Downfall of England*. London: Hurst & Blacknett Ltd.
Niemann, August. 1904a. *Der Weltkrieg, Deutsche Träume*. Leipzig: F W Vobach.
——1904b. *The Coming Conquest of England*. Translated by J. H. Freese. London: George Routledge & Sons.
Robida, Albert. 1887. *La guerre au vingtième siècle*. Paris: s.n.

**Secondary References**
Clarke, Ignatius F. 1966. *Voices Prophesying War 1763-1984*. Oxford: OUP.
——1995. *The Tale of the Next Great War, 1871-1914* Liverpool: Liverpool University Press.
——2001. *Disasters to Come* (British Future Fiction 7). London: Pickering & Chatto .
Davis, H W C and J R H. Weaver (eds). 1927. *Dictionary of National Biography 1912-1921*. London: Oxford University Press.
Gollin, Alfred M. 1960. *The Observer and J L Garvin 1908-1914. A Study in Great Editorship*. London: Oxford University Press.
Hindersmann, Jost. 1995. *Der britische Spionageroman: Vom Imperialismus bis zum Ende des Kalten Krieges*. Darmstadt: Wissenschaftliche Buchgesellschaft.
Lee Thompson, J. 2000. *Northcliffe. Press Baron in Politics 1865-1922*. London: John Murray.
Lopes, Antonio. 2004. '(Un)Masking the Self: The Hero in Edwardian Popular Fiction' . On line at: w3.ualg.pt/~alopes/Un-masking the self.pdf (consulted November 2004).
Mackenzie, Frederick A. 1921. *The Mystery of the Daily Mail 1896-1921*. London: Associated Newspapers Ltd.
St Barbe Sladen, N. 1938. *The Real Le Queux. The Official Biography of William Le Queux*. London: Eveleigh Nash.

# Ferdinand Freiligrath, William Wordsworth, and the Translation of English Poetry into the Conflicts of Nineteenth Century German Nationalism

*John Williams*

Wordsworth's reception in nineteenth century Germany was less extensive than other British Romantic poets; in the context of translation and conflict, however, Wordsworth's appearance in German anthologies merits careful study. This chapter shows that there was a greater knowledge of his work and reputation as a patriotic English poet than has previously been assumed. One of his chief admirers and translators of the mid nineteenth century, Ferdinand Freiligrath, was profoundly influenced by the political conflicts at the heart of the emerging German state. Freiligrath's selection and approach to the translation of Wordsworth's poems are considered in the light of the development of translation theory in early nineteenth century Germany, alongside the political and social impact of the French Revolution and Napoleonic wars. The influence of Friedrich Jacobsen, a devotee of English Romantic poetry in early nineteenth century Germany is also discussed. The chapter concludes with an assessment of the relationship between the reception of Wordsworth in late nineteenth century Germany and the evolving nature of political conflict as reflected in German foreign policy. Marie Gothein's biography and anthology of Wordsworth, published in 1893, are discussed in the context of a period of increasing strain in Anglo-German relationships.

Key words: Freiligrath, Wordsworth, translation, nationalism, poetry

## Introduction

Ferdinand Freiligrath (1810-1876) was a prolific and widely respected translator of English poetry into the German language. His political beliefs, however, were sufficiently outspoken to send him into exile on two occasions. This should alert us to the fact that his literary career - both as poet and translator - was inextricably bound up with political conflicts that were shaping the course of nineteenth century German national identity. "In the relations between two cultures" Bernhard Fabian has written, "a translation hardly ever presents itself as a simple 'action' or a straightforward 'process'" (Fabian 1991: 37). Lawrence Venuti has argued that where political and ideological conflicts are found, "they are always housed in the social institutions where translations are produced and enlisted in cultural and political agendas." (Venuti 1998: 29). Freiligrath's decision to translate poetry by William Wordsworth (1770-1850) as well as to publish him in English in Germany, provides an important opportunity to reflect on the complex nature of this process.

Wordsworth's career and reputation as a poet was profoundly shaped by his engagements with the political conflicts experienced in Britain from the 1780s through to his death in 1850. His poetry charts a complicated, often fraught and confused relationship with the contending claims of individual rights and liberties, patriotism, and respect for his Nation's past and its traditions, not least those relating to its religious foundations. In 1793, inspired by events in France and his reading of William Godwin, he began drafting an open letter in support of regicide. His brother Richard helped persuade him of the folly of publication. This was followed by a period when he began painfully to distinguish between what he now perceived as the shortcomings of Godwin's severely rationalist philosophical radicalism, and his own continuing, passionate commitment to the cause of political reform. This debate found outward expression through the composition in 1795-6 of his play, *The Borderers*. *The Borderers* was modelled in part on Schiller's *Die Rauber* of 1781. Schiller's play had first been enthusiastically publicised in England by Henry Mackenzie in 1788 (using a French translation), but by the early 1790s, political events had transformed it from an exciting example of literary *Sturm und Drang* into a dangerous piece of Jacobinical propaganda, and as such it was being vigorously attacked and condemned in the British press. As the war with Napoleon dragged on, Wordsworth's early radical republican ardour cooled. The degree to which he nevertheless continued to feel alienated from the political establishment of the day, however, remains a keenly debated issue (Williams 2005: 181-198).

Freiligrath was certainly not alone among German poets and intellectuals of the mid nineteenth century in becoming interested in Wordsworth's poetry. Johannes Scherr and Karl Elze, for example, both included Wordsworth in their widely disseminated anthologies from 1848 and 1853 onwards. Elze's anthology of early nineteenth century English and American poetry published the poems in English, with commentaries in German. It included eight poems by Wordsworth, making his contribution equal to that of Byron. The most popular poets were Tom Moore with 21 poems, and Felicia Hemans with 20. Scherr's anthology is entirely in German and includes just one poem by Wordsworth, 'We Are Seven', translated in a way that attempts a precise reproduction of the metrical arrangement and rhyme scheme of the English original. The translator was Karl Friedrich Ludwig Kannagiesser (1781-1861), an eminent academic and writer who also produced translations of Chaucer, Beaumont and Fletcher, Byron, Scott, Leopardi, and most notably, Dante. Scherr's anthology is of 'World Literature' and runs to 1,228 pages. The English section (second only in length to the German section) includes many of Freiligrath's translations. Given the eight Wordsworth poems in Elze's Anthology, the single Wordsworth poem in Scherr's *Bildersall der Weltliteratur* may conceivably be a reflection on the fact that Wordsworth had the reputation of being difficult to translate into German compared to many of his Romantic period compatriots.

Freiligrath undoubtedly emerges, however, as a key figure among German literary Anglophiles for the dissemination of Wordsworth's poetry in this period. In his essay of 1925 on Freiligrath as a translator of English Poetry, Gerald W. Spink notes him writing enthusiastically to Heinrich Kunzel in 1838 about how deeply Wordsworth's nature poetry had influenced him. Wordsworth "is wholly unsurpassable" (*"ganz unübertrefflic"'*) as a poet who knows and can express what a true feeling for Nature (*"Das Naturgefüh"'*) entails:

> Das Naturgefühl, das namentlich in Wordsworths Dichtungen weht, ist ganz unüberttrefflich, und denke noch immer mit stiller Freude an die Zeit zurück, wo ich ihn zuerst kennen lernte und mit ihm und Coleridge einsam Wald und Feld durchschweifte.
> (Spink 1925: 9)

## 1. Political Conflicts and the Reception of British Authors in Germany

Consideration of Freiligrath's formidable reputation as a translator of English poets into the German language, therefore, alerts us to the part which political conflict played in the reception of British authors in nineteenth-century Germany as it sought to establish a political and cultural identity and *Geist*. Wordsworth - never a poet to equal the popularity of many of his contemporaries in Germany - is a particularly interesting case in this respect.

As a poet who was anything but an automatic choice for German translators and editors, the reasons for turning to him will have tended to arise from a conscious decision to use a source text in a strategic manner. An awareness from the outset of Wordsworth's 'Englishness' made of his poetry a territory where it was possible to investigate conflict in various guises. This is to suggest that in Wordsworth's case we are looking at a significant departure from what was happening when English writers like Shakespeare, Byron, Moore, or Hemans, were taken up for translation. In their case, Venuti's claim seems wholly appropriate, "Foreign literatures tend to be dehistoricized by the selection of texts for translation, removed from the foreign literary traditions where they draw their significance." (Venuti 1998: 67) In Wordsworth's case, however, the evidence suggests that a far more complex process was taking place.

Freiligrath trained for a career in commerce. His reading of Byron and Hugo in particular inspired him as a teenager to write poetry in what he perceived to be the Romantic manner. He subsequently came under the spell of the political poetry of Georg Herwegh (1817-75), and began to use his own poetry to express increasingly radical political convictions. The success of his first collection of poems, published in 1838, encouraged him to devote all his energies to writing. By this time he was also translating and publishing

English poetry. The 1838 *Gedichte* includes French and English poetry translated into German. The poets represented provide us with an indication of the best known Romantic English poets in Germany, and his selection remained largely unchanged through repeated collected editions on into the 1850s. He had translated Coleridge's *The Ancient Mariner* around 1830, and went on to publish several editions of a Coleridge *Complete Works* (including one in 1877 with Doré's *Ancient Mariner* illustrations). The *Mariner* featured in all the collections of his own poetry, along with 26 poems by Tom Moore (by far the lion's share), slightly fewer poems by Scott, and a few each from Southey, Campbell, and Burns. Charles Lamb, Keats, and Felicia Hemans have one each. There are no poems by Wordsworth, but Freiligrath had published a translation of Wordsworth's 'Song for the Wandering Jew' (1800) in 1830 (Spink 1925: 9-11). Far more surprising than the absence of Wordsworth from the *Collected Poems*, might seem to be the omission of Byron. Along with Hemans and Moore, Byron became the most widely disseminated English poet of his generation in Germany at this time. But if we combine a knowledge of Freiligrath's political preoccupations with a consideration of an earlier, popular German account of the English Romantic poets, Byron's absence begins to look less puzzling.

Friedrich Johann Jacobsen published his *Briefe an eine deutsche Edelfrau, über die neuesten englischen Dichter* in 1820. At first sight, Jacobsen appears to endorse the widespread enthusiasm of his countrymen for the poet whose disdain for the 'simple' Wordsworth (expressed in *English Bards and Scotch Reviewers* of 1809) was well known. Byron's portrait was used as the frontispiece for the book, and besides devoting four chapters to him, Jacobsen refers to him throughout the 741 pages of text. Looked at more closely, however, we begin to appreciate that while Byron's lyric voice is praised unreservedly, his cynicism, particularly as it applies to a moral laxity and an indifference to patriotic commitment, is viewed as a flaw in his character that threatens to undermine the quality of his verse. Eudo C. Mason commented in 1959 that "[Jacobsen] is particularly at ease with Wordsworth's moral integrity, while he finds much in Byron (particularly the 'immoral parts' in Don Juan) unsettling." (Mason 1959: 124).

For all the problems that Jacobsen encountered with Wordsworth, a 'simple' poet claiming profound philosophical insight in a style that seemed peculiarly resistant to translation into the German language, he could not fault him on his patriotism. Wordsworth's love of country was made manifest in sonnets attacking the common aggressor, Napoleon. For a reader of Fichte's *Reden an die deutsche Nation* (1807), Joachim Heinrich Campe's *Wörterbuch der deutschen Sprache* (1807), and the equally high minded poetry of Ernst Moritz Arndt, Byron - beguiling as his lyrics might be - is suspect. Wordsworth - problematic in form and content as he could be for the German translator - undoubtedly merited serious study as a poet reflecting in his own way the potential conflict between art and politics, aesthetics and ideology, and language and national identity. Here was a volatile agenda comparable to that which had been increasingly exercising the minds of German writers since the influence of British authors had given way to the emergence of Germany's own Romantic Movement (Brown 2002: 82). Here too, in Wordsworth's experimentation with form and content, particularly available to Europeans readers after the Galignani edition of his *Poetical Works* (which included the Prefaces) came out in Paris in 1828, was evidence of an aesthetic, religious and political enquiry that complemented the German debate between Classicism and Romanticism conducted in the context of a burgeoning sense of a Germanic cultural identity. Wordsworth was granted two good length chapters in Jacobsen's book along with extensive quotations.

Freiligrath's knowledge of Jacobsen is beyond doubt, though as a German patriot, he probably did not need the *Briefe* to indicate the ways in which Byron was ideologically suspect, while Wordsworth remained worth the considerable labours his poetry demanded of its translator. Like Herwegh, Freiligrath's political sympathies were with the radical wing of reforming, middle class opinion. Germany can only be free, Freiligrath wrote in one of his political poems of 1844, when she is without Princes, "*Und frei nur ohne Fürsten*" (Freiligrath 1844). The political debate was inextricably bound up with a debate on the political function of language and literature, a key text for which had become Friedrich Schleiermacher's essay of 1813 on translation, *Über die verschiedenen Methoden des Übersetzens*. Fichte claimed that, though French occupation had robbed Germany of its political autonomy, "we have preserved our language and literature, and we will always remain a nation on this basis…" (Seeba 2003: 186). Jacobsen and Freiligrath cannot fail to have read the English poets with the words of Arndt's "Des Deutschen Vaterland" in mind:

> Only as long as you can hear the German tongue
> and praise the Lord in songs
> That's all!
> That's all that you, brave German, can call your own!
> (Seeba 2003: 187)

Their motives for and methods of translation will have been undertaken in the light of these issues.

By 1842 Freiligrath had achieved sufficient literary status to be offered a pension by Friedrich Wilhelm IV of Prussia. He accepted it, only to reject it two years later as it became increasingly clear that Friedrich was reversing his policies. This, and the publication of a volume of political poetry, *Ein Glaubensbekenntnis*, resulted in banishment (a fate shared with Herwegh) that took him first to Belgium, then Switzerland, and finally to London. He returned to Düsseldorf in 1848. As Paul Giles has suggested, in the period that links Romanticism to Modernism - from Byron to James Joyce - `exile` has been associated with `a form of intellectual empowerment` (Giles 2004: 31). Exile certainly informed Freiligrath's judgement in relation to his choice of poems for translation into German.

Freiligrath's *Gedichte aus dem Englischen* of 1846 (Freiligrath 1846a) was compiled in exile (though published in Germany). It marks the completion of his translation of Felicia Hemans' *The Forest Sanctuary*, a substantial poem of 169 stanzas, and it appears with 36 shorter pieces by Hemans. Hemans' work, it is worth noting, reflects throughout her keen interest in European poetry, drama and prose, and in its politics. With the case of Jacobsen in mind, it is also relevant to note that in later years, she moved from her enthusiasm for Staël, Byron, and Shelley, to become an admirer of the by then far more respectable and morally sound Wordsworth (Hemans 2002: 61). Headed with a quotation from Schiller's *Die Jungfrau von Orleans* and Coleridge's *Remorse*, Hemans described *The Forest Sanctuary* as a poem charting "the mental conflict, as well as outward sufferings" of a Spaniard in exile in North America with his child (Hemans 2002: 228). He is the victim of religious persecution in the sixteenth century. In addition to the poetry by Hemans (by now a widely translated author in Germany), Freiligrath's 1846 *Gedichte* contains six poems by Elizabeth Landon, three by Mary Howitt, one by William Cowper, eight extracts from Southey's *Thalaba* with three other poems, and one each from John Wilson, Barry Cornwall, Robert Monckton Milnes, Ebenezer Elliott and Tom Moore. Tennyson has fifteen poems, Longfellow four, and there are two by Wordsworth.

Freiligrath's Anglo-German reputation as a prolific poet and translator seems to have thrived on the basis of his appeal to a liberal, progressive readership. His choice of English poems for translation ensured that his target German readership would frequently be reminded of his own politically embattled situation. Whether in England or Germany, he donned the mantle of Wordsworth's alienated wandering Jew, and of Hemans' exiled Spaniard of *The Forest Sanctuary*. For Freiligrath, the act of translation appears to have been undertaken in the spirit of exploring the "unresolved state of tension" between what George Steiner has referred to as "resistant difference" and "elective affinity"; the translation will to a degree domesticate the source text, while the purpose of the finished translation remains dedicated to exposing its strangeness, its "resistant difference" (Steiner 1998: 413). German readers of Freiligrath's English translations were invariably to discover a more reflective and contemplative poetry than that likely to assail them when Freiligrath wrote his own German poetry. He thus appears to move beyond the theoretical framework that Schleiermacher constructed for his study of translation to the extent that he himself tends to identify with the author of his source text. Recalling Venuti's thesis that to analyse these conflictual processes fully, it is necessary to take into account the sociocultural context, it is important to appreciate Freiligrath's increasing independence when it came to both his choice of work for translation, and the method he adopted for translation (or indeed the decision to publish in English). Potential conflict between himself and publishers and editors receded as he himself gained increasing control over the production and marketing of his work.

From the bulk of the poetry he chose to translate, it is clear that Freiligrath would certainly have wished to challenge René Wellek's contention (made some 120 years later) that apart from Byron, no English Romantic poet "has the sense of ... life as Nothingness, of the artist as an outsider"; Freiligrath did not need to resort to Byron for a soul-mate in this respect, there were a number of others to choose from, including Hemans, and most certainly Wordsworth and Coleridge (Wellek 1965: 22). Wellek's view amounts to a repetition of Goethe's influential reading of Byron; however, it seems that this was by no means as widely accepted in nineteenth century Germany as it is often assumed to be (Saul 2000: 217).

What Wordsworth brought to Freiligrath's English pantheon was a profound sense of patriotism that linked love of country organically to nature itself. He also articulated an energetic opposition to the activities of autocratic foreign invaders. The two poems included in the 1846 collection are representative of his lyric note and his patriotic, political voice. The former is displayed in 'The Solitary Reaper', though we may be sure that Freiligrath's reading of it included an awareness of a political content that rarely if ever surfaces in the canon of Anglo-American criticism on this poem. Evidence to support this view is to be found in Elze's *Anthology*, where he groups 'The Solitary Reaper' with poems which have for the most part a very evident social and political purpose in the way they draw attention to the plight of the labourer; these include Elliott's 'Preston Mills', Hood's 'The Song of the Shirt', and E. B. Browning's 'The Cry of the Children'. These are all poems that engage with potentially explosive areas of conflict within a modern industrialising society.

## 2. Translating Wordsworth into German

'Yew Trees' (written in 1803 under the title of 'Ewtrees') marks Freiligrath's fascination with a poem that links patriotism to the poet's love of the natural world. Jacobsen had included this poem in his *Briefe*, quoting it (as was his normal method) in English, then translating it into a prose paragraph in a footnote. Wordsworth first published 'Yew Trees' in his 1815 *Collected Edition* (Wordsworth 1975: 146-7). The opening lines draw attention to the role played by the trees in supplying the longbows that had been used with such devastating effect against Germany's traditional foe:

> There is a Yew-tree, pride of Lorton Vale,
> Which to this day stands single, in the midst
> Of its own darkness, as it stood of yore:
> Not loth to furnish weapons for the bands
> Of Umfraville or Percy when they marched
> To Scotland's Heaths: or those that crossed the sea
> And drew their sounding boughs at Azincour,
> Perhaps at earlier Crecy, or Poictiers. (ll.1-8)

I am tempted to think that a reading of these lines was sufficient to set Freiligrath on the task of translation. As with Hemans' *The Forest Sanctuary*, Wordsworth's 'Yew Trees' takes its meaning from an idea that would be profoundly appealing to a German readership. The forest had long been a powerful symbol of German national identity. Commenting on early nineteenth century German literature and art, Simon Schama writes, "Religion and patriotism, antiquity and the future - all came together in the Teutonic romance of the woods. Figures asleep for centuries might stir into life, not least Germania herself". Elsewhere he points out that "by the time the German forest was being identified as the authentically native German scenery, much of it was fast disappearing under the axe", a fact that intensified the process of recreating the German forest through the "literary and visual imagination" (Schama 1996: 95, 107). The tree, a thing of beauty in its native landscape, may here become also a source of weaponry when it is time to go to war for your country. It is even possible that Freiligrath saw Wordsworth's Yew tree as a specific foil to Hemans' pessimistic comparison between an oak tree overwhelmed with vines and the failing political health of a nation in Part One, stanza xi of *The Forest Sanctuary*. I then imagine him becoming increasingly exasperated with Wordsworth as he struggled to translate the rest of the piece, determined, as was his practice (unlike Jacobsen) to retain the formal structures of rhythm and metre in his source text, and in this instance preserve one of Wordsworth's most interminably convoluted sentences that runs from line 14 for the remaining 24 lines of the poem. The act of translation has resulted in the poem itself becoming a site of conflict, the final, tangible evidence for which is that the reader is presented with four extra lines of German 'Yew Tree'!

Arguably, Freiligrath is here adopting Schleiermacher's preferred strategy as an *Übersetzer* translating an artistic text. In his *Über die verschiedenen Methoden des Übersetzens* of 1813, Schleiermacher recommends that the reader be given "the same impression that he as a German would receive reading the work in the original language" (Munday 2001: 27-8); the intention is to adopt an 'alienating' method of translation. Jeremy Munday summarises this as valorising the foreign and transferring it into the target language (*ibid*: 29). However, as the four extra lines of Freiligrath's 'Yew Tree' indicate, there remain complex tensions between rendering Wordsworthian blank verse poetic form into German, and reproducing at the same time anything like a faithfully Wordsworthian meaning. Here are the first eight lines of Wordsworth's poem, now become nine:

> Ein Eibenbaum, der Stolz des Lortonthals -
> Bis diesen Tag steht einsam er, inmitten
> Des eignen Dunkels, wie er vormals stand,
> Als er den Schaaren Umfraville`s und Percy's,
> Eh' sie nach Schottlands Haiden gingen, willig
> Geschosse reichte; oder jenen, die
> Das Meer durchKreuzten, und bei Azincourt,
> Vielleicht auch früher noch, bei Poitiers
> Und Crecy, dumpf die Bogen tönen liessen.

Freiligrath's German retains - as far as possible - the iambic pentameter discipline of the English blank verse line. Though blank verse is not in itself a problematic discipline for the German language, translating iambic pentameters from English, specifically when written in the way Wordsworth tended to manipulate the form, does clearly begin to create difficulties. Faced with the need to concede to an appropriate German word order, Freiligrath is prompted to relocate family and place names. The extra line that turns Wordsworth's eight into Freiligrath's nine in this passage begins to grow from line 4. By lines 6 and 7 it has become inevitable, by which time it is also clear that the conflicting demands of grammatical construction are putting increasing strain on the relationship between the source and target texts. This becomes very evident at the end of the passage, when Wordsworth chooses to disrupt the iambic beat in line 8, a process initiated by his use of the word "earlier" which problematises the scansion of "Crecy", and leaves "or Poictiers" to be read as though they were the final words of a prose sentence. Dismantling the metre in this way was a device Wordsworth did occasionally employ (it was a technique upon which Byron had poured scorn in *English Bards and Scotch Reviewers*); here it throws into dramatic relief the expansive, exclamatory lyric flow of the following two lines, where every syllable counts: "Of vast circumference and gloom profound / This solitary Tree!" Confronted with Wordsworth's metrical irregularities in line 8, Freiligrath works against his source text in a bid to retain a metrically orthodox line, moving "Poictiers" up to the previous line, bringing in the reference to "Crecy" after it, and finishing his ninth line with one easily assimilated extra syllable in "*liessen*". At the same time he translates Wordsworth's "drew their sounding bows" (line 7 in the source text) in a way that locates it in its appropriate place for his German readership, almost preserving the metre Wordsworth had chosen very deliberately to disrupt.

Conflict is ubiquitous in Wordsworth's poem, but a resolution of conflict is also implicit in the poet's representation of the Yew Tree as both a source of weaponry, and a natural object whose longevity epitomises steadfastness and continuity. Conflict is present in Freiligrath's identification with Wordsworth's subject matter, the heroism of patriotic warriors preserving their country's liberty; but it is also present in the difference that evolves as the poem moves from its location among the trees of England, a historical narrative that celebrates English nationhood in the English language, to a Germanic form of linguistic and cultural expression.

The political content of the 1846 *Gedichte aus dem Englischen* is primarily maintained through the poems by Ebenezer Elliott (1781-1849), the radical 'Corn-law rhymer', and (to a lesser degree) Robert Southey (1774-1843). Compared to Freiligrath's own style in political verse, however, it remains muted. Mary Howitt, one of the poets included, will have been made very aware of this when in 1846 Freiligrath presented her with a copy of his own *Ça Ira*. This is a small book of six politically incendiary poems, the first of which is set to the metre of the *Marseillaise* (Freiligrath 1846b). Two years after *Gedichte aus dem Englischen* was published, Freiligrath was back in Germany, continuing to write overtly political poetry in the wake of the 1848 revolutions. In 'Hamlet' (translated in the 1869 *Poems from the German by Ferdinand Freiligrath* by William Howitt, Mary's husband), he wrote:

> Deutschland is Hamlet! Solemn, slow,
> Within its gates walks every night,
> Pale, buried Freedom to and fro,
> And fills the watchers with affright.

I suggest that this is a darker rendering of Ludolf Weinbarg's description of Goethe's Faust in his *Ästhetische Feldzüge* of 1834: "Faust is Germany struggling to be liberated, indeed he is the liberated Germany as it anticipates the victory of its freedom." (Seeba 2003: 187) It should be noted, however, that by the time Freiligrath was writing, Shakespeare, of all the English writers, had acquired what was virtually a distinct German identity in consequence of repeated acts of translation.

We know that around this time Freiligrath's reading of English political poetry started to include the Chartist poet Ernest Jones. In 1848 his own defiant poem memorialising the victims of the fighting in Berlin, '*Die Toten an die Lebenden*', triggered his arrest for sedition. He was tried and acquitted, but soon after emigrated to England where he found work in the London branch of a Swiss Bank. He wrote on German literature, contributing frequently to *The Athenaeum*. By this time he was also corresponding, and on very familiar terms, with Karl Marx. Freiligrath eventually returned to Germany in 1868, and his final volume of poetry was published in 1876, the year of his death.

*The Rose, Thistle and Shamrock*, an anthology of English, Scottish, and Irish poetry, edited by Freiligrath, was first published in Stuttgart in 1853 (Freiligrath 1853). All the poetry is in English. There appear to have been at least five editions of this version, with Freiligrath's wife and his daughter Kate involved in the editing. The Preface to the revised 1874 edition notes that after more than 20 years in print, the anthology was still popular. This collection provides us with a reasonably reliable indication of which poems by Wordsworth had become familiar to an English reading German public in the 1860s and 1870s.

In Section 1, 'Poesy and the Poets', there are six poems by Wordsworth from a total of 52. These include 'Resolution and Independence', 'Scorn not the sonnet', 'To the Sons of Burns', and 'Composed upon Westminster Bridge'. Wordsworth is for the most part characterised in the *Anthology* as he is in this section, as a poet who produces verse in a reflective, lyrical mode. He has no poetry in the second or third section of the 1854 edition, but in Section 4, 'Society, Work and Progress', there are three extracts from *The Excursion*. It is here that, once again, issues of political conflict are given prominence.

*The Excursion*, first published in 1814, was intended by Wordsworth as the central section of his major work, a philosophical poem of epic proportions to be called *The Recluse*. He never completed the project, leaving the Nine Book *Excursion* (totalling 8,850 lines of poetry) to be read as his response to the major political and social issues confronting England in the early nineteenth century. Written throughout in Miltonic blank verse, it contains the observations of a small group of men on the recent history of the British Nation, not least the impact of the French Revolution, the fate of those who had been disappointed in their hopes for reform in the political life of Britain, and the consequences of the onset of industrialisation.

In the context of Wordsworth studies, *The Excursion* is an important measure of the extent to which Wordsworth continued to harbour disaffected views on the conduct of the British Government through the French Revolution period and on through the period of war with Napoleonic France that followed. The poem also contains a passionate critique of modern industrialisation and the consequent fate of those either drawn into factory labour, or thrown into rural poverty. Considered until relatively recently to signal unproblematically the poet's retreat into conservatism, Freiligrath's choice of extracts from *The Excursion* accords with more recent readings of the poem as one in which social, political, and religious conflict remain centre stage, and are far from being resolved in a manner that endorses the status quo (Williams 2002: 162-196).

Freiligrath turned to Book VIII, 'The Parsonage', for his extracts. The passage beginning at line 87 reflects on the effect on the countryside of industrial change:

> An inventive Age
> Has wrought, if not with speed of magic, yet
> To most strange issues. I have lived to mark
> A new and unforeseen creation rise
> From out the labours of a peaceful Land
> Wielding her potent enginery to frame
> And to produce, with appetite as keen
> As that of war, which rests not night or day,
> Industrious to destroy!

Freiligrath called this extract 'The Manufacturing Spirit'. The second passage is headed 'The Factory at Night', and begins at line 170:

> ... at the appointed hour a bell is heard
> Of harsher import than the curfew-knoll
> That spake the Norman Conqueror's stern behest -
> A local summons to unceasing toil!

Finally 'The Working Classes' begins at line 262: "Domestic bliss / (Or call it comfort, by a humbler name,) / How art thou blighted for the poor man's heart!" (Wordsworth 1959: 268, 270-1, 273).

Though the anthology contains many more poems that have liberal political and social themes, Wordsworth appears in the main as a lyric poet of nature and childhood. It is important to note, however, that in choosing to present *The Excursion* as a poem that explored the politics of class engendered by the factory system, Freiligrath departed from Jacobsen's reading of the poem. The *Briefe an eine deutsche Edelfrau* devotes an entire chapter to *The Excursion*, quoting from it at length. The passages Jacobsen chose, however, are very much in accord with the English Victorian reading of *The Excursion*, presenting it as a spiritual antidote to a view of the modern world as a place in danger of becoming engulfed by secularised political opinion and the worship of materialism. In this reading Wordsworth's philosophical appeal to the natural world as a guide to religious belief and social conduct depoliticises the poet in a way Freiligrath was not prepared to do.

Freiligrath's declared intention (stated in the Introduction to the 1853 edition of the Anthology) was that his collection of poetry should be "a welcome present to every lover of English poetry" in Germany, England and America. Genteel and politically neutral as this may sound, however, the idiosyncratic choice of *Excursion* extracts alone illustrates that political motivation born of the conflicts that marked the evolution of 19$^{th}$ century German nationalism were never far from the surface in Freiligrath's mind.

Though *The Rose, Thistle and Shamrock* consisted of poems in English, the issue of translation remains inimical to the political agenda of conflict that runs through Freiligrath's career. The technical problems of translating

Wordsworth into German - compared to Burns, Byron, or Hemans in lyric mode - has already been discussed. In her substantial biography and anthology of Wordsworth, published in 1893, Marie Gothein quoted Goethe on the generic problems of translating English into German: "If you replace the many short and striking monosyllabic English words with German compounds or many syllabic equivalents, all the power and effect of the words get lost" (Gothein 1893: vi-vii). Faced with these difficulties, Freiligrath, Gothein, and Andreas Baumgartner (whose 1897 anthology of Wordsworth's poetry was accompanied by a short biography) all opted to reproduce the rhythms and the sound of Wordsworth's poetry as best they could in the German language. An attempt at precision in this respect frequently forced them into a very free paraphrase of the sense of the lines. Some of Gothein's extracts from *The Prelude* are at first reading very difficult to place as a result of this. Freiligrath's rendering of 'Yew Trees' is another case in point.

Gothein, however, insists that it was not just the way that Wordsworth uses language that marks him out as '*durch und durch englisch*' (Gothein 1893: iii). For her - as for Freiligrath - there were equally important political issues involved. That phrase, '*durch und durch englisch*', occurs in a quotation Gothein used from the historian Leopold von Ranke (1795-1886). Ranke had used it in the course of a funeral oration he gave for another German Historian of his generation, J. M. Lappenberg (1794-1865). Ranke was recalling Lappenberg's enthusiasm for Wordsworth as a young man, and he goes on to say that it was not just the 'Englishness' of Wordsworth's poetry that intrigued Lappenberg and others in the years immediately following the fall of Napoleon, it was also his 'views', and his 'ideas'. To produce her biography Gothein worked closely with Professor William Knight, an influential figure in Wordsworth scholarship in England, absorbing an endemically English enthusiasm for the poet, then seeking to impart that strangeness to her German readers in a way that rendered it both familiar, yet still peculiar to its English cultural context. Gothein suggests that her German readers would do well to try and understand more about this most English of Englishmen, even if they fail to find his poetry as appealing as she clearly did. The European powers were taking increasingly careful stock of each other as the century drew to a close, and Jacobsen's, Freiligrath's, Gothein's, and Baumgartner's translated Wordsworth should be set in the context of the constant interplay between literary culture and politics throughout this period, and the various conflicts they reflected.

To begin to understand the nature of the English in the late nineteenth century, Gothein implies, you might do worse than add a study of the work of a very popular, patriotic English poet to your reading of Lappenberg. Lappenberg made his reputation in Germany as an archivist, and an historian of Anglo-Saxon England and England under the Normans. *A History of*

*England under the Anglo-Saxon Kings* was published in 1834, *A History of England under the Norman Kings* was published in 1857; both were translated into English by Benjamin Thorpe. Beyond the painstaking compilation of factual detail, Lappenberg is preoccupied by the processes of imperialism, and by the time Gothein was researching her life of Wordsworth, her interest in the poet does appear to be at least in part informed by her interest in the joint destinies of England and Germany as the century drew to a close.

Gothein describes how Lappenberg arrived in Edinburgh in 1817, aged 23. Educated in German Classical literature, he was excited by the discovery of what to him was a new 'cultural element' (*'neues Kulturelement'*), and - according to Gothein - "the enthusiasm for Wordsworth was in its genesis.... Crabb Robinson had written: 'You don't dare to praise Wordsworth in public, yet, but tête-à-tête you would admit, that you are one of his admirers.'" (Gothein 1893: iv) What had excited Lappenberg then might just as easily trouble many Germans of Gothein's generation. She alludes to a prophesy by De Quincey in his essay on Wordsworth, first published in *Tait's* Magazine in 1839, that the English language would colonise the world in the next 150 years, with the result that everyone would be reading *The Excursion*, and many of the shorter poems, with the ease and regularity that they now read Shakespeare.

**Conclusion**
To appreciate the impact of De Quincey's statement on Gothein, we need to appreciate the centrality of the issue of language in nineteenth-century German political history. In 1807, Joachim Heinrich Campe had written that in the midst of political chaos "the only remaining reason for hope" was the German language. In 1827 August Koberstein published a text book described by Hinrich C. Seeba as "tracing the history of German language and literature as the history of the Germans themselves." In 1854 Jacob Grimm undertook the *Deutsches Wörterbuch*, asking "what do we have in common but our language and literature?" (Seeba 2003: 184) This is the context for the literary, political, and historical labours of Jacobsen, Freiligrath, Lappenberg, Gothein, Baumgartner, and their contemporaries.

Seeba has discussed the particular significance of the part played in this debate by Georg Gottfried Gervinus in the 1830s. Gervinus' description of the historian's contribution to the evolution of nationhood through the study of literature is, to say the least, a remarkably expansive one. If we accept it as representative of a widely accepted view, then it will help to elucidate the full significance of the act of translation for Freiligrath and others:

> He [the historian] shows us the origin not just of one poem but of all poetic products from their time, from the circle of their ideas, actions, and fates. He demonstrates what in the poems reflects these times and what does not. He

explores the conditions of their production and reception and assesses their value accordingly. He compares them with the best examples of the genre at a particular moment and in a particular nation, when and where they came into being, and, expanding his horizon, with similar phenomena at other times and in other nations. (Seeba 2003: 194-5)

For an Anglophile translator of Freiligrath's generation, one moreover obliged spend many years of his life 'in other nations', the motivation to render Wordsworth's poetry into German was inextricably bound up with confronting political issues of patriotism and nationalism manifest within the restless and contested boundaries of a German identity that sought credibility both on the map of Europe, and in the minds of its progenitors. For Marie Gothein, bringing the work of an endemically English, patriot poet such as Wordsworth within the compass of the German language, was an act calculated to challenge a spirit of linguistic imperialism manifestly allied to the conflicting political imperial ambitions of Germany and England across the globe.

### References

Brown, Hilary. 2005. *Benedikte Naubert 1756-1819 and her Relations to English Culture*. London: Maney Publishing.

Elze, Karl. 1853. *Englischer Liederschatz aus englischen und amerikanischen Dichtern vorzugsweise des XIX. Jahrunderts mit Nachrichten über die Verfasser*. Dessau: Katz.

Fabian, Bernhard. 1991. *The English Book in Eighteenth-Century Germany* (The Panizzi Lectures 1991). London: British Library.

Freiligrath, Ferdinand. 1844. *Ein Glaubensbekenntnis*. Mainz: Victor von Zabern.

——1846a *Gedichte aus dem Englischen*. Stuttgart and Tübingen.

——1846b. *Ça Ira, Six Poems*. Herisau.

——1853. *The Rose, Thistle and Shamrock, A Book of English Poetry, Chiefly Modern*, selected and arranged by Ferdinand Freiligrath. Stuttgart, Edward Hallberger.

Giles, Paul. 2004. 'American Literature in English Translation: Denise Leverton and Others' in *PMLA* Vol. 119 No. 1: 31-41.

Gothein, Marie. 1893. *William Wordsworth, Sein Leben, Seine Werke, Seine Zeitgenossen*, 2 volumes. Halle: A.S. Verlag von Max Niemeyer.

Hemans, Felicia. 2002. *The Forest Sanctuary*, in *Felicia Hemans Selected Poems, Prose and Letters*, Gary Kelly (ed.). Ontario and Ormskirk: Broadview Press.

Jacobsen, Friedrich Johann. 1820. *Briefe an eine deutsche Edelfrau, über die neuesten englischen Dichter, herausgegeben mit über setzten Auszügen vorzüglicher Stellen aus ihren Gedichten und mit den Bildnissen der berühmtesten jetzt lebenden Dichter Englands*. Altona.

Lappenberg, Johann Martin. 1834. *A History of England under the Anglo-Saxon Kings*. Hamburg. Translated by Benjamin Thorpe, 1845, 2 volumes. London: John Murray.

——1857. *A History of England under the Norman Kings*. Hamburg. Translated by Benjamin Thorpe, 1857. Oxford: Oxford University Press.

Mason, Eudo C. 1959. *Deutsche und englische Romantik*. Göttingen.

Munday, Jeremy. 2001. *Introducing Translation Studies*. London: Routledge.

Saul, Nicholas. 2000. 'Aesthetic humanism (1790-1830) in Watanabe-O'Kelly (ed.) *The Cambridge History of German Literature*. Cambridge: Cambridge University Press.

Schama, Simon. 1996. *Landscape and Memory*. London: Fontana.
Scherr, Johannes. 1848. *Bildersall der Weltliteratur*, 2 vols. Stuttgart: Kröner.
Schleiermacher, Friedrich. 1813. *Über die verschiedenen Methoden des Übersetzens* in Robinson, Douglas (ed.). 1997. *Western Translation Theory from Heroditus to Nietzsche*: Manchester: St. Jerome.
Schmid, Susanne. 2004. 'The Act of Reading an Anthology' in *Comparative Critical Studies* Volume 1, Number 1-2: 53-69.
Seeba, Hinrich C. 2003. '*Trostgründe*: Cultural Nationalism and Historical Legitimation in Nineteenth-Century German Literary Histories' in *Modern Language Quarterly* 64 (2): 183-195.
Spink, Gerald W. 1925. 'Freiligrath as Translator of English Poetry', in *German Studies* 36. Berlin.
Steiner, George. 1998 (first published 1975). *After Babel: Aspects of Language and Translation*. Oxford and New York: Oxford University Press.
Venuti, Lawrence. 1998. *The Scandals of Translation: Towards an ethics of difference*. London and New York: Routledge.
Wellek, René. 1965. *Confrontations: Studies in the intellectual and literary relations between Germany, England, and the United States during the nineteenth century*. Princeton: Princeton University Press.
Williams, John. 2002. *Critical Issues: William Wordsworth*. Basingstoke and New York: Palgrave.
——2005. 'Britain's Nelson and Wordsworth's 'Happy Warrior': A Case of Cautious Dissent' in *Romanticism* 11.2: 181-198.
Wordsworth, William. 1959. *The Excursion*, in *Wordsworth's Poetical Works* volume 5. E. De Selincourt and Helen Darbishire (eds). Oxford: Clarendon Press.
——1975. *Poetical Works*. Thomas Hutchinson (ed.), revised by Ernest De Selincourt. Oxford: Oxford University Press.

# Translating the Enemy: A 'hip-hop' Translation of a Poem by the Russian Futurist Velimir Khlebnikov (1885-1922)

*Brian Chadwick*

This paper identifies the rhetorical and behavioral stylistics of playful confrontation which determine the global genre and 'relational aesthetics' of the text of Russian Futurism, and argues that a 'hip-hop' translation offers in a strong sense an adequate but non-unique homology. The notion of situatedness in relation to the original language text and its translation is examined. The conflict-determined contextuality of the original is underlined, parallels are drawn between the stress on orality, fluent delivery and address, and conclusions are drawn as regards the conflict generated by framing this translation idiom within a normative publishing canon signaled as "modern poetry in translation". A constructive mapping of the geographical and discursive boundary dislocations inscribed within the poem's structure by civil war onto semantic domains of ephemerality, instantaneity/ immanence and the fragile *powah* of the Word inherent in the "front line" positioning of high Rap poetry is outlined.

Key words: civil war, rap poetry, situatedness

| *"Kamennaia baba" – extract* | *Translation* |
|---|---|
| Mne mnogo l'nado? | Not verra much I am crammin fo' |
| Kovriga khleba | Just a loaf o bread |
| I kaplia moloka | an a drop of milk |
| Da eto nebo | plus as well de sky |
| Da eti oblaka | an a cloud or two! |

"An empire founded by war has to maintain itself by war." (Montesquieu 1689-1755)
"In whatever country we do battle it is always a civil war." (Napoléon Bonaparte)
"The violent effects of translation are felt at home as well as abroad." (Lawrence Venuti)

## Introduction

The paper has three sources or *causes*. These are: firstly, the author's translation of a group of poems and texts by the poet Velimir Khlebnikov (1885-1922), intended as a contribution to an anthology of English language translations of twentieth-century Russian poetry, *Ten Russian Poets* (Mc Kane 2004) (hereafter "TP"); secondly 'Issues raised by a 'rap' translation of a poem by Velimir Khlebnikov' (Chadwick 2004). The poem in question, in Russian 'Kamennaia Baba', literally 'Stone woman', translated as 'Rocking mama' (hereafter KB) was one of those proposed as part of the TP contribution. Thirdly, the invitation to contribute to a collection of essays on the theme of *Translation and Conflict*.

The above mentioned paper focused on the role a particular translation strategy played in foregrounding the *mood* of the poem and its aesthetic stance, which culminated in the poem's *vzryv*, a liberating explosion, brought about through the act of a butterfly settling on the eyes of a female stone carving, a transfigured representation of the violence and unpredictability of events contemporary with the poem's narration. This paper by contrast turns the problematic of its antecedent inside out, focusing in turn on the aesthetics and sociology of Futurism, as a movement informing the poet's own outlook, and then on the field of the poem's *signified*. In the present context, it addresses the issue of how translation variously renders and ideologically transforms the poem's realia, and how it functions as an agency in the ongoing project of evaluating, but also consolidating *and* contesting the meaning of these and the events this and other poems refer to.

The poem KB is dated 10 March 1919, with a degree of preciseness unusual for its author. Khlebnikov is one of the two generally acknowledged leaders of the predominantly literary movement known as Russian Futurism, the other "founding father" being the better known Vladimir Mayakovsky. The target language chosen for the translation was English, in one of its many vernacular variants, namely the by now utterly eclectic lingua franca of "rap" poetry. This version plundered its lexicon and syntax, broadly from London Jamaican and American hip-hop. The rationale for doing this took shape retrospectively; it was grounded in the perception that the "defining moment" of Russian Futurism was its playfully conflictual relationship with the existing literary and cultural mainstream.

## 1. Russian Futurism

This movement marked or engineered this relationship discursively in warlike terms, a relationship with the mainstream seen as non-negotiable difference, antagonism, and rupture, rather than the mutually compatible distance between non-antagonistic or indifferently co-existing alternatives. The differences were defined in terms of shifting but nevertheless sharply defined "positional" polarities with variously technical, sociological, ethnic or historical colouring, defining aesthetics or ideological procedures and stances[1]. These were selectively deployed to suit occasion, topos, or site, while constantly under the threat of encirclement, a circling, left to right displacement and resituation as cliché, fulfilling a fundamental *a priori* , the provisionality of the vernacular, its dissolution into obsolescence. This act was embodied in vernacular and disposable forms of street theatre and performance, cabaret, puppet shows, low-tech publications, the pamphlet, the film attraction, graffiti, daubing. This oppositionality was infectious - even "serious", non-futurist artists and *intelligenty* often willingly connived at their own subversion - the solemnities of Stanislavsky's landmark Chekhov and Gorky productions were regularly treated to farcical send-ups (*kapustniki*) by their own actors, while scholars of subsequent eminence like Roman Jakobson and Viktor Shklovsky contributed to Futurist "anthologies" and read papers at Futurist exhibitions, Shklovsky reading papers at art exhibitions urging the necessary value of nonsense and incomprehensibility.

Russian Futurism was defined not only by its conflictual aesthetics, but by a sociology driven by both class and ethnicity, a drive having a revolving-door relationship with the contemporary Eastern diaspora, as noted below. Both represent an overlay or remodelling of the vernacular (today's creole, patois, street-talk, jive) forming and reforming under the forces of immigration, diasporas, and labour mobilities. Early Russian Futurism was very conscious of the often abrasive street vernacular of an urbanising, recently rural proletariat, in its Russian variant constituted by internal immigration hailing equally from the Ukraine or Kazakhstan. The phenomenon of hooliganism in the first decade of the twentieth century was made much of by the outraged metropolitan St Petersburg Press (Neuberger 1993) and was, for that reason, highly valued by young poets, painters and radical scholars as linguistic, but also graphic and behavioural raw materials, to be "made strange", or to become the armature of the "secondary modelling" of "ordinary language" argued by Formalist scholars as constitutive of the literary process. "Like early modern peasants at carnival, the hooligans who infiltrated the main streets of the capital from their outposts on the city periphery" (*ibid.*: 143) displayed exaggerated forms of ordinary lower-class coarse behaviour in order to transgress social conventions and declare the autonomy of their own "uncultured" way of life. By seizing control of the street they temporarily created a space free of hierarchy" (*ibid.*: 63). Analogously the Futurists

> invaded the territory of 'proper art' with the coarse, crude, primitive, childlike and erotic, ....[in order to create] serious works of art that appropriated elements of the culture that society considered uncultured. (*ibid.*: 144)

In 'The Theme of the East in Khlebnikov' in *Narody Azii i Afriki* (Peoples of Asia and Africa), the literary scholars Loshchits and Turbin stress the physical and cultural importation of ethnicity, noting for example that whereas for the "elder generation", metropolitan Symbolists, often grandees born of the capitals' scientific or literary dynasties, closely linked to hegemonic European culture, "Asia" simply existed as an aesthetic theme, the Futurists in large part were themselves the

> offspring of an anarchic Russo-Asian element. Most of them came to literature from the periphery, arriving [in the metropolis] like outlanders, like a travelling circus or nomadic horde. They characteristically stylised their invasion of the capital cities as a medieval invasion. (*ibid.*: 150)

Khlebnikov himself was, in his own words. "born near Astrakan, in the *stan* [camp] of mongol nomads professing Buddhism", in a region which even now recalls a Noah's Ark of languages and peoples. As he puts it, in his veins Russian blood mingled with that of "Armenian and the Zaporozhian Cossacks". From early childhood, his ears became accustomed to the sound of Russian, Ukrainian and Tatar speech, and to "the extravagantly polyglot lexicon of the multilingual Babylon of the Russian South" (*ibid.*: 151).

## 2. Hip-hop

As regards the revolving door mentioned above, some Futurist stances find a provocative match in instances of the nomadic hybridization characterising much contemporary global hip-hop culture, which as periphery is internally and collectively pluralistic, defined as precisely in relation to the point singularities of the Centre and Empire as plains and valleys are to "their" mountain peak. Thus, one of the "dozens of Russian bands playing underground gigs in New York", the mighty Yoke is

> a rock band combining the broodingly poetic music of its homeland with New York influences from Latin percussion to Jamaican Rap [strengthened] by the addition of a rapper from Jamaica [who] has added a strangely appropriate counterpoint, ratcheting up the intensity of the smolderingly mysterious music. (Tanzer 2002)

Despite the surface remoteness, what the Futurist Khlebnikov, and Moratov, the Yoke's leader, share, is a kind of diasporic mobility, driven less by a Rimbaudesque nomadism than by the enduring imperatives of geopolitical metamorphoses - spun off into contemporary large-scale migrancies, having their own forms of expression: "after ten years away, lyrics like these are not exactly related to the feelings of living in Russia anymore - their personal statements about his experience as a migrant, an artist and a human being in the city" (*ibid.*).

Other reflections by Yoke's Muratov, on "what Russian culture is all about - mixing influences", an inevitable process in "the world's largest country, [which] has absorbed the influences of ethnic groups from gypsies in the East to Eskimos in the West, and every kind of ethnic music is played...." (*ibid.*) form an epochal refrain to Futurism's restless mobility, first during pre-revolutionary Russia's economic expansionism (led by foreign entrepreneurship and financed to a great degree by French, British, Belgian and German capital) then, after this "rehearsal", the navigation of the space and time contours of revolution and civil war - with interesting ideological equipment.[2]

In terms of its moments (activism, antagonism, nihilism, and agonism) the constituents of avant-garde confrontationism have classically and influentially been identified and provided with a typology by Poggioli's *Theory of the Avant Garde (*Poggioli 1968). Implicit in, but not central to

Poggioli's analysis, the military origin of the central metaphor - *avant-garde* - retains its most important defining feature in Futurist practice, that of positionality, of manoeuvres conducted behind enemy lines and on enemy territory. Thus it seemed to the translator of KB that an arguably viable translation "algorithm" would have as a fundamental postulate that the "situatedness" of the original language text is a prime fact requiring translation, especially in the case of a text with affiliations to a literary movement in which situatedness is so obviously a marked feature, and in which positionality is characterised not by continuity or embeddedness, but by rupture, rhetorically signaled as conflict; the term "algorithm" is used by Soviet translation theorist, T A Kazakova (1988), arguing that a bottom-up cottage industry "heuristics" rather than a top-down theorising of genre paradigms with attendant "algorithms" is determining in "normally obtaining" translation contexts with fuzzy definition (see the discussion of Venuti below for the politicization of the "heuristics" of normality).

The "distinct features" of rap with obvious affiliation to the above listing of Futurist polarities prompt considerations of an "algorithmic" kind regarding Futurist translation - emphasis on low-tech performance; elevation of Africa (as opposed to WASPness; see Khlebnikov's lexical politics, proscribing Latin roots); an emphasis on technical virtuosity ; its equally constitutive low-tech infrastructure; rhetorically skilful, ceremonious, usually ribald speech genres; "dialogic" forms of direct address - "toasting", "dissing", "snaps", i.e. taunts; supple code-switching techniques (again, a main device of Khlebnikov is a pervasive glossolalia); an emphatic militancy - witness NWA's (in)famous "Fuck Tha Police" being, ironically, "pumped out to a million listeners in Poland, Northern Czechoslovakia and the Western Soviet Union, at the very time it was "banned from airways of the US" (Morley 1992); in this connection, mention may be made of rappist artists like Chuck D, the leader of Public Enemy and spokesman for hip-hop, who often referred to rap music as "the CNN of African American youth", also Ice-T, controversial exponent of gansta rap, holding that "rappers have been reporting from the front for years" (Hill 1999: 106).

For both Futurism and rap music, the Word itself receives enormous stress as an agency, the vehicle and kernel of wisdom and the seat of power. *Slovo Kak takovoe*, "the Word as such", the title of a keynote Futurist manifesto of 1913, has resonance with "Yo word is yo bond" and "word to the mother", cited by Mufwene as "positive, reinforcing responses to something said or done". (Mufwene 1998: 208). Jah Bones, theoretician of London Jamaican hip-hop, notes that according to Rasta doctrine and reasoning "a language must have great significance in terms of its words, sounds and "powah", the "powah" is what gives Rasta strength and makes him formidable" (quoted in Sebba 1993:7). Mufwene carefully observes that while

> skilful use of African-American verbal traditions....will earn a person respect and recognition...[this is not to say] that African-Americans 'dis' [disrespect, discount] the written word, [but] as in other groups with a surviving oral tradition like native Americans, 'book learning' and written documents are believed to be limited in what they can convey or teach. (Mufwene 1998: 208)

Khlebnikov, less circumspectly, fulminated against the enemies "of word creation" and the "bookish petrifaction of language" perpetrated by the Russian intelligentsia, a leitmotiv running through some of his greatest poetry. Khlebnikov was devoured by a sense of the (conjunctural)

> power of the word [which resembles] the action of a light ray striking a powder magazine beneath some great capital, London, say....the detonation depends not on sheer force but the degree of accuracy... a weak and unintelligible word can destroy the world..." (Khlebnikov 1928-33, v.5: 207)

A notebook entry dated March 1921 raises, in a refracted form, the issue of the power of the word (I quote since it points to the domain of conflict which is the site of the poem in question):

> People have reckoned time in the blood of war and with the sword. Henceforth war will be ended when people have learnt to reckon time in ink. War has turned the universe into an inkwell of blood, and sought to drown the wretched and ridiculous writer in it. But the writer is seeking to drown the war in his inkwell, war itself - the clash of beliefs is the ring of wills. Who will win?

### 3. The translation of conflict

The above parallelism has been stressed partly in order to give some concrete sense to a notion of the "translation of conflict", however playful the enacted conflict in the given case thus far may have been. Both in the early aftermath of the Revolution and later, the pre-revolutionary "war games" played by the Futurists wired them to Bolshevik cultural requirements, adding a political dimension to their avant-gardism at a time when Bolsheviks such as Enlightenment Commissar Anatolii Lunacharsky were eagerly seeking cultural legitimation and welcomed practical input from whichever quarter. Implicit in the preceding discussion of Futurism is an argument for the sociolinguistic responsibility of literary translation, the urging of a need for translation to respect the *situatedness* of its source texts, especially when a literary practice problematizes its site, and assigns significance to conflict - when the normal conditions of textual reproduction are disrupted and when disruption is intentionally constitutive of the aggressor texts' semiosis. The Futurists played an exuberant game, assigning high aesthetic value to "rough" qualities, to things

> written [the Russian word "pisat" means to represent graphically, and denotes both writing and painting] and seen in the wink of an eye, the arranging of clumsy structures, tensile reading and writing, more awkward than greased boots or a lorry in the drawing room - a lot of knots, bundles and patches, jagged, grainy surfaces ...

(Kruchenykh cited in Khardzhiev 1976: 52)

Everything said so far bears on the problem of how the situatedness of an original language text may be translated. The mapping or translation of its theoretical or aesthetic keywords onto those of rap poetry begs questions regarding the degree of hospitality the host site may show towards a potentially foreign body. If an original text's situatedness requires translation, the translation's own situatedness requires definition. What can be said about the displacing of a vernacular idiom (rap) having a particular kind of roughness into the *foreigness* of a mainstream site of hegemonic culture, an overarching, global genre nameable as "published modern poetry in translation"? Here, one arrives at the second staging post of the "journey" being plotted by this paper, namely the proposed siting of this translation in particular.[3]

It can be said that the "rapping" of KB acquired a conflictual signification within the global text or discursive universe of which the *TP* anthology is a particular statement. Indeed, as the discussion of Futurism's posture above indicates, this was intended - its insertion is an essay in the transposition or metatranslation of that movement's "roughness" - how far however does the writ for rough translation run? While, historically and originally, this quality, or rather bundle of qualities was in Poggioli's usage "antagonistically" intended, the differences it constructs are not intrinsically or necessarily readable as conflictual, especially in a culture which celebrates difference, some would say of a non-signifying kind, suitable to the End of History (Derrida 1997). If conflict exists in this world, is it not obliged to do so in an outlawed and disavowed form?

The question receives an implicit and elegant response from James S Holmes, in support of his own, representative, one would say mainstream, view of requirements which poetry in translation should respect: "The average reader of a translation in English wants to find the kind of experience which has become identified with "poetry" in his readings of English Literature. The translator who wishes to be read must in some degree satisfy this want" (Holmes 1988: 14). Holmes cites a provocative observation by W H Auden to evoke the stuff of that experience:

> ...my own conviction is that in this age poetry can no longer be written in the High, even in the Golden Style, only in a Drab Style... By a Drab Style I mean a quiet tone of voice and a modesty of gesture which deliberately avoids drawing attention to itself as poetry with a capital P. Whenever a modern poet raises his voice he makes me feel embarrassed. (*ibid.*: 14-15)

Holmes further advocates a translation posture designed to achieve discursively an illusion of authenticity, the textual equivalent of *trompe-l'oeil* pictorial rhetoric: "like the poet [the translator] will strive to exploit his own creative powers, the literary traditions of the target culture, and all the expressive means of the target language in order to produce a verbal object that to all appearances is nothing more or less than a poem" (*ibid.*: 11). It is, clearly, beyond the scope of this paper, to argue in favour of the broad applicability of this "method" to the whole field of English language translation of modernist literature, here, poetry, and correspondingly refute its being dismissed as a case of special pleading. For the moment, I will simply signal the field of translation theoretics developed by Lawrence Venuti, claiming precisely this reach (and offering an opposed response to the "question"), which has been developed polemically but also has considerable empirical consistency and extends to "difficult" domains of modernist literature such as Pound's archaizing translations, and translation methods informed by French post-structuralism (elaborated in Chadwick 2004).

Venuti's discursive force-field situates the intuitivism of Holmes' prescription within a theoretical framework based on a historically inscribed opposition between "domesticating" and "foreignizing" translation strategies, the former threatening an "End of History" stasis in translation theory and practice. Thus, Holmes' comfortable heuristics are geopoliticised: "Anglo-American culture [remains] dominated by domesticating theories that recommend fluent translating" (Venuti 1995: 21). To achieve this fluency "translation is required to efface its second order status, with transparent discourse, producing the illusion of authorial presence, whereby the translated text can be taken as an original" (*ibid.*: 7). The corollary of this process is that the translator is rendered invisible: "The translator's invisibility at once enacts and masks an insidious domestication of foreign texts, rewriting them in the transparent discourse that prevails in English" (*ibid.*: 16-17).

In confronting the pressures towards fluency and transparency, translation faces hard choices: "the translator.... may submit to or resist dominant values in the target language... Submission assumes an ideology of assimilation at work in the translation process [...] Resistance assumes an ideology of autonomy, locating the alien in a cultural other [...]" (*ibid.*: 308).

The choice faced by the translator is between co-option or opposition. The former entails expert use of a "mediating technique" which disappears the translator, through which British and American publishing has successfully produced "cultures in the UK and US that are aggressively monolingual, unreceptive to the foreign, accustomed to fluent translations that invisibly inscribe foreign texts with English language values" (*ibid.*: 15), and "a cultural narcissism and complacency, an unconcern with the foreign that can only impoverish British and American culture and foster values and policies grounded in unequality and exploitation" (Venuti 1998: 89).

Opposition - the (ethical) antidote to this unidirectional centre-periphery textual traffic, and its consequential ethnocentric violence - is, for Venuti, embodied in a

> foreignizing translation [which articulates] the difference of the foreign text... by disrupting the cultural codes that prevail in the target language. In its efforts to do right abroad, this translation method must do wrong at home, deviating enough from native norms to stage an alien reading experience - choosing to translate a foreign text excluded by literary canons for example, or using a marginal discourse to translate it.
> (Venuti 1995: 20)

Hence the use of a foreignizing translation idiom in the case of this one poem served two purposes – and perhaps a third, more difficult, "situationist" purpose;

The first purpose was to confront the prevailing "Drab" tone of voice, and "modesty of gesture", which arguably even today sets the tone of modern and recent poetry and, following Holmes as discussed above, that of its translated simulacrum, a discreet kind of "ethnocentric violence" characterizing translated poetry at large, a rhetorical gesture which in neutralising overt violence (see 'liberal' disapprobation of Gangsta rap) sanctions a hegemonic "minus" violence of global reach.

The second purpose was to honour the Dionysian creative mode of the poet's writing, which intensifies following his self-discharge from the disintegrating Imperial Army in April 1917, and his literally peripatetic tracking of the theatres of often unsecured revolution and civil war - Khlebnikov wrote compulsively, a "graphomane" whose lips constantly and soundlessly "uttered" his writing gestures, as if in obedience to Rimbaud's famous slogan, *"Le dérèglement de tous les sens"* (except, for him, the derailing of an equally compulsive mathematical "sense" of numbers). The parallel with Rimbaud is tempting, but the opposition also is to be noted - Rimbaud's Faustian Ivan (Karamazov) and Khlebnikov's Parsifal-Alyosha are antipodes.[4]

Thus inserting this translation within a large number of translations in a more restrained and normative mode constitutes a "report" on the poet's "dionysian" mode of production, nourished by Futurism's abrasive or clowning outrances, via translation into a "speech mode" (rap poetry) equally dionysian. As a whole the translations intended for the *TP* anthology naturally gravitated towards a "High" or "Golden", in some cases archaizing mode, a re-enactment of Khlebnikov's peculiar resistance to "Drab" rendering, a separateness from his own mainstream contemporaries captured in a formula coined (and much quoted) by the eminent editor and commentator of his work, Yury Tynianov: "our single epic poet of the century" ("On Khlebnikov", in Khlebnikov *1928-1933*, I: 24).

This discussion has centred thus far on how the aesthetic and stylistic markers of the playful, "hooliganistic" conflict defining a movement having a sibling relation with its European fellows may be translated in a way that resists neutralisation and homogenization, their transmutation into the hegemonic code of "Drab" seriousness of their (here, metropolitan) target language - in fact how to preserve *grosso modo* the infrastructure of avant-garde literary practice. Parenthetically, the "war games" enacted by the multifarious acts of resistance of avant-garde practice recall Mikhail Bakhtin's evocations of the laughing principle of carnival, which at every point "doubles and parodies moments of serious-minded ceremony", subverts the "monolithically serious cultic forms of the established world order", and celebrates the "protean dynamism and transformative logic of a world turned inside out" (Bakhtin 1986: 291-304). Not to be lost sight of however is the regulatory function of the carnival - the world is turned upside down but for the time being only.

The issue of the situatedness of this translation has a larger, ideological dimension, discussed at length in works by Venuti, and alluded to above. The moment of the poem's writing is singular - a singularity reflected in the poem's weaving. This was an historically fleeting interval, from mid-November 1918 until approximately March 1919 when the Great Powers, through covert diplomacy, or overt military action, clearly identified the revolutionary soviet government as one not to be done business with (as an erstwhile ally and hopefully still malleable global partner) but to be crushed, when it began to be understood as an Enemy more considerable than a gang of ruffians to be cleared off the street, powerful enough to be labeled Evil with a good conscience, a moment when its Opponent was finally able, by reflection, to discern as yet in outline to be given precision in coming decades, its own true essence, the embodiment and guardian of the Free World. Vladimir Mayakovsky's poem '150, 000, 000' of October 1920, represents a diabolic carnival inversion of this manichean conflict in its formative phase.

The third, "difficult", purpose served by this translation idiom mentioned above concerns the situatedness of this translation within the poet's living, historical trajectory, at a conjunctural moment - 10 March 1919 - the events of which have been glimpsed "through" the foregoing discussion and which, as said below, is a moment of bifurcation, a historical forking of the ways - and a forking of the self. The facts of the trajectory of 1919 formed the ground imperatively requiring the construction of a kind of differential semiosis, whose signifiers were the styles (modes) of translation - code became message. At the beginning of 1919, Khlebnikov worked as a newspaper correspondent for the local (Astrakhan) newspaper *Red Soldier*. He wrote journalism of a kind suited to record his first-hand experiences of, for example, street battles in Moscow in 1918, the writing of prospectuses for local college courses, such as railway tunneling through the Himalayas and Sanskrit, and to urge visionary reconstruction incorporating sky screens, clouds on which war updates would be projected. Travelling near Kharkov across the British-fuelled war in the South, he wrote 'Kamennaia baba' and 'Night in a Trench' (discussed below), was admitted to a lunatic asylum to assess his military fitness for the (White) draft during the White summer advance on Moscow, where he wrote poetry in a grand, pastoral style emulating Pushkin. Prior to this, in May 1919, he produced a major theoretical text, 'Our Fundamentals' expounding a theory of language "exploding the deaf mute strata of linguistic silence" with a conclusion of great value for an understanding of the annihilating transformation (under pressure of civil war and the terrorism of forced allegiances) of the centredness of the self and its immersion in its own actualities, the real world, engendering another kind of fission or splitting: "we must bifurcate our being, be at once the scientist controlling the radiating waves and the tribes populating the rays' waveforms under the scientist's tutelage…" (Khlebnikov 1986: 632).

The dual aspect of the relationship of a source text to its translation, of the commission of original sin to the subsequent manning, or violation, of the ideological *cordon sanitaire* of containment, a relationship in which translation is theoretically free, in Venuti's sense, to choose to perform either the functions of illegal migrant or frontier guard, in dialogue with the Other, or policing the monologue of Empire - can most economically be identified in comparing two very different translations of the same segment of text, from a poem also by Khlebnikov, "Noch' v okope" - "Night in a Trench", seen by Vladimir Markov, key historian of Russian Futurism, as closely related, in both style and content, to 'Kamennaia baba'. Markov convincingly argues that the two poems have a kind of doppelganger relationship, and are two "recordings" from different physical and mythical vantage points, of the same military event (Markov 1962: 130-131).

## 4. Night in a Trench

'Night in a Trench' deserves at least a globally sketched background, this being also the background of KB. This poem, putatively contemporary with KB, narrates the period of waiting and subsequent military encounter, probably in Eastern Ukraine, in a landscape whose physical features recall descriptions of the South Russian steppe by Benedikt Livshits, chronicler of Hylaea, the adopted "Scythian" homeland of the most militant wing of Russian Futurism during its years (1911-1914) of glorious infancy. Red and White detachments, after a night of strung nerve-endings, did battle, one of any number, "watched" over by "three stone maids…flatly with dead eyes".

The year 1919 was global, since it was the year of the League of Nations Covenant and the Versailles Peace Treaty, and the maturing of the fatal, dissembling connivances following the Armistice of November 1918, leading not to peace but to Hot and then Cold war between the Great Powers and the "foul baboonery of Bolshevism" (Winston Churchill, from a speech at a Mansion House lunch on 19 February 1919, quoted in Kettle 1992, 3: 141). 1919 was the year when the monstrous features of the Enemy were clearly drawn and coalesced into a definite shape, traced in the minutes and papers of the Imperial War Cabinet, the War Office, the Foreign Office, and the Admiralty, in the diaries of major figures - Lloyd George, Winston Churchill, Robert Cecil, Lord Curzon, Balfour and others, in memoranda circulating among members of Chiefs of Staff and their Allied counterparts, the close liaisons maintained with Wilson, Clémenceau and others of the Big Four, the year when the "Great Game" underwent its final big Modernist metamorphosis, its moves obsessively plotted and materials for press circulation carefully considered. This was a time during which, when matters of European and World peace were being decided at the Paris Peace Conference in early 1919, "[…] individually and collectively the Big Four spent more time and energy on the Russian question than on any other major issue" (Mayer 1967: 284). When "what first appeared as a civil war waged on Russian territory between the Red Army and the armies of the 'white' generals now took on the shape of a war between the revolutionary soviet regime and the principal powers of the capitalist world" (Carr 1966: 123).

It was the year in which the military intervention of the Allied Powers in Soviet Russia reached its peak of intensity and commitment, nowhere more dramatically than in the Ukraine, where frontiers were at their geographically most shifting. For cartographers, the time dimension and the military vectors of a mapped terrain were more of the essence than its spatial configuration, one of the years of a period when "Kiev changed hands 16 times in 36 months" (Lincoln 1989: 303), geography's temporal dimension vividly illustrated in maps or "schemas" included in the volumes of the War Commissar Trotsky's civil war dispatches, (Trotsky 1924, maps 1-7, *hors texte*), the year of the founding Congress (2-6 March 1919) of the Third Communist International, when in his opening speech, Lenin outlined a translation "manual" (the word 'translation' is his) proposing equivalents of "proletarian democracy" and the "dictatorship of the proletariat", provocatively based on political realities… (Lenin 1963: 490).

The extract below, from "Night in a Trench", is a short section in which the poem steps aside from its main narrative and offers as it were in the margin a portrait of Lenin, a subsequent bone of contention for scholars and readers of Khlebnikov, because of its bearing on the poet's unorthodox and peculiarly "realized" understanding of the Bolshevik revolution. I offer the (transliterated) original language text (Khlebnikov 1986: 276). The first translation is published in Khlebnikov (1997: 161), the second, like KB, intended for, but finally not included in the TP Anthology referred to earlier. The difference between these versions is captured by the distinction discussed above between translations which are "domesticating" and those which are "foreignizing", the Schleiermacher-Venuti paradigm, we recall Venuti's excoriation of "linguistic imperialism", as historically the dominant trend in English language translation (Venuti 1995: 308).

*Translating the Enemy: A 'hip-hop' Translation of a Poem by the Russian Futurist Velimir Khlebnikov (1885-1922)*

| SOURCE | VERSION 1 | VERSION 2 |
|---|---|---|
| Molitve vernykh chernyshei | Driving out the chanting monks | De Man kick ass dem punkass monk |
| Iz khrama vetkhogo izgnav, | From their ancient holy choir | an all de bulljive auda temple |
| Siuda voiny uchit'ustav | To classrooms for the art of war | Fe geekin up an [to study] solijahs [soldiers'] law |
| Sozval liubimykh latyshei | The powers that be converted it | Em calling Lettish hardcore[true, steadfast] bredrin [brothers] |
| No on surovoiu rukoi | But HE with his uncompromising hand | An de Man widdim han [with hand] of iron |
| Derzhal zheleznogo puti | Holds a course along the iron way | keepin peeps [people] an de real line |
| Net, ia - ne on, ia ne takoi | No - I'm not like him, I'm not like that! | I ain't lak [like] him, not to em riddim |
| No chelovechestvo – leti | Mankind, fly! | But planet bredrin flyin high! |
| Litso Sibirskogo vostoka | His face has a Mongol cast | Luk de wicked grill frem eastern lan |
| Gromadnoi lob, izmuchennyi zabotoi | A massive forehead, creased with care | plus righteous dome stressd wid som static |
| I, ispytuia, vas pronzaiushchee oko | The questioning eye that sees right | eyz scopin bros wid slicin vizhun [vision] |
| O khate zhalitsia okhotoiu. | Through you - the farmstead his only care | Fe poor hood [poor neighbourhood] bredrin he an mishun [on a mission] |
| Ona adno, stezia zheleznaia | "The iron way's the only way! | An de real, de iron way |
| Doloi, beseda bespoleznaia | Too much idle talk | We cruzin [moving], no more he-said-she-said |

Points of contrast or ideological indices can be noted: "Mongol cast" and "powers-that-be" imply that a monolith with Asiatic characteristics is already in place, an anachronism which is readable in terms of the situatedness of the target language text (including importantly its targeted readership), domestically centred within its "hierarchy of cultural values". "Anachronism" is used advisedly to signal the fact that the text records a dynamic process of becoming and struggle (begging Lenin's question: who will win?) rather than celebration of an already monolithically installed "powers-that-be". A serious struggle - between a universally obtaining, yet utterly localised anarchism - whether a disorganised anti-bolshevism or a pro-bolshevism of a fantastic utopian or interested kind (peasants were often pro-Bolshevik but anti-Communist), and the "foul", centralised "baboonery" of a Bolshevik Council of People's Commissars concerned less with getting trains to run on time and more with organising an infrastructure capable of getting them on the rails, patching up destroyed, mined or worn out tracks, bridges, rolling stock and cracked boilers, and with inventing "import substitutions" for a country faced with blockade and military intervention, cut off from coal, wheat and oilfields and iron-smelting plants and lacking workers to man metal-working and machine shops... On the other hand, "Punkass monk", "Man" and "poor hood bredrin" signify an unambiguous alignment of sympathies less veiled than in the original, a tilting of translation's endemic perfidiousness in the opposite direction. This partisanship runs against the grain of the modulated discretion and "Drab" understatement valued by the targeted readership posited by Holmes-Auden. It is in fact inscribed in the particular "speech genre" of the given translation idiom, which has no trading currency able to handle notions of impersonality or ironizing detachment. The invitation to "luk dem Man", authorially voiced by a simulacrum MC, "toasting" the story-telling lyrics of a bastard sub-idiom ("Jafaikin") nodding in the direction of Jamaican Yardie talk invokes a mysteriously "other", Malcolm-X like figure with "powah", while "poor hood bredin" marks an abrupt shift from the *khata* (peasant hut) of the Ukrainian steppe to the urban ghetto and the Bronx projex, replacing the metonymy by its referent and installing poverty and deprivation as the core meaning of the image.

The trope is preserved in the first version; given the published context, "farmstead" subtly connotes the westward land colonization of North America - a best reverse translation would probably yield "*khutor*" rather than "*Khata*". "*Khutor*" was a parcellated agricultural estate with connotations of the Stolypin reform and land privatization ... Interesting also is the omission by Harvard's translator, Paul Schmidt, of the phrase "Lettish (ie. modern 'Latvian') hardcore bredin", of the second, itself a fairly literal rendering of his "*liubimykh latyshei*", (beloved Letts) of the original, referring to Red Latvian rifle detachments fiercely loyal to Lenin. Lastly and probably most revealingly, one notes the omission, in the Harvard translation, of the syntactical pivot and main signifier of authorial position within the extract, the conjunction "no"/"but"; its omission in the first version obliges a reading of the double exclamation "Net,...!/....leti! (NO.../(-) Mankind, fly!" as mutually reinforcing, and an intensification rather than an opposition and qualification; the second translation removes possible (but in its translator's view, formed after discussions with Russian native speakers, unlikely) ambiguities, including a negative reading of the verbal imperative "*leti*" (fly) by adding the qualifier "high".

Whichever side one is 'on', the example is an illustration of the elegant and involuted topology of the pathways linking the paired complex of "translation" and "conflict". Translations of conflict map into (ongoing) conflicts of translation. This quasi-mathematical domain requires orders of elaboration beyond the scope of this writing. By way of epilogue however, one would like briefly to point to features of its subtext for the sake of a kind of completeness, to fulfill a function of *enregistrement* or check-in.

First, this text itself - it seems that its objects - poetic and other texts of a modern revolution and civil war - are in themselves, uniquely in this writer's experience, global in their field of experience, and any remotely adequate discourse on them needs some "globalizing" procedures; a non-contextualising and purely particularistic analysis will play them false; whatever their genre - high poetry and crude propaganda alike - they figure forth, hyperbolically or, in the words of Lomonosov, a great universalising scholar of the Russian eighteenth-century Enlightenment, through "the excellent linkage of distant ideas", a globally expanded and historicized universe in which "Then" and "Now" are as active a pair of parameters as special notions of nearness and remoteness or geographical delineation and dissolution of boundaries; a naïve example serves as illustration, from a Petrograd Bolshevik leaflet, entitled 'Appeal by the women workers of the Vyborg District to sailors of the Baltic Fleet and Red Army men', 27 June 1919:

> The honest workers of their own countries do not wish to struggle against us. They are refusing to strangle their revolution and are rising against their oppressors. The flame of world revolution is licking with its fiery tongue the thrones of the executioners and exploiters. In the sea of revolution in which the soviet ship is sailing, other red ships are coming to its rescue. (Kupaigorodskaia 1981: 16)

This refers to the German and Hungarian revolutions, but also the multifarious acts of mutiny in the British and French armies, from the end of 1918 on, as well as "widespread disaffection... on the Clyde, in Scotland, in South Wales and other industrial centres of Great Britain." (see Carr 1966: 133-135).

As this writing proceeded, its "concept" seemed to become akin to the making of a baroque painting, in which the canvas is washed with dark or middling brown background. The act of painting consists in a progressive definition of detail by singular and highly specific high-toned patches and local opacities and highlights, a calligraphy of singular events - of water, vegetation, flesh, etc, which reveal the ground as an eternally pre-existing totality, the plenitude of nature, always and already real and perfectly known. Here, the ground of history, especially of a conflict of the given magnitude, as well as the ongoing project of creating an reinforcing its meaning, carried on through publishing and narratives of every kind, through diplomatic process and in extreme cases by military means, is perfectly known - by dint of tireless repetition. As "painter" one therefore needs only provide particulars, the rest comes into view, a bit of canvas becomes the forest depths, a limitless distance or a great storm, magically, without human intervention, known as perfectly as nature itself.

Every text - pamphlet, treatise or poem - appears as an encryption of the ground (horizon) rather than the highlighted foreground detail, and the briefer and more terse, the more encompassing the claim to totality - whose falsity is demonstrated by an endlessly redundant, exhaustive series of texts elaborately and reductively demonstrating the *trompe-l'oeil,* the illusory reality of this ground, and the reality - the dimensions of repression, aggression and violence said to underlie a dark world.

**Conclusion**

There exist yet other series of texts, often of a rare or initially confidential kind, in the face of which the totalitarian universe aestheticized by the baroque painter is put under strain; cracks appear. Personal memories, first hand accounts, etc - dispatches by *Manchester Guardian* Correspondent, Phillips Price for example, from Moscow in August 1918, observing in one which was stopped by the British Censor that

> one cannot be surprised of course that the governments of England, France and Germany should through the official agencies and their press centres endeavor to blacken the work of the Russian revolution ... living here, surrounded by the armed hosts of the European warlords, I am in a position to see more clearly than those outside this iron ring the power possessed by the ruling classes, whose designs include the strangling of this youngest of the governments of the toiling masses. (Price 1997: 141)

In another dispatch, dated Moscow 19 October 1918, also stopped by the British censor, Price states:

> After reading the English papers which have arrived here, I am at a loss to decide whether the persons giving information on Russia are deliberately fabricating news for their own political ends or are the victims of chronic nervous breakdowns. (*ibid.*: 150)

Arthur Ransome, then in Moscow, wrote:

> I love the real England, but I hate, shouting in daily telegrams across the wires from Russia, more than I hate anything on earth (except cowardice in looking at the truth) the intellectual sloth, the gross mental indolence that prevents the English from making an effort of imagination to realise what is happening beyond... (Ransome 1992a: 28)

H G Wells wrote that

> the writing of new books, except for some poetry and the painting of pictures, has ceased in Russia. But the bulk of the writers and artists have been found employment upon a grandiose scheme for the publication of a sort of Russian encyclopedia on the literature of the world. In this strange Russia of conflict, cold, famine and pitiful privations there is actually going on now a literary task that would be inconceivable in the rich England of today...In starving Russia hundreds of people are working on translations and the books they translate are being set up and printed... (Wells 1920: 47)

Wells again, finding himself in the midst of a meeting of the Central Organ of Revolutionary Government, the Petrograd Soviet, in contrast with any "atmosphere of weary parliamentarianism", noting "the peculiar thrill of a mass meeting ... some 200 people or so on the rostrum platform... naval uniforms, middle-class, working class costumes ... intelligent-looking women .... Asiatics .... unclassifiable visitors [while] the body of the hall was densely packed with people who filled not only the seats but the gangways and the spaces under the galleries ... two or three thousand men and women, all members of the Soviet ..." (*ibid.*: 115).

Over a year later, in 1920, Arthur Ransome commented on the effects of blockade and war

> the actual productive powers of Russia are ... sinking. But things are no better if we turn from the rye and corn lands to the forests. Saws are worn out, axes are worn out ... the shortage of transport cuts the production of wood fuel, the lack of which reacts on transport and on the factories and so on in a circle from which nothing but a large import of engines and wagons will provide an outlet. Timber can be floated down the rivers. Yes, but it must be brought to the rivers. Surely horses can do that, yes, but horses must be fed... (Ransome 1992b: 20)

Other documents record the lively discussions between British diplomat Picton Bagge, military attache Sidney Reilly and Polish financier Jarozynsky, of ambitious schemes of economic reconstruction, put to the Department of Overseas Trade, an offshoot of the Foreign Office, for an "Anglo-Russian combine, amounting to a take-over bid for the entire Russian economy", it being "important for the British Empire to draw extensively on Russian wealth"; the strategy would be to "secure controls of the big banks in Russia, the big transport companies and the insurance companies"; the main aim however was "far more imperial... control of the banks should mean both the economic and political control of Russia ... control of the grain trade" and ownership of "most mining, mineral and timber concessions ...British industries would be represented on the Russian bank boards by British subjects", who, Bagge suggested, should be "of the British Public School boy type ... live with selected families" to learn the language... "Prominent local politicians could also be employed at good salaries, when not actually in office ..." The Central Bank [controlled by British interests] would "run an intelligence network and control the Russian press" as well "as the Russian merchant fleet on the Black Sea, the Volga and the Caspian" (Kettle 1992: 425-426). Reilly, included because of his connections with American financial and industrial interests, records strong interest because of American postwar export stagnation, all of this from May 1919.

And other series - from the inner councils of State, for example the very detailed discussion by the British Cabinet's Eastern Committee, taking place earlier, in December 1918, focused on the political and military measures needed in the Caucasus and beyond, mainly to secure British control of the Baku oil-fields (Ullman 1968: 72-86); these and similar high-level (and confidential) discussions of state form a long series characterized by the obsessive working and re-working of imperial themes, and have more to say about this period and its subject than any amount of monographs on Bolshevik anarchy and its machinery of internal policing and one-party dictatorship. As Lenin observed in that month of March 1919, with contemporary overtones: "We are living not merely in a state but in **a system of states** [his emphasis]; and it is inconceivable that the Soviet republic should continue to exist for a long period side by side with imperialist states. Ultimately one or the other must conquer ..." (quoted in Carr 1966: 123).

Other series - meticulously itemizing the deep level of pre-revolutionary capitalist penetration of Russian mineral and industrial wealth - help to understand the depth of hatred of the Enemy and its foul baboonery, and why the poet was *hurtin fe* "just a loaf o bread an a drop o milk, plus as well de sky an a cloud or two!".

In the historiographical tradition relating to the Bolshevik revolution and Soviet Russia, this kind of *collage*, the baroque *limning* of highlighted particulars, simply does not occur, and probably is seen as bad manners. Histories of the Russian revolution do not approach it "from outside", from the point of view of the "system of states", and of the engagements by Western powers interested in the outcome. Those traditions are so densely implanted that engagement with them at their level of generality is unproductive. I offer the view that addressing them sideways through a linguistic and artistic discourse, here on the political axis of an art and its translation, is more interesting. The peculiarity and the interest in looking at the microstructures of decision-making and the manufacturing of consent is to see them at work. Allowed to "enter the public domain" when as it were the coast is clear, their discourses on power remain entirely contemporary, and have become bolder with the Enemy's defeat...

STONE WOMAN/ROCKIN MAMA    (Kamennaia baba)    10March1919.

> Ol man standin we de twisted stick
> an quiet like magic all aroun,
> an like waterwoman tickled pink,
> sittin an a mammath dead an lyin on de groun.
> An de old willow bark she all rustlin
> an whispa tales like people fe real -
> An yu stone age mammas standin like a slab,
> stan up in the field wid stone rock freakin
> reachin rite from de sky an to de sky.
> Dem mammas lukin tough an verra cruel,
> with beads roun de neck jus hacked no messin.
> An eagles in de sky dem no understan
> all de tales in stone of eastern land.
> Dem breed she stand with cool still smile,
> left on her own nevva knew her pappy.
> An on yu bosom like roun cobblestones

*Translating the Enemy: A 'hip-hop' Translation of a Poem
by the Russian Futurist Velimir Khlebnikov (1885-1922)*

de dew shine bright lak sucklin pappies.
De gallopin stone of de blackdread mamma
give de ol nite eagle quite a start,
an all her dreads flyin in de wind,
regulashun ridin, no janglin iron.
Luk de rocky mountains flauntin all they snow,
an dem congelated twistin of the ages' rockin.
an rocky high walls lockin in the babble
of all rushin water fallin an de plain.
Luk dem tree all a beggin an a prayin
to somebady lurkin doun in de clearin,
willin an beseechin
usin funky words dem got no names.
O poplar tree lovely, yu sweet black tree,
fe all dem fainin fe real cool evnins.
I hear yu sweet jive rustlin
an leaves all whisperin an swayin.
Somebady comin, ol "scratch 'n' scribblin",
dreads af gold an lips not movin.
What he be needin, dis wicked homeboy,
with silver murmur all roun him?
Weepin, Milky Way ain't my jurizdikshun?
"A hundred thousand wasted corpses groanin
all covered over in de cool fresh groun.
An I'm de last badass painter
writtin nameless horror of all de world.
Evva waitin fe blastin in my direkshun,.
What fe man, why yu packin?
an me with all that lovin fe all the peeple,
'Pan a time i livin in de steppe an de stones."
Sweet boy com sittin an with his hand,
spread the burnin book at his face's page.
So de moon he' give to weepin boy
a crust of bread made of evnin stars.
"Not verra much I am crammin fo',
jus a loaf of bread,
an a drop o milk,
plus as well de sky.
an a cloud or two!"
I love every milky hoochie mamma
an honey drippers slow to flower.
That me gon a hidin in de starry net,
in de wicked meshes of de Milky Way.
An when all rivers flowin blood,
an Vistula and Tiszla with the water crimson,
then de cipher numbers all grieving an a sobbin
jettin all over this poor planet.
There a cool butterfly with wings grown blue,
jus lik de eyz of stone mamma statue.
There she stan all grey an bare,
like she doomed te stan fe evva
someplace fe flies an bugs tek a rest,
luk her rocky hand pointin doun a doun doun
to honey love rules writtin in stone.

An her slaty eyes in de flat rocky slab
crude an cut with no def skilz.
Then de butterfly she com wingin doun
sittin on mamma eyes spreadin wide her wings,
crazy big wings coverin he eyz,
and de blue skies of de quiverin wings
givin good protection with her lacy lace,
splashin all he eyz with fire an crimson.
An de shimmer of de fire givin stoney mamma eyz,
an givin her dome som livin wisdom,
Eyz growin blue an he mind is a bloomin,
dem airy blue flyer he jus give de order.
Strawy dreads all flamin in de dark night time.
Wicked mamma carvin standin up, start jammin
rockin with he thunder.
'pan a time som blind bitch jus mindin sheep,
now cool mamma eyz like de badass blue flyer,
Milky Way endowin he with vizhun.
In de warzone, steel blastin, lead fly, no aggravashun,
an the flyers stony grave throwin off he chainz
im coffin fallin in de groun - liberashun
Hop hop rockin, coffin rollin to the sky!
Stony statue breakin, stars rockin an a rollin,
scopin dem sky like de blue butterfly.
Mind yo freakin stars an flamin sola systemz.
When he shoes fly rockin to the funky funky beat,
they writtin lines of fire jus like dem constellashunz
makin fire rainbows with evva juicin colours.
Give y'all living funky funkifaction
Now rocky steppe mamma she rockin on the real!
(Chadwick 2004)

---

1 For instance, (consonantal) roughness v (vocalic) smoothness, laughter v melancholy, matter (texture, faktura) v spirit (symbol, veil), East v West, street v salon, iconoclasm v the sacred, modernity v tradition (but not antiquity), the few v many (but not the people), the ephemeral v the eternal, speech (ellipsis) v script (punctilio), time v space, periphery v core, steppe v metropolis, handwriting v typography, nomadic v sedentary - the former term in each case motivating a confrontational approach to the creative act.
2 See for example the passage from a statement by Khlebnikov "on the nature of poetry", written in 1919-1920: "They say that only shopfloor workers can write work songs. Is that really true? Doesn't the essence of a poem consist in the departure from self and from the axis of one's own everyday life. Isn't a poem the flight from the "me"? Poetry is akin to flight, to cover the greatest number of versts (kilometres) of images and thoughts in the least possible time... Inspiration always plays the bard's origin false" (Khlebnikov 1986: 634).
3 In the event, KB was not included in *TP*. Khlebnikov remains adequately represented in the anthology by a group of other translations contributed anonymously. The reasons for the exclusion are not fully clear and in a strict sense are not pertinent to this discussion. These would concern Anvil's publishing profile, the then London publishing conjuncture, and marketing considerations.
4 See Dostoevsky's *The Brothers Karamazov*, I, book 1.

## References

Bakhtin, Mikhail. 1979. 'Problema rechevykh zhanrov' in *Estetika slovesnogo tvorchestva*, Moscow: Iskusstvo. 237-280.

——1986. 'Tvorchestvo Fransua Rable i naradodnaia kul'tura srednevekov'ia i renessansa. Vvedenie ('The Works of François Rabelais and medieval and Renaissance Popular Culture')' in *Literaturno-kriticheskie sta'i*. Moscow: Khudozhestvennaia literatura.

Carr, Edward H. 1966. *The Bolshevik Revolution*. London: Pelican. Vol. 3.

Chadwick, Brian. 2004. 'Issues raised by a 'rap' translation of a poem by Velimir Khlebnikov' in *Poetika iskanii ili poisk poetiki* , Proceedings of the Conference 'The poetics of questing, or the quest for a poetics' (Moscow 13-15 May 2003). On line: http://im-a-bitch.rajimsaragih.info/stone-woman-rockin-mamakamennaia-baba10march1919-t255-6-ol-man (consulted 15.10.2006).

Derrida, Jacques. 1997. *The Politics of Friendship* (tr. George Collins). Phronesis series, London and New York: Verso.

Dostoevsky, Fyodor. *The Brothers Karamazov, part I, book I*. London and New York: Everyman.

Hill, Patrick. B. 1999. 'Deconstructing the Hip-Hop Hype: A critical analysis of the *New York Times*' coverage of African American Youth Culture' in Winfield, Betty and Sandra Davidson (eds) *Bleep! Censoring Rock and Rap Music*. Westport: Greenwood. 103-112.

Holmes, James. 1988. *Translated: Papers on Literary Translation and Translation Studies*. Rodopi: Amsterdam.

Kazakova, T. A. 1988. 'Strategii resheniia zadach v khudozhestvennogo perevoda' (problem-solving strategies in literary translation) in *Perevod i interpretatsiia teksta*. Moscow: Institute of Linguistics of the USSR Academy of Sciences.

Kettle, Michael. 1992. *Russia and the Allies 1917-1920*. Vol. 3. London and New York: Routledge.

Khardzhiev, Nikolai (ed.).1976. *K istorii russkogo avangarda*. Stockholm: Gileia.

Khlebnikov, Velimir. 1986. *Tvoreniia*. Edited by Poliakov, M. Ia. et al. Moscow: sovetskii pisatel.

——1997. *Collected Works of Velimir Khlebnikov*. Vol. 3. Harvard University Press.

Kupaigorodskaia, A. P. 1981. *Oruzhem Slova – listovki petrogradskikh bolshevikov, 1918-1920*. ('The Weapon of Language – Petrograd Bolchevik leaflets). Moscow: Lenizdat.

Lenin, Vladimir Ilich. 1963. *Polnoe sobranie sochinenii* (Complete Works). Vol. 37. Moscow: Institut Marksizma-Leninizma.

Lincoln, Bruce. 1989. *Red Victory*, New York: Simon & Schuster.

Loshchits, Iu. M. and Vladimir N. Turbin. 1966 'Tema Vostoka v tvorchestve V. khlebnikova' (The Theme of the East in Khlebnikov) in *Narody Azii i Afriki* (Peoples of Asia and Africa). Moscow: Nauka. Vol. 4. 147-160.

Markov, Vladimir. 1962. 'The Longer Poems of Velimir Khlebnikov', in *University of California Publications in Modern Philology*. Vol. 62. 126-133.

Mayer, A. J. 1967. *The Politics and Diplomacy of Peacemaking. Containment and counterrevolution at Versailles 1918-1919*. New York: Knopf.

Mc Kane, Richard (ed.). 2004. *Ten Russian Poets. Surviving the Twentieth century*, Atlanta: Anvil Press.

Morley, Jefferson. 1992. 'Introduction' to Stanley, Lawrence (ed.) *Rap. The Lyrics*. London: Penguin.

Mufwene, Saliloko S. 1998. *African-American English: Structure, History and Use*. Londonand New York: Routledge.

Neuberger, Joan. 1993. *Hooliganism. Crime. Culture and Power in St Petersburg 1900-1914*. University of California Press.

Poggioli, Renato. 1968. *Theory of the Avant Garde*. Harvard: Harvard University Press.

Price, Morgan Philips. 1997. *Dispatches from the Revolution, Russia 1916*-1918. Foreword by Eric Hobsbawm. London: Pluto Press.
Ransome, Arthur. 1992(a). *Six weeks in Russia in 1919*. Introduction by Paul Foot. London: Redwords.
——1992(b). *The crisis in Russia: (1920)*. London: Redwords.
Sebba, Mark. 1993. *London Jamaican: a Case Study in Language Contact*. London: Longman.
Tanzer, Joshua. 2002. 'You ain't see nothin' nyet'. On line at: http://www.offoffoff.com/music/2002/yoke.php3 (consulted 11.06.2006).
Trotsky, Leo. 1924. K*ak vooruzhalas' revoliutsiia* (How the revolution armed itself). Vol. 2, part 1. Leningrad: Supreme Military Editorial Council.
Ullman, Richard. 1968. *Anglo-Soviet Relations 1917-1921*. Vol. 2. Princeton University Press.
Venuti, Lawrence. 1995. *The Translator's Invisibility*. London and New York: Routledge.
——1998. *The Scandals of Translation - Towards an Ethics of Difference,* London and New York: Routledge.
Wells, H. G. 1920. *Russia in the shadows*. London: Hodder & Stoughton.

# Part VI

# Conflict and the Translator in Fiction

# *L'Étrange destin de Wangrin* or the Political Accommodation of Interpretation[1]

*Sathya Rao*

Hero of Amadou Hampâté Bâ's novel *L'Étrange destin de Wangrin ou les roueries d'un interprète africain,* Wangrin is the perfect illustration of an interpreter forced to find his way between the French colonial authority and the West African colonized population. What is peculiar about this picaresque novel, written within the context of decolonization, is that it opens the way for an intermediary orientation which is neither a return to traditional values (Senghor) nor an apology of socialist revolution (Nkrumah). This middle term is that of a certain "accommodation" which lays the foundation of an unprecedented policy of translation. Indeed, Wangrin is said to master the Arabic language of Marabous, the French language of colonizers, and several local African dialects. Born under the protection of Gongoloma-Sooké, god of malice, he handles his destiny in such a way to capitalize on the various resources of his environment not without giving something to the disinherited. Considered as a saint by some critics and as a devil by others, Wangrin epitomizes the ultimate interpreter whose mastery of the various discursive territories is such that it transcends geopolitical and geolinguistic boundaries. The character imagined by A. H Bâ (whose life strangely resembles that of Wangrin) is the political, linguistic, and even economic agent of an original work of interpretation overwhelming the established discursive order. Neither conservative, nor idealist, Wangrin's policy of translation is simultaneously pragmatic and humanist. It maximizes translational, economical, and political profits while avoiding to get down to a certain level of loss which could be lethal.

Key words: colonisation, linguistic conflicts, storytelling.

## 1. Strategies of translation

Within the political context of French colonial settlement in Africa, the practice of translation could be suspected of either collaboration or resistance. Indeed, translating means simultaneously serving the colonizer's dominant language (in this case, French) and giving oneself the opportunity to manipulate it. Amadou Hampaté Ba's hero Wangrin embodies such a contradiction. Educated at the French colonial school (also called "school of hostages") yet familiar with both African and Muslim traditions, Wangrin works as an interpreter for the French colonial administration. However, instead of falling victim to his many contradictions, Wangrin is the perfect trickster: he has the ability to negotiate opposites. Like Hermes or Ulysses, Bâ's hero avoids overt conflicts, especially linguistic ones, by systematically resorting to his legendary ruse. As a result, the narrative economy of *L'Étrange destin de Wangrin* is no longer that of dualism. It is that of "in-between" (Bhabha) or ambiguity.[2] In other words, conflict as well as resistance are no longer a matter of brutal and inefficient oppositions (colonised/ coloniser, White/Black, writing/oral tradition, reality/fiction), but they require a good dose of strategy. Whilst locking itself within a sterile game of opposition, enunciation is constantly on the run, as though it were fighting to escape the inevitable. By inevitable, we mean at once the oppressor, destiny, the return of dialectics and the putting into writing of the story.

Once "laid down on a piece of paper", enunciation runs the quite foreseeable risk of being, in turn, ultimately manipulated. No wonder then that the reader asks himself if the narrator is the author, the hero of the novel or just a faithful friend reporting a true story. In this connection, the postscript to the novel speaks for itself:

> Depuis la parution de ce livre en 1973, certains malentendus sont apparus çà et là tant sur la personnalité réelle du héros que sur la nature même de l'ouvrage. Je ne sais pourquoi certains (et cela en dépit des précisions apportées dans l'Avertissement) s'interrogent : ce récit est-il une fiction, une réalité, ou un habile mélange des deux ? On admet généralement l'existence historique de celui qui s'était surnommé lui-même « Wangrin », mais on pense que j'ai dû « romancer » quelque peu sa vie, y introduisant même, pour corser l'histoire et lui donner une sorte de signification symbolique, un dosage subtil de tradition orale et d'événements surnaturels de mon cru. (Bâ 1992: 359)

> [Since the publication of this book in 1973, some misunderstandings have come out here and there about the real personality of the hero as well as on the nature of the book itself. I wonder why some (without paying attention to the pieces of information given in the foreword) keep asking themselves : is this narrative a fiction, a real story of a clever mix of both? Although, the historical existence of the one who called himself "Wangrin" is generally taken for granted, people think that I must have "romanticized" his life a bit by introducing a subtle dose of oral tradition, and supernatural events of my own invention in order to liven up the story, and endow it with a kind of symbolical significance,] (my translation)

As we will make clear, the act of writing itself is undermined by an inner conflict which can also be expressed in terms of translation. On the one hand, it is stricken by an ontological suspicion which can only be understood in the light of the peculiar relationship linking man to his word within the African context. On the other hand, writing allows both the re-composition and preservation of African oral tradition. The strength of such an ethical link contrasts with the anonymous materiality of the written text. In the same way, the true story of Wangrin challenges the traditional reading contract as well as the naïve realism typically granted to African writers. Significantly, the narrative begins with "a promise made to a man" (Bâ 1992: 7).

*L'étrange destin de Wangrin* stages the antagonistic condition inherent in the act of translating, that is: the forced respect due to the (colonial) authority of the Original and the possibility of its subversion. Wangrin is not only blessed by the gods, he knows how to supersede his destiny. Conning the oppressor is not simply and naively going against his will, it has to do with producing a knowledge or, rather, a translation, challenging that of the former. Both Wangrin's ability to overtake his destiny and Bâ's narrative discipline originate in this immanent or vernacular knowledge of Africa.

## 2. Conflict and ambiguity

Conflict of opposites constitutes one of the recurrent patterns of *L'Étrange destin de Wangrin*. The dualist scheme of conflict is contextually performed – that is, both expressed and mediated – through the recurrent pattern of ambiguity. The most obvious manifestation of ambiguity is the Bambara God Gongoloma-Sooké – also designated as "the confluence of opposites" – protecting Wangrin:

> Dans la mythologie bambara, Gongoloma-Sooké était un dieu fabuleux que l'eau ne pouvait mouiller ni le soleil dessécher. Le sel ne pouvait le saler, le savon ne pouvait le rendre propre. Mou comme un mollusque, pourtant aucun métal tranchant ne pouvait le couper.
> Les éléments n'avaient aucune prise sur lui. Il n'avait jamais ni chaud ni froid. Il ne dormait que d'un œil. Pour cette raison, la nuit avait peur de lui et le jour s'en méfiait (*ibid.*: 20).
>
> ["This god could neither be soaked by rain nor dried by the sun. Salt could not salt him, and soap could not clean him. Although he was as soft as a mollusc, no metal, however sharp, could cut through him.
> The elements did not affect him in the least; he never felt hot or cold. When he slept, he only closed one eye; because of this, he was feared by the night and mistrusted by day."]

Directing Wangrin's destiny even after his death, the leitmotif of 'ambiguity' can be associated with his unknown place of birth; ambivalent relation to French colonial authority; acute mastery of languages and speech; way of dealing with money or religion; and even with the controversial reception of his own life and deeds — not to mention Wangrin's Fulbe origin, which remains, historically speaking, a mystery for both African tradition and colonial ethnology:

> Les peuls – affirment les Bambaras – sont un surprenant mélange. Fleuve blanc aux pays des eaux noires, fleuve noir aux pays des eaux blanches, c'est un peuple énigmatique, que des capricieux tourbillons ont amené du soleil levant de l'est à l'ouest presque partout (Bâ 1991: 19).
>
> [Fulbes – claim Bambara people – are an amazing mix. White river flowing in the countries of black waters, black river flowing in the countries of white waters. It is an enigmatic people that capricious whirlwinds have brought from the rising sun of the East to the West almost everywhere]   (my translation)

Relying upon a system of oppositions, that can be roughly described as follows: Wangrin versus his initiation, Wangrin versus his colonial and African opponents, and Wangrin versus his destiny or himself, the narration finds its way out of conflict thanks to ambiguity. Indeed, the former opens up a "third space" within which the discourse can perform its Heraclitean work of subversion while escaping the dialectics of white French master and good Nigger. It is precisely within this non antagonistic space that the economy of language, knowledge, but also representation, needs to be reconsidered.

Moreover, ambiguity does not mean falsity. Wangrin is not a liar for the same reason that Bâ is not a storyteller. The dualist theory of representation and the type of judgment it produces are unable to assess the hero and author's complex performances. Within the African context, the fact of lying implies the rupture of the supernatural link between man and his words, and, therefore, the return of a tragic dualism. Significantly, Wangrin's decline is foreshadowed by his symbolic rupture or circumcision with both ancestors and traditions, as well as with his 'double' python and his protecting God. Furthermore, this rupture is accompanied by a process of acceleration: transgression of limits, excessive drinking, recklessness; not to mention the prophetic metaphor of the slippery slope which both heralds the hero's lethal drowning accident and depicts the inner damages caused by alcohol. To spin out the metaphor, destiny finally flows back on reality.

As Jean-Pierre Gourdeau (1980: 89) underlines it, Wangrin's own situation has to be considered within the archetypical conflict between the "functional discourse of the myth" and the "reiterative discourse history". Such a conflict obviously duplicates those between Original and translation, reality and fiction, and Coloniser and colonised. Strictly speaking, it is important to distinguish these two modalities of narrative temporality and speed although they are often intertwined. The symbolic or archetypal mode is directly connected to transcendence and consists in controlling destiny by means of supernatural knowledge. By way of contrast, the speculative or narcissistic mode consists in taking immediate pleasure from one's own possession. Stylistically speaking, it is remarkable to notice that the shift from one mode to the other results in a decreasing use of prolepsis and increasing use of analepsis (Rivia 1992: 59), as though the loss of contact with transcendence would diminish Wangrin's ability to master his destiny (or opponents). Easy money, alcohol, and Mrs Terreau constitute the exchange values of the speculative economy based upon the search for pleasure for its own sake. On the contrary, the symbolic economy allows convertibility between economic and spiritual capitals through charity, public pageants, and presents offered to Marabous.

In essence, the sinews of war are dualism and the speculative economy it establishes. Whereas Wangrin's philosophical performance manages to hold the opposites together, the rhetoric of rupture leads to all kinds of excesses.

More precisely, the latter lays the foundation for a colonial politics of discrimination (French coloniser .vs. African colonised) but also for an economy of discourse centred around pragmatic effects rather than symbolic content. To put it another way, since it is deprived of symbolic content, discourse has nothing to convey but its own exhilarating movement and illusion. As it is expressed in the root (*hal*) – meaning 'giving the power' – of the Fulfulde word for 'speech' (*haala*), verbal performance cannot be separated from its divine origin. Indeed, as Bâ recalls it, it is said of the first man, that it is from having spoken to God that *kiikala* brought its power (Bâ 1986: 100). Besides, prophecy intervenes directly in the narrative process as a kind of coded meta-discourse weaving together insightful prolepsis and analepsis. For example, let's remember Numu-Sama's prophetic words just after young Wangrin's circumcision:

> Je ne connais pas ta fin, mais ton étoile commencera à pâlir le jour où N'tubanin-kan-fin, la tourterelle au cou cerclé à demi d'une bande noire, se posera sur une branche morte d'un kapokier en fleur et roucoulera par sept cris saccadés, puis s'envolera de la branche pour se poser à terre, sur le côté gauche de ta route. A partir de ce moment tu deviendras vulnérable et facilement à la merci de tes ennemis ou d'une guigne implacable. Veille à cela, c'est là mon grand conseil. (Bâ 1992: 22).

> [I do not know how you will die, but I can see that your star will begin to set the day N-tubanin-kan-fin, the dove with a black ring round one half of her neck, comes to rest on the dead branch of a kapok tree in full bloom, cooing seven times distinctly, then leaves that branch and alights on the lefthand side of your path. From that moment on you will become vulnerable. From that moment on you will become vulnerable. You will be at the mercy of your enemies and ill-luck will dog your steps relentlessly. Guard against that moment; this is my advice to you.]

Broadly speaking, the conflict of interpretations is overcome on the basis of an intimate knowledge of both European and African linguistic, cultural, and political territories or networks of meaning. Not only does Wangrin speak a French "*couleur vin de Bordeaux*" but he masters various African dialects. However, far from being disinterested, Wangrin's decision of interpretation is oriented by his natural tendency to satisfy his own needs. The resulting economy of interpretation is based on a dialectical process of capitalisation of gains and redistribution to spiritual authorities, local population, and poor people. Significantly, one of the signs foreshadowing Wangrin's decadence is that:

> Il ne distribuait plus son argent aux pauvres avec la même prodigalité qu'autrefois. Certes, il ne refusait pas l'aumône, mais il était moins large et s'il habillait encore les veuves et les orphelins, ce n'était plus lui qui allait au-devant d'eux. (Bâ 1992: 312).

> [No longer so prodigal with the poor, he didn't of course refuse to give alms, but he was not as generous as he had been in former days and if he still clothed the widows and orphans who came to solicit his help, he no longer actually sought them out."]

Therefore, instead of being an end in itself, capital (be it economic or symbolic) finds its very meaning or value in its transmission, that is to say, both in the network of political alliances leading to profit and in its local redistribution.

In the end, the coloniser versus colonised conflict turns into a dynamic and original process of translation. Wangrin invests in the colonised world what he has learned from the colonial *episteme* while taking advantage of his acute knowledge of the colonised world in order to destabilise French colonial authority. Significantly, the latter cannot escape the ethnological description of its own 'customs' just as the knowledge of Africa needs a rigorous methodological framework to be carried on. It is precisely such a crossed-perspective that grants its originality to Bâ's 'ethno-literary' work. Using well-known traductological terms, Wangrin is neither a *cibliste* nor a *sourcier*. He is both at the same time: he is a sorcerer perfectly aware of the coloniser's target-language and a skilful administrator mastering the colonized's source-language. A certain number of collocations – compound words and metaphors – express this complexity: "*dialecte de mange-mil*", "*Blanc-blanc*", "*mine-piège*", "*le répond-bouche*", "*forofilon naspa*", "*français couleur vin de Bordeaux*", "*si besoin était, nous le ferions manger par la nuit*", "*Ses deux chevaux mangeaient du couscous fin et buvaient du lait*".

The enemy is not so much the colonial outsider as the "immanent" rupture leading to the disconnection with tradition. No wonder, then, that Bâ is so concerned about collecting oral traditions:

> Depuis plusieurs ruptures dans la transmission se sont produites : les promotions de militaires qui au cours des deux grandes guerres mondiales sont parties hors de leur pays, ont été souvent arrachées du même coup aux initiations qui devaient les brancher sur le grand tronc de la tradition. (Bâ 1986: 112)

> [since then several ruptures happened in the transmission : the contingents of soldiers that during the two world wars have left their country, were hence dragged away from ritual initiations that would connect them to great trunk of tradition]

If Wangrin knew how to take advantage of French administration, he has fallen victim to his exhilarating oblivion of tradition. The decentred 'topophony' of oral speech is based upon a dynamic economy of language favouring redistribution and translation of symbolic content rather than capitalisation. In other words, subverting both French colonial authority and knowledge essentially means using local power networks – such as marabous or African dialects –, which remain unknown to the oppressor.

## 3. From Interpretation to Science

Bâ's narrative work of 'recomposition' relies upon an epistemological assumption of coherence very similar to that used by the author to reconstruct the history of Fulfulde Empire in Macina:

> Au moment de l'écriture de l'ouvrage, je dus procéder à un nécessaire travail de montage et de coordination des différents témoignages et introduire partout où c'était nécessaire des textes de liaison, afin de donner à l'ensemble du récit un enchaînement cohérent. Ce fut là, à part le travail de traduction et de mise en forme, bien sûr, l'essentiel de mon apport personnel, ainsi que, par endroits, les descriptions des lieux. (Bâ 1992: 361).

> [When I was writing this book, I had to carry out to an essential work of montage and coordination of the different testimonies, and also introduce wherever it was necessary linking texts in order to give to the whole narration a coherent structure. That was, apart from the work of translation and imposition, of course, the bulk of my personal contribution, as well as, here and there, descriptions of places]

Such an assumption implies a theoretical re-elaboration or translation of the collected oral material into unified yet non totalitarian whole. This material is mostly composed of contradictory testimonies – be they those of Macinankes and Toucouleur, or those of the detractors and defenders of Wangrin – needing to be objectively assessed. The requirement of objectivity thereby provides a conciliatory solution to the narrative conflicts of interpretation. Besides, Bâ's strong claim for historical objectivity invalidates all attempts to reduce *L'Étrange destin de Wangrin* to a mere novel. Such a mistake can be explained by two reasons: firstly, western thought is unable to envision any continuity between the real and supernatural worlds; secondly, the ethnographer's discipline is confused with the author's creative genius. However, it is not possible to disconnect the text from the network of its underlying testimonies in order to 'capitalize' it solely in the phenomenological consciousness of the author. In other words, the narrative space of *L'Étrange destin de Wangrin* is conclusively Bâ's fertile imagination; it is, first and foremost, the intersubjective network of oral testimonies from which the novel proceeds.

Bâ's narrative gesture and Wangrin's ruse come from the same 'microscopic' knowledge of both the coloniser and colonised's discourses and territories. Such a knowledge contrasts with the coloniser's macroscopic one whose aim is to extend, in a narcissistic way, its own political, economical, sexual, etc, domination. In contrast to the latter, the former rely on an immanent knowledge of Africa informed by an intimate perception of its inner complexity. This understanding can be related to that of the "traditionalist" who, according to Bâ, is:

> Un 'généraliste' qui a des connaissances aussi bien dans la science des plantes, que dans celles des terres, propriétés agricoles ou médicinales, et dans la science des eaux, l'astronomie, la cosmogonie, la psychologie, etc. Il s'agit d'une science de la *vie et*

d'une science éminemment pratique, consistant à mobiliser les énergies disponibles au service de la vie. (Bâ 1986: 101)

[a generalist who has a good knowledge of the science of plants and earth, agricultural and medicinal properties, and of the science of water, astronomy, cosmogony, psychology, etc. It is a science of living things and a science eminently practical, consisting of mobilizing available energies for the promotion of life.]

Hence, an interesting analogy can be made between the dynamic network of oral speech, the "general" science of the traditionalist, and even T. Monod's universalist conception of natural science, the three of them being regulated by the same Humboldtian principle of life.

Bâ's originality lies in his attempt to re-organise – through a rigorous process of translation – the oral material into a written text. Because of its oral substrate, most African knowledge remained out of reach for colonial science, which could, therefore, let its imagination fantasize. In the case of Fulfulde traditions, the problem was as much historical as it was epistemological since, as the author puts it metaphorically, to deal with Fulfude matters is, for a European mind, to face profound chaos if one does not have the key and does not know the right door to open.

In order to elaborate his microscopic knowledge of Africa, Bâ reconciled ethnologic method and traditional African wisdom. Formed by Monod at the French Institute of Black Africa (IFAN) in 1942, Bâ became familiar with methods of investigation which allowed him to improve his work of collection and re-composition of oral sources. Following Théodore Monod's *Conseils aux chercheurs* and Marcel Griaule's *L'instrument pour l'ethnologie*, Bâ even wrote his own investigation manual. *L'Empire peul du Macina* and *L'Étrange destin de Wangrin* both rely upon the same requirement of scientific coherence. The latter can be understood as a narrative response to the conflict of interpretations. In the case of *L'Étrange destin de Wangrin* though, certain names and places have been slightly changed due to the promise made to Wangrin. From a methodological standpoint, Bâ insists upon the distinction between theory and practice. Theory is meant to unify and organise the chaotic stories patiently collected from traditionalists. As a whole, the theoretical work consists of re-organising narratives through the comparison of various and often contradictory testimonies. Within this process, the investigator may ask competent religious authorities for additional information. Funnily enough, the requirement of objectivity meets the traditionalist's concern for truth regarding his storytelling performance.

### 4. Beyond dualisms

*L'Étrange destin de Wangrin* gives to the notion of conflict an extension which exceeds the sole antagonism between oppressor and oppressed. Indeed, conflict designates the *dynamic* confrontation between coloniser and colonised, French language and African dialects, history and myth, ethnological method and African knowledge, written text and oral tradition, morality and immorality, etc. However, such a confrontation is not structured as a mere opposition; rather it takes place upon the complex discursive territory produced by local social, linguistic, political, and economic networks. Within this context, conflict has strong strategic content and describing both French colonial settlement and African realities as objectively as possible becomes an act of resistance. Science, translation, and writing are the objective means used to organise the chaotic local material; that is, the chains of signifiers formed and produced by African networks of oral communication. Indeed, they all pacifically gather and articulate antagonistic data within a coherent and non ideological narrative constituting, so to speak, the 'non colonial' knowledge and poetics of Africa.

---

1 Translated in English by Aina Pavollini Taylor as *The fortunes of Wangrin* (Nigeria : New Horn Press, 1987, mentioned as *FW*). The translation of the title deserves two comments : firstly, the choice of "fortunes" for "*l'étrange destin*" connects intertextually A.H. Bâ's novel with the tradition of nineteenth century English picaresque novel, one can think, for example, of Daniel Defoe's *The Fortunes and Misfortunes of the Famous Moll Flanders*. Secondly, no mention is made of the French subtitle « *Les Roueries d'un interprète africain*», which is for our purpose of major importance. Both decisions of translation tend to restrain prejudicially the mastery of Wangrin (and, to a certain extent, that of the translator himself) over his own actions. In other words, the first role is given to the hazards of fortunes rather than to Wangrin's science of anticipation.
2 In his remarkable introduction to the English translation of A.H. Bâ's novel, Abiola Irele puts the emphasis on the concept of ambiguity. Even though he explores its various dimensions within the narrative, Irele does not relate it to the notion of translation in particular, and to that of science in general. Far from being an evasive concept, ambiguity is a strategic performance or *savoir-faire* based on a rigorous knowledge of colonial practices.

**Primary references**
Bâ, Hampaté Amadou. 1992. *L'Étrange destin de Wangrin*. Paris: Éditions 10/18.
——1991. *Amkoullel l'enfant peul, mémoires*. Arles: A.C.C.T/Actes Sud.
——1987. *The fortunes of Wangrin*. Nigeria: New Horn Press.
——1986. 'La tradition vivante', in Ki-Zerbo, Jean (ed.). *Histoire générale de l'Afrique. Vol I. Méthodologie et préhistoire africaine*. Paris: Présence africaine/Edicef/ UNESCO, 99-112.

**Secondary references**
Aggarwal, Kusum. 1999. *Amadou Hampâté Bâ et l'africanisme*. Paris: L'Harmattan.
Bandia, Paul. 2001. 'Le concept bermanien de l' « Étranger » dans le prisme de la traduction postcoloniale', in *TTR*, 15(2): 123-139.
Devey, Muriel. 1993. *Hampaté Bâ. L'homme de la tradition*. Sénégal and Togo: LivreSud/NEA Togo.
Gourdeau, Jean-Pierre. 1980. 'L'Étrange destin de Wangrin : le mythe, l'individu, l'histoire', in *Afrique littéraire*, n°54-55: 89-91.
Makonda, Antoine. 1988. *L'Étrange destin de Wangrin. Étude critique*. Paris: Nathan.

Rivia, Sylvia. 1992. 'Les structures temporelles dans L'étrange destin de Wangrin d'Amadou Hampâté Bâ', in Jouanny, Robert (ed.) *Lecture de l'œuvre d'Hampaté Bâ*. Paris: L'Harmattan. 53-69.

# The Embedded Translator: a Coming Out Story

*Beverley Curran*

Translation has been a chronic trope employed in speaking of the mobility of cultural knowledges and information globally and their conversation, fragmentation, and reconstitution within specific histories and cultures. It is generally cast as a paradigm that opens out into a wider discussion, but the translator who emerges in the "fictional turn" of translation places emphasis on the particulars of place and history. This paper examines the embedded translator found in recent Canadian novels in English that explore World War II, its wake, and repercussions. It is my contention that a writer who situates the translator as a character or presence within his or her fiction and thus raises the visibility of that figure counters the paradigm of the "embedded" wartime journalist as a concentrated and exclusive source of information through resistance to a singular source in a monolingual tongue; and questions the simplification of complexity for the purposes of a pithy sound bite or easy understanding. The fictional translator in the texts by Michael Ondaatje and Kerri Sakamoto disrupt the habit of translation that prioritizes the comfort of the reader, and punctures the unviolated authority of a writer whose tongue is hegemonic and powerful and pervasive English-language media.

Key words: coming out, embedded translator, World War II.

## Introduction

I would like to consider the emergence or *coming out* of the translator as a fictional character or presence in contemporary Canadian anglophone writing, specifically in novels published in the 1990s. I call this growing presence a 'coming out' story not in order to 'sex up' the dossier of a figure hitherto largely ignored and left critically unexamined but to mark the increasing cultural significance of the translator, and, like any coming out story, signals the possible need for a retrospective re-reading of what precedes this emergence in search of why its identification was delayed. The two exemplary fictional translators I will discuss in this paper are found in Michael Ondaatje's *The English Patient* (1992) and Kerry Sakamoto's *The Electrical Field* (1998). Like many translators in the Americas, their practice takes place unofficially in marginal communities and its presence is unacknowledged or deliberately obscured by powerful media and institutions; its development eclectic; and its models often improvised (Gentzler 2002: 9). Memory and story are two important aspects of this translation activity that takes place off the official record and a conflict is often to be found when personal and public accounts rub against each other. Ondaatje's fictional translator is a charred somatic ruin, more a site than a figure, marking location as a crucial aspect of translation. *The English Patient* is set in Europe and the Libyan desert immediately prior and during World War II. It is peopled with a Hungarian count who prefers the status of "international bastard" to any nationality; two Canadians, an old thief and a young nurse; and a Sikh who is a bomb disposal expert in the British army. The fictional translator in *The Electrical Field* is a Japanese Canadian who finds herself as a child in the middle of conflict in Canada, which translates her from "citizen" to "enemy alien." Forcibly removed from the Pacific coast and interned in the wake of Pearl Harbor, decades later the fictional translator is still suffering from the effects of her community's drastic translation.

These damaged fictional translators and their stories will be compared with the notion of the journalist *embedded* in a war zone, whose reportage is monolingually insular but often mediated, like much of the news, by unacknowledged translators/interpreters. The *objective* reporter, particularly in a conflict zone, is as problematic as the *faithful* translator or the *neutral* interpreter. The translator is coming out in recent reportage (post-9/11) as well as in fiction, and is also involved in 'outing', as Mandarin translator Katharine Gunn was, leaking information considered sensitive and preferred hidden by governmental security agencies. Fidelity and the issue of the translator's loyalty are now considered clichés in translation studies, but they continue to be foregrounded in the representation of the translator in the news in areas of conflict.

## 1. The Conflicted Fictional Translator in *The English Patient*

Else Ribeiro Pires Vieira has observed a fictional turn in translation in Brazilian and Spanish Latin American (post)modern literature, where fiction has both provided theoretical parameters for translation and offered itself as an alternative source of theorization. Sherry Simon has noticed this fictional inscription of the translator, too, with particular reference to Québécoise writer Nicole Brossard's novel *Le désert mauve* (1996: 158-161), as an indication of just how central a Western intellectual and cultural preoccupation translation has become. In his examination of fictional texts where a second language is extensively deployed but already under translation, Leo Tak-Hung Chan suggests such texts signal a need to theoretically rethink translation. For example, Roman Jakobson's description of intralingual translation as rewording and designation of interlingual translation only as "translation proper" strikes Chan as too narrow when applied to texts that are not purely monolingual" (Chan 2002: 68). The deployment of translation within monolingual writers' works, such as the novels of anglophone Canadian writers Michael Ondaatje and Kerri Sakamoto, suggests an activity of even greater breadth and complexity. In less theoretical realms, when the US Department of Defense sponsors a conference on languages (Feal 2004: 4) and links the knowledge of multiple languages with national security, there seems little doubt that a linguistic "lack" in now being recognized by English speakers, regardless of global ubiquity of the language.

*The English Patient* raises issues of blockage, allegiance and agency, identity construction, and global and discursive migration. The narrative situates the fictional translator within a broad historical sweep and locates him at a specific and special moment in terms of history and translation: World War II. Major changes in translation practice took place immediately after the war, when it became professionalized, and even industrialized, through the creation of large international organizations, such as the United Nations (Brisset 2003: 103). World War II is significant in historical terms because of the magnitude of its powerful technology and degree of its horror; the psychic tremors of the Holocaust and the bombing of Hiroshima and Nagasaki continue to resonate. As the mayor of Hiroshima Akiba Tadatoshi said during the 2004 memorial service for A-bomb victims, "[T]he human race still lacks both a lexicon capable of fully expressing that disaster and sufficient imagination to fill that gap."[1] A sense of linguistic shortfall is a powerful presence in the construction of many of the fictional translators whom I have been looking at in my research, although it is seems to be absent in the English patient. In spite of painfully shedding his skin, he retains through his command of multiple languages membership in a polyglot professional class.

Ondaatje's fictional translator assumes that his own erudition and linguistic skills allow him to pursue his interest in geography in the Libyan deserts as if "he was alone, his own invention" (246).[2] This sense of free agency contradicts historical research which "rarely supports the view that translators are characterized by romantic alienation and freedom from culture, whatever their place of enunciation" (Tymoczko 2003: 201). The fictional translator in *The English Patient* operates within a mirage of self-sufficiency until pressures of the private and the political fissure his hermetic sense of self. In his nomadic explorations of the desert, the self-proclaimed "international bastard" (251) resists notions of national affiliations and personal ownership, but later, burnt beyond recognition, he is dependent on morphine and the care of Hana, a young Canadian nurse.

## 1.1 Translator's Block

The English patient lies embedded and immobile in a Tuscany villa in the waning days of World War II, on the cusp of significant changes in the world that he will not live to see. In fact, he spends most of his time thinking about the desert, remembering the woman he loved. He lives in the past, and is often described in archaic terms. For example, while Hana roams the house like a vagrant, the English patient is ensconced in a temporal and spatial elsewhere, reposing in his bed "like a king" (14), or a medieval knight:

> [H]e reposes like the sculpture of the dead knight in Ravenna. He speaks in fragments, about oasis towns, the later Medicis, the prose style of Kipling [...]. And in his commonplace book, his 1890 edition of Herodotus' *Histories* are other fragments – maps, diary entries, writings in many languages, paragraphs cut out of other books. [...] The references in his book are all pre-war [...]. (96)

The passage above deftly illustrates that the knowledge and skill of the English patient still allow him to slip from the desert to the Renaissance, or from Herodotus to Kipling, but physically he has reached an impasse. The intercultural traffic inscribed on his body is deadlocked. I would like to compare this position with the view Michael Cronin offers of the contemporary translator in *Translation and Globalization*:

> One of the most common experiences for translators is that of blockage. The word or expression or the equivalent allusion will not come, the textual whole somehow does not seem the right fit and try as you might, there seems to be no way out, the words refuse to come to your rescue. (2003: 93)

There is another condition of linguistic shortfall that I will call 'translator's block,' which is more than frustration about 'what gets lost in translation' or an inability to find *le mot juste*. Rather, it is a pained silence or stutter, awkward phrasing, and fragments of lost language used as translation strategies to register the effects of history – particularly assimilation– on the destruction of identities.

Translator's block is not registered on the tongue of the English patient, but is inscribed in his immobility and dependency on the kindness of strangers. Still, there is an implicit connection with the tongue, in the English patient's somatic condition if "patient" is allowed both its medical meaning and its designation in linguistics as a semantic role. In the latter case, "patient" refers to the entity undergoing a change of state or location through possession, acquisition, or exchange (Longacre 1983: 155-56). That is, as both translator and patient, the English patient performs the task of the translator while being translated.

Translator's block is more apparent in Miss Saito, the fictional translator in *The Electrical Field* that will be discussed shortly. She is ashamed of the way her community speaks English and hypercorrects her own utterances, remembering the humiliation of her inadequate linguistic performance, in Japanese and English, as an *ad hoc* translator for her family. Where languages have been suppressed, broken down, or disappeared, there is not just loss but damage. Gentzler observes:

> The effect of the past on the present though often erased or covered up by the monolingualism of English, often returns to haunt the present. For ethnic

> minorities in the Americas, this past and the language in which the stories are told, is becoming increasingly important to the communities to enable them to understand the present. (2002: 17)

In short, these are the basic conditions under which the fictional translator operates: there has been linguistic damage and translation is a mode of repair, a way of remembering.

## 1.2 The Technical Tools of the Translator

In addition to his burns, the English patient is also suffering from the painful discovery that "the earth's surface and its 'interesting geographical problems'" do not lie on the far side of human and financial behaviour (134), including military, economic, and emotional imperialism. In this sense, he shares a growing contemporary awareness that we all inhabit and are responsible for a complex and sensitive eco-system that influences and is affected by large cultural groupings found within it. As a technical rather than a literary translator, the fictional translator in Ondaatje's novel represents translation in a very different light. Most work done in translation lies outside the realm of literary and theoretical writing, yet "the cultural and intellectual stakes of non-literary translation are rarely spelled out in any great detail and are generally referred to only in the vaguest possible terms" (Cronin 2003: 2). The fictional translator in *The English Patient* is a lover of books, and a writer, but he describes himself as a "mechanic":

> Men had always been the reciters of poetry in the desert. And Madox – to the Geographical Society – had spoken beautiful accounts of our traversals and coursings. Bermann blew theory into the embers. And I? I was the skill among them. (241)

His first task of translation recounted in the novel is to identify a range of weaponry by touch. The link between the translator and technology is unmistakable, but the implications go further; "it is neither possible nor desirable to marginalize the technical in any proper definition of what it means to be fully human" (Cronin 2003: 3), nor is it wise to ignore translation.

Further, translation cannot be solely defined by its relationship with texts. The emergence of a translator as a character or presence in fiction marks an acknowledgement of the role of agent in the process. The technical translator in a literary work may signal a heightened awareness of the relationship of the translator, and his or her dependency on tools or "elements of the object world which translators use or have been affected by in their work down through the centuries" (*ibid.*: 10). Cronin explains the significance of this relationship as follows:

> Though tools are routinely described in an instrumental fashion in the periodical literature of translation technology, thinking on the relationship between translation

and the technosphere has been in the main underdeveloped. And yet like any other realm of human activity, it is impossible to conceive of translation outside the object world it inhabits. (*ibid.*)

This relationship is emphasized in *The English Patient* by intimately linking almost all the characters with tools that mark changes in technology in medicine, communication and war. The English patient has his translated text of Herodotus and a hearing aid; Hana has her drugs and hypodermic needles; Kip has his crystal set and tools for dismantling bombs. In other words, technology is an integral part of the daily life of the provisional community that comes together in the villa in Tuscany, as well as a crucial element in the construction of the fictional translator. In his relationships with texts, people, and technologies, the fictional translator is found at the centre of powerful cultural tensions.

Translation and technology also play a key part, of course, in the conflict in Iraq. In order to help present a positive picture of the service being rendered by their troops, the Bush administration devised the idea of embedded journalism. "Put reporters and photographers in the heart of the action, they figured, and they'll help depict the sacrifice that [their] troops [were] making. [...] Little did they imagine what might happen if the true embeds, the soldiers themselves, had cameras" (Cahan 2004: 15). Defense Secretary Donald Rumsfeld complained about the lack of control in

> a wartime situation in the Information Age [...] where people are running around with digital cameras and taking these unbelievable digital photographs [of, for example, the night shift at Abu Ghraib Prison] and then passing them off, against the law, to the media.
> (*ibid.*)

There is a new force in the world: the amateur. As a photographer in possession of technology that cannot be controlled, the amateur is a loose cannon and not to be trusted. The lay translator in possession of a "dangerous" language is similarly under suspicion. In Iraq, for example, available translators are not necessarily seasoned or even trained professionals. As one *fixer* describes the situation:

> Now many people are coming to the hotels where journalists stay to find work. New people. I don't know who they are. The teacher is coming for work, the doctor is coming for work. The university professor is coming to work as a fixer – because it's good money. There's a general who served in the army in the time of Saddam, and now he's a translator. (Gettleman 2004: 289)

Reporters such as Jeffrey Gettleman are attached to the mainstream media, but operate in the "Red Zone" in Baghdad, where they "are in daily contact, through their Iraqi staffs, with the nightmare the Iraqi people are experiencing" (Ignatius 2006: 10). Although linguistic mediation is clearly implied, such journalists have far less upbeat stories to report than the "embedded" journalist, or those in the Green Zone, where official American versions of the conflict circulate. In either zone, the Western journalist is increasingly dependent on the Iraqi reporter, as translators and blog authors, who has English. Notions of "objective" reporting from this one-sided position are as shaky as the pacts of neutrality and fidelity assumed as the ethical basis of work in interpreting and translation. Certainly these are not in operation under such pragmatic working conditions as the conflict in Iraq, but are they ever really applicable?

**1.3 Trusting the translator**
The loyalty issue is also a great concern regarding the translators and interpreters working at the Guantanamo Bay US Navy Base. Investigations into security breaches at the prison centre on the hiring of a US translator and how the translator who was "already under investigation got secret clearance and was allowed onto the base, and how a second translator managed to leave with classified information" (*The Daily Yomiuri* 2004: 'US probes'). According to the article, the other suspects currently under investigation are a couple of Muslim chaplains. The translators had been hired as contract workers by the San-Diego-based Titan Corporation, and both are Arabic translators. They are charged with lying to federal agents; espionage and aiding the enemy; and suspicion of aiding the enemy. They say they are innocent.

The demand for "qualified linguists" at Guantanamo Bay is high as there are over 200 interrogators working in 17 languages. About 70 translators are involved in the interrogations of the 660 detainees at the base's Camp Delta prison camp, and most of the detainees are suspected of links to the Al-Qaida network or the ousted Taliban regime. However, the translators themselves – most of them Arabic interpreters -- also pose a security risk. "You can have the most secure cells and an isolated military base, but if you don't control the people who come on the base, you have a serious problem," cautions Matt Levitt, terrorism analyst and senior fellow at the Washington Institute (Cahan 2004: 14). The prison attempts to contain and control can be seen more broadly as the attempts of a paranoid nation to reassure itself it is a "self contained entity that controls itself by suspecting everything else" (Abel 2004: 1242). The translator with an inaccessible and crucial other language embodies a counter-narrative; and his or her presence in the prison embeds it there, where it can circulate.

To return to Ondaatje's novel, when the English patient is interrogated by the British in 1944, his seared condition and inability or unwillingness to identify himself were not exceptional: "At that time of the war there were hundreds of soldiers lost from themselves, more innocent than devious. [...] The burned pilot was one more enigma, with no identification, unrecognizable" (95). He played with their inability to identify him as a traitor or ally, but the interrogating officers found "[e]verything about him was very English except for the fact that his skin was tarred black, a bogman from history" (96). The illegible body, untranslatable, is an obstacle to recognition. Clem Robyns has observed

> If we define a discourse as a set of messages viewed by their producers or receivers as linked because they rely partly on a common set of norms, the awareness of such common codes is possible only via confrontation with their absence, namely, with other discourses. (1994: 406)

The common codes the interrogators use to identify an Englishman seem to be based on criteria of skin and tongue. The English patient manipulates the missing skin factor to keep his identity, in personal and cultural terms, uncertain. Much later it turns out that his tongue has furnished very effective linguistic camouflage, for "the English patient is not English" (163), but a Hungarian count, Ladislaus de Almásy, one of the great desert explorers, who acted as a desert guide for German spies during the war.

With Almásy's personal history attached, the questionable loyalties of a translator conflate with those of a traitor. Once again, the semantic roles of "agent" and "patient" are both apparent, but this time "agent" is accented by its connection to espionage. The link here between the translator and fidelity and issues of loyalty is an ubiquitous one:

> The stock commonplaces of literary pundits all bear on the dubious textual morals of translators. The ritual invocation of *belles infidèles*, *traddutori*, *traditori* and the omnipresent dictum of poetry being what gets lost in translation suggest that translators are basically not to be trusted and that translation is a somewhat dishonest enterprise. (Cronin 2003: 68)

*The English Patient* is about betrayals in love and war, but the concept of fidelity comes under question as a sturdy cornerstone that clarifies the task of the translator. In fact, the figure of the fictional translator suggests that the notion of fidelity as a "static essence" is burnt out: "If translators are agents of change in a culture, then it would seem that infidelity, not fidelity, must be their constant preoccupation" (Cronin 2003: 68). In actual reportage, however, translators continue to be among the usual suspects when it comes to issues of loyalty.

Whereas the flawless English of the fictional English patient could be put to positive use in dealing with interrogators suspecting his allegiances, in the war in Iraq, such proficiency can be a liability. Public displays of "foreign" language proficiency are full of risk. *The Times* correspondent Stephen Farrell maintains that for journalists "[a] little Arabic is good, [but] too much leaves you open to accusations of being CIA or Israeli spies" (Farrell 2004: 14). Iraqi translators working for the British journalist "do not tell their neighbours who they work for" and, on call 24 hours a day, "they will not answer the mobile phone if it rings in a taxi or a dubious area of the city, so as not to be heard speaking English." For foreign reporters like Farrell, the translator offers both linguistic and somatic camouflage. As the journalist glibly reports, they local translator provides a useful human shield. While he rides in the back seat of an "invisible" Korean car, "[t]wo Iraqis [sit] in the front seat, driver and translator, to satisfy casual observers." Through the translator, the reporter is able to shift his or her national affiliations. As one fixer explained, "I never say the journalist is from America. I say he's French or Canadian or from Chechnya" (Gettleman 2004: 289). But disguises are sometimes ignored and when a reporter is killed, his translator may be killed, as well.

If fictional translators are agents of change, and patients, as well, how are they operating in Anglophone writing in late modernity? And why is their presence so often awkward, unreliable, and even painful? I suggest that those who speak only English feel their monolingualism a liability in spite of the language's powerful global influence. Ondaatje's fictional translator, however, is certainly not just registering anglophone angst. The English patient, after all, is not English. Being Hungarian suggests he speaks "in translation" throughout this novel. In spite of his formidable linguistic gifts, Almásy is in the double bind of any minority language translator: letting a dominant language like English take over, he becomes less and less "recognizable;" resisting the powerful dynamic, however, can mean being sidelined in linguistic stasis. The use of English is commonly taken to be one of the distinctive features of globalization and Anglophone cultural hegemony. The fictional translator in Ondaatje's *The English Patient* is a complex and suggestive construction that positions translation as a process carried out by non-native English speakers, which means that these agents are always English 'patients', in translation themselves.

## 2. The camp translator in *The Electrical Field*

The English patient can talk the talk but not walk the walk: that is, although an unidentifiable somatic wreck, he is "recognized" as English through his command of the language. In Kerri Sakamoto's novel, *The Electrical Field*, the situation is reversed. The fictional translator speaks only fragmentary Japanese, but her body keeps being read before she can speak. *The Electrical Field* roots itself in insecurity, "a radically insecure subjectivity [...] swaying between divergent possible selves and vulnerable to manipulation" (Sinfield 1992: 64). Sakamoto's novel is set in the mid-70s when many Japanese Canadians still resisted the idea of Redress and a national collective identity because it painfully reminded them of their stigmatized status as such in the 1940s. In fact, the term "Redress" was a largely unfamiliar one, stirring in the "social cauldron of [...] a period parked by the emergence of identity politics, in which the ideology of assimilation was [being] subsumed by a new buzz word, 'multiculturalism' (Miki 1998: 202). The figure of the translator in *The Electrical Field* exemplifies the problematic of identity and community among Japanese Canadians psychically and linguistically damaged by that uprooting and dispersal. The faulty, suggestive, and ironic play of Miss Saito's Japanese translation offers, like camp talk, "textures of negotiation" (Harvey 2001:128) that keeps both the author and the reader attentive to possible and alternative meanings of the translator herself.

Written and published post-Redress,[3] the novel considers the problematic relationship that Japanese Canadians have with their Japanese identity and uses traces of the Japanese language as a code of community to revive that cultural connection. The evident bitterness of the linguistic relationships in *The Electrical Field* dampens and even contradicts the celebration of hybridity and its linguistic play promoted by, for example, Homi Bhabha or Salman Rushdie in both critical and creative writing. The "damaged" fictional translator is closer to the position of the border-crossing, code-switching *mestiza* articulated by Gloria Anzaldúa, who finds hybridity "a difficult and precarious political situation and [painful] psychic experience. The hybrid individual is marginalized everywhere, often vilified, and usually full or self-doubt" (Alcoff 2006: 256), and links this insecurity to forms of violence. Even with this more sobering approach, Anzaldúa has been criticized for being "too utopian for a concrete reality that has always been informed more by border enforcers than border crossers" (Castillo 2006: 260), and certainly *The Electrical Field* sees racialized and linguistic boundaries set up within the nation's borders

In terms of readership, Sakamoto has her immediate community in mind,[4] but Miss Saito, her fictional translator, is part of the *nisei* community, is oriented towards a Japan that she has never seen and a language and culture that she has almost forgotten. Because her translation necessarily stages loss, its performance becomes a method for "pretending an identity into existence" (Apter 1999: 134); Miss Saito's "Japanese" identity can then be recognized as a translation effect. Sakamoto uses traces of the Japanese language as a code of community to revive a cultural connection. At the same time she creatively configures a translator who is neither professional nor in possession of the linguistic competency necessary to be an effective interpreter. Miss Saito reaches out from the restrictive 'poverty' of her community's halting use of English as a vernacular and vehicular language for Japanese, which, in the cultural field of the *nisei* community, she sees as a mythical tongue.

Considering their respective perceptions of their own community, Sakamoto's project as an author and Miss Saito's "intentions" as a translator are very much at odds, but in both cases, the deployment of Japanese insists that the secret of a submerged and eroded Japanese identity be not only divulged but employed to share a dark story. Operating under the constraints of recent history that accelerated assimilation, Miss Saito inadvertently works at the confines of her identity by working with a language that belongs to someone else. Although she resists being politicized, as a translator she demonstrates "the role play[ed] by language for the *agent*, the person who acts, even though intention is not fully present in itself" (Spivak 2000: 397). Gayatri Spivak has called for a "foreignizing" translation that gives the reader "a tough sense of the specific terrain of the original" (2000: 405), but has in mind a translator so thoroughly at home in that language that she can speak "by choice or preference, of intimate matters in the language of the original" (404). Similarly, Lawrence Venuti, in his desire to jointly illuminate both the translator and the departure text, proposes "foreignizing" as a strategy "that registers the irreducible differences of the foreign text" (Venuti 2000: 341) through innovative lexical choices, register, and style that require linguistic command. The fictional translator's relationship with the Japanese language in *The Electrical Field*, however, is limited, and consists largely of intimate terms related to the body. In other words, the performance of the fictional translator in the novel borrows language piecemeal and improvises identity in a manner that is rather queer. In fact, it will be seen that in this "play of surfaces feigning substance" (Harvey 2000: 456), Miss Saito enlists camp strategies to enact her identity.

**2.1 Redress or Crossdress? Camp Translation Strategies**
In "Notes on Camp" (1964), Susan Sontag sees Camp as an apolitical aesthetic mode devoted to artifice, and a sense of life as theatre. As she explains:

> Camp sees everything in quotation marks. It's not a lamp, but a 'lamp'; not a woman, but a 'woman.' To perceive Camp in objects and persons is to understand Being-as-Playing a Role. (Sontag 1964)

It is difficult to describe the history of Japanese Canadians without seeing everything in scare quotes, including the term 'Japanese Canadian'. For example, the term can be applied to a body marked by the actual experience or psychic duress of the internment camps and signified by a discourse that translated 'citizen' into 'enemy alien'. 'Evacuation' was a euphemism used by the government to describe the uprooting and internment of Japanese Canadians, who eventually employed the word in their own narrative descriptions. It is a term that makes a socially engineered crime a natural disaster, and renders 'internment' a protective safety precaution and the 'camp' a mountain getaway.

Thus the "camp" experience of interned Japanese Canadians leads to a "camp" sensibility that is "alive to a double sense in which some things can be taken," not as a "split-level construction" of literal and symbolic meaning, but "the difference [...] between a thing meaning something, anything, and the thing as pure artifice" (Sontag 1964). The internment camp and its inhabitants stage an artificial identity, and its unstable terms simultaneously negotiate, like any translation, "the problematic of the crossing" (Harvey 2003: 4). Under such circumstances, "the body is not a 'being,' but a variable boundary" (Butler 1990: 139). The 'evacuation' confounds the boundary in Canadian history between inclusive and exclusive citizenship, in which the 'inner' (Japanese) Canadian citizen is expelled and becomes an outer 'enemy alien'.

The particular contours of the event of 'evacuation' are marked by the physical ex-pulsion and re-pulsion that "founds and consolidates culturally hegemonic identities along sex/race/sexuality axes of differentiation" (Butler 1990: 133). The 'excretory function' becomes "the model by which other forms of identity-differentiation are accomplished. In effect, this is the mode by which Others become shit" (*ibid.*: 136). (It is also how being Muslim becomes synonymous with being a terrorist). The term 'evacuation' then is not just a euphemism, but, more seriously, a fabrication that is then translated into the actual fabric of individual lives. Since this fabricated identity is an effect of governmental and media discourse, then the task of the camp translator is to subvert and displace the distinctions between a discourse of authentic and dubious linguistic and cultural origins. Instead of employing the collective language of Redress to be recognized as a loyal "Canadian" instead of a suspect "Japanese," Miss Saito performs the role of a camp translator "in a state of continual incandescence – a person being one, very intense thing" (Sontag 1964), reduced and excessive. She embodies and enacts an arrested pulsion, an aching desire to be translated beyond the rejection or embrace of citizenship.


**2.2 "Outing" An Identity**
The first use of Japanese by Miss Saito, the fictional translator and narrator of the novel, is *nihonjin*: "we nihonjin, we Japanese" (1), an inclusive reference to Japanese born in Canada and unable to speak Japanese. The novel continues to investigate the permutations of that identity in terms of community, language, race, gender, and stereotype. The fragmentary and even faulty use of Japanese in this novel is a strategy for "outing" a Japanese identity strategically downplayed by Japanese Canadians under pressure to assimilate, as well as by the Redress Movement itself in order to effectively make its case against the Canadian government as wronged citizens.[5] At the same time, this outing of a Japanese identity is "thoroughly consonant with putting on an act" (Apter 1999: 136) because most of the linguistic and cultural connections have already been lost. It is a performance Sakamoto intends primarily, if not exclusively, for the Japanese-Canadian community

of *nisei* and *sansei*, whose "significant, distinctive condition" (Interview) finds them removed from their Japanese heritage through the passing of the generations and an assimilation forcefully accelerated by internment: not fluent in Japanese but racially marked.

Meanwhile, in "apparently homogenous Japan," Sakamoto observes, "where a thriving population has little knowledge or interest in foreign-born *nikkei* [6] and their experiences elsewhere, it is another case of mistaken identity: racially inconspicuous, but culturally different" (Interview). In Canada they are Japanese; in Japan, foreign; theirs is a contingency-based identity that never seems to fit. Particularly among the *nisei* population, a lack of language, humble rural roots, and limited educational opportunities have all fostered a sense of inferiority as both Japanese and Canadians. Miss Saito's performance of translation with limited linguistic means is very close to what Walter Benjamin describes as the task of the translator; it is "a gesture towards a restoration of what seems to have come before and, precisely within that move towards reestablishment, the incompletability of that gesture" (Jacobs 1999: 9). Although Miss Saito translates under linguistic constraint, she has her cake by savouring the crumbs.

Sakamoto's novel consolidates a distinct Japanese-Canadian literature through deliberate intertextual reference to Joy Kogawa's *Obasan*, but it just as surely is looking for ways to open up the parameters of that literature. As Sakamoto explains, *Obasan* is "the seminal book on internment -- it documents that history while poetically inscribing the personal, political, and spiritual -- and in so doing, has cleared a path for other writers to tell stories related, but not confined to, that story" (Interview). As another middle-aged unmarried woman, Miss Saito, the fictional translator in *The Electrical Field* evokes the figures of Naomi Nakane and Aunt Emily in *Obasan* and replicates the stereotype of the lonely spinster schoolmarm. In fact, she theatricalizes more than replicates the stereotype, in her insistence on "Miss" status and frequent reference to her own sensitivity, describing herself as "a finely tuned receptacle for others' impulses and confidences" (4). In personal terms, we can call the highly strung Miss Saito a camp construction, while in historical terms, we see her identity is, like that of other *nisei* caught up in internment, deconstructed by the camps. Her theatricalization is an extravagant gesture in circumstances of constraint.

Burdened by the daily care of her bedridden senile father and cowed by the past, Miss Saito has felt the impediment of a missing tongue and a sense of disfigurement like missing teeth. Although neither bilingual nor in control of either English or Japanese, she has endured the humiliation of being forced to assume the role of the family's inadequate linguistic mediator, especially when the family had to relocate as the internment camps closed down.

> On-ta-ri-o, Papa kept saying with his pitiful accent. He'd wanted to come east but all he could do was huddle behind me [...]. I was the first-born, born here; they pushed me out

> to the big city to the world, thrusting my homely face to it when they were afraid. Now that it wasn't just *nihonjin* in the shack next door or down the road of the camp. Ask this, say that, while they hung back. I didn't know the right words to say, in English or in Japanese. I cringed at how I stumbled along, each sentence gaping like a mouth with missing teeth. (51-2)

Miss Saito's personal humiliation is part of a communal humiliation, specifically the internment and forced relocation of the Japanese Canadians that Kogawa evokes so powerfully in *Obasan*. The mouth with missing teeth that characterizes Miss Saito's early performances as a translator is thus aligned with the image of the shacks in the internment camp with their "crooked doors like rotting teeth and their peeling burnt tar paper skin" (296). Missing teeth and rotten teeth, of course, are not synonymous, but they both distort attempts to take a sure and incisive critical bite. The architecture of internment reveals the rot in the construction of an unblemished Canadian history, while the fictional translator in Sakamoto's text works the gap where words are missing from the narrative to dislocate the conversation with both *Obasan* and the historical moment of internment in order to resume it as a psychic legacy rendered in the spatial terms of an electrical field. The novel revolves around an inter-racial murder (a Japanese neighbour and her white lover) motivated by marital infidelity, but the psychic constellation implicates the national crime of internment in the commission of the personal one.

In a more theoretical iteration, these missing teeth can be likened to "non-sites within the texture of a territorialized universe" that "position an impasse and turmoil within representation [...] which nonetheless takes on the properties of an agency of translation" (Cohen 2003: 111). The 'afflicted' translator comes into view and her performance with missing teeth makes history visible. "In the space between the teeth, in the "fault," what is expressed is not only a grimace of loss, for those gaps deface the complacent grin of the "natural(ized), unifying discourse of 'nation', 'peoples', or authentic 'folk tradition', those embedded myths of a culture's particularity" (Bhabha 1994: 172). Sakamoto's fictional translator operates in the rictus in a parodic performance of both "transparent" reality and the articulate author as "an enunciative space" (*ibid.*: 180). Missing teeth or a stutter may mar a linguistic performance and thus be subject to derision, but they do not fail to indicate a 'faultline' in representation. Miss Saito, as a "character," resents her neighbour Yano's attempts to have her seek redress as a member of a wronged community, but as a "translator" she still challenges a subjectivity that is based on a belief in "autonomous, self-determining" individuality by foregrounding subjectivity as "an effect of cultural production" (Sinfield 1992: 36). And when the cultural production is translation, subjectivity is discontinuous and disrupts what 'goes without saying': the local is 'foreignized' so that Japanese Canadians like Miss Saito can 'out' their ingrained sense of themselves as inferior translations even if they cannot restore their linguistic and cultural losses.

Further, in both the image of the translator and that of the makeshift camp, there is a parodic evocation of the "bilingual and multilingual writers, especially bricoleurs of European languages who have gone even beyond Joyce in playing games with language" (Chan 2002: 61). The translator shaped by contingency and operating under constraint dislodges the aesthetic of autonomy, the artist "all by himself but beholden to no one" (Jameson 1991: 307). These images also qualify the celebration of hybridity that Fredric Jameson describes as "playing with the boundary like a loose tooth" (1991: 363), finding carnivalesque humour in the "inside-out" spaces, and getting high on disorientation. If the value of "uncertainty, displacement, [and] the fragmented identity" has been theoretically recognized, there are nevertheless circumstances where the matter has not been one of "willful psychic positioning but of an upheaval in the deep material of the self" (de Courtivron 2003: 3). As I have said, the particular liminal condition of being a *nisei* links a sense of inferiority, as a Canadian and as a Japanese, with the issue of authenticity, "and suffering in either case. Not Canadian enough to stay out of the camps; not Japanese enough to go 'home' to Japan with ease; and not Japanese enough to be exotically compelling" (Interview). The writer wishes to articulate a hybrid identity forged out of cultural and linguistic detritus, but to do this necessarily involves imagination and exaggeration. Miss Saito sits at her window, looking out at a world that seems to have passed her by, leaving her with memories she would rather forget, a senile father to look after, and a lack of sexual experience. While Miss Saito is both repressed and oppressed, "her creative outlet, what saves her, or at least allows her to survive, is her voyeurism. She feeds vicariously off what she observes through her window, and importantly, she theatricalizes it" (Interview). In other words, the fictional translator in *The Electrical Field* is a deliberate representation of a drama queen.

**Conclusion**
The fictional translator in the texts by Michael Ondaatje and Kerri Sakamoto disrupts the habit of translation that prioritizes the comfort of the monolingual English reader, while puncturing the "chaste compactness" (Benjamin 1968: 91) and authority of the writer whose own and sole tongue is hegemonic. It is my contention that when writers such as Ondaatje and Sakamoto situate a translator as a character or presence within his or her fiction they raise the visibility of that figure. This, I believe, counters the paradigm of the "embedded" wartime journalist as a concentrated and exclusive source of information through resistance to a singular source in a monolingual tongue; and questions the simplification of complexity for the purposes of a pithy sound bite or easy understanding.

In newspaper reports concerning the war in Iraq, the translator may or not be acknowledged until he or she is kidnapped or a casualty. Even then, reports may identify the foreign journalist but not the local translator whose family probably reported them missing. However, not all translators in Iraq are local. Kim Sun II, who was found beheaded in Iraq in June 2004, is described in one report as a "South Korean who worked for a company that supplies the US military" (*Yomiuri* 2004: "US journalist, translator disappear"). In another report (*Yomiuri* 2004: "S Korea hostage") he is more specifically identified as a translator, "an Arabic speaker and evangelical Christian." The translator's body was found clad in an orange jumpsuit similar to those worn by prisoners in US detention camps like Guantanamo Bay. In war zones everywhere, it seems the loyalty of translators remains a fundamental issue.

---

1 *The Daily Yomiuri*, 7 August, 2004: 3.
2 Page numbers appearing without the author's name refer to the novel, *The English Patient* and then *The Electrical Field* respectively, under discussion.
3 The Japanese Canadian Redress movement sought compensation from the federal government for the internment of citizens of Japanese descent following the bombing of Pearl Harbor. The Redress Movement came to a successful conclusion in 1988.
4 Sakamoto says, in a January 2000 interview, "My first audience was the Japanese Canadian community [although] it was not a point to be exclusive." Throughout this paper, references to "Interview" are to this personal interview.
5 As Theodore Goosen explains, "not a single act of sabotage or treason had been committed in Canada by a Japanese Canadian; the expropriation of property and the dispersal of the community to internment camps had been both unjust and strategically unnecessary. But at the time of the Redress Movement, maintaining this position (reflected in the title of Ken Adachi's history of the Japanese Canadians, *The Enemy That Never Was* [1976]), required that experiences and individuals who might compromise the "official narrative" had to be excluded" (63).
6 A Japanese word meaning "of Japanese descent" applied to those living outside Japan.

## References

Abel, Marco. 2004. 'Don DeLillo's 'In the Ruins of the Future': Literature, Images, and the Rhetoric of Seeing 9/11' in *PMLA* 118(5): 1236-1250.
Alcoff, Linda Martín. 2006. 'The Unassimilated Theorist' in *PMLA* 121 (1): 255-259.
Anzaldúa, Gloria. 1987. *Borderlands/LaFrontera: The New Mestiza.* San Francisco: Aunt Lute.
Apter, Emily. 1999. *Continental Drift: From National Characters to Virtual Subjects.* Chicago and London: University of Chicago Press.
Benjamin, Walter. 1968. 'The Storyteller' (tr. Harry Zohn) in *Illuminations* (ed. Hannah Arendt). New York: Harcourt, Brace & World. 83-109.
Bhabha, Homi. 1994. *The Location of Culture*. London and New York: Routledge.
Brisset, Annie. 2003. 'Alterity in Translation: An Overview of Theories and Practices' (tr. Donna Williams and Michele Healy) in Petrilli, Susan (ed.) *Translation, Translation*. Amsterdam, New York: Rodopi. 101-127.

Butler, Judith. 1990. *Gender Trouble: Feminism and the Subversion of Identity*. London: Routledge.
Cahan, Richard. 2004. 'Digital technology permits more photos, wider impact' in the Chicago Tribune supplement in *The Daily Yomiuri* (29 May 2004: 15-16).
Castillo, Debra A. 2006. 'Anzaldúa and Transnational American Studies' in *PMLA* 121 (1): 160-265.
Chan, Leo Tak-Hung. 2002. 'Translating Bilinguality: Theorizing Translation in the Post-Babelian Era' in *The Translator 8* (1): 49-72.
Cohen, Tom. 2003. 'Trackings' in Jacobs, Carol and Henry Sussman (eds) *Acts of Narrative*. Stanford: Stanford University Press. 110-129.
Cronin, Michael. 2003. *Translation and Globalization*. London and New York: Routledge.
*Daily Yomiuri, The*. 2004. 'US probes Guantanamo for leaks' (August, page unavailable), 'US Journalist, Translator disappear in south Iraq: South Korean reporter detained' (Date and page unavailable),
——'S Korea hostage beheaded' 24 June: front page.
de Courtivron, Isabelle. 2003. 'Introduction' in de Courtivron, Isabelle (ed.) *Lives in Translation: Bilingual Writers on Identity and Creativity*. New York: Palgrave Macmillan. 1-9.
Farrell, Stephen. 2004. 'Survival guide to working in a war zone' in *The Times supplement, The Daily Yomiuri* (12 September 2004: 14).
Feal, Rosemary G. 2004. 'Mapping Languages in the United States' *MLA Newsletter* (Fall): 4-5.
Gentzler, Edwin. 2002. 'What's Different about Translation in the Americas?' *CTIS Occasional Papers* (2): 7-17.
Gettleman, Jeffrey. 2004. 'Dispatches from a Disaster' *GQ*, 4 December: 284-298.
Harvey, Keith. 2000. 'Translating Camp Talk: Gay Identities and Cultural Transfer' in Venuti, Lawrence (ed.) *The Translation Studies Reader* .New York and London: Routledge. 446-467.
——2003. *Intercultural Movements: American Gay in French Translation*. Manchester: St Jerome Publishing.
Hoffman, Eva. 2003. 'P.S.' in de Courtivron (2003): 49-54.
Ignatius, David. 2006. 'Journalists in Baghdad's Red Zone risk lives to tell the truth' in *The Daily Yomiuri* (2 April 2006).
Jacobs, Carol. 1999. *In the Language of Walter Benjamin*. Baltimore and London: The John Hopkins University Press.
Jakobson, Roman. 2000. 'On Linguistic Aspects of Translation' [1959] in Venuti (2000): 113-118.
Jameson, Fredric. 1991. *Postmodernism: Or, the Cultural Logic of Late Capitalism*. Durham: Duke University Press.
Kogawa, Joy. 1994. *Obasan* [1981]. New York: Doubleday.
Longacre, Robert E. 1983. *The Grammar of Discourse*. New York: Plenum.
Miki, Roy. 1998. 'Unclassified Subject: Question Marking 'Japanese Canadian' Identity' in *Broken Entries: Race Subjectivity Writing*. Toronto: The Mercury Press. 181-204.
——2005. *Redress: Inside the Japanese Canadian Call for Justice*. Vancouver: Raincoast Books.
Ondaatje, Michael. 1993. *The English Patient* [1992]. Toronto: Vintage Books.
Robyns, Clem. 'Translation and Discursive Identity' in *Poetics Today* 15(3): 405-528.
Sakamoto, Kerri.1998. *The Electrical Field*. Toronto: Vintage Canada.
Simon, Sherry. 1996. *Gender in Translation: Cultural Identity and the Politics of Transmission*. London and New York: Routledge.
Sinfield, Alan. 1992. *Faultlines: Cultural Materialism and the Politics of Dissident Reading*. Oxford: Clarendon Press.
Sontag, Susan. 1964. "Notes on Camp." On line at: http://www.bradleypaul.com/sontag.html (consulted July 2006).

Spivak, Gayatri Chakravorty. 2000. 'The Politics of Translation' [1992] in Venuti, Lawrence (2000): 397-416.
Tymoczko, Maria. 2003. 'Ideology and the Position of the Translator: In What Sense is a Translator 'In Between'?' in Calzada Pérez, Maria (ed.) *Apropos of Ideology: Translation Studies on Ideology – Ideology in Translation Studies*. Manchester: St Jerome Publishing. 181-201.
Vieira, Else Pires. 1998. 'New Registers for Translation in Latin America' in Bush, Peter and Kirsten Malmkjaer (eds) *Rimbaud's Rainbow: Literary Translation in Higher Education*. Amsterdam, Philadelphia: John Benjamins Publishing Company. 171-195.
Venuti, Lawrence (ed.). 2000. *The Translation Studies Reader*. London and New York: Routledge.

# Part VII

# The Translator's Visibility

# The Translator's Visibility: the Rights and Responsibilities Thereof

*Carol Maier*

The last decade has brought increased visibility for translators. Though the number of books published in English translation is no greater and reviews of translation still seldom give full attention to the translator, with the growth of information technology and of translation studies as a discipline, academic translators have gained in "usefulness." Also, recent world events have prompted a heightened awareness of the need for qualified translators and interpreters. But are translators fully aware of, or prepared for, the responsibility and the multiple possibilities for conflict that such visibility entails? I think that they are not, or at least some are not, to judge from the defensive nature of their response to reviews of their work, or from comments about the appropriateness of translators engaging in political activities that might seem to contradict the conventional metaphor of translation as a bridge. Translators seem disinclined to discuss this lack of preparedness, focusing their efforts, albeit to some degree understandably, more on their rights than their responsibilities. So this is a discussion of the ways in which translators are currently being called to account for their work, ways in which they are being drawn into unanticipated conflicts. I will refer to several incidents from my own experience as a translator. I will also discuss the case of several fictional translators, for example, Dr. Pereira, the protagonist of Antonio Tabucchi's *Pereira Declares*. An invisible Portuguese translator, Pereira suddenly finds himself conscious in a new way of the events occurring in the world around him. Consciousness here is inseparable from conscience, as both Pereira and the reader are led to realize; and Tabucchi's novel can serve as an excellent point of departure for a discussion of the responsibilities and accountability that translators today must assume.

Key words: accountability, conflict, responsibility, translator fiction, visibility.

> "For a fleeting instant her mind was vast enough,
> strong enough, to inhabit both afternoons at once. . .
> hovering between one consciousness and another."
> (Mary Yukari Waters, *The Laws of Evening*)

Just a scant two decades ago, Lawrence Venuti (1986) could publish what proved to be a groundbreaking essay about the translator's invisibility, and Naomi Lindstrom (1989) could note that not only would academic translators like to see their work more recognized, they "would like to identify with. . . certain faculty members who perform useful services". The last two decades, however, have brought significant changes for translators, who now find themselves in more visible situations, doing work undoubtedly considered "useful". The number of books published in English translation has not increased significantly and reviews of translation seldom give full attention to the translation, much less the translator, but the growth of information technology and of translation studies as a discipline has meant increased status for academic translators. Recent world events have also prompted global awareness of the need for qualified translators and interpreters.

The translator's visibility has increased in a very real professional sense then, and translators welcome that visibility, as well they should. However, I find myself wondering if translators are aware that for translation to become fully visible as both a profession and a practice it will be necessary for them to address the multiple possibilities for conflict that visibility can involve? My hunch is that they are not ready for that challenge, or at least translators in the United States are not, to judge from the defensive nature of their letters in response to reviews of their work. The same conclusion can be reached by talking to translators about the appropriateness of translators engaging, as translators as opposed to individuals, in political activities that might seem either to reinforce the frequent association of translators with traitors or to run counter to the opposing but equally frequent definition of translators as cultural ambassadors who make communication possible in spite of difference. In fact, to judge from most discussions among translators of which I'm aware, their efforts to increase visibility have focused on increasing the rights and their skills rather than explaining their profession. Given the low esteem in which translators have long been held, this focus is understandable. At the same time, however, if translation is to be well understood, whether by readers, publishers, or translators, it is essential that the complex, even conflictive nature of translation be thoroughly explored.

Consequently, my comments here will address some of the ways in which translators are currently being called to account for their work, ways in which they are being drawn into conflicts both internal and external that they had not anticipated and for which they may not be prepared. In order to do that, I will discuss briefly the cases–the stories--of a several fictional translators. I will also discuss a few incidents of conflict from my own experience–my own story--as a translator. Although to use such stories is to risk falling into anecdote, I share Douglas Robinson's belief (1999) that, when woven into theoretical exploration, anecdotal material can prompt abstract consideration that abstraction by itself often renders difficult, if not impossible. In addition, as an instructor of translation who is continually in the position of disabusing students of the notion that meaning can be neatly conveyed between speakers or languages, and as a practising translator, I am increasingly convinced that it is incumbent on translators and translation scholars to develop ways of representing translation that make visible the destabilizing, even shattering effect that translation can have on a translator.

(1) "What she couldn't explain amounts to a theory
of sorts. . . . ." (Martha Ronk, "Vertigo")

Although I don't know if what I cannot explain about the effect of translation on a translator amounts to a theory, or even a sort of theory, I do know that when I came to that line in Martha Ronk's poem (2004:13), I felt certain that Ronk was probing a destabilization akin to the one that I have been thinking and writing about for some time. Ronk's long poem is structured around fragments from G. W. Sebold's novel *Vertigo*, and the line quoted above occurs in a section that follows "So they say this world is what happens; but they do not say what the person is like to whom it happens." How true that is of discussions about translation, I found myself thinking as I recalled recent debunking of the "between" as a metaphor for translation. Maria Tymoczko's insistence (2003)–in my opinion, fully justified–that translators, even when they engage in acts of resistance, are firmly rooted in one culture, one position, rather than somewhere in the middle of two came to mind immediately. I thought also of Zrinka Stahuljak's meticulous explanation of how both the metaphor of conveyance and the metaphorization of "translation" itself not only obscure the inevitable multiplicity of polysemy of a text (Stahuljak 2004: 41) but also work toward what she describes as a "hegemonic, undemocratic global discourse" (Stahuljak 2004:33).

Yes, I thought, but what about the translator as an individual? If "between" is not an acceptable metaphor, how might an individual translator conceptualize and discuss the vexed interactions that can be obliterated in conventional descriptions of translation? Here, two responses occurred to me. The first was to suggest that translators devise an alternate metaphor or metaphors, such as that of the translator as intersection, which Sue-Ann Harding has explored in her essay about resistance (2004). Drawing on Tymoczko's work and, in particular on a comment by Anthony Pym in *Methods of Translation History*, Harding has used the metaphor of the intersection to represent the translator's role graphically and to show how the network that translators make collectively "could be extended to include people other than translators" (2004: 12).[1] Her graphical representation is compelling to me because it allows one to think of translators as beings that are embedded in a context and as such are points of contact and connection, although they can also, paradoxically, be points of resistance and conflict.

Curiously, the second response that occurred to my question about "bringing together" returned me to the notion of the between, even as it provided an alternative to it. I say this because, if translators are in fact intersections or points of contact, they are also intermediaries, and in order to make visible the possible conflicts that their mediating activity involves, it might be useful to probe that conflict more deeply than translators are wont to do. To do this, I would argue, it is not necessary to focus on either the impossibility of articulating and conveying meaning or on the polarities between which translators are commonly thought to convey meaning. On the contrary, one can focus on the translator as he or she finds that to become a point of contact can involve becoming a point of conflict. One can examine the experience of a translator at moments when the practice of translation jolts a translator into a new awareness of the situation in which he or she is embedded–an awareness that, albeit in an unstructured way, suggests a principle, a "theory of sorts" about the practice of translation and the translator's experience of being –in the sense of both existence and location– in the middle.

(2) "Mais traduire n'est pas qu'une belle prouesse technique, c'est une façon d'être.
(Dominique Grandmont, *Le Voyage de Traduire*)

Thanks to Rosmary Waldrop's *Lavish Absence* (2002), in which she writes in depth and detail about her translations of the work of Edmund Jabès, I was led to Grandmont's *Le Voyage de Traduire* (1997). To engage in translation, Grandmont explains–and it is important to note that she uses *traduire*, the verb, and not *traduction*, the noun–"is a strange voyage from which one may not return" (1997: 9).[2] What strikes Waldrop is the strangeness of that voyage, the "travail" it involves, and the high "stakes" it implies. What struck *me*, however, when I located Grandmont's book and read her discussion, was the definition of translation as a way of being. The definition reminds me, of course, of Walter Benjamin's "form" or "mode" and of the questions that Benjamin's words always raise for me (1969: 70). At the same time, though, linked as it is with a possibly endless voyage, it also takes me in a different, more compelling direction, and I think of a passage in Rosa Chacel's *Ciencias naturales* in which the narrator, a translator, stands at night on the deck of a trans-Atlantic ship and reflects in the darkness about the leit motif of "sublime high tide" (*la excelsa pleamar*) and the human inability to tolerate boundlessness, not so much because of the events it might hold as because of the total uncertainty with which one finds oneself (Chacel 1988:7). If translating is a way of life, I think, it is not possible for a translator to predict where he or she might be headed, and it seems to me that a translator would do well to "go out [on the journey] prepared," as Waldrop suggests (2002: 44), although prepared not so much in Waldrop's context of sheer hard work as in Chacel's context of the unknown, and what I sense is Grandmont's context of attitude–the way of being–that guides the way that one lives one's life.

And how does one live one's life as a translator? In the area of professional ethics, with respect to one's clients and readers, the question is one that translators discuss increasingly in both practical and professional terms. And in this area, examples come to mind quite readily, in the form of numerous essays, conversations, and conference discussions. What occurs to me in a more powerful, more personal way, though, are the dilemmas of several fictional characters who are suddenly made aware of the uncertainty that translation can mean for them. No doubt because I was reading Anne Patchett's *Bel Canto* at the same time that I was reading Waldrop's book, I thought immediately of Gen, the Japanese interpreter who was "surprised to find his hands trembling" as he translated the demands of the hostage-takers who held him prisoner, along with a large group of others: "He could never remember an instance when what he was translating had actually affected him" (Patchett 2001: 61).

Suzy Park, the young Korean-American protagonist of Suki Kim's *The Interpreter* (2001), also came to mind. I remembered Park making up her own questions in the Bronx Criminal Court when the district attorney's uninformed, insensitive probing prompted her at first to rephrase his words and, ultimately, to replace them as her client's answers suggested to her that he possessed information that pertained to her family (93-99). And I remembered Dominique Green, the protagonist of *The Interpreter*, by Suzanne Glass (2001), as Green sat in an interpreting booth and purely by chance heard a conversation between two conference attendees, one of whom had forgotten to turn off his microphone. The information she hears those delegates exchange could possible save lives, one life in particular, but "A voice in my head," Dominique says, "was screaming at me.'Your vows of confidentiality are as solemn as the Hippocratic oath'" (8).

Each of those incidents in which an interpreter is forced to rethink the definition of responsibility affected me as much when I remembered them as they had when I first read the novels in which they appeared. The fictional character that entered my thoughts most forcefully, however, was Dr. Pereira, the protagonist of Antonio Tabucchi's *Pereira Declares* (1996). An ageing journalist, Pereira is employed by a second-rate Lisbon newspaper. The year is 1938, the Spanish Civil War is raging, Salazar's dictatorship prevails in Portugal, and the country is described by the narrator as "gagged" (1996: 5). Pereira's task at the newspaper is to compose the culture page, for which he writes essays and translates nineteenth-century stories from the French. When the novel opens, he is an unassuming individual who prefers not to sign his translations, defines his job as "culture" (*ibid.* : 61), has never taken an interest in politics, and spends a great deal of time thinking about death and wondering about the immortality of the soul. His life changes radically, however, when he comes in contact with a young Italian writer who is involved with assisting the Spanish Republic. Pereira cannot explain why, but the young man reminds him of the son he never had. He befriends him, and through their association becomes aware of both the situation in Spain and the extent of the censorship that exists in his own country.

Gradually Pereira becomes emboldened to resist that censorship, and this he does through translation, which, he learns, can lead one to explore conflict within oneself, to sign–declare–onself, and to take responsibility for one's actions. Pereira's trajectory is one of an intense inner conflict that begins with a desire to repent of his life as he's lived it so far. Initially he merely alludes to this desire in the culture page, through a translation of Balzac's "Honorine," a tale of remorse that he says he read as a tale that in some way was autobiographical for him. His translations grow increasingly politicized, however, when he publishes Alphonse Daudet's "The Last Class" and begins to work on Georges Bernanos's *Diary of a Country Priest*. Eventually his involvement with the young Italian writer leads Pereira to write a piece himself that will make it impossible for him to continue to working on the newspaper or to continue living in Portugal. Although Pereira writes this piece as a journalist, and it is not one of the pieces that he has translated that marks his emancipation, translation has played a key role in making that emancipation possible. Through his work as a translator he has ventured into the previously uncharted "sublime high tide" of his conscience and his times. It is a voyage that strengthens him as an individual even as it puts him in danger as a citizen. What the consequences of his actions will be, the reader is not told. Rather, the narration ends with Pereira's open act of rebellion, and both he and the reader are left at a crossroads, a point between.

(3) "Behind Me–dips Eternity/ Before Me–Immortality/ Myself–the Term between–"
    (Emily Dickinson, #721)

Those lines are from Emily Dickinson's poem number 725 (1960: 353). I find them pertinent to both the point at which Tabucchi leaves his protagonist and his reader and to the translator's experience. In particular, I am drawn by the word 'Term', in the opening lines of the poem, by 'Maelstrom', and 'Crescent', which appear in the final lines (1960: 354), and by the vague nature of the two polarities between which the speaker is located. Like the narrator in Chacel's *Ciencias naturales*, the speaker in Dickinson's poem is situated at a sort of four-way intersection formed by the co-incidence of four directional uncertainties. Before and behind looms the unknown; behind and below lies a suggestion of descent and depth; before and above are connotations of ascent; above and below there is water, since 'maelstrom', read literally, is a 'whirling stream'. Surrounded by boundlessness, the speaker is located not so much between polarities as among them. Sailing a tiny craft in total darkness under a stormy sky, the speaker seems to express a sensation that is less one of duality than of bewilderment.

Or, perhaps, it would be more accurate to say that in the final stanza of the poem Dickinson expands the 'Term between' of the first stanza by turning into a more complex "among." This change is important because it implies a dissolution of polarities that, paradoxically, creates a possibility for survival. In the absence of any light, the speaker apparently feels so lost that an object pronoun ('Myself') is used instead of the subject pronoun that one would expect, so that in the middle is 'me', not 'I'. At the same time, however, the speaker's craft is a crescent, a mere sliver, to be sure, but one that suggests waxing and a glimmer of light. Even if that light is not visible in such darkness, the crescent itself suggests change, fertility, and growth. It also suggests that the speaker's 'Term between' is a limited period of time that lasts only a few days of any given month. The crescent may convey bewilderment, then, but it also hints at a cyclical motion that subsumes polarities. As such, it assures the speaker of what, in her essay on bewilderment, poet and novelist Fanny Howe has described as "an actual approach . . . a way to settle into the unresolvable" (2003: 14). Howe is not writing about Dickinson, but her comments about bewilderment are helpful here, because she explains convincingly that, as "a complete collapse of reference and reconcilability," bewilderment "breaks open the lock of dualism . . . and peers out into space" (*ibid.*: 15).

With respect to Dickinson's poem, it is important to note also that the 'Term between' is not only a non-static point in space and time, it is also an element of language, a word. Although the speaker of that word does not possess the transcendent power enjoyed by the divine Word–the size of the speaker's craft implies a reference to the speaker's lack of accomplishment as well as to the smallness of the vessel–as a word, the speaker not only has but *is* a way out. Because the speaker can speak or write and, as both Tabucchi's Dr. Pereira and recent translation-related discussions of the between suggest, when the point between is explored fully, what appear to be absolute polarities can be experienced as multiplicities. Unfortunately, however, in the case of translation, polarities are all too frequently reinforced, albeit passively, from a lack of discussion, or because of a translator's inability or unwillingness to examine either the complex, possibly conflictive junctures at which translators often find themselves or the affects that translation can have on a translator.

> (4) "The pieces included here. . . were written in an English for which I take 'final' responsibility. . . . When and where I would choose to follow his [the poet's] urging that I 'trust the text enough to betray it' was my decision . . . when I found myself grazing what might be termed the 'last frontier' in a translator's practice, . . . I believe there were instances when I took issue with the text in ways that made full betrayal [in the poet's sense] impossible". (Carol Maier, "Translator to Reader", *Refractions* by Octavio Armand)

Those words were written by me some ten years ago when I prepared the translator's introduction to my translations of Octavio Armand's *Refractions* (1994: 6). At the time that I wrote that introduction I was struggling with my feelings about my work with Armand, a Cuban-born poet whose family left Cuba a couple of years after the Revolution. An admiration for his daring, creative use of language had led me to translate many of his poems and essays. Although he and I frequently held opposing opinions about political issues, I respected his views, which were always presented with a thoughtfulness and clarity that I often found lacking in the arguments of people who disagreed with him and considered him just one more *gusano* and excluded him from discussions of Latin American exile

By the time I wrote the introduction to *Refractions*, however, my feelings about translating Armand's texts had changed considerably. Ironically, attitudes toward Cuba on the part of the North American left had begun to soften, but I found myself increasingly impatient with some of the differences that existed between my own attitudes and Armand's, in particular attitudes about sexuality. I have written before about those differences and my response to the conflict that I've experienced with respect to Armand's work, and by returning to the conflict here my intent is not to repeat my previous discussion. My reason for returning is the following: When I wrote before about my differences with Armand and the conflicts that can arise between a translator and a text or its author, I argued for a more complex image of translation than that usually held by translators, one that would encompass diversity and conflict as well as communication–one not dissimilar to that described by Stahuljak in her essay (2004). My affirmation of that image has not weakened. However, my understanding of the difficulties in realizing that image have altered considerably, as has my thinking about what it means for a translator to take responsibility for her work and her understanding of translation. In this context, the passage from the introduction to *Refractions* that figures as the epigraph to this section, specifically the acceptance of final responsibility that I state there, troubles me persistently.

I say this because increasingly I see that, although I took responsibility for the words in the introduction to *Refractions*, I avoided the responsibility–in both that and in my previous essay–of articulating what it can mean emotionally for a translator to translate collaboratively and conflictingly at the same time. Of course, the introduction to *Refractions* may well not have been the appropriate place for such a discussion, but in my previous essay I could have probed my feelings more deeply and written about them more clearly. Moreover, I could have documented those feelings with passages from my journals, in which I find comments such as this one about "being pulled into a collaboration I both resist and respect. . . on the one hand I want to run from that collaboration, on the other hand it seems necessary because. . . of the typically 'Cuban voice' [that's neither] in [n]or out of Cuba. . . too open for one, to closed for the other." In my journal there are also comments about sexuality that demonstrate succinctly my ambivalence about empathizing with Armand as a marginalized, hence feminized, writer vis-à-vis forums about exile and Latin American literature. However, I find those comments in the same journal entry that I find an expression of intense anger concerning an essay titled "Ramming the Page," in which Armand mentions his sympathy for and identification with a woman being violated, in this instance by a physician who inserted his instruments into her vagina and "read her like a page", as if Armand did not realize that at the same time he was sympathizing with the rammed woman but also writing about the page as the one who rammed. Even so, another, nearby, entry contains my observation that "translation as abrasion can be extraordinarily enlightening". In short, then, I realize now that when I wrote previously about translating Armand's work I evaded writing a truly candid examination of my feelings– whether for myself or for a reader. I also realize that not doing so became increasingly troubling to me and that it had implications for my work as a translator and for my thinking about translation theory, practice and pedagogy.

I have not returned here to my work with Armand, however to push further on my feelings about the work that he and I did together and write out an examination of one translator's conscience, but to be able to focus more sharply on a 'between' defined less by polarities than on the potential conflict within individual translators and among translators as a group. To do that, I'm going to jump ahead a few years in time from my introduction to *Refractions* to the morning in June of 2002 when I turned on my computer and read a message from Mona Baker about her decision to remove two members from the board of *The Translator* because of their affiliation with Israel universities. At the time I read Baker's message, I was acquainted with her position about the Palestinian-Israeli conflict and I was following the press coverage of the boycott of Israeli institutions. Nevertheless, I was taken aback by Baker's decision. Over the course of the next days, as I read the outpouring of responses to which Baker's decision had given rise and thought through my own response, I felt troubled by several issues. At the time, the most pressing of those issues concerned whether an action such as the one Baker had taken was appropriate and effective–in a political way - and whether, if thoroughly understood, the decision could be considered anti-Semitic. It was on the basis of my thinking about those two issues, I decided to remain on the board of *The Translator*; and the abundant correspondence and large number of clippings in my file indicate that most of the many people who expressed an opinion about Baker's decision formed their opinions on the same basis.

There was a third issue, however, that troubled me, and that was its appropriateness and, ultimately, its effectiveness, in a sense related to translation. What, I wondered, is a translator to do when she finds that, apparently, she is fostering not communication and collaboration but its opposite? Coincidentally, while I was wrestling with this question, I was reading a piece by poet Anna Carson called "The Light of Towns". "Towns", that piece begins, "are the illusions that things hang together somehow," and to illustrate her statement Carson has written a series of poems about such towns as "Town of the Wrong Question", or "Wolf Town", or "Town of the Sound of Twig Breaking", or "Town I Have Heard of". "The position you take in this may separate you from me", Carson wrote. "Hence, towns. And then scholars" (1995: 94). And in my journal I noted that "a translator is always positioned, always sees from, sees as; sees both alone and accompanied. . . . so that, yes, Carson is right, a scholar takes a position. But what about a translator, since a translator's position is not only one that at least to some extent includes more than one town but is also one that shifts continually? How can a translator be the mediator she has considered herself to be and declare herself a truly loyal citizen of one town or another? How does a deliberate effort to inhabit multiple and perhaps conflicting towns affect a person who tries to do that?"

Those are not rhetorical questions but questions that, to work responsibly, translators need to address far more fully than they have in the past, especially when translators and interpreters are increasingly being placed at intersections far more troubling than the ones I've mentioned so far.

(5) "[I]n one of the great ironies of the era . . . . A distinguished translator . . . happened to be Jewish".(Lila Azam Zanganeh, "*Mein Kampf*: The Italian Edition")

The "great irony" referred to in those sentences is the hiring of a Jewish translator for the Italian translation of *Mein Kampf,* although the contract between the Germans and the Italian Office of Foreign Affairs stipulated "that the Italian translator not be a Jew" (Zanganeh 2004: 35). To my way of thinking, another great irony here is that although Lila Azam Zanganeh, the author of the piece, mentioned the fact of Treves' Jewishness, she did not include even a comment about how Treves must have felt as he worked on this project or about how translating *Mein Kampf* might have affected him not only as a translator but also as a human being.

If it were uncommon to find that discussions of what could only be uncomfortable translation experiences lack comments about the translator's discomfort, Zanganeh's essay would not be noteworthy in this context. Unfortunately, however, this type of omission is more the norm than the exception in such discussions. Consider, for instance, two articles in a recent issue of the American Translators Association (ATA) *Chronicle*. In the first, Nancy Schweda Nicholson (2004) reviews Suzanne Glass' *The Interpreter*. Although the principal intrigue of the novel concerns the ethical decision that agonizes the protagonist, Nicholson mentions that dilemma only in passing and focuses her comments instead on the ways in which the Glass has and has not offered a realistic portrayal of an interpreter's practice, working conditions, and status. Similarly, and I believe, more telling, is the second *Chronicle* piece, in which Tanya Gesse (2004) interviews Peter Less, who worked in 1946 as an interpreter at the Nuremberg trials of Nazi war criminals, despite the fact that his parents and other family members had died at the hands of the Nazis. When asked how he maintained the necessary neutrality, Less stated only that "It wasn't easy . . . you could not let your feelings interfere with your job. You were to interpret as faithfully as possible. . . . So we did" (47). Interviewer Gesse asked Less one further question about his possible dis-ease: "At the recent International War Crimes Tribunal of Slobodan Milosevic," she said, "interpreters received psychological aid to deal with the descriptions of atrocity they had to interpret. Did you receive any psychological aid?" Less replied that he had not, that there was no such aid available at the time. "[B]ut," he said, "we were young, and we could dissociate ourselves from our job" (2004: 47).

It is possible, of course, that Less responded as he did not because he had truly been able to distance himself from a painful situation as because he felt reluctant or unwilling to discuss his experiences. However, neither of his responses indicates either reluctance or refusal. Moreover, his comments parallel those of many other interpreters who have spoken publicly about their feelings in situations of conflict. I am thinking in particular of the North American interpreters and translators who have worked in Iraq during the current conflict and whose work has received unprecedented attention because of both the lack of qualified linguists and the abuses that have been documented in Abu Ghraib and other prisons. Despite that increased attention, however, even when afforded an opportunity to examine the need to treat another human being in a way that compromised–or at least challenged–their definition of "human" translators and interpreters have not spoken out in detail about the conflict they might have experienced. Perhaps, as Chris Mackey (2004) explains in *The Interrogators*--an account of his experiences as an interrogator in Kahandar shortly after the attacks in September, 2001–, "Most of the interrogators truly detested the prisoners they faced . . . and saw them as complicit in the attacks" (175). Even so, however, and despite his observation that interrogators "get a much closer look at the enemy" (175), and may hate the enemy even more than combat soldiers, on several occasions Mackey acknowledges that the prisoners are "humans. And their sins don't always make it easy to be dishonest yourself, even if it's for the greater good" (175-76). To "engage in cynicism, dishonesty, and deception," he says, "in quantities that would be considered pathological in the real world, day after day 'takes its toll'" (231). That's as far as Mackey goes, however.

Not to press further is Mackey's prerogative, but I don't believe that it is the prerogative of translators and translation scholars if they want both to understand the translator's experience fully and to make that experience visible. Even though comments such as Less' or Mackey's provide little insight into the affects of mediation, there are indications that translators and interpreters who work in conflictive situations suffer great turmoil. Reportage on this turmoil is scant, but several instances come to mind. Courtney Angela Brkic (2003), for instance, in the introduction to her short story collection *Stillness*, writes of her work as a translator with a forensic team in Bosnia in

1996, where "in the mosque and on-site... the faded words were written in a language that I could understand, and I carried them in my head long after providing translations" (2003: xiii).

Iraqi translators employed by the US military, in the few opportunities North Americans have been able to hear from them directly, tell of feelings similar to and even more poignant that Brkic's, since they have to hide their employment in order to protect themselves when they're off the base, as well as mediate between Iraqis and North Americans. At least one such interpreter in Mosul has said that he refused to interpret "when $101^{st}$ soldiers beat Iraqis without justification" (in Tyson 2004: 10) and that he and other interpreters threatened to resign when the abuses at Abu Ghraib were shown on television. Few refusals such as this one have made their way into the North American media, but a similar situation was narrated by Hyder Akbar (2004), a young North-American translator raised in the US, who refused to translate in the interrogation from which he "came away... feeling something like despair" (37).[3]

Reading Akbar's comments and copying his words onto my draft reminds me of an article by Zrinka Stahuljak that concerns translators who worked in the 1991-92 war in Croatia (2000). Stahulajak's article is the only one that I've found that directly addresses the affect on translators working in what I would call limit situations, and I want to mention it here by way of a conclusion. A translator, Stahuljak writes, working in situations such as the one she studied must translate "an actual borderline conflict... that produces in the translator a violent internal conflict: she is torn between allegiance to her native country and professional neutrality" (2000: 43). This translator, Stahuljak argues has "been excluded from the theory of translation" (2000: 51), in which she must be reinscribed as a witness who has worked "between testimony and translation" (2000: 43); and without full knowledge of her and her circumstances, our understanding of translation is incomplete.

Most translators and interpreters are not serving–and will not serve–in situations as highly conflictive as the one described by Stahuljak. However, many translators and interpreters do or will work in situations in that establish the framework from which such situations may develop. Moreover, albeit in less extreme ways, all acts of translation hold the possibility for the translator to be affected in ways he or he did not anticipate. Consequently, situations like the one discussed by Stahuljak, must be factored into any explanation, any theory of translation and, in the context of my comments here, into any metaphor for translation. The spatial metaphor of the between–with its variants of the overlap and the intersection–has been proved inadequate for that task. This means that translators and translation scholars need to be searching for and experimenting actively with other ways of conceptualizing. If one focuses one's attention not on the borders but on the between itself, that between can expand both horizontally and vertically and become a sort of unbordered boundlessness that evokes more a journey than a place. After all, as Grandmont has suggested, translating is a voyage, and perhaps by stressing it as a verb, an action that occurs in a re-defined between, the complexity and potential conflict of translation can be made more visible. Given the increasing need for translators and interpreters world wide, and the challenges and dangers faced by many translators and interpreters, it is incumbent on translators and translation scholars not only to advocate for the rights of translators but to accept the responsibility of acknowledging and addressing the presence of conflict as an integral part of much translation practice.

---

1 My thanks to Sue-Ann Harding for permission to refer to and cite her paper.
2 Here I have used Waldrop's translation (p. 44).
3 Although the precarious position of Iraqi translators is still far from appreciated fully in the West, since this essay was written, Western journalists have begun to acknowledge their dependence on and at times close friendship with their translators and interpreters. See, for example, Michael Goldfarb's book about Ahmad Shawkat (2005) and the efforts of the *Christian Science Monitor* (2006) on behalf of Allan Enwiya (*Monitor* Staff Reports), the interpreter for Jill Carroll who was killed at the time of Carroll's abduction.

## References

Akbar, Hyder. as told to Susan Burton. 2004. 'Interrogation Unbound' in *The New York Times Magazine*. (11 July 2004: 17-18).
Armand, Octavio. 1994. *Refractions* (tr. Carol Maier). New York: Lumen Books.
Benjamin, Walter. 1969. 'The Task of the Translator" (trans. Harry Zohn) in Arendt, Hannah (ed.) *Illuminations*. New York: Schoken Books. 69-82.
Brkic, Courtney Angela. 2003. *'Stillness' and other Stories*. New York: Farrar, Straus & Giroux.
Carson, Anne. 1995. 'The Life of Towns' in *Plainwater: Essays and Poetry*. New York: Knopf. 91-111.
Chacel, Rosa. 1988. *Ciencias Naturales*. Barcelona: Seix Barral.
Dickinson, Emily. 1960. *The Complete Poems* (ed. Thomas H. Johnson). Boston: Little, Brown.
Gesse, Tanya. 2004. 'Interview with a Legend' (Interview with Peter Less) in the *The ATA Chronicle* September: 44-48.
Glass, Suzanne. 2001. *The Interpreter*. South Royalton, Vermont: Steerforth Press.
Goldfarb, Michael. 2005. *Ahmad's War, Ahmad's Peace: Surviving under Saddam, Dying in the New Iraq*. New York: Carroll & Graf.
Grandmont, Dominique. 1979. *Le Voyage de Traduire*. Creil: Dumerchez.
Harding, Sue-Ann. 2004. 'Sites of Resistance'. Unpublished Paper.
Howe, Fanny. 2003. 'Bewilderment'. *The Wedding Dress*. Berkeley: University of California Press, 2003. 5-23.
Kim, Suki. 2003. *The Interpreter*. NY: Farrar, Straus & Giroux.
Lindstrom, Naomi. 1989. 'Translation and Other Academic Endeavors' in *Hispania* 72.3: 587-588.
Mackey, Chris and Greg Miller. 2004. *The Interrogators*. New York: Little Brown.

*Monitor* Staff Reports. 2006. 'Helping Jill Interpret Iraq' in *The Christian Science Monitor* (31 March, 11).
Nicholson, Nancy Schweda. 2004. Review of *The Interpreter*, by Suzanne Glass in the *ATA Chronicle* September: 53-56.
Patchett, Anne. 2001. *Bel-Canto*. New York : HarperCollins.
Robinson, Douglas. 1999. 'Nine Theses about Anecdotalism in the Study of Translation' in *Meta* 44 (2): 402-408.
Ronk, Martha. 2004. '*From* Vertigo' in *American Poetry Review* November/December: 13-14.
Stahuljak, Zrinka. 2000. 'Violent Distortions: Bearing Witness to the Task of Wartime Translators" in *TTR: Traduction, Terminologie, Rédaction* 13 (1): 37-51.
——. 'An Epistemology of Tension'in *The Translator* 10 (1) (2004): 33-57.
Tabucchi, Antonio. 1996. *Pereira Declares* (tr. P. Creagh). New York: New Directions.
Tymoczko, Maria. 2003. 'Ideology and Position of the Translator: In What Sense is the Translator 'In-Between'?' in Calzada Pérez, María (ed.) *Apropos of Ideology: Translation Studies on Ideology - Ideology in Translation Studies*. Manchester: St. Jerome Publishing. 181-201.
Tyson, Ann Scott. 'Caught in Crossfire in Iraq' in *The Christian Science Monitor* (15 September, 10).
Venuti, Lawrence. 1986. 'The Translator's Invisibility' in *Criticism* 28 (Spring): 179-212.
Waldrop, Rosmary. 2002. *Lavish Absence: Recalling and Reading Edmond Jabès*. Middletown, CT: Weslyan University Press.
Waters, Mary Yukari. 2003. *The Laws of Evening: Stories*. New York: Scribner.
Zanganeh, Lila Azam. 2004. '*Mein Kampf*: The Italian Edition' in *The New York Times Book Review* (7 November 2004, 35).

# Notes on Contributors

**María Calzada Pérez** is a lecturer in translation and English at Jaume I University (Castellón, Spain). She has published widely, and is author of *La aventura de la traducción: Dos monólogos de Alan Bennett* (2001), a book on translating Alan Bennett's *Talking Heads*. Her articles include contributions to *Target*, *Meta*, *Text*, *Babel*, and *Perspectives: Studies in Translatology*. She is editor of *Apropos of Ideology: Translation Studies on Ideology – Ideologies in Translation Studies*. Her main research interests are in translation and ideology, corpus studies and European Parliamentary texts, advertising and pedagogy.

**Brian Chadwick** is a translator and artist who also researches in twentieth century Russian history. He is a former lecturer at the Chelsea School of Art, where he used language translation strategies to serve as a basis for event-based projects involving translations within and across linguistic, visual and accoustic media. His many translations range from Brecht and Eisenstein dialogues, Russian futurist poetry and poetics, soviet film theory, and French revolutionary archival material. He has published in both art and education journals, and in anthologies of modern poetry in translation. His recent work includes a project on web-based micronation, and the Nanostate. In 2005 he gave a symposium, entitled 'Writing Europe', in Kiev which was sponsored by the British Council.

**Red Chan** is a lecturer in Translation and Cultural Studies at the University of Warwick. Her research is in translation studies and interpreting with reference to contemporary Chinese literature and culture. She has given numerous talks and conference papers in the U.K. and abroad, and her publications include: 'Leaving the World to Enter the World: Han Shaogong and Chinese Root-seeking Literature*'* in *China Information: A Journal on Contemporary China Studies* (2006), '*Twentieth-Century Chinese Translation Theory: Modes, Issues and Debates*' in *The Translator* vol.11, no.2 (2005), "Translation, Nationhood and Cultural Manipulation: the Case of China' in *Europe and the Asia-Pacific* (2003), all translations in *Use Me, Shoot Me, Destroy Me: The Story of a Psycho Cowgirl*, and the translation of 6 chapters *in Chinese Women Organizing: Cadres, Feminists, Muslims, Queers* (2001).

Notes on Contributors

**Beverley Curran** is an associate professor teaching linguistic, cultural and media translation in the Department of Creativity and Culture at Aichi Shukutoku University in Nagoya, Japan. She is currently researching theatre translation in theory and performance in post-Meiji Japan. Articles on the fictional translator in Australian and Canadian writing, lesbian writing, and Canadian literature have appeared in collections and journals such as *Canadian Literature*, *Style*, and auto/biographical studies. Her collaborative translation of Nicole Brossard's *Journal intime* was published in 2000.

**Mila Dragovic-Drouet** is a translator and interpreter who works between French and Serbo-Croat. She has published translations in architecture, the history of art, psycho-analysis, French classical works, and on literary theory. A member of the Serbian Translators Association, in the 1990s she worked at the Embassy of the European Union at Belgrade, with teams of journalists, and with U.N. humanitarian missions. She has taught at the University of Rennes and in Paris at INALCO (Institut National des Langues et Cultures Orientales).

**Ian Foster** is a Lecturer in German at the University of Salford. He has published numerous articles on Austrian literature and culture from the 1870s to the present day, including contributions on Ferdinand von Saar, Peter Altenberg and Joseph Roth. In 2002 he edited a volume on Arthur Schnitzler: *Zeitgenossenschaften / Contemporaneities*. He has special interest in military themes and the *fin-de-siècle* - his most recent work includes articles on Christoph Ransmayr and on fiction on military themes in the context of Anglo-German relations before 1914.

**Piotr Kuhiwczak** is Associate Professor in Translation and Cultural Studies at the University of Warwick, and he has lectured and taught both in the U.K. and abroad. His research lies in translation studies and comparative literature. His current research projects are the study of the translation of the Holocaust memoirs and testimonies, and censorship on writing and translation in Central and Eastern Europe. He is co-editor of a volume of essays *A Guide to Translation Studies* (2007), and his other publications include: 'Outwitting the Politburo. Politics and Poetry Behind the Iron Curtain', in *Cold War Literature* (2006), 'Left Untranslated: On the function of the "untranslatable" in literary texts' in *Forum* (2005), 'The Troubled Identity of Literary Translation' in *Translation Today* (2003), 'Buried in Translation' in *The Cambridge Quarterly* (2002), and *Successful Polish-English Translation: Tricks of the Trade (1998)*.

**Carol Maier** is professor of Spanish at Kent State University, Ohio, where she is affiliated with the Institute for Applied Linguistics. Her research interests include translation theory, practice, and pedagogy, and she has published translations of work by Octavio Armand, Rosa Chacel, Severo Sarduy, and María Zambrano, amongst others. Her current translation projects include work with Nuria Amat and Nivaria Tejera, as well as further work with Armand, Chacel, and Sarduy. She is also editing a homage volume to the late Helen R. Lane and co-editing a collection of essays about teaching literature in translation.

**Paschalis Nikolaou** obtained his PhD in Literary Translation at the University of East Anglia. His research interests lie in translation as experiment and experience, and in the relationships between life-writing and literary translation. His reviews, articles and translations (including one on "Odysseus Elytis's 'An Oral Self-Portrait' have appeared in *Modern Poetry in Translation, The London Magazine* and *In Other Words*. His poems have appeared in poetry magazines in Greece and the UK. He is the author of an essay entitled 'Notes on Translating the Self' in *Translation and Creativity: Perspectives on Creative Writing and Translation Studies (2006)*. He is currently co-editing a 'Selected Poems' of Nasos Vayenas, and a volume of essays on literary translation.

**Jerry Palmer** was Professor of Communications at London Metropolitan University till 2005. He has authored seven books, including *Spinning Into Control. News Values and Source Strategies* (2000), and *Media at War: the Iraq Crisis (*2000). His other publications include: 'Le 'news management': gestion de la publicité ou gestion des actualités?' in *COMU 4*, 'News values' in *The Media: an Introduction* (1997/2001), 'Les négociations en amont: les associations caritatives anglaises et les médias' in *Télévision et Exclusion* (2002), 'The press reporting of European Economic and Monetary Union in four countries' in *Transnational Communication in Europe (* 2000), 'Formes d'engagement et stratégies communicationnelles', in *L'Engagement* (forthcoming 2006), 'Le Secret et les Stratégies Communicationnelles' in *Autour du Secret* (2005), 'Source Strategies and Media Audiences: Some Theoretical Implications' in *Journal of Political Marketing 3* (4) (2004), '"Our Eyes and Our Ears": Journalists and Fixers in Western media reporting of the Iraq Crisis' in *Journalism* (forthcoming), 'L'Islam, les Médias et la Guerre' in *Questions de communication* (2006).

**Sathya Rao** is assistant professor in French translation at the University of Alberta. He is the author of numerous articles and book chapters on translation theory, erotics of translation, postcolonial theory, Francophone literature and cinema including: "Comment la philosophie doit-elle penser l'Autre de couleur ?" in *Ethiopiques*, n°74, 1st semester (2005), "Towards a Non-Colonial Theory of Translation" in *Traces: a Multilingual Series of*

*Cultural theory* (2005); "Le point de vue de la théorie unifiée de l'Afrique et son envolée dans le champ de la traduction" in *De l'écrit africain à l'oral. Le phénomène graphique africain* (2006); and "Quelques considérations éthiques sur l'invisibilité du traducteur ou les vertus du silence en traduction" in *TTR*, XVII, n°2, (2006).

**Myriam Salama-Carr** is Professor of Translation Studies at the University of Salford. She is the author of *La Traduction à l'époque abbasside* (1990) on the development of medieval Arabic translation, and has published numerous articles on the history and didactics of translation, including contributions to *Translating Others* – both Volumes 1 and 2 - (2006), *Intercultural Communication Studies* (2006), *Social Semiotics (2007)), La théorie Interprétative de la traduction II* (2005), and *The Medieval Translator VIII* (2004). She was the organiser of the conferences on *Translation and Conflict* in 2005 and co-organiser of its sequel in 2006.

**Jun Tang** is Associate Professor of Translation Studies at the College of Foreign Languages, South China University of Technology. Her research interests lie in translation and comparative cultural studies. She has conducted two research projects in translation studies sponsored by the central government. Her monograph, *Bilingual/Bicultural Perspective of Translation* appeared in 2002. Since 1999 she has published about 30 articles and presented 4 conference papers in English or Chinese on the ethics of translation, globalization and translation, and theoretical translation studies.

**Roberto A. Valdeón** is Senior Lecturer in English Studies at the University of Oviedo. He is the author of *Las novelas de E. M. Forster: una revisión intertextual* and *Spanish Texts for Translation*, and over forty other articles on EFL and translation. These include: "The CNN en Español News" in *Perspectives: Studies in Translatology*, "The Translated Spanish Service of the BBC" in *Across Languages and Cultures*, and "Inserts in Screen Translation" (forthcoming). He is the coordinator of a European Grundtvig project (2006-08). His most recent interest lies in audiovisual and media texts and their translation into Spanish.

**John Williams** is Professor of Literary Studies at the University of Greenwich. His first book, *William Wordsworth: Romantic Poetry and Revolution Poetry*, was published in 1989 by Manchester University Press. Since then he has contributed volumes on Wordsworth to the Palgrave Macmillan *Literary Lives* series (1996), and to the *Critical Issues* series (2002). He also edited the 1993 Macmillan *New Casebook* on Wordsworth. His most recent publication is `Britain's Nelson and Wordsworth's `Happy Warrior`: a Case of Cautious Dissent`, published in *Romanticism* 11.2

(2005). He is currently researching the reception of Wordsworth's poetry in 19th century Germany for a book to be published shortly.

**Lawrence Wang-chi Wong** is Professor of Chinese and translation studies at the Nanyang Technical University, Singapore, where he is also the Dean of Humanities, Arts and Social Sciences, the Director of Humanities and Social Sciences. He is also Professor at the Department of Translation, The Chinese University of Hong Kong, as well as being the Director of Research in Translation. His main research interests are in translation studies and literary studies in modern China. He has published over ten books, two of which are on the translation history of modern China.

# INDEX OF NAMES

**A**
Abel, Marco  239, 248
Achilles  82, 88, 91-93
Adachi, Ken  248n
Adorno, W. Theodore  66, 72
Aggarwal, Kusum  231
Ai Han Zhe (see Gutzlaff)  46
Aitchison, Jim  150, 162
Akbar, Hyder  264-265
Al Sadr, Moqtada  22
Al Shehari, Khalid  151, 159, 162
Alcoff, Linda Martín  242, 248
Allan, Stuart  101, 117
Andric, Ivo  32, 40
Andromaque  88
Anzaldúa, Gloria  242, 248
Apter, Emily  163, 242, 244, 248
Armand, Octavio  259-261, 265
Arndt, Ernst M  186-187
Arrojo, Rosemary  100, 117
Auden, W. H.  205, 212
Aznar, José Maria  99

**B**
Bâ, Hampaté Amadou  5, 223-230, 231n.
Baker, Mona  8, 8n, 103, 105, 109-112, 117, 261
Bakhtin, Mikhail  208, 219
Balfour, Robert  210
Balzac, Honoré de  258
Bandia, Paul  231
Bao Peng  41, 49, 51-54
Barker, Sebastian  93n
Barnett, Robert  125, 128
Barnstone, Willis  93n, 94

Barthes, Roland  4, 8, 151, 159, 163
Bassat, Lluis  150, 163
Bassnett, Susan  1, 8, 135-136, 147, 150, 163
Bauman, Janina  63, 70, 72n, 72
Baumgartner, Andreas  195-196
Beasley, Ron  151, 163
Beaugrande, Robert de  102, 117
Beaumont, Francis  184
Beaumont, Peter  27
Beeching, Jack  45, 55
Beigberder, Frédéric  150, 154, 163
Bell, Allan  99, 101, 105-106, 108, 117
Benjamin, Walter  245, 247-248, 256, 265
Berger, John  154-155, 163
Berger, Warren  150, 156, 159, 163
Berman, Antoine  6, 8, 71, 73
Bernanos, Georges  258
Bernard, William Dallas  51, 55
Bespaloff, Rachel  82, 90, 94
Bhabha, Homi  223, 242, 246, 248
Biardzka, Elzbieta  31, 40
Bigelow, Bruce  16, 27
Bingham, John Elliot  52, 54, 55
Bismarck, Otto von  169
Blatchford, Robert  174, 182
Bleibtreu, Carl  177
Blomberg, Sven  154
Bloom, Harold  92-94
Boase-Baier, Jean  93n

## Name Index

Boldrick, John  16-17, 27
Bones, Jah  203
Borges, Jorge Luis  80, 94
Borkgren, Sherrlyn  16, 27
Botelho, William  43
Boulet, Jim  16, 27
Bourdieu, Pierre  7
Brisset, Annie  235, 248
Brithnoth, 179
Britton, Roswell  43, 55
Brkic, Courtney Angela  263-265
Brock, Peter  35
Broomhall, Marshall  55
Brossard, Nicole  234
Brown, Hilary  187, 197
Browning, Christopher  62, 72
Browning, E. B.  189
Brownlie, Siobhan  100, 117
Bueno, Antonio  150-151, 153, 163
Bugarski, Ranko  40
Burck, Charlotte  69, 73
Burgess, Heidi  152, 156-158, 163
Burns, Richard  93n
Burns, Robert  186, 195
Buscal, John  72n
Bush, George  120
Bush, W. G.  92, 120, 153
Butler, Judith  244, 248
Byron, George G.  184-189, 191, 195

### C

Cahan, Richard  238-239, 249
Caillé, Pierre-François  32, 40
Calzada, María Pérez  4
Campagna, Jod  16, 27
Campbell, Stuart  103, 117
Campbell, Thomas  186
Campbell-Bannerman, Henry  172-173
Campe, Joachim H.  186, 196
Campos, Haroldo de  150
Camus, Albert  38

Cao Feng  130n, 131
Carne-Ross, Donald  75, 81-82
Carr, Edward H.  210, 213, 216, 219
Carroll, Jill  265n
Carson, Anna  261-262, 265
Carter, Ronald  108, 117
Castillo, Debra A.  242, 249
Cecil, Robert  210
Chacel, Rosa  256, 265
Chadwick, Brian  5, 199, 206, 208, 219
Chan, Leo Tak-Hung  234, 247, 249
Chan, Red  4
Chandler, Daniel  163
Chang Hsinpao  44, 49, 55, 55n
Chapman, George  76-77
Chaucer, Geoffrey  184
Chekhov, Anton  200
Cheney, Dick  153
Chesney, George  169-171
Chesterman, Andrew  103, 116, 117
Chomsky, Noam  154-155, 162-163
Chuck, D  203
Churchill, Winston  158-159, 210
Clarke, Ignatius F.  170, 173, 182
Clémenceau, Georges  210
Clinton, Bill  120, 128-129
Clinton, Hillary  4, 119-120, 122-130, 146
Coates, Austin  47, 55
Cohen, Tom  246, 249
Coleman, Peter T.  152, 163
Coleridge, Samuel T.  186, 188-189
Collins, Randall  152, 163
Collon, Michel  31, 35, 39n, 40
Cook, Elizabeth  93-94, 94n
Cook, Guy  150-151, 163
Cornwall, Barry  188

Courtivron, Isabelle de  247, 249
Cowper, William  188
Creon  92
Cronin, Michael  13-14, 27, 33, 40, 153-154, 157-160, 162-163, 236-237, 240, 249
Curran, Beverley  5-6
Curzon, George  210

**D**

Dai, Sijie  121, 130
Danesi, Marcel  151, 163
Dante, Alighieri  184
Daudet, Alphonse  258
Davis, Aeron  15, 27
Davis, H.W.C.  177, 182
Defoe, Daniel  231n
Delcassé, Théophile  172
Delisle, Jean  32, 40
Deliyannis-Easty, Harina  90
Dent, Lancelot  52-53
Dérens, Jean-Arnault  39n, 40
Derrida, Jacques  205, 219
Deutsch, Morton  152, 163
Devey, Muriel  231
Diamodes  88
Dibb, Michael  154
Dickinson, Emily  258-259, 265
Dinan, Stephen  16, 27
Döblin, Alfred  63, 73
Doré, Gustave  186
Dostoevsky, Fyodor 218n, 219
Driant, Édouard (Capitaine Dranrit)  170, 182
Dragovic-Drouet, Mila  2-3, 32, 40

**E**

Edmonds, Sibel  7
Eitel E.J.  53, 55
Eliott, T. S.  79, 81
Elliot, Charles  48
Elliot, George  52
Elliott, Ebenezer  188-189, 192

Elze, Karl  184, 189, 197
Endacott, George B.  50, 55
Engelking, Barbara  64, 73
English, Ron  156
Enwiya, Allan  265n
Ernest, Stefan  64, 73
Erskine Childers, Robert 172, 182
Espiner, Mark  89, 94
Even-Zohar, Itamar  1, 8
Eyre, Richard  87-88, 95

**F**

Fabian, Bernhard  183, 197
Fagles, Robert  77, 94
Fairbank, John  49, 51, 55
Fairclough, Norman  4, 99-102, 104, 107, 115, 117
Farrell, Stephen  240-241, 249
Fawcett, Peter  77, 95
Fay, Peter W.  50, 55
Feal, Rosemary G.  235, 249
Felman, Shoshana  68-69, 73
Feng, Liu  126-127
Feuilherade, Peter  16, 18, 27
Fichte, Johann G.  187
Field, Cyril  172
Filipovic, Zlata  32, 40
Finkelstein, G. Norman  61, 69, 73
Fisher, John  174-175
Fisher, Ronald  152, 156, 163
Fletcher, John  184
Ford, Carolyn  129n
Foreman, Jona  17, 27
Foster, Ian  5
Fowler, Roger  4, 8, 117
Fox, Chris  154
Freiligrath, Ferdinand  5, 183-197
Freiligrath, Kate  193
Friedman, Thomas L.  153
Friedrich Wilhelm IV  187

**G**

Garwood, Paul  16, 27
Gentzler, Edwin  3, 9, 233, 236,

249
Gervinus, Georg G. 196
Gesse, Tanya 262-263, 265
Gettleman, Jeffrey 238, 240-241, 249
Giles, Paul 187-188, 197
Gladstone, W. E. 82
Glass, Suzanne 257, 262, 265
Goddard, Barbara 163
Godwin, William 184
Goethe, Johann W. 189, 192, 195
Goldfarb, Michael 265n, 265
Goldhagen, Daniel 62, 73
Gollin, Alfred M. 175, 182
Goosen, Theodore 248n
Gopegui, Bélen 150, 163
Gorky, Maxim 200
Gorman, Lyn 117
Gothein, Marie 183, 195-197
Gourdeau, Jean-Pierre 226, 231
Grandmont, Dominique 256, 264-265
Greenspan, Henry 67, 73
Grimm, Jacob 182n, 196
Grimm, Wilhem 182n
Gross, Jan 62, 73
Gu, Zhangsheng 46, 55
Gulick, V. Edward 44, 56
Gunn, Katherine 7, 234
Gutzlaff, Charles 41, 45-48, 50, 53-54, 56

**H**

Hall, Stuart 102, 117
Halliday, Michael A. K. 105, 111, 117
Hao, Yen-P'ing 52-53, 56
Hampaté Bâ, 232
Harding, Sue-Ann 255, 265, 265n
Harris, Brian 2, 8
Hartley, John 105, 117
Harvey, Keith 242-244, 249
Hasan, Ruqaiya 105, 111, 117

Hatim, Basil 100-102, 108, 117, 163
Heaney, Seamus 92, 95
Heath-Robinson, William 174, 179
Hector 88
Heller, Zoë 62, 67, 73
Hemans, Felicia 184-186, 188-190, 195, 197
Hendzel, Kevin 20
Hermans, Theo 1, 8, 150, 163
Hermes 223
Herodotus 236, 238
Herwegh, Georg 185, 187
Hill, (Doctor) 44, 45n
Hill, Patrick B. 203, 219
Hilsum, Lindsay 20, 27
Hindersmann, Jost 182
Hirsch, Marianne 3, 8
Hodges, Nan Powell 48, 56
Hoey, Michael 105, 117
Höfle, Hermann 64
Hoffman, Eva 249
Hoggard, Liz 91, 95
Hollis, Richard 154
Holmes, James S. 205-207, 212, 219
Homer 75-78, 80-84, 86, 90-92, 94
Hood, Thomas 189
Howard, Michael 20, 27
Howe, Fanny 259, 265
Howitt, Mary 188, 192
Howitt, William 192
Hsu, Immanuel 44, 56
Hugo, Victor 185
Hunter, William 42-45, 55n, 56
Huntingdon, Samuel 1-2, 8
Hurley, Andrew 80
Hurtado González, Silvia 108, 118
Hussein, Saddam 18, 26n

**I**

Ignatius, David 238, 249
Irele, Abiola 231n
Irving, David 62, 72
Izetbegovic, Alija 30, 39n
**J**
Jabès, Edmund 256
Jackson, Andrew 48
Jackson, Guy 118
Jackson, Michael 156
Jacobs, Carol 245, 249
Jacobsen, Friedrich 183, 186-190, 194-197
Jakobson, Roman 201, 234, 249
Jameson, Fredric 138, 147, 247, 249
Jarozynsky 215
Jellico, John 177
Jervis-Jones, William 182n
Jia, Wenbo 147
Jones, Ernest 192
Joyce, James 93, 160, 188, 247
**K**
Kahn, Joseph 122-123, 125, 128, 130
Kaldor, Mary 152, 157, 163
Kannagiesser, Karl 184
Karaindrou, Eleni 90, 95
Kazakova, T. A. 203, 219
Keats, John 186
Kellman, Steven 71, 73
Kellner, Douglas 151-152, 163
Kepinski, Antoni 72
Kertesz, Imre 63, 71, 73
Kettle, Michael 209, 215, 219
Khardzhiev, Nikolai 205, 219
Khlebnikov, Velimir 5, 199-204, 207-210, 218n, 219
Kilbourne, Jean 150, 154, 163
Kim, Suki 257, 265
Kim Sun II 248
Kimmel, Paul R. 152, 157, 165
Kipling, Rudyard 236
Klein, Naomi 150, 163

Klemperer, Victor 65, 73
Knight, William 195
Knyvet, Wilson 177
Koberstein, August 196
Kogawa, Joy 245-246, 249
Kosinki, Jerzy 69
Krauss, Robert M. 152, 163
Kruchenykh 205
Kuhiwczak, Piotr 3, 40
Kunzel, Henrich 185
Kupaigorodskaia, A. P. 213, 219
Kursk, Ivan 85
**L**
La Capra, Dominic 68, 73
Lamb, Charles 186
Landon, Elizabeth 188
Lane, W. Ronald 150, 164
Lanzmann, Claude 68, 73
Lappenberg, Johann 195-197
Lash, Scott 153
Lasn, Kalle 156, 163
Lattimore, Richard 77
Laub, Dori 73
Le Baron, Michelle 4, 135-136, 147, 163
Le Queux, William 5, 169, 171-179, 182
Lederer, Marianne 37, 40
Lee Thompson, J. 171-172, 182
Lefevere, André 1, 8-9, 135-136, 147
Lenin, Vladimir Ilich 210-211, 216, 219
Leociak, Jacek 64, 73
Leopardi, Giacomo 184
Less, Peter 262-263
Lessing, Doris 81
Leung Chung-yan 48-51, 55n, 56
Levi, Primo 65-66, 73
Levitt, Matt 239
Lewis, Wyndham 79, 95
Li Yimin 130n
Li Ying 130n, 131

*Name Index*

Liang Fa 43
Liang Jinde 43-44
Liang Tingnan 53, 56
Liaou Ahsee (see William Botelho) 43
Lin Chongyong 52, 56
Lin Yongyu 54n, 56
LinYutang 140, 147
Lin Zexu 42-44, 49, 51-54, 54n, 56
Lincoln, Bruce 210, 219
Lindsay, Hugh 47
Lindstrom, Naomi 253, 265
Lipstadt, Deborah 72
Liu Kang 138, 145, 147
Liu, Lydia H. 56
Liu Minshan 130n
Livshits, Benedikt 209
Lloyd George, David 210
Logue, Christopher 3, 75-91, 93, 93n, 94, 94n
Longacre, Robert E 236, 249
Longfellow, Henry W. 188
Lopes, Antonio 170, 182
Loshchits, Iu M. 201, 219
Lumley, Bob 99, 107, 118
Lunacharsky, Anatolii 204
Luo Lin 130n
Lutz, Jessie 56
Lynch, Timothy 152-153, 164
**M**
Mackenzie, Frederick A. 171, 182
Mackenzie, Henry 184
Mackey, Chris 263, 265
Maier, Carol 6, 259
Makonda, Antoine 231
Malcolm X 212
Mao Tse-Tung 127-128
Marina, José Antonio 149, 162, 164
Marinetti, Filipo T. 94n
Marjoribanks, Charles 47

Markov, Vladimir 209, 219
Martín, Jacinto 150, 153, 164
Marting, Susan 16, 27
Marx, Karl 192
Mason, Eudo C. 186, 197
Mason, Ian 100-102, 108, 117
Matson, (Major) 172
Mayakovsky, Vladimir 200, 208
Mayer, A. J. 210, 219
Mayers, William F. 41, 56
Mayoral, Roberto 149, 164
Mc Kane, Richard 119, 199, 219
Mc Leane, David 117n
Mengele, Josef 66
Merlino, Jacques 31-32, 38, 40
Meschonnic, Henri 6
Meyer, Michael 103
Miall, Hugh 152, 164
Miki, Roy 242, 249
Miller, Greg 265
Milosevic, Slobodan 31, 263
Molina, Rueda, Beatriz 164
Monckton Miles, Robert 188
Monod, Théodore 230
Montesquieu, Charles-Louis 199
Montgomery, Martin 105, 117
Moore, Tom 184-186, 188
Moratov, Illias 202
Morley, Jefferson 203, 219
Morrison, Elizabeth Armstrong 56
Morrison, John 48-51, 54-55, 55n
Morrison, Robert 41, 45, 48
Mufwene, Saliloko S. 203-204, 219
Munday, Jeremy 190, 197
Muñoz, Francisco A. 152, 156, 164
Murat, Joachim 85
Murray, Hugh 42
**N**
Napier, William John 45, 48

Napoleon  85, 183-184, 186, 195, 199
Napthine, Anne  160, 164
Nash, Walter  108, 117
Neuberger, Joan  201, 219
Neuforge Charles  35
Newmark, Peter  29, 31, 40
Nicholson, Nancy Schweda  262, 266
Niemann, August  177, 182
Nikolaou, Paschalis  3
Nixon, Richard  120
Nkrumah, Kwame  223
Nord, Christiane  109, 118
Norris, Margaret  79, 94n, 95
Northcliffe, Lord (Alfred Harmsworth)  169, 171-172
Novak, Dave  153
Nudler, Oscar  7, 9

**O**

O'Kane, Henry  13-14
Olk, Harald  100, 102, 108, 118
Ondaatje, Michael  6, 233-235, 237, 239, 241, 247, 249
Oschlies, Walter  66, 73
Outcherlony, John  55n, 56
Owen, David  31, 32, 40

**P**

Palmer, Jerry  2, 15, 17, 26n, 27-28
Paquette, Jean  45-47, 56
Parker, Peter  44
Patchett, Anne  257, 266
Patroclus  88
Paulson, Gunnar S.  72n
Pavollini, Taylor Aina  231n
Pedro, Raquel de  150, 164
Peeters, Jean  115, 116, 118
Picton Bagge, John  215
Plunkett, John  27
Poggioli, Renato  202-203 205, 220
Pollack, Sydney  8n

Pope, Alexander  76-77, 84, 94
Pottinger  50-51, 54
Pound, Ezra  78-79, 84-85, 93n, 94n, 95
Priam  88
Price, Morgan Philips  214, 220
Prothero, Mitchell  16, 28
Pushkin, Alexander  209
Puurtinen, Tiina  101, 117
Pym, Anthony  1, 6, 9, 255

**Q**

Qi Shan  44, 51-52, 54
Qi Ying  51, 56
Qian, Qichen  145
Qing, Jiang  127
Quincey, Thomas de  196

**R**

Rabadán, Rosa  109, 118
Ramonet, Ignacio  154-155, 164
Ranke, Leopold von  195
Ransome, Arthur  214-215, 220
Rao, Sathya  5-6
Reagan, Ronald  120,
Reich-Ranicki, Marcel  64-65, 73
Reilly, Sidney  215
Reinmann, Cordula  152, 164
Ricoeur, Paul  72-73
Ride, Lindsay  41, 48, 56
Ride, May  41, 48, 56
Riefenstahl, Leni  92
Rimbaud, Arthur  207
Rivia, Sylvia  226, 231
Roberts (Lord)  174
Robida, Albert  174, 182
Robinson, Douglas  1, 9, 170, 254, 266
Robinson, Mark  150, 164
Robyns, Clem  240, 249
Ronk, Martha  254-255, 266
Rossi, Cecilia  93n
Rosslyn, Felicity  76, 95
Rotzoll, Kim  151, 164
Rubin, Michael  17, 28

*Name Index*

Rumsfeld, Donald 238
Rushdie, Salman 242
Russell, Bertrand 80
Russell, J. Thomas 150, 164
**S**
Sabra, Hani 16, 27
Said, Edward W. 136, 137, 147
Sakamoto, Kerri 6, 233-234, 241-242, 244-247, 248n, 249
Salama-Carr, Myriam 9
Salazar, Antonio de Oliveira 257
Samary, Catherine 39n, 40
St Barbe Sladen, N. 172-173, 175, 182
Saul, Nicholas 189, 197
Schama, Simon 190, 198
Schelesinger, Philip 99, 107, 118
Scherr, Johannes 184, 198
Schiller, J. C. F. 184, 188
Schleiermacher, Friedrich 5, 187-188, 190, 198, 210
Schmid, Susanne 198
Schmidt, Paul 212
Schulz, Hans 182n
Scott, Clive 93, 93n
Scott, Walter 184,186
Sebba, Mark 203, 220
Sebold, G. W. 255
Seeba, Hinrich 187, 192, 196-198
Seguinot, Candice 151, 164
Seleskovitch, Danica 29, 35, 37, 40
Sengor, Leopold 223
Shakespeare, William 185, 192, 196
Shakir, Abdullah 151, 164
Shan, Qi 44, 52, 54
Shawkat, Ahmad 265n
She Ying 49
Shelley, Percy 188
Sheyholislami, Jaffer 118
Shklovsky, Victor 201
Shukang Ku 129n

Simon, Sherry 234, 249
Simpson, Paul 101, 118
Sinclair, John 118
Sinfield, Alan 81, 95, 241, 246, 249
Slater, John 151, 164
Snell-Hornby, Mary 135, 147
Soanes, Catherine 118
Sontag, Susan 243-244, 249
Sophocles 92
Southey, Robert 186, 188, 192
Soza, Samuel 16, 28
Sperry, Paul 16, 28
Spielberg, Steven 70
Spink, Gerald 185-186, 198
Spivak, Gayatri Chakravorty 243, 250
Staël, Germaine de 188
Stahuljak, Zrinka 255, 260, 264, 266
Stam, Robert 164
Stanislavsky 200
Steiner, George 1, 5, 9, 66, 73, 76-77, 91-93, 94n, 95, 188, 198
Stevenson, Angus 118
Storace, Patricia 68, 73
Subramanyam, Aishwarya 93n
Sullivan, J.P. 78, 95
Sun Limei 129n, 131
Szpilman, Andrzej 70
Szpilman, Wladyslaw 69, 70, 73
**T**
Tabucchi, Antonio 253, 257-259, 266
Tadatoshi, Akiba 235
Tanaka, Keiko 151, 164
Tang Jun 4
Tanzer, Joshua 202, 220
Tatum, James 88, 95
Taylor, Aina P. 231n
Taylor, Charles 13
Taylor, Gary 16, 27

Taylor, Lisa 117n, 118
Teng Ssuyu 56
Tennyson, Alfred 93, 188
Terrill, Ross 127, 131
Thatcher, Margaret 117n
Thiéry, Christopher 39-40
Thorpe, Benjamin 195
Ticknor, Benjamin 48
Tolkien, J. R. R. 128
Toury, Gideon 1, 9, 109, 116, 118
Traugott-Tamm 175
Treves, Angelo 262
Trotsky, Leo 210, 220
Tudjman, Franjo 30, 39n
Tumber, Howard 17, 26n, 28
Tuo Hunbu 52, 54, 56
Turbin, Vladimir N. 201, 219
Twitchell, James B. 150, 164
Tymoczko, Maria 3, 9, 235, 250, 255, 266
Tynan, Kenneth 81, 91
Tynianov, Yury 207
Tyson, Ann Scott 264, 266
**U**
Ullman, Richard 215, 220
Ulysses 223
Underwood, Simeon 78, 94n, 95
Urry, John 153
**V**
Valdeón, Roberto 3-4, 108, 118
Valdés, Cristina 151, 164
van Dijk, Teun A. 99, 101, 118
Vatell, Emerich de 42
Venuti, Lawrence 1, 5-6, 9, 78, 95, 183, 185, 188, 198-199, 203, 206-210, 220, 243, 250, 253, 266
Vermeer, Hans J. 109, 118
Vidal, Bernard 118
Vieira, Else 150, 164, 234, 250
Von Kleppen 180
**W**

Wadensjö, Cecilia 13-14, 28
Wakefield, Xanthe 75, 82
Waldorff, Jezry 70
Waldrop, Rosmary 256-257, 265n, 266
Waley, Arthur 47, 50, 53, 56
Washburn, David 16, 20, 28
Waters, Mary Yukari 253, 266
Watt, A. P. 175
Weaver, J. H. R. 177, 182
Weinbarg, Ludolf 192
Wellek, René 189, 198
Wells, H. G. 214-215, 220
Welsh, Frank 50, 56
Wesołowska, Danuta 66, 73
Wilde, Oscar 160
Wilkomirski, Binjamin 69
Wilhem II (Kaiser) 169, 172, 174
Wilhem IV (of Prussia), Friedrich 187
Williams, John R. 5, 184, 193, 198
Willis, Andrew 117n, 118
Wilson, H. W. 177
Wilson, John 188
Wilson, Woodrow 210
Wodak, Ruth 103
Wodehouse, P. G. 174
Wolf, Michaela 103, 118
Wong, Lawrence 3, 49, 54n, 56
Woodford, Kate 118
Wordsworth, Richard 184
Wordsworth, William 5, 183-198
Wu, Harry 123-124
**XYZ**
Xiao Xie 45, 57
Xiaoping Deng 121
Xu Jun 129n
Xu Shidong 45, 50, 57
Yao, Steven G. 78, 93n, 95
Yilibu (I-li-pu) 50-51

*Name Index*

Yuan Dehui 43-44, 55n
Yuan Nan 130n, 131
Yuchueh Chung 129n
Zambrana, Rafael 150, 165
Zang Zude 126
Zanganeh, Lila Azam 262, 266
Zhang Xi (Chang Hsi) 50-51,
    55n, 57
Zhao Ziyong 52
Zheng Zianshun 53, 57
Zhu Rongji 144-146
Zlateva, Palma 117